Essential Vectorworks Skills for Scenic and Production Designers

Essential Vectorworks Skills for Scenic and Production Designers is an accessible textbook that covers the digital skills of 2D drawing, 3D modeling, rendering, drafting, and design presentation, providing aspiring designers with an invaluable toolkit to quickly and efficiently hone their craft.

Modeled after learner-centered teaching practice and based on USITT drafting standards, this book is structured around six carefully selected core projects. It introduces key terms and commands, tools, techniques, and procedures for drawing, modeling, rendering, drafting, and design presentation with Vectorworks. Each chapter begins with key commands and a set of learning objectives that will be explored. The design exercises and projects that follow invite the reader's active participation in the learning process. Along with step-by-step instructions, 240 illustrations (including student work samples), and three insightful interviews with professional designers, this book also contains open-ended projects that encourage the reader to explore new ways of scenographic expression and creatively apply commands and techniques to solve example design problems.

This textbook is for use in scenic design, drafting, model making, and rendering courses in university theatre and media programs, and may be of interest to emerging professional scenic designers or scenographers for theatre, opera, and concert performances, production designers or art directors in the film and television industries, themed exhibition designers, and theme park designers.

Essential Vectorworks Skills for Scenic and Production Designers includes access to a wealth of online resources, including 15 videos with step-by-step instruction, six files in vwx or PDF formats for additional exercises and projects, and a video of student work samples.

Ming Chen is Professor of Theatre and Resident Scenic Designer at Kennesaw State University. She has over 30 years of university teaching experience in scene design and is a member of United Scenic Artists, Local USA 829, actively working in the professional world as a scene designer. She is the author of *Visual Literacy for Theatre*, a textbook on theatrical designs, and a major contributor to *ArtsTrends USA*, a bilingual book on performance designs. She authored and co-authored a dozen articles published in peer-reviewed journals, such as *Theatre Topics*, *TD&T*, and *American Review of China Studies* in the U.S., *Theatre Arts and EPerformance* (Shanghai Theatre Academy, China), *Theatre Arts Journal* (online, Tel Aviv University, Israel), as well as *Scenography International* (online). She is the recipient of a categorical award at the Prague Quadrennial for her co-design of the set for *Titus Andronicus*, an Excellence in Scene Design award from The Kennedy Center American College Theatre Festival for her set design for *Good Person of Szechwan*, and a Distinguished Professor Award (2023), as well as two Outstanding Book awards (for *ArtsTrends USA* and *Visual Literacy for Theatre*) from Kennesaw State University.

Essential Vectorworks Skills for Scenic and Production Designers

Drawing, Rendering, Modeling, Drafting, and Presenting

Ming Chen

Routledge
Taylor & Francis Group
NEW YORK AND LONDON

Designed cover image: Scene Design for Rent created in Vectorworks by Ming Chen with a background photo by dan_prat

First published 2025
by Routledge
605 Third Avenue, New York, NY 10158

and by Routledge
4 Park Square, Milton Park, Abingdon, Oxon, OX14 4RN

Routledge is an imprint of the Taylor & Francis Group, an informa business

Library of Congress Cataloging-in-Publication Data
Names: Chen, Ming (Computer graphics designer), author.
Title: Essential VectorWorks skills for scenic and production designers : drawing, rendering, modeling, drafting, and presenting / Ming Chen.
Description: New York, NY : Routledge, 2024. | Includes bibliographical references and index.
Identifiers: LCCN 2024015700 (print) | LCCN 2024015701 (ebook) | ISBN 9781032209906 (hbk) | ISBN 9781032209890 (pbk) | ISBN 9781003266242 (ebk)
Subjects: LCSH: Theatres--Stage-setting and scenery--Computer-aided design. | VectorWorks. | Computer-aided design--Computer programs. | Computer graphics--Computer programs.
Classification: LCC PN2091.S8 C495 2024 (print) | LCC PN2091.S8 (ebook) | DDC 792.02/50285--dc23/eng/20240409
LC record available at https://lccn.loc.gov/2024015700
LC ebook record available at https://lccn.loc.gov/2024015701

ISBN: 978-1-032-20990-6 (hbk)
ISBN: 978-1-032-20989-0 (pbk)
ISBN: 978-1-003-26624-2 (ebk)

DOI: 10.4324/9781003266242

Typeset in Century Gothic Pro
by KnowledgeWorks Global Ltd.

Access the Support Material: resourcecentre.routledge.com/books/9781032209890

To my husband, daughter, friends, and students

Contents

How to Use This Book?

To meet the current and future market demands in theatre and entertainment industries, this book pioneers a systematic approach and multimedia delivery of the subject in question to empower aspiring scenic, production, theme park designers, and art directors with digital competency and a skillset essential to their training while nurturing their impulse to explore and discover. If you want to work as a designer or art director for theatre, opera, concerts, films, television, theme parks, and/or trade shows in the future but have little or no prior knowledge and experience using Computer-Aided Design software, this book is for you.

The book packet contains 10 written chapters, more than 240 illustrations, including student work samples, 3 interviews with professional designers and art directors, 15 instructional videos, 6 readymade templates for exercises and projects, and an additional video containing student work samples. It covers subjects ranging from an introduction to Vectorworks to various Vectorworks skills for drawing, modeling, rendering, drafting, and presentation with light, camera views, and animation. You will be introduced to Vectorworks resources, commands, tools, techniques, and working methods and procedures. You will learn 2D drawing, 3D modeling, rendering, drafting, and ways to present your designs all in one course, as opposed to several separate courses. You will experience and marvel at the amazing work this power tool, Vectorworks, can do for you. With an emphasis on Vectorworks techniques, the step-by-step instructions on "how to do" come in both text and video formats. You will acquire the techniques with your preferred learning mode (reading, listening, watching, or a combination of them) and at your own pace through repeated reading of the text or stopping and rewinding the video.

Below is a suggested procedure for using this book for each chapter.

- Read the Abstract to understand what to expect in the chapter.
- Read the Learning Objectives to gain insight into what you will learn from going through the chapter.
- Read the main text to gain knowledge on the subject covered in the chapter while picking up key vocabulary, commands, concepts, and techniques.
- Follow the step-by-step instructions in the Technique section of the chapter to practice the relevant techniques, methods, and procedures. You can watch the video with the text version of the Technique open for reference. You can stop and rewind the video or repeatedly read the text as needed. You can find the video(s) for the chapter on resourcecentre.routledge.com/books/9781032209890 (under a folder named Videos). Some chapters have two or three videos to accompany the text on techniques. To practice the techniques, sometimes you will be prompted to use readymade templates also available on resourcecentre.routledge.com/books/9781032209890 (under a folder named Appendices).
- Selectively do the exercises available in the Experiment and Practice section of the chapter to learn more techniques, explore various ways of using the commands and techniques learned previously, and/or test what you have acquired in the main text of the chapter.
- Work on a project, if applicable, to demonstrate your ability to creatively apply what you have learned in previous chapters.

Although designing with digital means will eventually allow you to work more efficiently and effortlessly, the learning process of getting there could be tedious and even frustrating at times due to technical glitches and abnormal issues. So, patience is much needed during the learning process. The good news, however, is that, while working to solve the problems at hand, you can take comfort in the thought that you will come out of the problem with more knowledge and skills, which will benefit you and save you time in the long run. Remember the Chinese proverb "More haste, less speed" and remember that it would usually take people several years to learn a set of skills essential to scenic and production designers by hand to the level that you are trying to reach in a semester.

Modeled after best teaching practices (learner-centered), the author of this book applies various teaching pedagogies, which include but are not limited to the following:

- Teach key concepts and techniques in different ways, with repetitive patterns and progressive fashions, so that you can retain the knowledge and have a smooth and progressive learning experience.
- Align learning objectives, activities (such as exercises and projects), and assessments (such as nongraded tests with keys and project evaluation criteria) for you to successfully reach your learning objectives.
- Structure the book content around meaningful projects, aiming at developing your competency to solve real-world design problems.
- Conceive projects to cover skills required of your professional training and arrange them in a progressive order based on the level of difficulty and complexity.
- Deliver the content through multimedia means to alleviate your anxiety over learning and using new technology.
- Expose you to a wide variety of related industries that employ artists with digital skills through interviewing working professionals in these industries.
- Set clear expectations and provide pathways to help you succeed in your projects.
- Use work samples from your peers to challenge and inspire you to explore new ways of solving the given problems.
- Design projects with open-ended solutions to encourage you to experiment and discover.

I hope that the above guidance helps and that you will enjoy the journey of learning the essential skills of Vectorworks!

Acknowledgments

The process of writing this book is both arduous and rewarding, because it involves trial-and-error, experiments, and discoveries. During this long journey, many people have come to my aid.

First, I would like to thank my publisher, Stacy Walker, who recognized the potential value of the book, made meaningful suggestions for the book title, and encouraged and supported me along the way. I have also been deeply impressed by the professionalism and attention to detail Senior Editorial Assistant, Lucia Accorsi, exhibited throughout our collaboration. I would like to thank her for her attentiveness to my book project and her watchful eye.

The reviewers and editors of this book, though anonymous to me, helped me shape the book to where it is now. I am indebted to them for providing thoughtful comments and feedback on the draft of my book.

I could not be more thankful for the moral and financial support that I received from the Kennesaw State University Center for Excellence in Teaching and Learning and Focal Press and Routledge – Taylor & Francis Group, without which this book is not possible.

My appreciation is also due to Nemetschek Group for graciously allowing me to use Vectorworks name, icon, logo, and screenshots in my book.

For many years now, I have been a beneficiary of Vectorworks four-day workshop training by Donald Ward. I have been using the techniques taught in the workshop in classroom teaching and in my scene design projects. It was his workshop that planted the seed of this book in me. For him and his inspiration, I express my sincere gratitude.

The three distinguished designers/art directors, Even Alexander, Han Lixun, and Matthew L. McCoy, whom I interviewed for the book, took the time out of their busy schedules to correspond with me through WeChart and email to bring professional insight into the application of digital means in a wide variety of design industries. They also allowed me to grace the pages of my book with images of their award-winning designs. I am grateful for their significant contributions to this publication.

Last, but not least, I would like to take this opportunity to recognize my students in Design Skills classes, especially in the past few years, for their valuable contributions to this book. They modeled the book's intended audience for me, challenged me with problems they encountered during the learning process, provided me with feedback for my draft of the Technique sections, worked hard to demonstrate their digital proficiency and creativity through class projects, and allow me to use their works done in Design Skill classes as Student Work Samples in this book. It was for this group of students that I started creating instructional videos during the COVID pandemic when we were compelled to offer online courses. This book is the result of my ongoing conversations with them. I am deeply thankful for their involvement in this book project.

CHAPTER 1
Introduction to Vectorworks

Vocabulary

Design
Draft
Scale
Plan
Ground Plan/Floor Plan
Section
Cross Section/Centerline Vertical Section
Elevation
Orthographic Projection Drawings
Top View
Front View
Side View
Graphical User Interface
Shading
Solid Modeling
Building Information Modeling

Learning Objectives

- Get familiar with drafting terms and conventions.
- Outline the history of drafting and the highlights of the breakthroughs in CAD technology.
- Cite industries and disciplines utilizing VW as a tool to develop designs.
- Articulate reasons for using VW to develop digital literacy in drawing, modeling, rendering, and drafting.
- Memorize names and locations of major drawing tools on VW Application Window.
- Demonstrate ability to properly setup a drawing environment before starting a project.
- Practice VW drawing behaviors and navigation techniques in VW working environment.

The Background

What is Vectorworks?

Vectorworks (VW) is a type of CAD or CADD software. CAD stands for Computer Aided Design, whereas CADD is the abbreviation of Computer Aided Design and Drafting. Speaking of the difference between design and drafting, to ***Design*** is to give life to an idea generated from the need to solve problems, while to ***Draft*** is to draw a design mechanically. Drawing a set of technical plans is a very important part of the design process, but just a part.

Why CAD Now?

The technical skill set required of a scenic or production designer bears close resemblance to those required of an architect, interior designer, or a landscape designer. For instance, the output of a scenic or architectural design would include sketches, models, renderings, and technical drawings, namely drafting. In fact, the fundamental drafting standard applied in scenic and production design industries has been based primary on the standard established in architecture industry.

DOI: 10.4324/9781003266242-1

For centuries, architects and scenic designers have been drawing, painting, making 3D models, and drafting by hand. However, owing to the rapid development of computer technology, designers working in both industries nowadays can draw, paint, make models, and draft plans without even lifting a pencil. In his article titled "Shaping the City," Roger K. Lewis, a columnist of Washington Post, observes, "In architecture offices today, you rarely find a drafting board with a parallel bar, rolls of tracing paper, measuring scales, triangles, drawing templates or boxes of pencils and markers. Instead, you see a workstation with a flat-screen monitor, keyboard and mouse…" (Lewis). Using CAD to draft plans on personal computers has started since 1982. But most people resisted to practice digital drafting until 1990s for various reasons, including those who believed that one must learn hand drafting before using CAD, because drawing with hand is a coordination of eye, brain, and hand, which cannot be replaced by drawing with a computer. Lewis argues, "Computer-aided-design (CAD) has transformed architectural design methodology, not because it eliminates manual drawing, but because it allows architects to compose stacks of drawings at every stage of design. Architects can show clients countless design variations, create realistic renderings and graphic simulations, and produce detailed construction documents" (Lewis).

To understand what happened in the design field to make CAD an indispensable tool for the designers today, let us examine the evolution of drafting and the breakthroughs of our generation.

Pre-CAD

From the amphitheater of Ancient Greece (Fig. 1.1), the permanent stages of Medieval France (Fig. 1.2),

Figure 1.1 *Greek Theatre*. Hellenistic Theatre at Priene (modern Turkey), capacity: 6500, ca. 340 BCE (Photo by Christopher de Lisle. CC BY-SA 4.0 via Wikimedia Commons).

Figure 1.2 *Medieval Theatre*. Frontispiece painted by Hubert Cailleau in 1577, showing the stage design for *The Passion and Resurrection of the Savior* performed in Valenciennes in 1547 (PD-US via Wikipedia).

the Renaissance indoor theatres of Italy (Fig. 1.3a), and the 19th-century theatres of England (Fig. 1.3b) to the contemporary movie sets (Fig. 1.4), no matter how small or grandeur, simple or complex, the process of creating architectures, sceneries, and film sets has always started with an idea communicated to the builder through drawings.

The history of architectural drawings can be traced back to the ancient Egyptian and Mesopotamian eras (2700 BCE). The earliest drawings are often bird's eye view of a building or a site, some of which were drawn to ***Scale***. To ***Scale*** is to use a small increment on a plan to represent a measured foot on the realized product. For example, a drawing done in half-inch-scale means the use of half inch on a

Figure 1.3a *Renaissance Theatre*. Illustration, page 69, from *De architectvra libri qvinqve*, 1569. Drawing by Sebastiano Serlio (1475–1554). Source notes: "blocks cut by G. Chrieger". Typ 525.69.781, Houghton Library, Harvard University (PD-US via Wikimedia Commons).

Figure 1.3b *Drury Lane Theatre*. Interior of Theatre Royal, Drury Lane ca. 1808: This engraving was published as Plate 32 of *Microcosm of London* (1808) (see File:Microcosm of London Plate 009 – Billingsgate Market.jpg). Authors: Thomas Rowlandson (1756–1827) and Augustus Charles Pugin (1762–1832) (after) John Bluck (fl. 1791–1819), Joseph Constantine Stadler (fl. 1780–1812), Thomas Sutherland (1785–1838), J. Hill, and Harraden (aquatint engravers) (PD via Wikimedia Commons).

Figure 1.4 *Contemporary Movie Set*. Interior of The Green Dragon Inn (Hobbiton movie set for the *Lord of Ring*) Conceptual Design by Alan Lee. Photo by Pseudopanax (PD-US via Wikimedia Commons).

plan to represent one measured foot in the realized product (1/2″ = 1′–0″). The plan shown on the lap of the statue of Gudea (Fig. 1.5), the ruler of Lagash in Mesopotamia (c.2200 BCE) and The Zhaoyu Burial Site Plan (Fig. 1.6) found in Hebei Province, China (c.300 BCE) are two examples of earliest scaled ground plan known to humankind.

Architecture plans from the early Renaissance were found using a triad drawing system to express

Figure 1.5 *The Statue of Gudea*. Gudea, prince of Lagash, is portrayed in the statue named "the architect with map." The statue was dedicated to the god Ningirsu. Curved into his lap is the scaled plan of his palace that he has commissioned. The statue was carved out of Diorite in c.2200 BCE (Louvre Museum, Paris, France) (PD via Wikimedia Commons).

architect' ideas of the building structure. This triad system includes plans, sections, and elevations, each is a non-perspective drawing outlining the building from a specific viewpoint. A ***Plan***, often referred to as a ***Ground Plan*** or a ***Floor Plan*** in theatre, is a drawing describing what you would see if you were to cut off the building or scenery horizontally and look the building directly downward. A ***Section***, often referred to as ***Cross Section*** or ***Centerline Vertical Section*** in theatre, is a drawing describing what you would see if you were to cut off the building or

Figure 1.6 *The Plan of Zhaoyu Burial Site*. Dated ca. 300 BCE, the Zhaoyu Burial Site Plan was found in the tomb of Zhongshan Kingdom, China. On the copper plate inscribes the imperial edict promulgated by King Zhongshan for the construction of the burial. The ground plan show on the plate includes the names and dimensions of three large tombs and two middle tombs, as well as the distance between the site and the four Royal Palaces. The scale of the plan is 1:500 (CCBY-SA 4.0 via Wikimedia Commons).

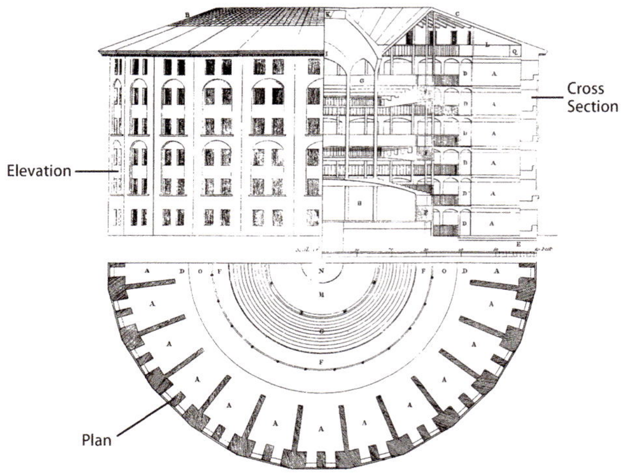

Figure 1.7 *Drawings Using Triad System*. Architectural drawings using a triad system, combining elevation, section, and plan. Drawings by Willey Reveley of Jeremy Bentham's proposal for a Panopticon prison, 1791 (PD via Wikimedia Commons).

scenery vertically and look to the open side of the building. An ***Elevation*** is a drawing of the building describing a specific side of the building. (The details of these plans will be discussed in Chapter 7 – Types of Drafting.) Fig. 1.7, a proposal for a Panopticon prison, features a combination of elevation, section, and plan.

In theatre, a 3D set unit is often communicated to a technical team through a series of ***Orthographic Projection Drawings*** which showing various sides of the set unit in a systematic fashion (Fig. 1.8).

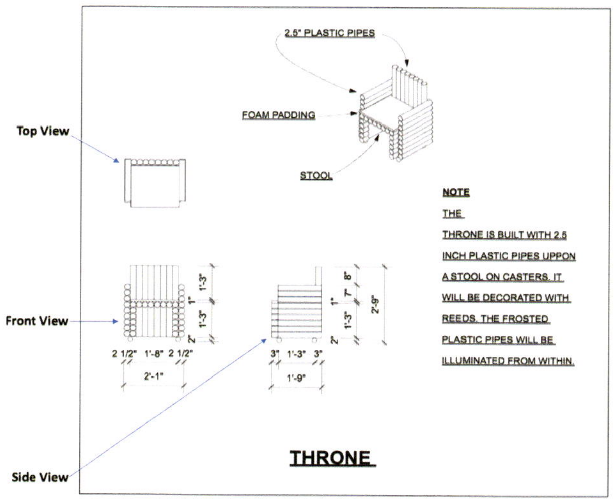

Figure 1.8 *Orthographic Projection Drawings*. Orthographic projection drawings of a throne for The *SpongeBob Musical*.

A ***Top View*** is a drawing that describes a 3D object viewing from above; a ***Front View*** is a drawing that tells a 3D object viewing from the front; a ***Side View*** is a drawing that expresses a 3D object viewing from a side. Architects, engineers, and other designers have been using this triad system to get their design ideas across to their clients, other artistic team members, and builders for the past 800 years.

In the early days, people would inscribe their plans of the buildings onto tablets made of stones, bronze, clay, and wood. Later, these inscribed tablets were replaced by ink on parchments or coarse paper as these materials were lighter and easier to carry around. Back then, the parchments were made from prepared skins of animals and coarse paper was made from linen, cotton, or papyrus plants. Parchment and coarse paper were switched over to vellum when blueprint reproduction process was available. Subsequently, vellum yielded to smooth paper as Xerox printing became common place. For millenniums, while media used to produce such construction drawings evolved over time, how designers work however had stayed the same: Drafting by hand, employing lines as elemental geometry construction to communicate with builders and clines.

Emergence of CAD

Starting from the late 1950s, the development of artificial intelligence has made several breakthroughs that profoundly changed the way the designers work. With the original intention of digitalizing the drafting process, the technological advancements instead led us now to a place where designers can create drawings, models, renderings, and drafting all on computer. These traditionally seen as different forms of work can now be seamlessly integrated for projects, owing to the scientists and computer programmers. Below are a few highlights of these breakthroughs. (Note: This list is far from exhaustive. There are numerous inventions in between, which made these highlights possible.)

- ***Digitalization of Drafting***: The history of CAD can be traced back to the year of 1957, when Dr. Patrick J. Hanratty developed PRONTO, the first commercial numerical-control programming system known as the precursor of CAD, according to Adam Beck, the author of "60 Years of CAD Infographic: The History of CAD since 1957" (Beck).

Previously, computer programs were designed for military purposes and used by large aerospace, engineering, and information technology companies like Lockheed, General Motors, and IBM. At the beginning, the program merely served as a digital form of a drawing board, with designers and drafters drawing lines in a 2D design digital environment.

- ***Graphical User Interface***: A graphical user interface (GUI) is an interface through which a user interacts with electronic devices, such as computer or smartphone, by using icons, menus, and graphics. In 1963, while working on his Ph.D. thesis in MIT, Ivan Sutherland developed a computer program named Sketchpad. In his article titled "An Introduction to Human – Computer Interaction," Mike Sharples credited Sutherland as one of the "Pioneers of HCI" and of "a few visionaries who imagined new ways of working with computers" and "has had a strong influence on present-day methods of interaction with computers" (Sharples 294). Sketchpad broke the grounds on several front. It was the first design program utilizing GUI, exploring human-computer interaction (e.g., a light pen used on a computer monitor), and introducing computer object-oriented programming. Sutherland's Sketchpad inspired and laid the foundation for the further development of 3D modeling and rendering software in the digital world of design.
- ***Shading***: In computer graphics, shading refers to the rendering of surfaces on a mathematically defined object. Andrew Glassner of Microsoft Research Lab, who published extensively on computer graphics, attributed Henri Gouraud and Bui Tuong Phong for the shading techniques as we seen today: "Two of the most famous graphics techniques, derived from shading algorithms by Henri Gouraud and Bui Tuong Phong, have been implemented in hardware and software worldwide" (Glassner 83). In the early 1970s, Henri Gouraud and Bui Tuong Phong discovered the techniques at the University of Utah. The discoveries significantly contributed to the power of current rendering and presentation capacity in CAD software. Lagend has it, in 1975, Martin Newell, a computer graphics researcher at the University of Utah, created a mathematical model of a teapot to test computer graphics. The Utah Teapot, or Newell teapot, later became a standard reference object and an "in-joke" in the computer graphics community (see Fig. 1.9).

Figure 1.9 *Utah Teapot*. A contemporary rendition of the legendary Utah teapot model developed by Martin Newell and modified by Jim Blinn. Image contribution by Dhatfield (CC BY-SA 3.0 via Wikimedia Commons).

VW uses a teapot in the menu bar as its icon for rendering.

- ***Solid Modeling***: As one of the many modeling types and an important one, Solid Modeling is the computer modeling of 3D solid objects. Romulus, the first solid modeling software, is widely known as the invention of Ian Braid, Charles Lang, Alan Grayer and the Shape Data team. The group released Romulus in 1978 Cambridge, England. According to the DBpedia, "It was the first commercial solid modeling kernel designed for straightforward integration into CAD software" ("Romulus [Modelling Kernel]"). This technology opened the door for the mainstream 3D modeling mode that we see in CAD today
- ***CAD for PC***: Before the 1980s, mainframe computers and CAD software were too expensive for general industry and individuals and the digital programs were mainly developed for the use in aerospace, automotive, and electronic industries. Therefore, even though 3D modeling software continued to improve in the 1970s, the beneficiaries of these technological inventions were still very limited. In 1982, Autodesk founded by John Walker released AutoCAD, the first CAD software made for PC instead of mainframe computers. This move, along with the IBM's introduction of PC in 1981, made digital drawing tools accessible to general industry and individuals, including architects and scenic designers. As a result, CAD started to gain its popularity.
- ***BIM (Building Information Modeling) Technology***: In 1984, Radar CH (later ArchiCAD) headed by Gábor Bojár released the first BIM software for PC. The software enhanced designer's workflow

and made the creation and management of information data much easier and more efficient. It allowed seamless communication and collaboration among clients, members of artistic team, and builders in every stage of the entire project, from brainstorming ideas, design, construction, to operation.

- ***CAD for Mac***: The further expansion of the CAD application to include Mac users occurred in 1985, owing to Richard Diehl, the founder of Diehl Graphsoft that developed MiniCAD (later Vectorworks). MiniCAD was the best-selling CAD software among Mac users.
- ***3D Modeling***: In the same year when MiniCAD came into being, Autodesk began to offering AutoCAD 3D, a software program that empowers the users to create 3D virtual models in solid, wireframe, or surface, and render it in a photorealistic fashion.

The breakthroughs highlighted above make it possible nowadays for the designers to create impressive renderings of a project with speed, ease, accuracy, and a gentle learning curve.

Design with CAD Software Versus Design with Hand (pros and cons)

So far it is still true that the invention of CAD has not eliminated hand drafting because drafting manually is more intuitive. However, more and more designers have started switching design by hand to design with CAD largely due to the software's much improved accessibility, efficiency, productivity, and project outcome.

- ***Accessibility***: Although CAD technology is more advanced and sophisticated today than it was in the 1970s and 1980s, it has become increasingly user friendly. For some software, you can just pick up and explore on your own. With technical sophisticated programs, a few days of workshops can take you further along on the path to successfully use the program to model, render, and draft. The learning curves can be even gentler than that of manual drafting. For example, drafting manually takes lengthy practices to draw lines of different weights with clarity, consistency, and accuracy. But with CAD, after you select the tool and the line weight, every line you draw will be crisp, clear, and consistent. Similarly, for hand drafting, it takes time and effort to learn how to make orthographic projection drawings correctly, how to place them in the right positions, and how to align them evenly. In CAD environment nonetheless, these tasks only requires that you memorize and locate a command; the computer will do the trick for you. A series elevations are only a few mouse-clicks away.
- ***Efficiency***: Working with CAD is more efficient, especially considering its features, such as duplicate, undo/redo, import/export, retrieve stock objects and images, to name a few. In manual drafting, these tasks could be painstakingly time-consuming, daunting, and even costly. A small error might mean that you would have to redo the entire drawing.

  In CAD, objects can appear on different layers and assigned to different classes, but they are all integrated as one project. A modification in project can be done once, and CAD software can automatically update all layers of the design affected by the modification. Unlike manual drafting which propels the designer to update changes on all relevant pages one by one, working with CAD is certainly more efficient in that regard.

  Traditionally, for a single design project, designers produce sketches, renderings, models, and technical drawings all by hand as separate works, each with a different set of media. It takes time and consumes material. With CAD, on the other hand, designers work more efficiently. They can now easily and quickly make rough plans, construct models, render them in texture and color, and generate technical drawings all in one virtual setting. The works are built on one another in a progressive manner and unified by digital means without extra cost, except for drafting which usually needs to be printed on paper for construction.

  In addition, many CAD programs offer designers a higher degree of efficiency by providing them with BIM capacity. This allows clints, members of artistic and managerial teams, builders working collaboratively, and even remotely over the cloud. There are no physical boundaries among all parties involved.

- ***Productivity***: CAD can be more accurate, because designers can input numerical numbers and fractions to draw and modify the objects. If components conflict geometrically, CAD can alert the designer and recompute its shapes and dimensions instantly. It even gets better when a model is finalized, CAD can generate any types of conventional technical drawings by a few mouse clicks. Then, the technical drawings are ready to be dimensioned and annotated for printing. These features in CAD, along with many others, reduce the time to draft for construction, and in turn, increased the designers' productivity.

  Working with BIM technology, all parties involved in a design/construction project no longer need to be physically present in one place and even at the same time; the software allows all involved to form better network collaboration remotely. Professionals "save time considerably when they can work remotely on a project together," Lorilai Greene, a staff writer for Architecture Lab indicates (Greene). A report by Steve Jones at Dodge Data & Analytics, which was released in 2017, shows 70% architects in the United States believe that BIM has helped to "reduce project error" and "data fraction," 56% architects claim that it helped to "increase client satisfaction with greater project visibility and input" (Jones 5), and 75% think that it increased the speed of their "decision-making" (Jones 10). In short, BIM technology has boosted architects' productivity.
- ***Project Outcome:*** The main goal of all CAD users is to deliver a better visualization to their clients and team members, which best express their ideas of form, color, and texture. With the exceeding moldability of its modeling tools, its photorealistic rendering capacity, and its powerful presentational faculty, ranging from projection views to animated walkthrough of a model enhanced by light and shadow, CAD can certainly help designers to reach their goals.

Why Vectorworks?

There are numerous versions of CAD available on the market today. After being compared with some of the most used software in the profession, such as AutoCAD, Fusion 360, and Sketchup in the following aspects, VW emerges as the optimal choice overall for prospective and professional scenic and production designers to develop digital literacy in drawing, modeling, rendering, drafting, and presentational skills required by their professions.

- ***Level of User Friendliness***: Although VW is not as intuitive as Sketchup, it is a more solid and accurate program to produce technical drawings, which is an important part of a design product. Modeling with Sketchup on the other hand, though fast and efficient, tends to be less accurate. As compared to AutoCAD, a more solid and accurate program for structural design and construction, VW is more user friendly and has a shallower learning curve.
- ***Basic Functions and Key Strengths***: While most CAD programs these days, including Sketchup, AutoCAD, and Fusion 360, can assist designers to perform basic functions of 2D drawing, 3D modeling, rendering, and drafting, each program has its unique strengths and limitations. Fusion 360 is more suitable for engineering and product design. AutoCAD is almost a default program for architects and builders as its technology is solid for structural design and construction. Vectorwork's strengths in rendering, 3D printing, and build-in BIM, as well as industry-specific Workspaces make it a preferred choice for theatrical designers. The Build-in BIM feature allows fluid communication and seamless collaboration among the team members in every step during the creative and production processes. Inside the program's various workspaces, VW organizes tools, commands, and resources into industry-specific sets. Based on his research, Niall Black, Technical Director of National Theatre of Scotland, suggests that "Vectorworks is the theatre Standard" (Black 4). He points out, "The adoption of Vectorworks is consistent in the UK and USA and this is not by accident. Most of the world's leading lighting designers work in these two markets adopted them and as a result have created a methodology that others follow. In return, Vectorworks has worked with them to generate copious paperwork which is now indispensable to many Production Electricians" (Black 2).
- ***Compatibility***: By nature, theatrical productions depend heavily on close collaboration among all parties involve. For example, the works of lighting

designers and video designers build on the plans created by scenic designers. It would be ideal for all three designers to use the same software, or at least software that could import/export compatible file formats. Since VW is a default software for lighting and video designers, the preferred choice of software for scenic designers is deemed obvious. Still, unlike Sketchup, which has limited options to import/export most used file formats, the long list of file formats VW can import from and export to, especially DXF/DWG share by AutoCAD, makes the software even more attractive, as the various import/export file format options allow for easy communication even among collaborators using a different software package.

- ***Reliability***: VW (previously MiniCAD) is a reliable and steadily growing software that stands the test of time. It is the first CAD Program for Mac users. It enjoys a long and sustained success since its inception in 1985, especially in the entertainment design industry. According to an article published in Architects' Journal, "MiniCAD has been around for a long time. Renamed, its new incarnation brings high-level object functionality to both MacOS and Windows users" (AJ Contributor).
- ***Cross-Platform***: Vectorworks can run on both Mac and PC computers.
- ***Affordability***: Not as affordable as Sketchup, Rhino, and even Fusion 360, the cost of Vectorwork software is however competitive to that of AutoCAD, Solidworks, and 3ds Max and Cinema 4D. That said, VW does offer free educational version of the program to students and teachers studying or working in educational institutions. (Refer to next section "How to Acquire an Educational Copy of Vectorworks Design Suite" for details.)
- ***Tech Support and Training Resources, Workshops, and Online Instructional Videos***: VW provides its user with a strong online tech support team categorized by their functions. The company regularly offers workshops at different level of CAD competency to train and guide its customers. In addition, the high-quality online instructional videos on various subjects also help the users of the software to lessen their learning curves.

It goes without saying, CAD is only a tool to aid designers during their design processes. However, the power of the tool cannot be underestimated. With the rapid development of computer technology, VW has the potential to profoundly transform the scene design curriculum in universities. Courses traditionally offering technical skills to scenic design students, such as model making, scenic rendering, and drafting, can now all be covered in one umbrella – that is to learn essential VW skills for scenic and production designers.

How to Acquire an Educational Copy of Vectorworks Design Suite?

If you are a student or a teacher involving in a design-oriented study program, you are eligible to claim a license to download an education copy of Vectorworks Design Suite software on your own computer for free. The steps are simple. All you need to do is to create an account on Vectorworks Student Portal by providing an email address and a password, submit a copy of your student or faculty ID, wait a few days for the company to verify your ID and, after you get a permission notice in your email, download Vectorworks Design Suite to your computer. The license allows you to download the software on a few different computers but will not let you use the software on two or more computers simultaneously.

To acquire an educational copy of Vectorworks Design Suite, go to https://customers.vectorworks.net/education and follow the instructions provided on the website.

Technique 1 – Drawing Setup and Navigation

In this section, you will learn how to prepare a proper working environment for your drawings, how to navigate around VW drawing environment, and how to save your drawing files. These include starting a project, resetting drawing preferences, drawing setup, saving documents, arrangement of application window, navigation technique, and drawing behavior. The following step-by-step instructions are also available in digital video format. You can find the video named "Chapter 1_Video" on resourcecentre.routledge.com/books/9781032209890 (under a folder named Videos). During the excises, you can stop and rewind the video at any time to learn the techniques at your own pace.

Arrangement of Application Window

Application Window Overview

After you have downloaded the VW software on your computer and opened a file for the first time, the Application Window (Fig. 1.10) shows you a default setting with frequently used tools and commands in an open position and arranged logically. The bars are located on the top of the drawing area. Those include Top Menu bar (the first line), VW Version bar (the second line), File Name Tab bar (the third line), View bar (the fourth line), and Tool Mode bar (the fifth line). The Recourse Manager bar is a floating bar which can be expanded into a window by hoovering over your mouse on the bar. In the middle of the Application Window is the Drawing Area, which is surrounded by the major palettes on the left, bottom, and right sides of the area. These palettes include Basic (top left), Tool Sets (middle left), Attributes (bottom left), Snapping (bottom-right), Object Info (top right), and Navigation (lower right). Carefully study the name and location of each palette to acquaint yourself with your drawing environment. That said, however, you can customize the arrangement of the palettes to your liking.

To help you quickly identify the tools available in Basic palette and Tool Sets. VW provides display options for the tools. If you click the dropdown menu located on the top-right corner of the tool palettes, you can choose among View Tool As… "Icons", "Icons and Text," or "Text." "View Tool As Icons and Text" is especially helpful if you are not familiar with what the icons look like for each tool.

Docking and Undocking Palettes

1. To undock a palette, click and drag the top (gray) bar of the palette to a new location.
2. To dock a palette, click and drag the top (gray) bar of the palette to where you want the palette to be. You will get a screen hint when a blue bar appears. If you release your mouse button when the blue bar appears at the docking location, the palette will dock.

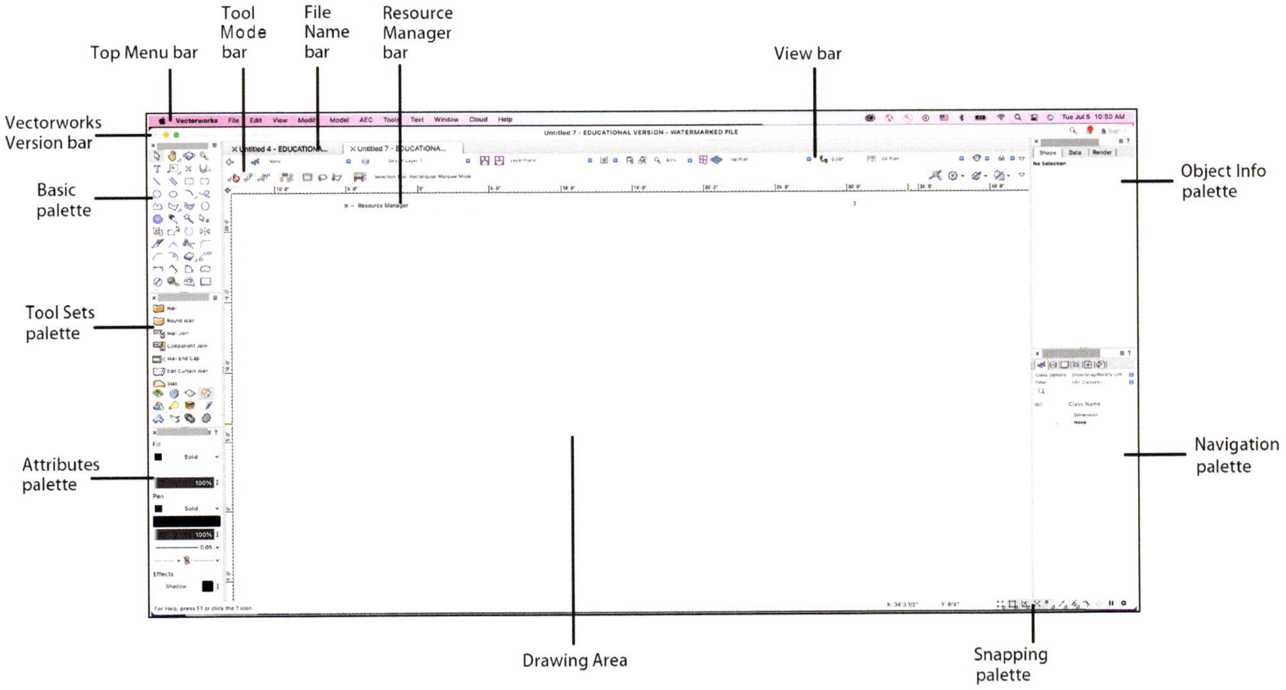

Figure 1.10 *VW Application Window*. A screenshot of VW Application Window 2022.

Note: The palettes contain major tools for your drawing. Leave them open all the time. If for some reason, you need to close them or have accidentally closed them, you can get them back by going to Window – Palettes. On the Palettes dropdown menu, you can check to open any palette on the list.

Navigation Technique

VW offers tools, commands, and options to allow the users to get around a drawing fairly easily.

Move a Document

Command: Basic palette – Pan tool
Shortcut: H

1. To move a document on your drawing board, press the space bar on your keyboard while dragging the document from one place to another.
2. As an alternative, if you have a middle button on your mouse, you can hold the button instead of pressing the space bar while dragging the document around.
3. A third option is to move the document by invoking Pan tool located on the Basic palette. The shortcut for the Pan tool is the H key on the keyboard.

   Note: The benefit of using middle mouse button or space bar is that you can move the document around even if you are in the middle of a drawing.

Switch Views

Command: Basic palette – Flyover tool
Shortcut: Shift+C

1. If you have a numeric keypad on your keyboard, you can use it to switch views from one direction to another:
   a. 0 = Top/Plan View
   b. 1 = Left Isometric View
   c. 2 = Front View
   d. 3 = Right Isometric View
   e. 4 = Left View
   f. 5 = Top View
   g. 6 = Right View
   h. 7 = Rear Isometric View
   i. 8 = Back View
   j. 9 = Right Rear Isometric View
2. As an alternative, you can also use Flyover Tool located on the Basic palette to drag the object to a customized viewing direction and angle. The shortcut for the Flyover tool is the Shift+C key on the keyboard.

   Note: You can also switch views by evoking Projection view tools and Walkthrough tools. These will be covered later in this book.

Zoom In and Out

Command: Basic palette – Zoom
Shortcut: C

1. The most intuitive way to zoom in and out of a drawing is to scroll up and scroll down in the middle of your mouse.
2. A less intuitive option for zoom is to use Zoom Tool located on the Basic palette. The shortcut for the Zoom Tool is C key on the keyboard. There are two modes available on the mode bar after you select the Zoom Tool.
   a. If you select the first mode (marquee mode), you can use Marquee tool (available in the Basic palette) in a click and drag mode to zoom in a specific area on the drawing.
   b. If you select the second mode (interactive mode), you can click and hold your mouse, then push your mouse forward (for zoom in) or drag your mouse backward (for zoom out).
   c. Aside from the previous zoom options, you can also press certain keys to zoom your drawing to a specific range. These alternatives can be very handy during the drawing process.
      - Fit to Page Area: Press Ctl+4 for Window users (Comd+4 for Mac users)
      - Zoom-Fit to Object(s): Select the object(s), then press Ctrl+6 for Window users (Comd+6 for Mac users)
      - Center the object(s): Select the object(s), then press Ctrl+3 (Comd+3 for Mac)
   d. Keyboard shortcut Z is used for magnifying the details of a drawing. To Zoom in on a specific part of a drawing, hoover over your mouse to the part in question and press Z key on the keyboard. This permits you to see the small details in that specific part of the drawing more clearly.

Note: If you do not know what an icon or a symbol in VW program stands for, you can hoover over your mouse to the icon or symbol for a couple of seconds, VW gives you a short description including its name and function. If you want a more complete answer, go to Help located on the Top Menu bar, select "What's This." A question mark appears alongside your mouse indicator. This means that now you can click on any icon, symbol, or text in the program and VW will lead you to an answer in its online help menu.

Before you start using the software, you need to make a few choices to prepare a drawing environment that is most suitable for the work you set out to accomplish.

Starting a Project

1. To start a design project, double click on the VW icon to open the software.
2. Click "OK" to acknowledge the educational version of VW program.
3. When the program opens, you will see a blank document. If not, go to Top Menu bar, select File. In the dropdown menu, select New.
4. When a dialog box opens, prompting you to create a blank document, click "OK."

Resetting Drawing Preferences

1. To reset your drawing preferences, go to Tools (on Top Menu bar) – Options – VW Preferences. (As an alternative, you can go to Top Menu – VW – Preferences. In VW, there are always different ways to reach to the same goal.)
2. When a popup window comes up, click on Session (on the left column of the window).
3. Click on the "Reset Saved Settings" button. When a dialog box appears, click "OK."

   Note: You do not need to reset drawing preferences for every project you do, but you should know where the settings are located and how to reset saved setting to default settings. You can change other setting preferences in this window and save them at any time.

Drawing Setup

Document Setup

1. To setup a document, go to File – Document Setting – Document Setup.
2. When a dialog box appears, make the following selections.
   a. In Drawing Units, click on the Edit button.
      i. When a dialogue window opens, click on Dimension located on the left column of the window.
      ii. In the Units dropdown menu, select Feet & inches.
      iii. In Fraction Precision, select 1/8″ and click "OK" to save the setting.
   b. In Layer Scale, click on the Edit button.
      i. When a dialogue window opens, under Imperial, select ½″ scale.
      ii. Click "OK" to save the setting.
   c. In Drawing Area, click on the Edit Button.
      i. When a dialogue window opens, on the left column, check "Show page boundary" and uncheck both "Show page breaks" and "Show watermarks."
      ii. On the right column, check "Choose size unavailable in printer setup."
      iii. In the "Size" dropdown menu, select "US Arch D" for a standard drafting sheet (36″ × 24″) and click "OK" to save the setting.
   d. In the Drawing Grids, click on the Edit Button.
      i. When a dialogue window opens, under Snap Grid, check Symmetrical.
      ii. Type 1/8″ in the X slot and click "OK" to save the setting.
      iii. Click "OK" again to save the document setup.

Workspace Setup

1. To setup your disciplinary workspace, go to Tool – Workspace – Architect

   Note: Each Workspace has a set of tools, commands, and resources customized for a specific discipline. You may choose either Architect, Designer, Landmark, or Spotlight, depending on the type of work you are engaged in at the moment. You may also switch from one Workspace to another during the drawing process.

Snapping Preference Setup

1. To set Snapping Preferences, go to Tool – Options – VW Preferences.
2. When a dialog window opens, click on Interactive (on the left column of the window).
3. Check all boxes except for the first box – full screen cursor box – and click "OK."

Layer Setup

Note: In VW, "Layer" is intended to help you to organize various components of your design in different physical elevations. This subject will be stipulated in great length in Chapter 5 – Layers, Classes, and Build-in Objects.

1. To create a new Design Layer, click on the Layer icon located on the left side of the View bar. An "Organization" dialog box appears.
2. Click on "New." A New Design Layer box shows up. Give a name to your design layer and click "OK" to close the box.
3. In Organization dialog box, select the layer you just created and click "Edit", an Edit Design Layer dialog box appears.
4. Click on "Scale…". A Layer Scale window opens with a list of available scales.
5. Check ½" (scale) then click "OK" to close the window. Click "OK" again to finish the set up.

Class Setup

Note: "Class" is another organizational tool in VW. Unlike "Layer" however, "Class" is intended for you to categorize the various components of your design, using attributes available in the program. This subject will also be stipulated in great length in Chapter 5.

1. To create a new class, click on the Class icon located at the left end of the View bar.
2. When an "Organization" dialog box comes up, give a name to the class, and click "OK." An Edit Class(es) window opens.
3. In this window you can make choices for this class.
4. Click "OK" to close the Edit Class(es) window, and "OK" again to finish the setup.

   Note: As an alternative, you can use the Layer and Class icons located on the Navigation palette (low right corner of the Application Window). To access Active Layer Scale, Layer Options, and Class Options, you can right click (for Window users) or Ctrl + Click (for Mack Users) and make the selections.

Saving Documents

Save a File

1. To save a file onto your computer hard drive, go to File – Save as…
2. When a dialog box opens, type "Test" in the "name" slot, select "desktop" in the "where" dropdown menu, and click "Save" to save the file onto your computer desktop. You need to remember the name and the location in which you saved your file so that you can find it later.

   Note: It is wise to save your project right away and very often, just in case something unexpected happen to your file during the drawing process. In fact, the "autosave" feature in VW Preferences allows to set how often you want to save your file. Say, if you set the "autosave" on 15 minutes, the program will automatically prompt you to save your up-to-day file every 15 minutes. To save a file is to save a copy of your work on your computer in a default file format. In VW, the default is vwx file format.

Save a File as a Template

1. To save a file as a template for repeated use in the future, start with a blank document.
2. Set up the file with all the desired elements.
3. Go to File – Save As Template.
4. Enter a name for the template with the ".sta" template extension.
5. Select an appropriate template folder in which to place the file and click "OK."
6. To use the template, go to File – New.
7. When the dialog box opens, select "Use document template."
8. In the dropdown menu, select the template you want to use and click "OK."

Export a File

1. To export your file onto to your computer, go to File – Export. In the dropdown menu, select PDF.
2. When a dialog window opens, make sure that the file format is PDF.
3. In Resolution slot (on the right column), type "300 (DPI)." Then click "Export." A dialog box appears, asking you to name your file and designate a location to save your file in.
4. Name your file "Try PDF."
5. Select "Desktop" in the "where" dropdown menu and click Save.

   Note: By now, you should have two files saved on your computer. One is a vwx file named "Test" and the other is a PDF file named "Try PDF." Open them to verify that your documents are saved in the desired formats. You can export files to a different format. This means that you can share with people who work in a different software than VW. VW offers a long list of formats you can export to.

Drawing Behavior

VW operates on a click-click system as opposed to click-and-drag system. Click once, click twice, click three times, and continuous clicks. Here are some examples.

1. Click once: Text Tool is a one-click tool. You can click once and finish your typing.
2. Click twice: Rectangle Tool is a two-click tool. You can click once and let go of the mouse. After you type in the dimensions, you can click the second time to finish the drawing.
3. Click three times: Circle Tool by three points mode (3rd on the mode bar) requires three clicks.
4. Continuous clicks: The Polygon Tool is a continuous click tool.

Note: There are only a few situations in which you need to Click & Drag in VW program. This includes selecting objects with Marquee Mode, moving objects, using Pan Tool and Flyover Tool. Using Walkthrough Tool and Polygon Tool (to drawing curves) also need to click and drag. These will be covered later in this book.

Experiment and Practice

Application Window

Fill in the blanks with the appropriate names shown in Fig. 1.11. Each name can only be used once.

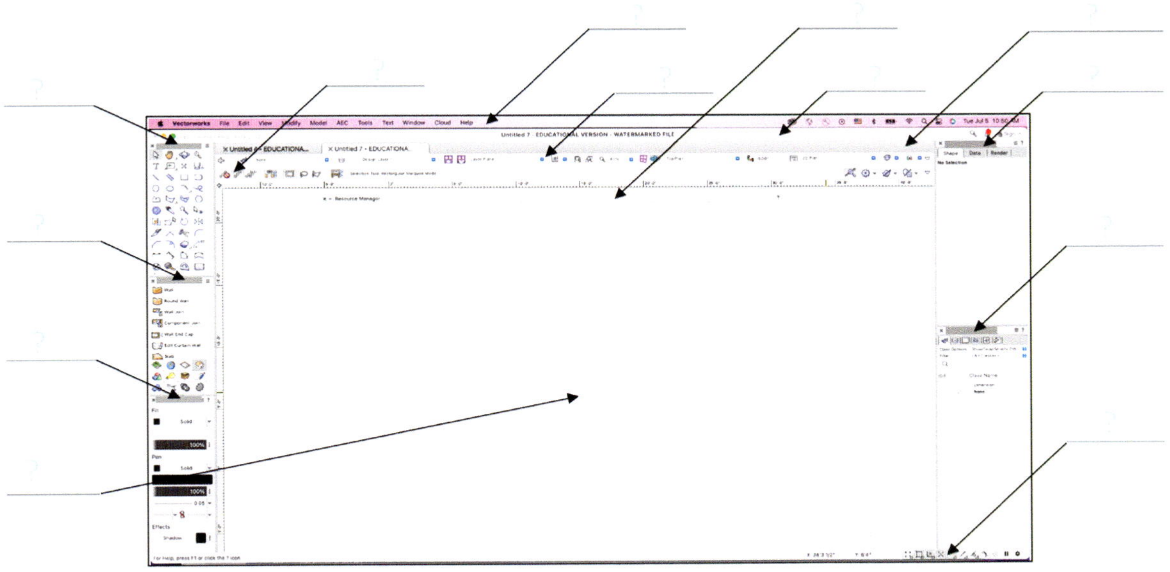

Can you name them

Snapping
Attribute
View
Navigation
Resource Manager

Top Menu
Object Info
Drawing Area
Vectorworks Version

Tool Mode
Basic
Tool Sets
File Name Tab

Figure 1.11 *Naming Game Chart*. A naming game chart created for the player to get familiar with Vectorworks' Application Window.

Drawing Behavior

This treasure-hunting game asking that you find two or more drawing tools in your drawing environment (not listed under ***Drawing Behavior*** in Technique 1), which behaves the way as described in each of the categories listed below. Put the names of the tools in the relevant categories.

1. Two-click tool:
2. Three-click tool:
3. Continuous-click tool:

Drawing Setup and Saving

Create a document and make the following choices.

1. Document Setup
    a. Unit: Feet & Inches
    b. Fraction Precision: 1/16″
    c. Size: US Arch D (36″ × 24″)
    d. Snap Grid: symmetrical and 1/8″
2. Workspace Setup
    a. Workspace: Architect
3. Layer Setup
    a. Layer Scale: ½″

Save your document as a Template in ".sta" file format and name this file as: ½″ Scale Template.

Create another document and make the following choices.

1. Document Setup
    a. Unit: Feet & Inches
    b. Fraction Precision: 1/8″
    c. Size: US Arch D (36″ × 24″)
    d. Snap Grid: symmetrical and 1/8″
2. Workspace Setup
    a. Workspace: Spotlight
3. Layer Setup
    a. Layer Scale: ¼″

Save your document as a Template in ".sta" file format and name this file as: ¼″ Scale Template.

File Export

1. Open your ½″ scale template.
2. Use Circle Tool to create three circles of different sizes.
3. Zoom to fit the three objects in the window.
4. Export the file into a PDF file.
5. In Export Range, choose "current view."
6. In Resolution, choose "300" DPI.
7. Click "Export" button.
8. Name the file "Three Circles."
9. Save the file on your Desktop.

Bibliography

AJ Contributor. "Cad That's Not Mini Anymore." *The Architects' Journal*, 11 July 2020, https://www.architectsjournal.co.uk/archive/cad-thats-not-mini-anymore.

Beck, Adam. "60 Years of CAD Infographic: The History of CAD since 1957." *CADENAS PARTsolutions*, 10 Mar. 2022, https://partsolutions.com/60-years-of-cad-infographic-the-history-of-cad-since-1957/.

Bentham, Jeremy. Fig. 1.07 *Drawings Using Triad System*. 1791. Public Domain, via Wikimedia Commons.

Black, Niall. "CAD Comparison – A View from a Production Manager." *The Envelope Room*, Creative Scotland, 7 July 2020, pp. 1–7, http://www.enveloperoom.org.uk/uploads/2/2/8/6/22863594/cad_comparison_short_read.pdf.

Black, Niall. "CAD Comparison – A View from a Production Manager." *The Evelope Room*, Creative Scotland, 7 July 2020, pp. 1–11, http://www.enveloperoom.org.uk/uploads/2/2/8/6/22863594/cad_comparison_long_read.pdf.

Cailleau, Hubert. Fig. 1.02 *Medieval Theatre*. 1577. Public Domain, via Wikipedia Commons.

Cangminzho. Fig. 1.06 *The Plan of Zhaoyu Burial Site*. ca. 300 BCE. Heibei Provincial Museum. January 9, 2018. CC BY-SA 4.0, via Wikimedia Commons.

Dhatfield. Fig. 1.09 *Utah Teapot*. June 30, 2008. CC BY-SA 3.0, via Wikimedia Commons.

Glassner, A. "Situation Normal [Gourand and Phong Shading]." *IEEE Computer Graphics and Applications*, vol. 17, no. 2, 1997, pp. 83–87.

Greene, Lorelai. "Best CAD Program for Architects: All You Need to Know." *Architecture Lab*, 8 Mar. 2022, https://www.architecturelab.net/cad-program-for-architects/.

Jones, Steve. "Leading the Future of Building Connecting Teams." *Dodge Data & Analytics*, 2017, pp. 1–27, https://damassets.autodesk.net/content/dam/autodesk/www/campaigns/You-can-Subscription/aec-smart-market-brief-connecting-teams-en.pdf.

Lewis, Roger K. "Shaping the City." *The Washington Post*, WP Company, 11 Feb. 2011, https://www.washingtonpost.com/wp-dyn/content/article/2011/02/11/AR2011021103539.html.

Lisle, Christopher de. Fig. 1.01 *Greek Theatre*. ca. 340 BCE. September 30, 2018. CC BY-SA 4.0, vis Wikimedia Commons.

Nemetschek Group. Fig. 1.10 *VW Application Window*. Vectorworks. 2022.

Nemetschek Group. Fig. 1.11 *Naming Game Chart*. Vectorworks. 2022.

Pseudopanax. Fig. 1.04 *Contemporary Movie Set*. 15 Jan. 2018. Public Domain, via Wikimedia Commons.

"Romulus (Modelling Kernel)." *DBpedia*, https://dbpedia.org/page/Romulus(modelling_kernel). Accessed 15 June 2022.

Rowlandson, Thomas, et al. "File : Microcosm of London Plate 032 - Drury Lane Interior 1808.JPG." *Wikimedia Commons*, commons.wikimedia.org/wiki/File:Microcosm_of_London_Plate_032_-_Drury_lane_interior_1808.jpg. Accessed 26 Oct. 2023.

Serlio, Sebastiano. Fig. 1.03a *Renaissance Theatre*. 1569. Public Domain, via Wikimedia Commons.

Sharples, M. "An Introduction to Human – Computer Interaction." *Artificial Intelligence*, M. A. Boden (ed), London: Academic Press, 1996, pp. 293–323.

Unknown. Fig. 1.05 *The Statue of Gudea*. ca.2120. Louvre. March 19, 2018. Public Domain, via Wikimedia Commons.

CHAPTER 2

Two-Dimensional Drawing

Vocabulary

Smart Points
Tool Modes
Cartesian Coordinate System
Polar Coordinate System
Fixed Handle Point
USITT
Line Weights
Vertex Mode
Inner Boundary Mode
Outer Boundary Mode
Chamfer
Duplicate Array
Add Surface
Clip Surface

Learning Objectives

- Memorize the names and locations of basic 2D tools, commands, and resources.
- Practice 2D drawing, editing, modifying, and rendering techniques.
- Demonstrate the ability to create a variety of 2D shapes and render them in patterns and colors through innovatively applying tools, commands, resources, and techniques available in the VW 2D drawing environment.

In the early days, CAD programs were intended to help designers draft plans in a digital 2D capacity. Some users nowadays still use Vectorworks to do the drafting work without going through a 3D digital modeling process. However, the professionals who know how eager to take full advantage of the immense capacity that the current VW program has to offer. After building a digital model, designers can now command the VW program to generate 2D orthographic projection drawings from the 3D model through an automated process. The benefits of CAD, 3D Modeling, and BIM were elaborated in the previous chapter.

The Purpose of 2D Drawing in Current VW Environment

Since creating technical drawings in 2D fashion deems out of date in our time, one might ask what the 2D programs in VW are there for. For scenic and production designers, learning to draw in the VW 2D program is neither learning to draft nor learning to design graphics in a traditional sense; rather, it is the elemental step in the learning process of modeling in a 3D form. In other words, 2D drawing has become a starting point for building 3D models because, when the model is done, the 2D drafting is automatically generated by a given command. In light of this,

DOI: 10.4324/9781003266242-2

you will follow the instructions in this chapter to learn how to draw in 2D and get familiar with some of the basic tools and commands available in VW to prepare yourself for modeling in a 3D form.

2D Tools, Commands, and Resources

Most of the 2D drawing tools, such as the Line Tool, Circle Tool, and Mirror Tool, reside in the Basic palette. The tools that help you draw more precisely, such as Snap to Object and ***Smart Points***, were stored in Snapping palette. Most of the 2D rendering tools, such as Solid or Pattern and various Color choices, are available in the Attributes palette. As the name implies, "Edit" (Top Menu bar) hosts editing commands, such as Undo, Redo, and Duplicate. Similarly, modifying commands, such as Trim, Join, and Clip Surface, are placed under the umbrella of Modify (Top Menu bar). You can find resources, such as 2D symbols of doors and tables and title block templates, in Resource Manager (floating bar). The functions of the Object Info palette run across all areas discussed above, including 2D drawing, editing, modifying, and rendering.

Although available for use in a 2D environment, some of these tools, commands, and resources are not exclusively designed for 2D drawings; they can be used to model and render in a 3D environment. For instance, you can use the command Duplicate to duplicate both 2D shapes and 3D forms. The Color tool can also be applied to 2D shapes and 3D forms.

Vectorworks offers far more 2D tools, commands, and resources than we can cover in this chapter. Hopefully, knowing the scope limitations of this book will encourage you to explore more possibilities of what you can do with VW software on your own.

Before diving into 2D drawing and rendering techniques, let us examine some features unique to each palette that we will be using.

Basic Palette

Drawing Tools, Tool Modes, and Tool Preferences

Basic palette contains a variety of tools for you to draw lines and shapes of different types. Some of these tools not only let you draw lines and shapes but

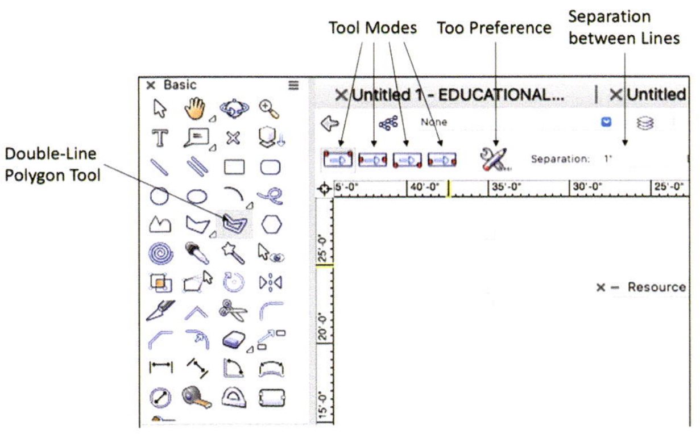

Figure 2.1 *Tools_Modes_Preferences*. A screen shot of VW Basic palette with Double-Line Polygon Tool selected, revealing choices on the Mode bar.

also allow you to pick how to draw them (***tool modes***). Furthermore, it offers you opportunities to input more specific perimeters for the item you will be drawing. For example, if you click on the Double-Line Polygon Tool, you will see four different drawing modes appear on the mode bar. You can hoover over your mouse to see what each of them entails. In addition, you can input the size of the separation between the two lines. You can even set other preferences by clicking on the Tool Preference icon (Fig. 2.1).

Hidden Tools

It is good to know that there are more tools available on the Basic palette than they appear. These tools are hidden behind some of the tool icons. The hidden tools are hinted with a small triangle on the lower right corner of these icons. If you select a tool and press the small triangle by it, you can then see and select what is hidden (Fig. 2.2).

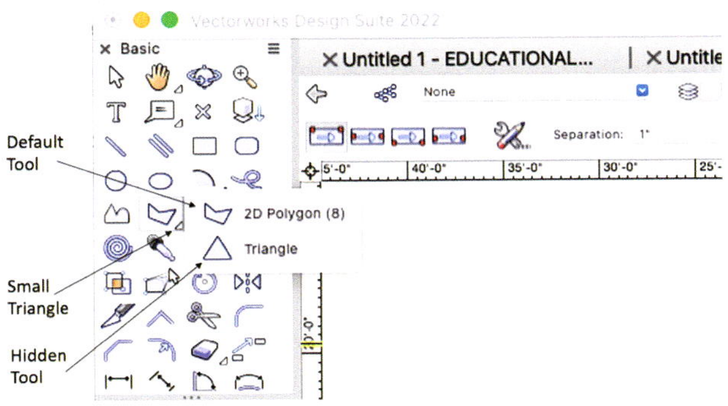

Figure 2.2 *Hidden Tools*. An example of hidden tools, revealing a Triangle Tool icon hidden behind a Polygon Tool icon.

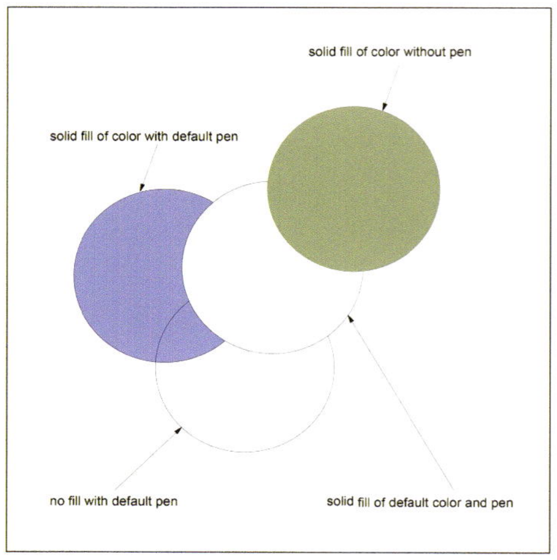

Figure 2.3 *Pen_Fill_Color*. A diagram showcasing choices on pen, fill, and color.

Attributes Palette

In Attributes palette, you can choose how you treat the lines and shapes you drew. (Fig. 2.3 Pen_Fill_Color)

For instance, you can draw a shape filled with a checkboard pattern in black and green colors. You can use another color for the outline of the shape, or even turn off the shape's outline.

It makes sense that the default setting for the shape tool is a black line encircling a white space. However, when you draw with polyline tools, you expect to see no fill in between lines, but it turns out the space in between the lines is also filled with white. Please do remember, if your intention is to draw lines as opposed to shapes, you can switch from Solid fill to None on the Attributes palette (Fig. 2.4).

The attributes you select before drawing a shape will stay as defaults until you restore the previous defaults or select new attributes. For example, if you select a pattern in the Fill slot for the rectangle you are about to draw but forget to restore the previous default for Fill after you draw the rectangle, the next time you draw a shape, the shape will assume the pattern you selected for the rectangle. Turning on a patterned Fill before drawing is beneficial if you intend to draw a bunch of shapes with the same patterned as Fill. That said, if you want to draw only one shape with this patterned Fill, draw the shape first with the default fill. While the shape is

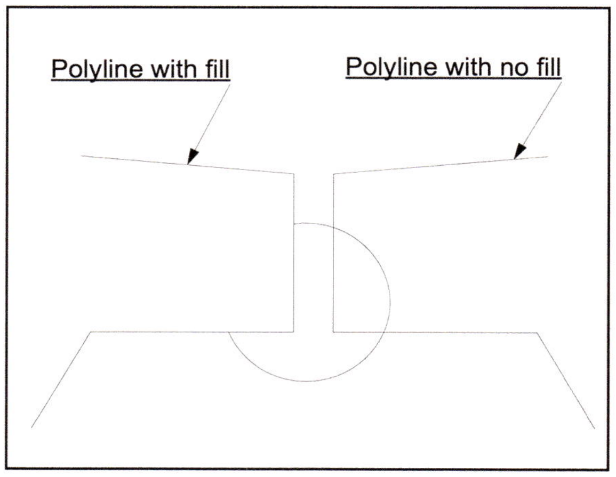

Figure 2.4 *Solid or None*. A diagram explaining the difference between "Solid" and "None" in Fill choices. The shapes on the left and right of the circle both overlap the circle. The shape drawn with solid fill on the left covers part of the circle, while the shape drawn with no fill on the right reveals the circle nestled behind.

still selected, switch the default Fill with a patterned Fill. In this way, when you draw your next shape, the Fill of the new shape will assume the default Fill. This is a general rule for all attributes displayed on palettes.

Snapping Palette

There are many choices for snapping a line, a shape, or a dimension to a certain place in a drawing. The most helpful tool could be Smart Points. When Smart Points is turned on, you can place your cursor at a point on your drawing and hold it for a set moment (a couple of seconds or so), the point of your chosen position will be lit with a red square to indicate that a smart point is temporary set. You can then get a hint of vertical or horizontal reference lines that will help you to align lines, shapes, and dimensions with the position of the Smart Points. You can set up to three Smart Points for reference in any drawing moment.

Object Info Palette

Cartesian and Polar Coordinate Systems

If you draw a diagonal line in the drawing area and click on the Shape tab of the Object Info palette, you will see three options to display the dimension information regarding the line. The one on top with a cross in the middle of a square (binding box indicator) gives you the measurements of the width

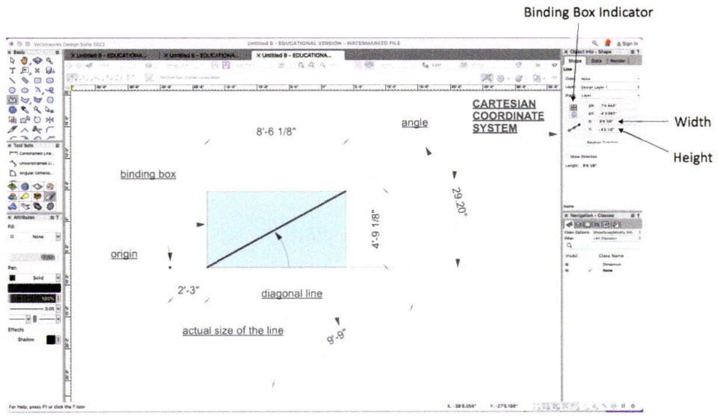

Figure 2.5 *Cartesian Coordinates*. An annotated diagram explaining how Cartesian Coordinate System works.

and height the line occupies using the ***Cartesian Coordinate System***. It does not give you information about the accrual length of the line (Fig. 2.5).

If you switch to the second one from the top (***Polar Coordinate System***), it will show you the exact length and angle (starting from the 3 o'clock position) of the line. It also tells you where the fixed handle point of this line is located from the origin on the page (Fig. 2.6).

You can change the fixed handle point to a new position, the system will recalculate the position of the line based on the distance between the origin and the new position of your fixed handle point.

In Polar Coordinates, south and west are negative zones; north and east are positive zones. For example, if you were to draw a rectangle starting at the upper left corner and finishing at the lower right corner. The width dimension is a positive number because the motion is eastward. The height dimension is a negative number because the motion is southwards.

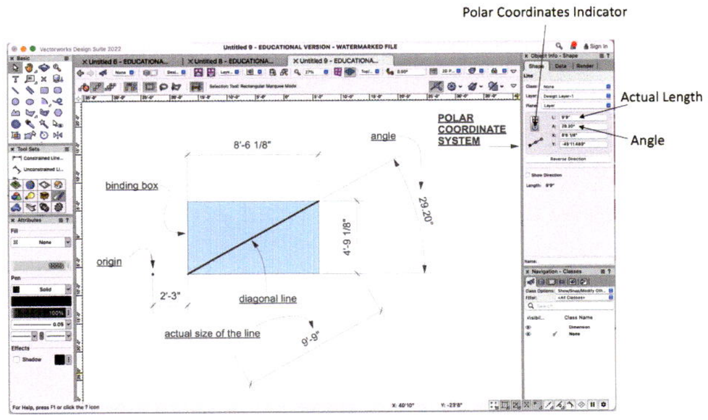

Figure 2.6 *Polar Coordinates*. An annotated diagram explaining how Polar Coordinate System works.

Another example regarding positive and negative zones in Polar Coordinates is the use of the Rotate Tool. If you try to rotate a horizontal line counterclockwise, you will need to type in a positive number. However, if you try to rotate a horizontal line clockwise, you will need to type in a negative number.

Handle Points

Another use for the fixed handle point is when you need to change the dimensions of your drawing. When you input a new dimension number in the Object Info palette, if you choose the left handle as the fixed handle point, your drawing will either expand or shrink on the right side of the shape, but the fixed handle side will remain in the original position.

Lines and Symbols

Lines and Symbols are the building blocks of designers' drafting language. They have special meanings for the professionals who need to read them. The United States Institute for Theatre Technology (***USITT***), the largest professional organization in the U.S and Canada for theatrical designs and technology, sets the drafting standard in our field. For example, according to the USITT drafting standard, various line types and ***lines weights*** (thickness of line) are assigned to draft different objects. For instance, to express the centerline of the theatre, you need to use a long line that alternates one long-dash and one short-dash and end the line with a centerline symbol. To draw set units, a solid medium-weight line is needed. In the following section (Technique 2), you will learn how to access stock symbols, line types, and line weights. The conventions for using them will be elaborated in the later chapters.

Technique 2 – Two-Dimensional Drawing

In this section, we will play with some of the most used tools, commands, and resources available in VW to see how they work in a 2D drawing environment. If you are not familiar with the icons in the Basic palette, please click on the dropdown menu located on the top-right corner of the palette and select "View Tool As – Icons and Text," as this will help you quickly identify the tools you need for the following exercises. Note: The following step-by-step procedure is also available in a digital video format. You can find the video named

"Chapter 2_Video" on resourcecentre.routledge.com/books/9781032209890 (under a folder named Videos). During the exercises, you can stop and rewind the video at any time to learn the techniques at your own pace.

2D Drawing Tools

Line Tool

Command: *Basic – Line Tool*
Shortcut: 2 (on the keyboard)

Note: The line tool is a double-click tool. In between the two clicks of drawing a line, VW lets you press the "Tab" key on your keyboard to enter the dimensions and angles of the object you are drawing. Continuously clicking the "Tab" key will allow you to see all your choices and make your selections.

To prepare for the drawing, open the file named "Try" which you saved on your computer desktop previously. It is a blank vwx. document in ½" scale.

To draw a straight line, do the following:

1. Select Line Tool on the Basic palette to invoke the tool.
2. Click once on the Drawing Area and lead your cursor in the direction you want your line to go.
3. Click on the "tab" key located on your keyboard. This will let you input the length and angle of the line.
4. Type 10′ in the L (length) slot.
5. Click on the tab again to toggle your option to the A (angle) slot.
6. Type 30 for the angle.
7. When the 10′ line lands at a counterclockwise 30-degree angle, press Enter (on the keyboard) to lock down the line and then make the second click to complete the drawing of a straight line.

As an alternative to the method described above. You can follow the instructions below to achieve the same result.

1. Select Line Tool on the Basic palette to invoke the tool.
2. Click once on the Drawing Area, lead your cursor in the direction you want your line to go, and click the second time.
3. Go to the Object Info palette.
4. Make sure the Polar Coordinate System (the icon looking like a target sign) is selected and the ***Fixed Handle Point*** (the icon looking like a bar with three handle points) is in the left position.
5. Type 10′ in the L (length) slot.
6. Type 30 in the A (angle) slot. The line is now completed.

Double Line Tool

Command: *Basic – Double Line Tool*
Shortcut: Alt+2 (for Windows) Option+2 (for Mac)

1. To draw a double straight line, select Double Line Tool on the Basic palette to invoke the tool.
2. On the Tool Mood bar, type 6″ in the "Separation" slot.
3. Click once on the Drawing Area and lead your cursor in the direction you want your line to go.
4. Click on the "tab" key and type 10′ for the length.
5. Click on the tab again and type 15 for the angle.
6. When the 10′ line lands at a counterclockwise 15-degree angle, press Enter to lock down the line and then make the second click to complete the drawing of a double straight line.

As an alternative, you can also draw the double line and change the dimensions in the Object Info palette later.

Rectangle Tool

Command: *Basic – Rectangle Tool*
Shortcut: 4 (on the keyboard)

1. To draw a rectangle, select Rectangle Tool on the Basic palette to invoke the tool.
2. Click once on the Drawing Area and lead your cursor in the direction you want your rectangle to go.
3. Click on the "tab" key located on the keyboard. This will let you input the width and height of the rectangle.
4. Type 10′ in the W (width) slot.
5. Click on the tab again to toggle your option to the H (height) slot.

6. Type -6′ for the height of the rectangle. The reason for the -6′ is because you want your second click to land on the lower right corner of the rectangle, which is south-towards in the Polar Coordinate System.
7. Press Enter to lock the input.
8. Click the second time to finish your drawing of the rectangle.

As an alternative, you can draw a rectangle and adjust its dimensions later in the Object Info palette.

Note: Drawing in the Object Info palette using Polar Coordinates brings extra advantages. First, you can add, subtract, multiply, or subdivide dimensions using symbols and add on numbers. (+ for plus, – for minus, * for multiply, / for subtraction). Now, let us try it.

1. Draw a 4′ (wide) × 3′ (tall) rectangle.
2. In the Object Info palette, behind 4′ in the width slot, type + 2′ and press Enter, and behind 3′ in the height slot, type +1′ and press Enter. The rectangle is now 6′ × 4′. You can try to subtract, multiply, and divide the numbers the same way as you did for plus.

Secondly, you can make a choice on where you want to anchor your rectangle. For instance, if you want to place your rectangle on the ground and centered, select the lower middle point as your anchor point. If you do so, no matter how you want to add or subtract the numbers, the rectangle will stay centered and grounded.

Finally, you can draw the overall size of an object (e. g., A room) by adding up the dimensions and entering them one by one in the width and height slots of the Object Info palette (e.g., 10′ + 6′ + 3′6″ + 5′ … wall, window, door, and another wall…). The computer will do the math and draw a rectangle based on its overall dimensions for you.

Selection Tool

Command: *Basic – Selection Tool*
Shortcut: X (on the keyboard)

1. By now, you should have several lines and shapes in your Drawing Area for selection.
2. Click on the Selection Tool located on the Basic palette.
3. Click on a line to select it.
4. Press and hold the Shift key while you continue to click on a double line and a rectangle to select them.
5. Deselect everything by clicking on an unoccupied/negative space in your Drawing Area.
6. Click on the Selection Tool again to select a group of objects by first clicking on the top-left corner of the group.
7. Hold and drag your mouse to the lower-right corner of the group, and then release the mouse. You will see that a group of objects has been selected.
8. Deselect everything again by clicking on a negative space in your Drawing Area.
9. Click on the Selection Tool again. This time, you will choose the objects more selectively by using the Marquee selection modes.
10. Click on Lasso Marquee mode, located on the Mood bar.
11. Click on the top-left corner of the group of objects you want to select.
12. Hold down and drag your mouse to include every object you want to select. Since the tool is so intuitive and organic, you have more flexibility in picking the objects using this mode.
13. When everything you want to select is within the lassoed area, double click the mouse to complete your selection.

    Note: The Polygon Marquee Mode located next to the Lasso Marquee Mode assumes the same function. The only difference is that the selection path of the polygon tool is straight, as opposed to the flexible winding path of the Lasso Marquee Mode. To deselect the select object(s), double click the “X” key on the keyboard.

Smart Points

Command: *Snapping – Smart Points*

1. To align two objects in space, click on the Smart Points tool located on Snapping palette.
2. Click on the Selection Tool.
3. Pick up an object by the points you want to align with a position on another object.
4. Drag the object to let the two points meet.
5. Wait for a few seconds to activate Smart Points.

6. Drag the object to a new location alongside the guidelines provided by the Smart Points tool.
7. When the object has moved to a place you want, release the object to complete the alignment.

Circle Tool

Command: *Basic – Circle Tool*
Shortcut: 6 (on the keyboard)

To draw a circle, click on the Circle Tool located on the Basic palette. There are many modes to draw a circle in a VW environment, depending on what you know about the circle. Here are a few examples.

Radius Mode

1. If you know the radius of the circle, select Radius Mode.
2. Click on the Drawing Area to place the center of the circle.
3. Click on the Tab key and type 3′ (the radius) in the L slot.
4. Press Enter and make the second click (or press Enter again) to finish the drawing.

Diameter Mode

1. If you know the diameter of the circle, select the Diameter Mode.
2. Click on the Drawing Area to locate the left side of the circle.
3. Click on the Tab button and type 6′ (the diameter) in the L slot.
4. Press Enter and make the second click (or press Enter again) to complete the drawing.

Circle from Three Lines Mode

1. If you know neither radius nor diameter but want to have a circle fit in a region, you can draw three lines to define the region.
2. Draw three lines.
3. Click on Circle from Three Lines Mode.
4. After the mode is selected, click on the lines one by one. The lines will be lit in RED as you click on them.
5. After you have finished the three clicks, move your cursor towards the middle of the circle. A circle image appears.
6. Click on the circle to finish the drawing.

Arc Tool

Command: *Basic – Arc Tool*
Shortcut: 3 (on the keyboard)

1. To draw an arc, select the Arc Tool located on the Basic palette.
2. Several mode icons appear on the Mood bar.

Radius Mode

If you know the radius, the start-point, and the sweep of the arc, select the first mode, Radius Mode. You will

1. Use Tab button to insert the radius of the Arc in the L slot and the start point of the arc in the A slot, and then press Enter.
2. After a Sweep slot is available to you, insert the degree of the sweep, and press Enter to complete the arc.

Three Points Mode

If you do not know the radius of the arc, select the second mode, Three Points Mode. You will click three points to define the arc.

Tangent to Line Mode

The third mode, Tangent to Line mode, can be used as a French Curve. Click and move your mouse to a place where the tangent appears, then click again and move your mouse to the opposite side of that curve.

Center Mode

The fourth mode, Center Mode, allows you to adjust the bow or radius of the arc.

Freehand Tool

Command: *Basic – Freehand Tool*
Shortcut: Alt+5 (for Windows) Option+5 (for Mac)

Freehand Tool is the most intuitive tool in the VW drawing environment. Like a pencil or pen, you can just select the tool and move your mouse to draw anything freehand with it. The result will be as organic as an organic line or shape can be (Fig. 2.7).

Tools with such flexibility will never impede your creative impose and intuition as some people might assume. Rather, you will get all the benefits of a digital line or shape. For example, your freehand digital drawings can be duplicated, rotated, and mirrored with incredible ease and speed.

Figure 2.7 *Freehand*. A digital study of Grace Lu's pencil drawing titled *Evelyn*, using VW Freehand Tool, to illustrate the intuitive nature of the tool.

Polyline Tool

Command: *Basic – Polyline Tool*
Shortcut: 5 (on the keyboard)

Polyline Tool is a continuous click tool.

1. To draw a polyline, select Polyline Tool on the Basic palette.
2. The line will continue as you continue to make clicks.
3. The line will end with a double click (Fig. 2.8).

2D Polygon Tool

Command: *Basic – 2D Polygon Tool*
Shortcut: 8 (on the keyboard)

2D Polygon Tool is also a continuous click tool. As soon as you click on the tool, three modes appear on the Mode bar. They are Vertex Mode, Inner Boundary Mode, and Outer Boundary Mode

Vertex Mode

1. To draw a polygon in ***Vertex Mode***, select the 2D Polygon Tool located on the Basic palette.
2. Use continuous clicking to define the Vertexes of the polygon.

Figure 2.8 *Polyline*. An example of digital one-line drawing using Polyline Tool.

3. If you made a mistake, double-click the Delete key on the keyboard to go back one step in the drawing process. Do not switch tools in the middle of the drawing process.
4. Click the last time to enclose the polygon.

Inner Boundary Mode

Inner Boundary Mode allows you to draw a negative space enclosed by positive shapes.

1. Click on the 2D Polygon Tool.
2. Select ***Inner Boundary Mode***. An Eyedroper Bucket icon replaces your cursor.
3. Click on the enclosed negative space. A shape of the negative space is created and selected.

Outer Boundary Mode

Outer boundary Mode lets you create a shape defined by the silhouette of a group of shapes.

1. Click on the 2D Polygon Tool.
2. Select ***Outer Boundary Mode***.
3. Like the Lasso Marquee tool, this tool will let you click and drag to select a group of shapes. When you complete the selection. The group of shapes is combined into one single shape.

Eyedroper Tool

Command: *Basic – Eyedroper Tool*
Shortcut: Shift+E

To pick up an attribute or attributes from one shape and drop it/them to another shape, do the following.

1. Select the Eyedroper Tool located on the Basic palette.
2. Move your cursor to the shape from which you want to pick up the attribute(s).
3. When the shape is lit in RED, click on the shape to pick up the attribute(s).
4. Press and hold the Alt key (for Windows) or Option key (for Mac) to toggle the mode on the mode bar from Pick up Attributes Mode to Apply Attributes Mode.
5. Click on the shape you want to apply the attribute(s) to complete your task.

Select Similar Tool

Command: *Basic – Select Similar Tool*

With Select Similar Tool, you can select objects that are similar to the object you click.

1. Click on the Select Similar Tool located on the Basic palette.
2. Click on the object that has the attributes of other objects that you want to select (e.g. shape, texture, color, etc.). The objects with similar attribute(s) in the drawing will be selected based on the default setting (type).
3. To change the default setting, double-click on the Select Similar Tool to make your choices.

Reshape Tool

Command: *Basic - Reshape*
Shortcut: - (hyphen)

1. Select a polygon you want to reshape.
2. When the vertex handles on the polygon appear, click on the Reshape Tool located on the Basic palette.
3. Move Polygon Handles mode will let you reshape your polygon by moving its handles.
4. Switch the mode to Add Vertex Mode, you can then add vertex to the shape for more handles by which to reshape.
5. Switch the mode to Delete Vertex Mode, you can then delete a vertex from the shape for reshaping.

Rotate Tool

Command: *Basic – Rotate Tool*
Shortcut: Alt+= (for Windows); Option+= (for Mac)

1. To rotate an object, select the object.
2. Select the Rotate Tool located on the Basic palette.
3. Use the tool to draw an axis about which to rotate.
4. Make the second click at the end of the line and drag the axis around to make the rotation. A ghost image appears to display the status of the rotation.
5. When the object is rotated to your desired angle, make a third click to complete the rotation.

If you know the angle of rotation, you can double click on the Rotate Tool. When a dialog box comes up, enter the angle of the rotation, and click "OK."

Mirror Tool

Command: *Basic – Mirror Tool*
Shortcut: = (on the keyboard)

Mirror Tool lets you draw mirror images on the opposite side of a central dividing line, whether it be a horizontal line, a vertical line, or a diagonal line.

To mirror an image or half of an image, do the following:

1. Select the image you want to mirror.
2. Click on the Mirror Tool.
3. Draw a centerline by click-click the mouse. In between the two clicks, you will see a ghost mirror image on the opposite side of the line you are drawing.
4. After you finish the second click, the mirror image is complete.

Split Tool

Command: *Basic – Split Tool*
Shortcut: L (on the keyboard)

With the Split Tool, you can split a long line into short lines and a shape into parts. There are tree modes on the Mode bar for this tool.

Point Split Mode

1. To split a line into two, select the Split Tool located on the Basic palette.
2. Select Point Split Mode on the Mode bar.
3. Hoover over your cursor on the line, the line becomes HOT (RED).
4. Click on a point in the line where you want the line to split.
5. To see the result of the split, deselect the line by clicking on the Selection Tool and then clicking on a negative space in the Drawing Area.
6. You can now click and drag a part of the line away.

Line Split Mode

1. To split a shape into two, select the Split Tool.
2. Select Line Split Mode.
3. Use click-click to draw a line across the shape to indicate where you want the shape to split. After you make your first click, the shape becomes HOT.
4. Make a second click to draw the line.
5. Deselect the shape by clicking on the Selection Tool and then clicking on a negative space in the Drawing Area.
6. Now, you can click and drag a part of the shape away to see the result of the split.

Line Trim Mode

1. Select Split Tool.
2. Select Line Trim mode. This is a three-click mode.
3. Use click-click to draw a line across the shape to indicate where you want the shape to split. After you make your first click the shape becomes Hot.
4. Make a second click to draw the line.
5. Move your cursor up-and-down and side to side to reveal a directional arrow along the line. The arrow points to the part that you want to retain after splitting. You can change the direction of the arrow to decide which part of the shape you want to keep.
6. After you make the third click, the part you do not want to retain will go away by itself.

Trim Tool

Command: *Basic – Trim Tool*
Shortcut: Alt+Shift+L (for Windows); Option+Shift+L (for Mac)

When you make a line to meet another line, if you draw a line that is longer than you need, this is when the Trim Tool comes in handy.

1. Draw two lines that intersect with each other.
2. Select the line that goes across the line that you want to trim off.
3. Click the Trim Tool located on the Basic palette.
4. Hoover over your cursor on the line you want to trim a part off. The line turns Hot.
5. Click on the part that you intend to trim off. VW will do the trick for you.

Chamfer Tool

Command: *Basic – Chamfer Tool*
Shortcut: Alt+7 (for Windows); Option+7 (for Mac)

To ***chamfer*** is to cut away a right-angled edge or corner to make a symmetrical sloping edge.

If you select Chamfer Tool on the Basic palette, three drawing modes are available at your disposal. Standard Mode let you mark a Chamfer position. Split Mode splits lines at Chamfer end points. Trim Mode trims off the excess lines at chamfer endpoints. The procedures are the same. The only difference is the selection of a different mode on the mode bar and the result will be different. Let us try Trim Mode.

Trim Mode

1. Select Chamfer Tool.
2. Click on Trim Mode.
3. Input measurements for the chamfer endpoints (first line position and second line position).
4. Hoover over your cursor on the first line. When it turns HOT, make your first click
5. Hoover over your cursor on the second line. When it turns HOT, make your second click to complete the action. The corner has gone away by itself.

Offset Tool

Command: *Basic – Offset Tool*
Shortcut: Shift+- (hyphen)

1. To draw an offset line(s), first, draw a squiggly line using the Polyline Tool.
2. Select Offset Tool located on the Basic palette.
3. Make sure Offset by Distance Mode on the Mode bar is selected.
4. Input the measurements in the Distance slot (still on the Mode bar)
5. Decide which side of the squiggly line you want to place your offset line(s) and click on that side. Every click you make will result in one more offset line on that side of the squiggly line (Fig. 2.9).

Note: In case some of the offset lines are blocked by the solid fill, go to Attributes palette to switch the Fill from Solid to None.

Symbol Insertion Tool

Command: *Basic – Symbol Insertion Tool*
Shortcut: Alt+0 (for Windows); Option+0 (for Mac)

Aside from drawing objects on your own, you can insert readymade symbols from the VW symbol library residing in Resource Manager, and even edit them. Some of the symbols allow editing, while others do not.

1. To insert a 2D symbol, click on the Symbol Insertion Tool located on the Basic palette.
2. Expand the Resource Manager bar into a window by hoovering your cursor over the bar.
3. On the top of the window, click on the dropdown menu located in the middle of the bar and select All Recourses if it is not already selected.
4. In the Search slot on the right, type "table and chairs" and press Enter. Table and chair symbols appear in the middle column of the window.
5. Click on Event Table 5ftx3ft and Chairs. A larger version of the symbol appears in the preview window on the right column.
6. Click once on the Drawing Area.
7. Move your cursor away and around the center of the symbol to decide the angle at which you want to set this group of furniture, then make a second click to place the symbol.
8. Continuous clicking on the Drawing Area will make you more copies of the same symbol. To get out of the Symbol Insertion Tool, press the "X" key on the keyboard.

Figure 2.9 *Offset*. An example of digital drawing with Offset Tool.

2D Editing Tools

Note: The commands used to edit 2D drawings are also available to edit 3D models.

Undo and Redo

Command: Edit (on the Top Menu bar) – Undo
Shortcut: Ctrl+Z (for Windows); Cmd+Z (for Mac)
Command: Edit (on the Top Menu bar) – Redo
Shortcut: Ctrl+Y (for Windows); Cmd+Y (for Mac)

If you make a mistake during your drawing process, VW will let you undo multiple times of your most recent actions.

1. To undo the previous step, go to Edit on the Top Menu bar.
2. On the dropdown menu, select Undo.

If you regret the action(s) you have just undone, VW will let you retrieve the action(s) multiple times.

1. To redo the previous step, go to Edit.
2. On the dropdown menu, select Redo.

You can set the number of times you want to undo and redo in VW Preferences. That said, occasionally, you may not be able to undo some of the actions. Please refer to VW online help for details.

1. To set the number of undos and redos, go to Tools, located on the Top Menu bar. In the dropdown menu, select Options – Vectorworks Preferences…
2. When the Preferences window appears, click on Sessions (located on the left column of the window).
3. Type the maximum number of Undos and click "OK."

Duplicate

Command: Edit (on the Top Menu bar) – Duplicate
Shortcut: Ctrl+D (for Windows); Cmd+D (for Mac)

1. To Duplicate an object, select the object.
2. Go to the Top Menu bar and click on Edit.
3. In the dropdown menu, select Duplicate. A copy of the object appears near the original object.

Duplicate Array

Command: Edit (on the Top Menu bar) – Duplicate Array
Shortcut: Ctrl+Shift+Alt+D (for Windows); Cmd+Shift+Option+D (for Mac)

With the command ***Duplicate Array***, you can make choices on the number of duplicates and the way these duplicates are arranged in relation to each other in space.

1. Draw a circle (1′ radius)
2. Select the circle.
3. Go to the Top Menu bar and click on Edit.
4. In the Dropdown menu, select Duplicate Array. A dialog window pops up.
5. In Shape dropdown menu, select Rectangular Array.
6. Insert the following information.
   a. Number of Columns: 3
   b. Number of Rows: 3
   c. Distance Between Columns: 3′
   d. Distance Between Rows: 3′
   e. Unselect Rotate Duplicates if it is selected
   f. Original Object: check "Retain" if it is not already checked.
7. Click "Ok" to complete the duplication.

Note: In the result image, you will notice that, although your choices on the distance between both columns and rows are 3′, the actual distance between the edges of the circles is only 1′. This means that VW is counting the distance between columns and between rows by the center points of the circles. Hence, when you measure the distance, you need to include the dimension of the object you want to duplicate (Fig. 2.10).

Now, let us try to make duplicates in a circular array.

1. Draw a circle (1′ radius).
2. Select the circle.
3. Go to the Top Menu bar and click on Edit.
4. In the Dropdown menu, select Duplicate Array. A dialog window pops up.
5. In Shape dropdown menu, select Circular Array.
6. Inset the following information:
   a. Number of Duplicates: 12
   b. Angle Between duplicates: 30
   c. Original Object: uncheck "Retain."
7. Click "OK" to complete the duplication (Fig. 2.10).

Figure 2.10 *Duplicate Array*. An example of creating patterns with "Duplicate Array" commands.

2D Rendering Tools

In VW 2D environment, you can apply color, pattern/texture, and shadow to the lines and shapes you draw. You can adjust the opacity of these attributes. You can even apply an image found outside of the VW program to a shape. Most of the 2D rendering tools reside in the Attributes palette. Fig. 2.7 provides you with the names of the bars in the attributes palette (Fig. 2.11).

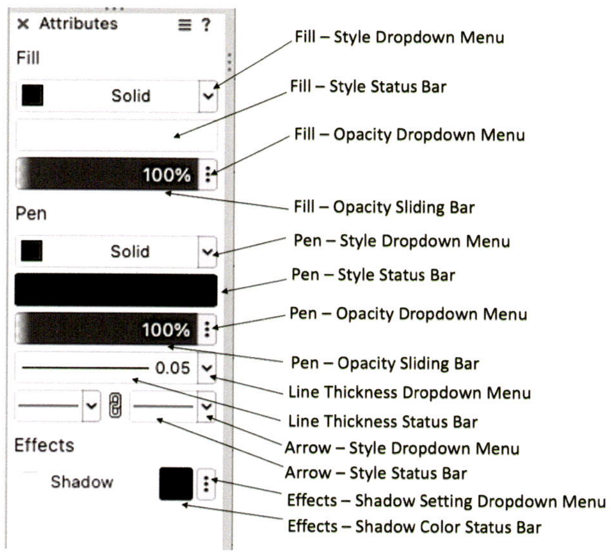

Figure 2.11 *Attributes Palette*. An annotated Attributes palette.

Fill

Fill Color

1. To apply a color to a shape, select the shape.
2. Go to the Attributes palette. Make sure that Solid is selected in the Fill – Style Dropdown Menu (Fig. 2.11).
3. Click on Fill – Style Status Bar (Fig. 2.11). A color chart appears in a dialog window.

   Note: In the Fill Color and Pen Color dialog windows, VW offers two color charts. Classic Vectorworks Colors, located on the top of the list, offers numerous color swatches with brilliant colors; Standard Vectorworks Colors, located at the bottom of the window, contains more muted color choices.

4. Click on a color swatch of your choice. The color shows up on the Fill – Style Status bar as well as on the shape that you selected.

Note: If your client and construction team use AutoCAD, to ensure that your color choices are comparable to the colors available in AutoCAD, you might want to look for colors in AutoCAD and find their RGB color values, then come back to VW to input the RGB values of these colors in the Custom color window, as AutoCAD has limited color choices (255 colors) and their standard colors do not necessarily match Standard Vectorworks Colors.

Fill Pattern (Texture)

1. To apply a pattern (texture) to a shape, select the shape.
2. Go to the Attributes palette and select Pattern in the Fill – Style Dropdown Menu (Fig. 2.11).
3. You can make choices on the existing patterns by clicking on the Fill – Style Status Bar (Fig. 2.11) and clicking on the pattern of your choice. Your choice will be reflected on the Fill – Style Status Bar as well as on the shape you selected.

Fill Opacity

1. To adjust the opacity of the fill. Select a shape that is filled with color or pattern or both.
2. Click and push the Fill – Opacity Sliding Bar (Fig. 2.11) back and forth horizontally to see the changes in the shape you selected.

Note: The Opacity Sliding Bar in the Fill section is also available in the Pen section.

Pen

Line Color

1. To change the color of a line or lines that enclose a space, select the line or shape.
2. Go to the Attributes palette. Make sure that Solid is selected in the Pen – Style Dropdown Menu (Fig. 2.11).
3. Click on the Pen – Style Status Bar (Fig. 2.11).
4. When a color chart appears, select the color you want.
5. You may also get rid of the line by selecting None in the Pen – Style Dropdown Menu.

Line Type

1. To choose a type of line with which you draw, select Line Tool on the Basic palette.
2. Draw a line and make sure that it is selected.
3. Go to the Attributes palette, select Line Type in the Pen – Style Dropdown Menu.
4. Click on the Pen – Style Status bar, a library window pops up.
5. On the left column of the window, select Vectorworks Libraries – Defaults – Attributes – Line Types.
6. Click on _Default Line Types.vwx, a list of line type icons appears in the middle column.
7. Select the line type you want. A detailed view of the line type is displayed in the preview window located on the right column.
8. Click on Select to confirm your choice. The active line in your drawing now assumes the line type you selected.
9. If you want to draw a bunch of lines with that line type, deselect everything by clicking on a negative space on the Drawing Area before going to the Attributes palette to make your Line Type choice.

Note: If you choose a line type before selecting a specific item in your drawing, this line type will become the default line type until you actively make the change.

Line Thickness

1. To make a choice on the thickness of the line(s) you draw, select the line or shape.
2. Go to the Attributes palette, click on the Line Thickness Dropdown Menu (Fig. 2.11).
3. Select the line thickness you want. The active line or shape now assumes the thickness of the line you selected. Your choice will also be reflected on the Line Thickness Status Bar (Fig. 2.11).

Shadow Effects

1. To apply a shadow effect to the line or shape of your choice.
2. Select the line or shape.
3. Go to Attributes – Effects and check the Shadow box.
4. Click on Effects – Shadow Setting Dropdown Menu (Fig. 2.11). A dialog window pops up.
5. Input 2″ in the Offset slot, 1″ in the Blur slot, 75% in the Opacity slot, and 315 in the Angle slot.
6. Click on Effects – Shadow Color Status Bar (Fig. 2.11). A color chart appears.
7. Select the color you want for your shadow if you do not like the default shadow color, which is black (Fig. 2.12).

Image

1. To apply an existing image to a shape, save an image in JPEG format onto your desktop. Memorize the dimensions of the image. For example, 8′ (w) × 4′ (h).
2. In VW Drawing Area, draw a rectangle that has the proportion of the image you want to import. For example, 8′ × 4′ or 16′ × 8′ or 4′ × 2′ etc.
3. Go to File (on the Top Menu bar) – Import – Import Image File…
4. When a dialog window appears, locate the JPEG image you have saved on your desktop, select the file, and click on "Open."
5. When another dialogue box pops up, click "OK" to accept the default.
6. When the image arrives at your Drawing Area, it may not be the same size as the rectangle you drew due to unmatched file resolutions, but it will have the correct proportion.

Figure 2.12 *Shadow Effects*. An example of creating and manipulating shadow effects using tools available in Attributes – Effects.

Figure 2.13 *Imported Image*. This is an example of using combined commands of Linear Duplicate Array, Gradient Fill, and Import Image.

7. Drag the image onto the rectangle. if the image is smaller than the rectangle, use the Selection Tool to adjust the size of the image to fit the Rectangle.
8. Select both the Rectangle and the Image.
9. Go to Modify (on the Top Menu bar) – Group. The rectangle and the image become one group.
10. If the image is larger than the rectangle when it arrives on your Drawing Area, drag the image on top of the rectangle.
11. Go to Modify (on the Top Menu bar) – Send – Send to Back.
12. Now you can use the Selection Tool to adjust the size of the image to fit the rectangle.
13. While the image is still selected, go to Modify – Send – Send to Front.
14. Select both the image and the rectangle.
15. Go to Modify – Group. The rectangle and the image become one group (Fig. 2.13).

2D Modification Tools

Send

Command: Send (on Top Menu bar) – Send to Front (Forward, Back, or Backward)
Shortcuts
Send to Front: Ctrl+F (for Windows); Cmd+F (for Mac)
Send Forward: Ctrl+Alt+F (for Windows); Cmd+Option+F (for Mac)
Send to Back: Ctrl+B (for Windows); Cmd+B (for Mac)
Send Backward: Ctrl+Alt+B (for Windows); Cmd+Option+B (for Mac)

Send commands located on Top Menu bar – Modify are designed for you to adjust objects' relative depth position. The Send dropdown menu displays four choices: Send to Front, Send Forward, Send to Back, and Send Backward. You can use any of them to maneuver the objects depth position until they display in a correct order.

1. Draw one circle, one rectangle, and one triangle, overlapping one on top of another.
2. Select the object on the top of the stack.
3. Go to the Top Menu bar – Send – Send to Back
4. Go to the Top Menu bar – Send – Send Forward.
5. Repeat the command "Send Forward" to bring the object back to the top of the stack.

Rotate

As an alternative to using the Rotate Tool in the Basic palette, you can use the Rotate command under Modify located in the Top Menu bar to give a specific angle of rotation to complete the action.

1. Draw an irregular polygon using the Polygon Tool located on the Basic palette.
2. Select the object.
3. Go to the Top Menu bar to select Modify – Rotate.
4. In the dropdown menu, select Rotate Left 90° to see the result.
5. Go to the Top Menu bar to select Modify – Rotate again.
6. In the dropdown menu, select Flip Horizontal to observe the difference.
7. Go to the Top Menu bar to select Modify – Rotate again.
8. In the dropdown menu, select Rotate…
9. This time, a dialog window appears, allowing you to give a specific angle to rotate the object.
10. Type -30 in the Angle slot. As a result, the object will be rotated at a clockwise 30-degree angle (refer to Polar Coordinates).

Trim

Command: Modify (on the Top Menu bar) – Trim
Shortcut: Ctrl+T (for Windows); Cmd+T (for Windows)

As an alternative to using the Trim Tool located on the Basic palette, you can use the Trim command found under Modify in the Top Menu bar. The process is similar.

1. Draw two lines that intersect each other.
2. Select the line that goes across the line that you want to trim off.
3. Select Modify located on the Top Menu bar.
4. In the dropdown menu, select Trim.
5. Click on the part you intend to trim off. VW will do the trick for you.

Join

Command: Modify (on Top Menu bar) – Join
Shortcut: Ctrl+J (for Windows); Cmd+J (for Mac)

Join command will bring together two potential intersect-lines.

1. Draw two lines that are close in position but are not touching each other.
2. Select the two lines.
3. Go to the Top Menu bar and select Modify.
4. In the dropdown menu, choose Join. You'll see the lines extend in order to come together as an entity.

Add Surface

Command: Modify (on the Top Menu bar) – Add Surface
Shortcut: Ctrl+Shift+Alt+A (for Windows); Cmd+Shift+Option+A (for Mac)

The ***Add Surface*** command allows you to combine several shapes into one shape.

1. Draw several shapes as if they were components of a building
2. Select all the shapes.
3. Go to Modify, located on the Top Menu bar.
4. Select Add Surface. The shapes join to become one shape.

Clip Surface

Command: Modify (on the Top Menu bar) – Clip surface
Shortcut: Ctrl+Shift+Alt+C (for Windows); Cmd+Shift+Option+A (for Mac)

The ***Clip Surface*** command lets you make holes and cuts in existing shapes. If you select two shapes, one on top of another, the "clip surface" command will cut the shape on the top into the shape at the bottom.

1. Draw one large shape and two smaller shapes.
2. Place two smaller shapes on top of the large shape.
3. Select all three shapes.
4. Go to the Top Menu bar and select Modify.
5. In the dropdown menu, select Clip Surface.
6. Deselect all by clicking on a negative space in the Drawing Area.
7. Select the two smaller shapes if they are not yet selected.
8. Move the two smaller shapes away to reveal what has happened to the large shape.

Group

Command: Modify (on the Top Menu bar) – Group
Shortcut: Ctrl+G (for Windows); Cmd+G (for Mac)

1. To group shapes, draw a bunch of shapes.
2. Select all the shapes.
3. Go to the Top Menu bar and select Modify.
4. In the dropdown menu, select Group. All the shapes become one group. You can now move them and rotate them as one entity (Fig. 2.14).
5. To edit the group, double-click on the group.
6. When the edit window appears, make changes to the group and Click on the Exit Group button.

Ungroup

Command: Nodify (on Top Menu bar) – Ungroup
Shortcut: Gtrl+U (for Windows); Cmd+U (for Mac)

1. To ungroup a group of shapes, select the group.
2. Go to the Top Menu bar and select Modify.
3. In the dropdown menu, select Ungroup. All the shapes that were grouped as a unit have now become individual shapes.

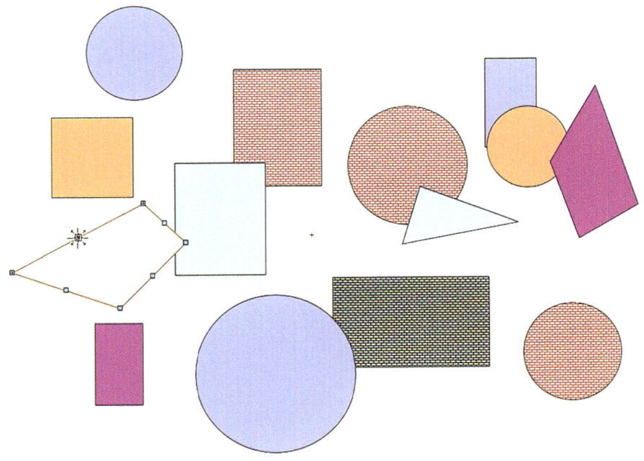

Figure 2.14 *Group*. This image demonstrates various, shape, color, texture created by using tools and command available in VW 2D drawing environment.

Experiment and Practices

1. Take a few minutes to locate the following tools and commands:
   a. Duplicate Array
   b. Offset
   c. Smart Points
   d. Redo
   e. Line thickness
   f. Selection
   g. Join
   h. Pattern
   i. Mirror
   j. Eyedrop
2. Create two 2D images (non-figurative preferred), each demonstrating the application of at least 2 drawing tools and 2 rendering tools.
3. Create an image or pattern that showcases color contrast and gradation.
4. Within the perimeters given below, create an outline of a building viewing from above.
   a. Drawing Scale: ¼″ = 1′ – 0″
   b. Drawing Size: US Arc D (36″ × 24″)
   c. Drawing in Top/Plan View (default view)
   d. Overall Building Dimension: 64′ (w) × 40′ (h)
   e. The drawing must include an open-air courtyard within the building boundary.
   f. In the middle of the courtyard, there must be a centerpiece (a fountain, a tree, or a sculpture) illustrated in the drawing by the use of a symbol found in the VW symbol library.

Bibliography

Lu, Grace, *Evelyn* (pencil drawing). (Fig. 2.7 *Freehand Drawing: Evelyn* – A digital study by Ming Chen), 2023.

Nemetschek Group, Fig. 2.1 *Tools_Mode_Preferences* (a Screen Shot of the Application Window), Vectorworks, 2022.

Nemetschek Group, Fig. 2.2 *Hidden Tools* (a Screen Shot of the Application Window), Vectorworks, 2022.

Nemetschek Group, Fig. 2.5 *Cartesian Coordinates* (a Screen Shot of VW Application Window), Vectorworks, 2022.

Nemetschek Group, Fig. 2.6 *Polar Coordinates* (a Screen Shot of VW Application Window), Vectorworks, 2022.

Nemetschek Group, Fig. 2.7 *Attributes Palette* (a Screen Shot of VW Application Window), Vectorworks, 2022.

CHAPTER 3

3D Modeling, Rendering, and Visualization

Vocabulary

Extrude
Push/Pull
Tapered Extrude
Multiple Extrude
Extrude Along Path
Sweep
Add Solids
Subtract Solids
Split
NURBS Curve
Deform
Render
Import
View
Projection
Render Mode
Layer Plane
Working Plane

Learning Objectives

- Memorize the locations and functions of the basic 3D modeling, rendering, and visualization tools and commands.
- Practice 3D modeling, rendering and visualization tools and commands, techniques, and processes by following instructions available in both text and video forms.
- Demonstrate your ability to create original 3D forms by innovatively applying the modeling, rendering, and visualization tools, commands, techniques, and processes.

When a shape expands into a new dimension in space, it becomes a form. While shapes are fundamental structural units for 2D designs, such as graphic design and fabric design, forms are essential to the work of 3D design. Sculpture, architecture, interior design, and scenic design are such examples. This chapter covers topics on modeling, rendering, and visualization of 3D forms, including geometric and organic forms. In the VW working environment, you can use tools and commands to create 3D forms from scratch; you can adopt and edit 3D forms available in the program; and you can also import and edit digital forms found outside of the program. The emphasis of this chapter, however, lies on the 3D modeling, rendering, visualization tools, commands, resources, techniques, and processes, aiming to empower, guide, and encourage you to innovatively apply them in the creation of your own 3D forms. Topics on inserting, importing, and editing readymade objects and symbols will be covered in the next chapter.

3D Modeling – Tools, Commands, and Resources

3D modeling commands are located in the top menu bar under *Model*. Most 3D modeling tools reside in *Tool Sets – 3D Modeling* and *Basic* tool palette.

DOI: 10.4324/9781003266242-3

The ***Extrude*** command allows you to transform a 2D shape into a 3D form. You can turn a circle into a cylinder by providing a height dimension. Alternatively, you may choose to extrude a shape in a more tangible way. By invoking the ***Push/Pull Tool*** and switching to a 3D view, you are enabled to drag the center point of the circle to a new dimension to directly transform the circle into a cylinder. If you want to create a trapezoid from a square, you use the command ***Tapered Extrude***. Your choices of the height and the angle of the tapper will determine the way your trapezoid looks to the viewer. The command ***Multiple Extrude*** permits you to extrude multiple shapes at the same time and turn them into a more complex form. The stack order, the types and sizes of the shapes employed, as well as the positions of the shapes in relation to each other, are important factors that will affect how the 3D form will eventually turn out. The result of ***Extrude Along Path*** often astonishes the beginning users of the software. Applying this command to create an object is not unlike a magician conjuring up a rabbit out of thin air. The use of a hollowed circle in conjunction with a squiggly line, for instance, can produce a pipe, a basket, or a water slide, depending on what type of line you draw and whether you choose the line or the circle to be the path for extrusion. (See examples in Fig. 3.24 and Fig. 3.25.) Similarly, ***Sweep*** is a command you use to create an object circling around a center core, such as a vase or a bottle. You create a profile of an object, invoke the command, and VW will do the rest of the work for you. (See an example in Fig. 3.13.)

Aside from various ways of extrusion, VW offers you commands to work in both additive and subtractive methods of modeling. Like an architect, you can combine elemental building blocks to create complex structures via the application of ***Add Solids***. Contrarily, you can chisel away bits and pieces of a solid block to carve out the silhouette of a 3D form by employing the command ***Subtract Solids***. With this command, you can cut a corner of, bunch a hole from, or make a dent in a solid block like the way a wood sculptor works (see Fig. 3.1).

Another intuitive solution to the problem of subtract solids is the use of ***Split Tool*** found in *Basic* palette (see Fig. 3.2).

In addition, if your intention is to create organic forms, you may want to explore the ***NURBS Curve Tool*** and the ***Deform Tool***, both residing in *Tool Sets – 3D Modeling*. NURBS are mathematical representations of 3D geometry that can accurately describe any shape or form. The organic form of the glass roof-like form shown in Fig. 3.3 showcases the visual effect that these tools can offer.

Figure 3.1 *Add and Subtract*. An example of using *Add Solids* to combine 3D forms and using *Subtract Solids* to chip away solids from 3D forms. *Push/Pull Tool* is an alternative to the two commands.

Figure 3.2 *Split*. An example of using *Split Tool* to provide dissect views of hollowed pipes.

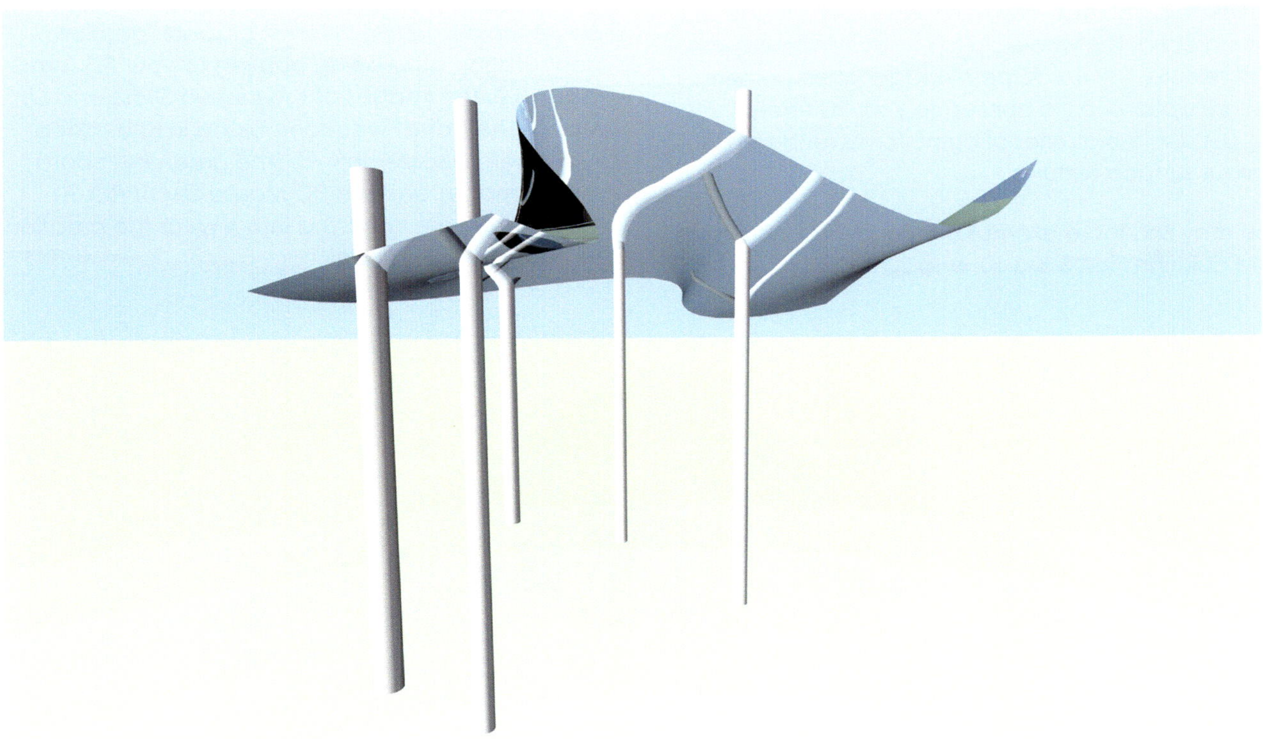

Figure 3.3 *NURBS Curve & Deform*. An example of using *NURBS Curve Tool* and/or *Deform Tool* to create an organic form.

Texture and Color Rendering of 3D Forms

The word ***Render***, in VW context, can refer to the application of texture or color to 2D shapes or 3D forms. It can also refer to the visualization of form, texture, and color in various degrees of detail as is used in ***Render Mode***. (See next section: Visualization of 3D forms.) The tools you use to render color and texture in 2D shapes distinctively differ from those you use to render 3D forms. In VW, all tools in the *Attributes* palette only execute on 2D shapes, with the exceptions of "Solid" in *Fill Style* and "Color" in *Solid Fill Color*, both of which render in either 2D or 3D modes. Similarly, except for "Class Texture" in *Object Info – Render*, which works on both 2D and 3D forms, all available textures in *Object Info – Render – Texture* only render on 3D forms.

To apply textures to your 3D forms, you can do a search in *Resource Manager* for the type of texture you want to render an object with. After a texture is selected, you may assign either a specific side of the object or the whole object to be rendered with that texture. VW *Resource Manager* offers numerous texture options to be applied to your 3D forms. Fig. 3.4 displays a series of cubic forms rendered in various surface textures.

You may find more examples of rendering in textures and colors in Figs. 3.5, 3.10, and 3.13.

To apply an existing texture to a 3D form, you also need to consider the scale of the texture in relation to the scale of the 3D form. By right-clicking your mouse on the texture icon found in *Resource Manager* and selecting "edit," an *Edit Texture* window will appear to allow you to adjust the scale of the texture to suit that of your object.

If none of the textures available in the VW program serve your particular needs, VW provides a venue for you to import an image of a texture that you find outside of the program so long as the image is saved in a format importable to the VW working environment. The ***Import*** command under the *File* menu offers a list of image formats that are compatible with VW for import. You can import the image by choosing "New Resource" in *Resource Manager* and selecting *Renderworks Texture – Image*, and then import the image you saved on your computer to the *Resource Manager*. The image can then be edited in terms of scale, transparency, and reflectiveness before being applied to the surfaces of your 3D form. It can even be edited in terms of scale, position, and rotation after being applied to your 3D form. In Fig. 3.6, the images of the *Broken Glass* and *La Mano* (*The Hand*) were combined in Photoshop. Along with *Disassembly-12* (the green keyboard matrix image) and the *PC Mouse DM1 PRO 3D Model*, they are imported into VW for the creation of the virtual set model.

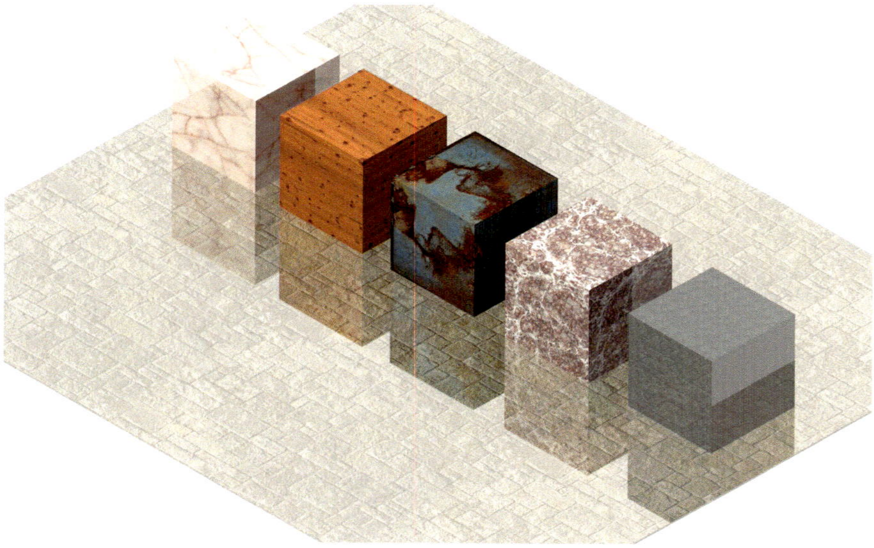

Figure 3.4 *Texture Blocks*. An example of applying various VW stock textures on the surfaces of 3D forms.

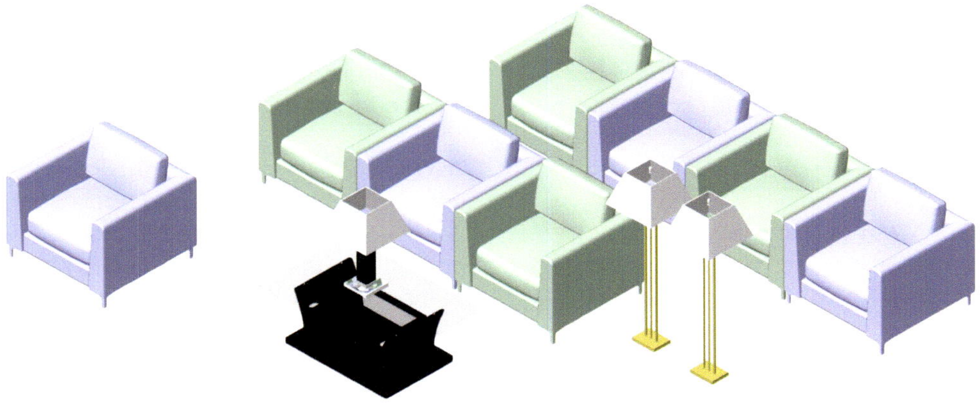

Figure 3.5 *Interior Furniture*. An example of pastel colors existing in *Attributes* palette being applied to the sofa symbols found in VW library.

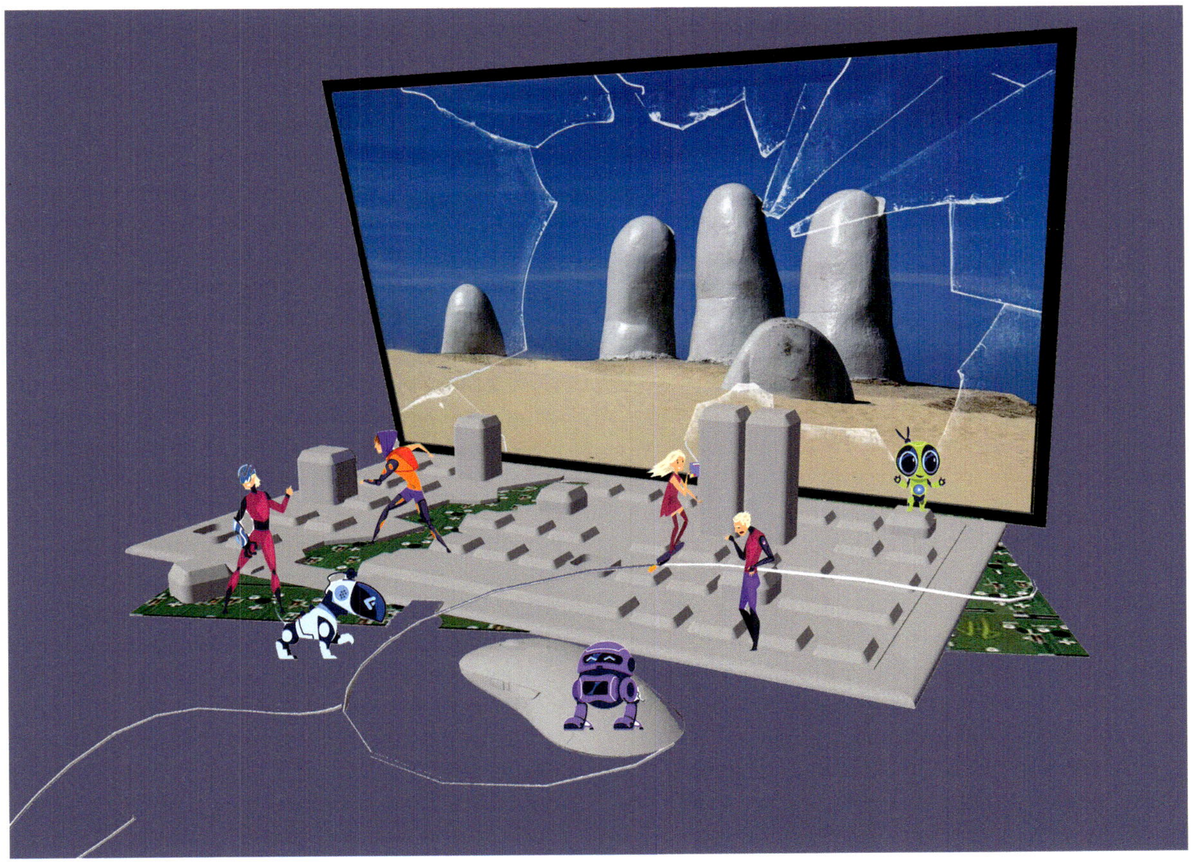

Figure 3.6 *Imported Images*. A display of a virtual set model created by including 2D and 3D images imported from outside of VW program; PC Mouse DM1 PRO 3D Model by Łukasz Szopa; Disassembly-12 by TechPowerUp (CORSAIR K63 Wireless Mechanical Keyboard Review); La Mano by Chilean artist Mario Irarrázabal (photo credit: www.luxurypunta.com); Broken Glass by Omelchenko Andrii, 2019.

While wood grain texture is considered suitable for a spindle chair in a performance of realistic style and a glass texture brings out the brilliance of a diamond with well-proportioned cuts, contemporary designers, however, often intentionally disjoint the normal relationships among design elements, such as color, form, and texture, in order to make a conceptual point. VW makes these new ways of artistic expression effortless. The glass texture applied to the roof-like form in Fig. 3.3 is such an example.

Since the rendering of colors in 2D designs and 3D designs is the same in VW, you may refer to the previous chapter for the rendering of colors on 3D forms.

Visualization of 3D Forms

Visualization here refers to the viewing and presentation of the 3D forms. Visualization happens all the time during and after your modeling and rendering processes. To show an image of a 3D form, VW offers a variety of options, including visualization in various viewing angles/directions, projections, and rendering modes. You may select these options either from ***View***, located on the top menu bar or on the *View bar* along the top of the application window.

The first set of options regards viewing angles and directions. *Top/Plan* view is the only 2D view of the object. It is the view you would normally start the modeling of a 3D form and often go back to during your modeling process, because this is the only view that displays the positional relationship among all the objects in a straight-on, non-perspective, 2D view of the 3D form. Other standard viewing directions and angles include *Top* view, *Front* view, *Right* view, *Left* view, *Back* view, and *Bottom* view, as well as various *Isometric* views. These views are all 3D views. Furthermore, you may choose to customize a view by invoking the *Flyover* tool located in both *Basic* palette and *Tool Sets – 3D Modeling* and intuitively turning a 3D form to the desired viewing direction and angle. Viewing angle and direction choices reside both in *View – Standard Views* on the top menu bar and on the *View* bar.

The second set of options allows you to view and display your 3D form in a variety of ***Projections***, including orthogonal projections, perspective projections, and oblique cavalier projections. *Projection* choices reside both in *View – Projection* on the top menu bar and on the *View* bar.

In addition, VW offers a variety of rendering modes, which you can also access either through *View – Rendering* located in the top menu bar or through *Render Mode* located on the *View* bar. In a modeling process, the three most popular modes of rendering are *Wireframe*, *Shaded*, and *Final Quality Renderworks*. The *Wireframe* is the fastest render mode of the three because, in this mode of rendering, the object is presented as a network of polylines. Fig. 3.7 is an example of 3D forms rendered in *Wireframe* mode.

However, in practice, most people want to see the 3D form they are creating as a solid. Therefore, *Shaded* mode is most likely to be set as the default mode for 3D rendering. You can set or change the default setting by going to *Tools – Options – Vectorworks Preferences* and selecting the *3D* tab. Comparing to *Final Quality Renderworks*, *Shaded* render mode renders significantly faster. Although lacking in details, you may still see colors and, sometimes, textures (depending on the type of texture) presented in this mode of rendering. As the name implies, *Final Quality Renderworks* exhibits the most smooth and detailed rendering work amongst. This mode can take a significant amount of time for the rendering to complete when the 3D form is complex. For this reason, *Final Quality Renderworks* is used prudently during the creation process of complex forms, but more often in the presentation of them to others. Fig. 3.8 showcases the glass texture rendered in the mode of *Final Quality Renderworks*.

The importance of mastering the skills of 3D modeling, rendering, and visualization for set designers can never be overemphasized because our contemporary theatre prefers scenery comprised of 3D units to those comprised of 2D flats, owing to Adolphe Appia and Gordon Craig, who lit the touch for the staging reform of the late 19th century. 3D sceneries nowadays influence actor's physical movements in numerous ways. Actors can walk around, walk under, and step on the top of a set unit. This demand for set design brought the skills of 3D modeling and rendering to the forefront of the design process. 3D forms are the building blocks a set designer uses to fashion visual edifices that tell stories.

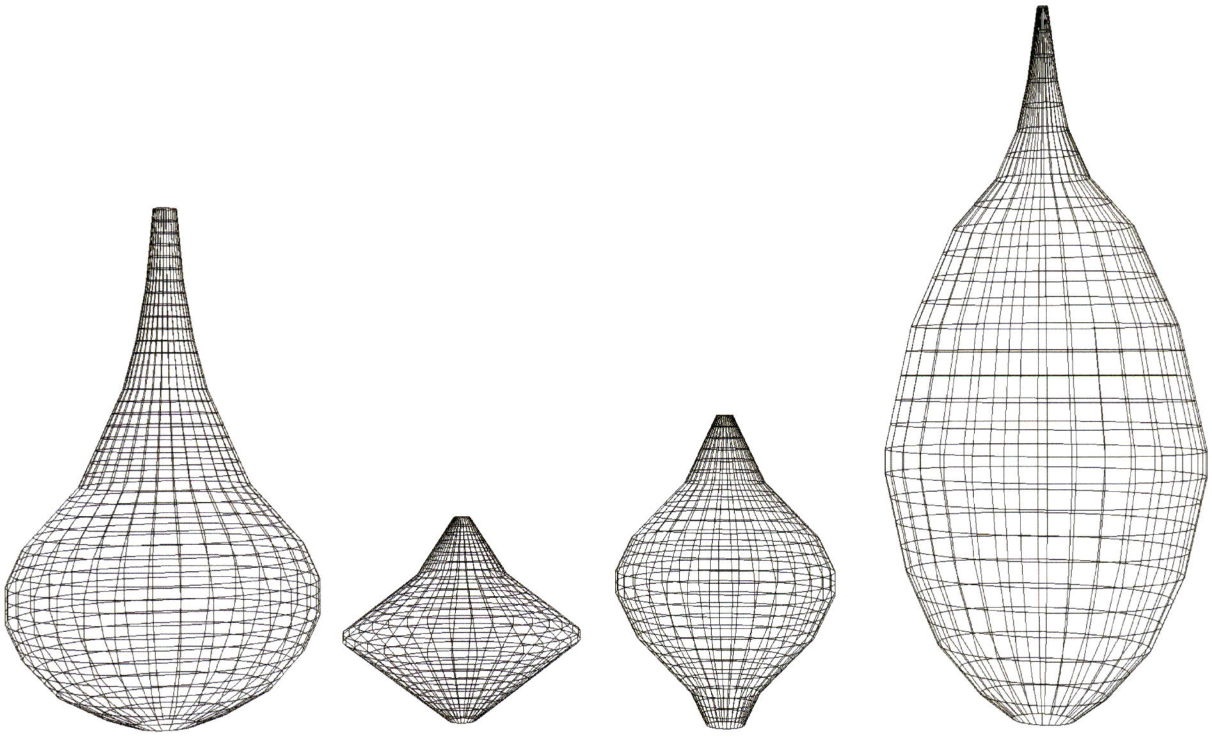

Figure 3.7 *Teardrops_Wireframe*. An example of rendering 3D forms in *Wireframe* render mode.

Figure 3.8 *Crystal Teardrops*. An example of glass texture applied to a 3D form and rendered in *Final Quality Renderworks* render mode.

Technique 3 – 3D Modeling, Rendering, and Visualization Techniques

This section covers 3D modeling, rendering, and visualization techniques. You will become familiar with the tools, commands, and processes associated with these techniques. The following step-by-step instructions are also available in digital video format. You can find the video named "Chapter 3_Video" on resourcecentre.routledge.com/books/9781032209890 (under a folder named Videos). During the exercises, you can stop and rewind the video at any time to learn the techniques at your own pace.

3D Modeling Technique

Extrude

Command: *Model – Extrude*
Shortcut: Ctrl+E (Windows); Cmd+E (Mac)

1. Open a ½″ scale drawing template.
2. In *Top/Plan* view, draw a circle (radius: 2′).
3. Go to the top menu bar, select *Model – Extrude*. A dialogue window pops up.
4. Give a number to the height (height: 4′) and click "OK."
5. See the result in an *Isometric* view.
6. In the *Object Info* palette, you can adjust the radius and height (Extr) of the solid.

Tapered Extrude

Command: *Model – Tapered Extrude*
Shortcut: Ctrl+Alt+U (Windows); Cmd+Option+U (Mac)

1. In *Top/Plan* view, draw a rectangle (size: 4′ × 6′).
2. Go to *Model – Tapered Extrude*. A dialogue window pops up.
3. Give a number to the height (height: 9′)
4. Give a number to the angle (taper angle: 5°) and click "OK."
5. See the result in an *Isometric* view.
6. In the *Object Info* palette, you can adjust the angle of the taper and the height of the solid.

Multiple Extrude

Command: *Model – Multiple Extrude*
Shortcut: Ctrl+Alt+E (Windows); Cmd+Option+E (Mac)

1. In *Top/Plan* view, draw multiple shapes overlapping or close to each other.
2. Select all the shapes you just drew.
3. Go to *Model – Multiple Extrude*.
4. Give a number to the height.
5. See the result in *Front* view.
6. In the *Object Info* palette, you can adjust the overall height and profile of the solid.

Extrude Along Path

Command: *Model – Extrude Along Path*
Shortcut: Ctrl+Alt+X (Windows); Cmd+Option+X (Mac)

1. In *Top/Plan* view, select the *Circle Tool* in *Basic* palette and draw a circle (radius: 6″).
2. Draw a smaller circle (radius: 5″) on the same axis as the existing circle.
3. Select both circles.
4. Go to the top menu bar to select *Modify – Clip Surface*. The smaller circle will cut into the big circle.
5. Take the smaller circle out of the big circle to hollow out the big circle and delete the smaller circle.
6. Select the *Polyline Tool* in the *Basic* palette and draw a squiggly line.
7. Select both the polyline and the hollowed-out circle.
8. Go to *Model – Extrude Along Path*. A dialogue box appears.
9. If the curved line is highlighted in RED, click "OK" to execute the command. But, if the circles are highlighted in RED, click "Next" to switch the highlight to the curved line, and then click "OK" to execute the command.
10. If your default render mode is *Wireframe* and you want to see the tube rendered in solid, go to the teapot icon located on the *View* bar to select *Shaded* in the dropdown menu. If you want to change the default render setting to Shaded, go to *Tool* (on the top menu bar) – *Options – Vectorworks Preference*. Then select "3D", where you can change the default render mode to Shaded.

Sweep

Command: Model – Sweep…
Shortcut: Ctrl+Alt+W (Windows); Cmd+Option+W (Mac)

1. In *Front* view, draw a rectangle. (height: 8′; width: 2′6″)

2. Go to *Tool Sets – 3D Modeling* and click on *Set Working Plane Tool*.
3. Click on the rectangle to turn it into a working plane (highlighted in purple).
4. Invoke the *Polyline Tool* in the *Basic* palette and make sure the *Corner Vertex Mode* is selected.
5. Draw a shape of half-vase inside the rectangle, starting the polyline from the upper left corner, working clockwise, and ending the polyline at its starting point to close the line by double-clicking the mouse. During the drawing process, use click-click mode to draw straight lines and click-drag mode to draw curves.
6. After the shape of a half-vase is complete, select *Offset Tool* from *Basic* palette.
7. Make sure the *Offset by Distance Mode* on the mode bar is selected. Type 0.2″ in the *Distance* slot to give thickness to the wall of the vase.
8. Click once inside of the half-vase shape.
9. Create a rectangle to cover the top wall of the half-vase (overlapping the offset vase shape).
10. Create another rectangle to cover the left wall of the half-vase (overlapping the offset vase shape).
11. Select the two rectangles you just created as well as the offset half-vase shape.
12. Go to *Modify – Add Surface*. The three shapes become one shape.
13. Select both the combined shape and the half-vase shape you previously created.
14. Go to *Modify – Clip Surface* to hollow out the half-vase.
15. Delete the combined shape and then the rectangle that you previously created to reveal the true profile of the vase.
16. Select the profile of the vase and go to *Model – Sweep*… A dialogue box appears.
17. Click "OK" to accept the default. A 3D vase is thus complete.
18. See the result in an *Isometric* view.

Push/Pull

Command: *Tool Set – 3D Modeling – Push/Pull Tool*
Shortcut: Shift+R (Windows); Shift+R (Mac)

1. In *Top/Plan* view, draw a circle (radius: 2′).
2. Select the *Push/Pull* tool in the *Tool Sets – 3D Modeling*
3. Go to an *Isometric* view.
4. Hover over your mouse to highlight the circle in RED.
5. Click and drag the center of the circle to the desired height. Release your mouse to complete the modeling. This is a more intuitive way of creating a cylinder than using *Extrude* command.

Add Solids

Command: *Model – Add Solids*
Shortcut: Ctrl+Alt+A (Windows); Cmd+Option+A (Mac)

Automatic Method

1. In *Top/Plan* view, draw a square (4′ × 4′).
2. Extrude the square into a cube (4′ × 4′ × 4′).
3. Select the Circle Tool and check to see if the Active Plane located on the *View* bar is in "Automatic" mode. If not, click on the "Look at Working Plane" button next to it, then select the "Automatic" mode in the Active Plane dropdown menu.

   Note: ***Layer Plane*** is different from ***Working Plane***. Every VW layer has an internal layer plane associated with it. This plane is sometimes referred to as the "ground plane," as it provides a constant reference to the objects in the layer. In contrast, the Working Plane can be moved and rotated to align with different objects and surfaces when modeling in 3D. Every drawing also has an internal Working Plane. The default orientation of the Working Plane is invisible, as it is the same as the active Layer Plane (see Fig. 3.9).

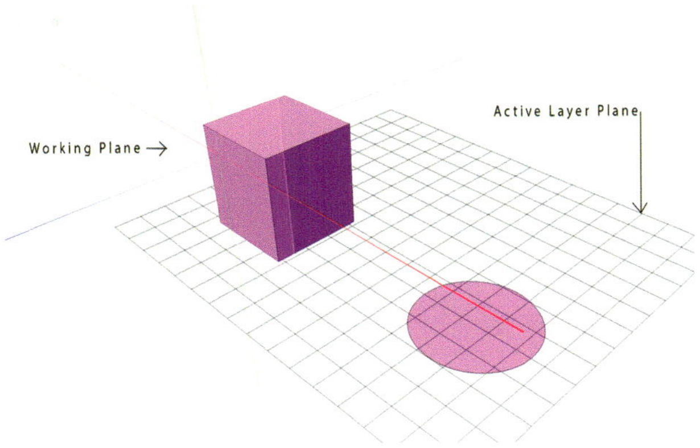

Figure 3.9 *Working Plane vs. Layer Plane*. A diagram showing the difference between Working Plane and Layer Plane.

4. Create a circle (dia.: 2′) in the middle of the cube.
5. Extrude the circle into a cylinder (height: 3′).
6. Go to an *Isometric* view to see the result.
7. Select both solids.
8. Go to the top menu bar and select *Model – Add Solids*. The two solids become one.

Bottom Z (Bot Z) Method

1. In *Top/Plan* view, draw a square (4′ × 4′).
2. Extrude the square into a cube (4′ × 4′ × 4′).
3. Select *Circle Tool* and confirm the *Active Plane* located on the *View* bar is in the *Layer Plane* mode.
4. Create a circle (dia.: 2′) in the middle of the cube.
5. Extrude the circle into a cylinder (height: 3′).
6. Go to an *Isometric* view to see the result. You will find that the cylinder is invisible.
7. Click the B key (X-ray key) on the keyboard to reveal the hidden lines, the cylinder appears as selected. If not, click on the *Select* icon in the *Basic* palette. Deselect the cube and reselect the cylinder.
8. Go to the *Object Info* palette and input 6′ in the *Bot Z* slot to elevate the cylinder. You will see the column appear at the top of the cube.
9. Select both solids.
10. Go to the top menu bar and select *Model – Add Solids*. The two solids become one.

Subtract Solids

Command: *Model – Subtract Solids*
Shortcut: Ctrl+Alt+S (Windows); Cmd+Option+S (Mac)

Subtract Solids in Top/Plan View (2D View)

1. In *Top/Plan* view, draw a square (9′ × 9′).
2. Extrude the square to create a cube (height: 9′).
3. Ensure the current view of the working plane is on Layer Plane and draw a circle (5′ diameter) in the middle of the cube.
4. Extrude the circle to create a cylinder that is taller than the cube (height: 10′).
5. See the 3D form in an *Isometric* view.
6. Select both the cube and the cylinder.
7. Go to *Model – Subtract Solids*. A dialogue box appears.
8. Make sure the Retain Subtracting Objects box is unchecked.
9. If the cube is lit in RED, click "OK" to execute the command. If the cylinder is lit in RED, click the forward arrow to select the cube, then click "OK" to execute the command. In any case, you want the object you need to retain lit in RED.

Subtract Solids in Front View (3D View)

1. Switch to a *Front* view of the previously created form.
2. Select *3D Modeling* tool on the *Tool Sets*.
3. Click on the *Set Working Plane* tool (Planer Face Mode) to select the tool.
4. Click on the front surface of the cube.
5. Draw a circle (5′ diameter) in the middle of the cube.
6. Extrude the circle by -10′ to make sure the new cylinder you are creating cuts into the cube.
7. View the result in an *Isometric* view.
8. Select both the cube and the cylinder.
9. Go to *Model – Subtract Solids*.
10. When the cube is lit, click "OK" in the dialogue box to execute the command.
11. You may also use the *Flyover Tool* to view the result from customized angles.

Split

Command: *Basic – Split Tool*
Shortcut: L (Windows); L (Mac)

1. In *Top/Plan* view, draw a rectangle (width: 9′; height: 1′).
2. Go to *Model – Extrude*. Type 9′ in the Extrusion slot and click "OK."
3. Switch view from *Top/Plan* view to *Front* view.
4. Go to *Tool Sets – 3D Modeling* and click on *Set Working Plane Tool*.
5. When the 9′ × 9′ square is lit in purple, click on this plane.
6. Draw a 3′ × 3′ square, overlapping the upper right corner of the previous square. This will give you a horizontal mark 3′ from the right edge and a vertical mark 3′ from the top of the large square.
7. Verify the current projection in the *View* bar is on *Orthogonal*.
8. While the large square is selected, click on the *Split Tool* located in the *Basic* palette and select Line Trim Mode on the mode bar.
9. Click once on the top edge of the large square at point 3′ from the right edge.
10. Click the second time on the right edge of the large square at point 3′ from the top edge while observing the large square being lit with RED lines. Then, you will see an arrow appear in the center of the line you just drew.

11. Make your third click towards the center of the large square. This will cut off a corner from both squares.
12. If the corner is still retained, deselect both shapes, select the corner, and drag the corner to a new location.
13. Delete the remaining small reference triangle.
14. See the result of the split in an *Isometric* view.

Helix-Spiral

Command: *Model – 3D Power Pack – Create Helix Spiral…*

1. In *Top/Plan* view, draw a straight line (Length: 20′).
2. When the line is selected, go to *Model – 3D Power Pack – Create Helix Spiral…* A dialogue window appears.
3. Make sure the option of Using Turns is selected.
4. Insert the following information:
   a. Turns: 4
   b. Start Radius: 7′
   c. End Radius: 2′
   d. Start Angle: 30
5. Click "OK." A spiral line appears.
6. Draw a small circle (diameter: 6″)
7. Select both the spiral line and the circle.
8. Go to *Model – Extrude Along Path*. A dialogue box appears.
9. If the spiral line is lit in RED, click "OK" to execute the command. If the circle is lit in RED, click "Next" to select the spiral line. Then, click "OK" to execute the command.
10. Switch to the Front view. Select *Modify – Rotate – Rotate…* when a pop-up window appears, insert –90 in the angle slot. This will turn the spiral into a downward spiral.

Deform

Command: *Tool Sets – 3D Modeling – Deform*

Taper Solid

1. In *Top/Plan* view, click on *Regular Polygon Tool* in *Basic* palette.
2. Create a six-sided polygon (radius: 3′).
3. Extrude the polygon (height: 12′).
4. Switch to an *Isometric* view.
5. Click on the *Deform Tool* located in *Tool Sets – 3D Modeling*.
6. Click on *Taper Solid Mode* located on the mode bar.
7. When your mouse hovers over the object, the object is lit in RED.
8. Make your first click on the solid to invoke a directional arrow.
9. Make your second click on the solid to locate the center of the taper.
10. Move your mouse around to determine the direction of your taper, then make the third click.
11. Move your mouse again on the directional track to decide if you want your solid to taper in or out and how much it tapers. Then make your fourth click to see the result.

Twist Solid

1. Go to Edit on the top menu bar and select *Undo* in the dropdown menu to undo the taper.
2. While the *Deform Tool* is still selected, click Twist Solid Mode located on the mode bar.
3. Hover over your mouse to light the 3D form in RED, and make a click to claim the solid.
4. Click the second time to locate the center of the twist that you are about to make.
5. Move your mouse out and around the center and make a third click to locate the start point of the twist.
6. Move your mouse around the center to determine the direction and degree of your twist, and make the fourth click to see the result of the command.

Bulge Solid

1. To prepare for your *Bulge Solid* command, undo the twist performed previously on the 3D form.
2. While the *Deform Tool* is still selected, click Bulge Solid mode located on the mode bar.
3. Hover over your mouse to light the 3D form in RED, and make a click to claim the solid.
4. Click the second time to locate the center of the bulge that you are about to make.
5. Turn your mouse around and make the third click to determine the direction of the bulge.
6. Drag your mouse to decide if you want the solid to bulge or contract and how much the solid will bulge or contract, and make the fourth click to see the result of the command.

NURBS Curve

Command: *Tool Sets – 3D Modeling – NURBS Curve Tool*
Shortcut: Shift+7 (Windows); Shift+7 (Mac)

NURBS Curve 1

1. In *Top/Plan* view, draw a square (5′ × 5′).
2. Extrude the square into a rectangular prism (height: 8′)
3. Click on the *Render Mode* arrow located next to the teapot icon.
4. In the dropdown menu, select *Shaded Options*… A dialogue window appears.
5. Choose "Very High" in the Detail Slot. Click "OK" to close the window.
6. Click on the *Render Mode* arrow again to select *Shaded* to render your 3D form.
7. Switch to *Right Isometric* view.
8. Go to *Tool Sets – 3D Modeling* and click on the *NURBS Curve Tool* while the object is still selected. Be sure the Interpolation Point Mode on the mode bar is also selected.
9. Draw an arch in the left panel of the prism, starting with the first click on the lower left corner of the left panel. Click the second time on the top middle point of the left panel. Your third click should be on the lower right corner of the left panel (refer to Fig. 3.10).
10. Draw an arch on the right panel of the prism by making the first click on the top middle point of the right panel and the second click on the lower right corner of the right panel (refer to Fig. 3.10).
11. While the modeling is still going on, switch to a *Left Rear Isometric* view and continue your arches on the new left and right panels of the prism.

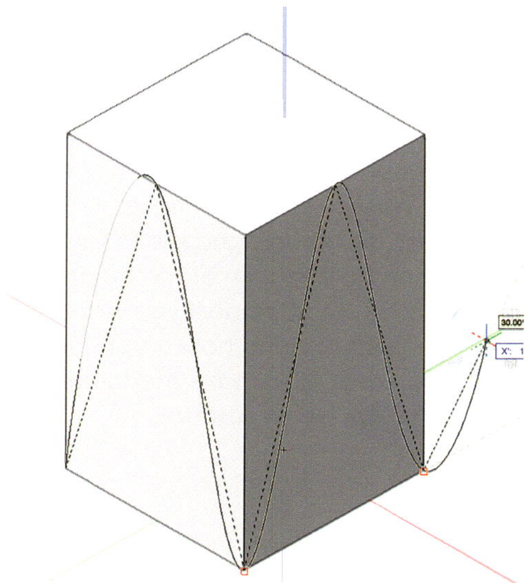

Figure 3.10 *NURBS curve.* A diagram for Step 9 and Step 10.

12. When you are about to complete your arches on all four panels of the prism, make sure that your last click meets the first click you made when you started this modeling process.
13. Select the rectangular prism and delete it. A 3D NURBS curve appears.
14. Select the curved line by double-clicking on it.
15. Zoom ("z" key on the keyboard) to the last click you made and move the reshape handle (the small blue square) around to snap it onto the blue square handle of your first click.
16. Go to *Model – 3D Power Pack – Create Surface from Curves*. A 3D form appears.
17. Go to *Basic* palette and select *Flyover Tool*.
18. Drag you mouse to see the 3D form in various angles.

NURBS Curve 2

1. In *Top/Plan* view, draw a rectangle (8′ × 12′).
2. Extrude the rectangle into a rectangular prism (height: 3′)
3. Switch to *Right Isometric* view.
4. Go to *Tool Sets – 3D Modeling* and click on the *NURBS Curve Tool* while the object is selected. Ensure the Interpolation Point Mode on the mode bar is also selected.
5. Draw a continuous, squiggly line that runs across all four panels of the prism. Make sure that the position of the first click meets that of the last double-click to enclose the 3D NURBS curve.
6. Select the rectangular prism and delete it. A 3D NURBS curve appears.
7. If needed, select the line by double-clicking on it and zoom in on the last click to adjust the position to meet the position of your first click.
8. Go to *Model – 3D Power Pack – Create Surface from Curves*. A 3D form appears.
9. Go to the *Basic* palette to select the *Reshape Tool*.
10. Select Move NURBS Surface U Vertices Mode found in the mode bar.
11. Move some NURBS points into new positions to see the changes.
12. Go to the *Basic* palette and select the *Flyover Tool*.
13. Drag your mouse to see the 3D form from various angles.

3D Visualization Technique

Viewing Angles and Directions

Note: The *Current View* dropdown menu resides in the *View* bar. The default viewing angle and direction is *Top/Plan* view, the only 2D view in the dropdown list.

1. With a 3D object(s) available on your drawing, click on the *Current View* dropdown menu and select *Front* to switch your viewing direction to a front view.
2. Click on the *Current View* dropdown menu and select *Right Isometric* to switch your viewing angle/direction to a *right isometric view*.
3. Click on the *Flyover Tool* located on the Basic palette to select the tool.
4. Click and drag your mouse to an angle/direction from which to view your 3D object(s).

Viewing Projections

Note: The *Current Projection* dropdown menu is located on the *View* bar.

1. With a 3D object(s) available on your drawing displayed in an *Isometric* view, click on the *Current Projection* dropdown menu and select *Normal Perspective*.
2. Switch the projection to a *Narrow Perspective* to see the difference.
3. Switch the projection to a *Wide Perspective* to see the difference.
4. Switch the projection to *Orthogonal* to see the difference.

Render Modes

Note: The *Current Render Mode* dropdown menu is located on the *View* bar (next to the teapot icon).

1. With a 3D object(s) available on your drawing displayed in an *Isometric* view, click on the *Current Render Mode* dropdown menu and select *Wireframe* to see the result.
2. Switch the *Current Render Mode* choice to *Shaded* to see the result.
3. Switch the *Current Render Mode* choice *to Final Quality Renderworks* to see the difference.

3D Rendering Technique

Render a 3D Form in Color

Command: *Attributes palette – Solid Fill Color* (color bar)

1. Click on *3D Modeling* in *Tool Sets* and select the *Sphere Tool*.
2. Click drag your mouse to create a sphere (10′ radius).
3. While the sphere is selected, go to the *Object Info* palette and click on the Render tab. Make sure that the "Class Texture" in the Texture dropdown menu is selected.
4. Go to the *Attributes* palette and click on the color bar to select an existing color to render the sphere.

Render a 3D Form in Texture

Command: Object Info – Render – Texture – Resource Manager (if applicable)

1. While the sphere is still selected, go to the *Object Info* palette to select *Render* tab.
2. Switch "Class Texture" in the Texture dropdown menu to "Texture."
3. Click on the up/down arrow to conduct a search for "marble."
4. Marble icons appear in the search result window.
5. Click on Stone Marble Pink 04 RT.
6. Click on the "Select" button.
7. The sphere is now a marble ball!

Render a 3D Form in Image

Command: *Resource Manager – New Resource – Renderworks Texture – Image – Import an Image File*

1. Download a landscape image onto your desktop. (JEPG format is preferred.)
2. Make a note of the size of the image. For instance: 5″ (h) × 7″ (w).
3. In *Top/Plan* view, create a rectangle that is proportional to the size of the image. For example: 10′ (h) × 14′ (w) or 20′ (h) × 28′ (w).
4. Extrude the rectangle by 1″.
5. While the 3D form is selected, go to *Resource Manager*, click on New Resource, and a Create Resource window will appear.
6. Select "Renderworks Texture" and click on the "Create" button. An Edit Texture window appears.
7. Give a name to the image you are about to import.
8. In the Color dropdown menu, select "Image." A Choose Image window appears.
9. Make certain "Import an Image file" is selected and click "OK."
10. Locate the image you previously saved on your computer desktop, select it, and click "Open." The image you selected appears in the Edit Image Color window.

11. Click "OK" to import the image. The image appears in the Edit Texture preview window.
12. In the Edit Texture window, make the size of the image equal to the size of the 3D object. For example, type 10′ in the Image Size slot. Type 10′ in the Obj Size slot. This ratio allows only one image (as opposed to repeated images) to be shown in the preview window.
13. Click "OK".
14. Go to Object Info – Render and select texture if the image has not yet appeared on your 3D object.
15. Click on the arrow in the Texture window to select the image that you have just imported. If it is not shown on the display panel, do a search for the image to select it.
16. You can now adjust the scale, position, and rotation of the image to your satisfaction in *Object Info* palette.
17. For some images, you might need to switch the *Current Render Mode* to *Final Quality Renderworks* to see the result.
18. To add a frame to the painting, create a profile of the frame and a rectangle around the painting, and use the *Extrude Along Path* command to complete the task.
19. You can also apply a texture to the frame and view the result in Final Quality Renderworks.

Experiment and Practice

Creating a Diamond

Figs. 3.11 and 3.12 illustrate different renditions of the Blue Diamond, one of the diamonds is rendered in Wireframe render mode; the other is rendered in Final Quality Renderworks render mode.

1. Go to the Top Menu bar and select *File – New*, a popup window appears. Click "OK" to create a blank document
2. Click the *Regular Polygon Tool* in the *Basic* palette and change the Number of Sides perimeter located in the mode bar to 8.
3. From the center of the page, draw a polygon.
4. Go to the *Object Info* palette to adjust the size of the polygon (X:1/8″; Y: 1/8″)

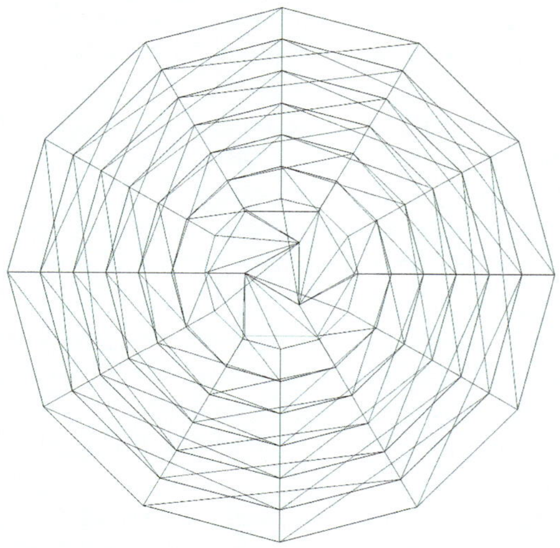

Figure 3.11 *Diamond_Wireframe*. An illustration of how a diamond rendered in *Wireframe* looks in *Top/Plan* view.

Figure 3.12 *Blue Diamond*. An illustration of how the diamond rendered in *Final Quality Renderworks* looks in *Front* view.

5. While the polygon is still selected, click on *Offset Tool* in the *Basic* palette.
6. In the mode bar, choose Offset by Distance and set the distance in ¼″
7. Click outside of the polygon (near the lower right corner of the page) 10 times and inside of the largest polygon once.
8. Click to select the last polygon you created, right-click your mouse, and select "Rotate…". A popup window appears.
9. Type 22.5 as the rotation angle and click "OK."
10. Press "x" key twice to deselect the polygon.
11. Use the *Selection Tool* (click and drag) to select all the polygons (or press Ctrl+A on Windows; Cmd+A on Mac to select them).
12. Go to *Model* in the top menu bar and choose *Multiple Extrude*. A pop-up window comes up.
13. Type 3″ in the Extrusion slot and click "OK."
14. To add texture to the diamond form, go to the *Object Info* palette and click on *Render*.

15. In the Texture Dropdown menu, choose "Texture."
16. Click on the existing texture icon to access the *Resource Manager*. Make sure "All Resources is selected. Search "Glass" in *Resource Manage*. A bunch of glass types will appear as a result.
17. Double-click on Glass Blue 03 RT.
18. To view the result of your model, switch to the *Front* view (or any other 3D view). Then, go to the teapot icon, select *Final Quality Renderworks*, and wait for a few moments to allow render time.

Creating a Spindle

Figs. 3.13 and 3.14 illustrate different renditions of wooden spindles, Twin Spindles (Fig. 3.13) are rendered in Wireframe render mode; Wooden Spindle (Fig. 3.14) is rendered in Final Quality Renderworks render mode.

1. Go to *File – New*. A pop-up window appears. Click "OK" to create a blank document
2. Click the *Circle Tool* in the *Basic* palette to select it.
3. Draw a circle (dia. 1 ½").
4. While the circle is still selected, click on the *Offset Tool* located in *Basic* palette.
5. Check Offset by Distance on the mode bar and type 0.1 in the Distance slot.
6. Click 5 times outside of the circles.
7. Copy and paste the largest circle, and place the copy exactly on the top of the largest circle.
8. Click twice on the midpoint of the circle.
9. Press the "x" key twice to deselect the circles.
10. Use the *Selection* tool (click and drag) to select all the circles.

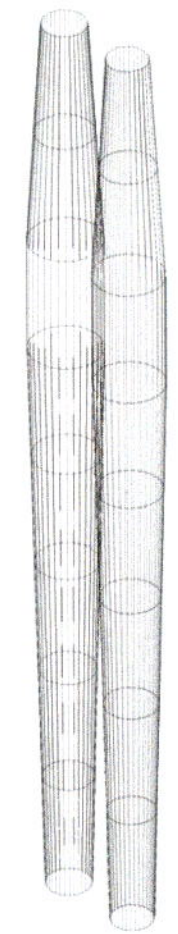

Figure 3.13 *Twin Spindles_Wireframe*. Twin Spindles rendered in a Wireframe render mode.

Figure 3.14 *Wooden Spindle*. A wooden spindle rendered in *Final Quality Renderworks* render mode.

11. Go to *Model – Multiple Extrude*.
12. When the popup window appears, type 3' in the Extrusion slot and click "OK."
13. To view the result of your extrusion, switch to a *Front* view.
14. To apply a wood texture to the spindle, select the spindle and go to *Resource Manager*.
15. Make sure "All Resources" is selected in the dropdown menu and conduct a search for "wood."
16. When the wood icons appear in the *Resource Manager* window, double-click on "Wood (arrowayWood 055 Cedar Lebanon 1)- Vert" to select it. Right click on the icon to select "Import." A pop-up window appears. Give a name to the texture, make sure "Preserve folder hierarchy" is checked, and click "OK."
17. To see the result of your texture rendering, click on the teapot icon and select *Final Quality Renderworks*.

Creating a Wine Glass

Fig. 3.15 shows the result of the following procedure.

1. In *Front* view, use the *Line Tool* found in the *Basic* palette to draw a straight vertical line as the center axis of the wine glass.
2. Click on the *Polyline Tool* found in the *Basic* palette and make sure Corner Vertex Mode in the mode bar is selected.
3. Draw the profile of a wine glass, using click-click for straight lines and click-drag for curves.

Figure 3.15 *Wine Glass*. The result of using *Sweep* command in the creation of a wine glass.

4. Go to *Model – Sweep…* to execute the drawing of a wine glass (solid).
5. Double-click on the solid to gain access to the Sweep Profile edit window.
6. Select *Offset Tool* in *Basic* palette.
7. Make sure Offset by Distance Mode on the mode bar is selected.
8. Type the relative thickness of the glass in the Distance slot (also located on mode bar).
9. Click once inside the glass profile.
10. Add two rectangles (one on the top and one on the left side of the glass profile) overlapping the offset shape in order to hollow out the solid.
11. Select the offset shape and the two rectangles.
12. Go to *Modify – Add Surface*. The three shapes become one shape.
13. Select both the profile shape and the newly combined shape.
14. Go to *Modify – Clip Surface*. The true profile of the wine class is complete.
15. To see the result, click on the Exit Sweep Profile button and select an Isometric view.

Creating a Balustrade from Scratch

Fig. 3.16 shows the result of the following procedure.

1. Draw a 10′ (w) × 9″ (h) rectangle, extrude it by 3″, and set the Bot Z at 0.
2. Draw a 6″ × 6″ square, extrude it by 2″, and set the Bot Z at 3″.
3. Snap the center of the 3D form to the vertical center of the rectangle and, horizontally, 3″ away from the left edge of the rectangle.
4. Draw the following circles from the same center point in an order as shown below.
   a. A 2.5″ (dia.) circle
   b. A 4″ (dia.) circle
   c. A 4″ (dia.) circle
   d. A 2.5″ (dia.) circle
5. Select all four circles. Go to *Model – Multiple Extrude* to extrude the form by 1.5″.
6. Go to the *Object Info* palette to set the Bot Z at 5″.
7. Snap the center of the 3D form to the center of the previous square.
8. Draw a 2.5″ circle, extrude it by 0.5″, and set the Bot Z at 6.5″.

Figure 3.16 *Balustrade from Scratch*. An example of balustrade created from scratch using basic tools and commands available in VW.

9. Snap the center of the 3D form to the center of the previous circles.
10. Draw the following circles from the same center point in an order as shown below.
    a. A 2.5″ (dia.) circle
    b. A 4″ (dia.) circle
    c. A 4″ (dia.) circle
    d. A 2.5″ (dia.) circle
11. Select all four circles. Go to *Model – Multiple Extrude* to extrude the form by 1.5″.
12. Go to the *Object Info* palette to set the Bot Z at 7″.
13. Snap the center of the 3D form to the center of the previous circles.
14. Draw a 2.5″ circle, extrude it by 0.5″, and set the Bot Z at 8.5″.
15. Snap the center of the 3D form to the center of the previous circles.
16. Draw the following circles from the same center point in an order as shown below.
    a. A 2.5″ (dia.) circle
    b. A 3.5 (dia.) circle
    c. A 4.5″ (dia.) circle
    d. A 5″ (dia.) circle
    e. Another 5″ (dia.) circle
17. Click on *Offset Tool* in *Basic* palette.
18. Double-click on Offset Tool Preference located on the mode bar.
19. When a pop-up window appears, make the following choices.
    a. Method: Offset by Distance.
    b. Distance: 0.15″
    c. Duplication: Duplicate and Offset.
    d. Wall Offset: Offset from Center Line, and "Smooth Corners." Then, click "OK."
20. Click on the center of the circle 8 times, and then draw a 2.5″ (dia.) circle.
21. Select all the circles in this group.
22. Go to *Model – Multiple Extrude*. A dialog box appears.
23. Extrude the form by 9″, set the Bot Z at 9″, and snap the center of the 3D form to the center of the previous circles.
24. Draw the following circles from the same center point in an order as shown below.
    a. A 2.5″ (dia.) circle
    b. A 3″ (dia.) circle
    c. A 3″ (dia.) circle
    d. A 2.5″ (dia.) circle
25. Select all the four circles, extrude them by 0.5″, set the Bot Z at 1′6″, and snap the center of the 3D form to the center of the previous circles.
26. Draw a 2.5″ circle, extrude it by 0.5″, set the Bot Z at 1′6.5″, and snap the center of the 3D form to the center of the previous circles.
27. Draw a 2.75″ circle, extrude it by 0.25″, set the Bot Z at 1′7″, and snap the center of the 3D object to the center of the previous objects.
28. Draw a 3″ × 3″ square, extrude it by 0.5″, set the Bot Z at 1′7.25″, and snap the center of the 3D form to the center of the previous circles.
29. Switch to a *Front* view to see the baluster you have just created.
30. If the forms are all connected vertically, switch back to *Top/Plan* view.
31. Select all but the largest rectangle in the drawing.
32. Go to *Model – Add Solids*. The individual 3D forms become one baluster.
33. While the baluster is still selected, click on the *Mirror Tool* located in *Basic* palette.
34. Draw a vertical line aligned with the center of the largest rectangle to produce another baluster on the opposite side of the rectangle.
35. Draw a horizontal reference line between the centers of the two balusters and then delete the baluster located on the right end of the rectangle.
36. Press the "Shift" key while you select both the remaining baluster and the reference line.
37. Go to the *Edit* menu located on the top menu bar and select *Duplicate Along Path*…. A pop-up window appears.
38. Click on "Number of Duplicates," Type "10" in the slot, click "Preview" to view the result, and click "OK" to exit the window.
39. Delete the horizontal reference line.
40. Draw a 10′ × 9″ rectangle, extrude it by 3″, set the Bot Z at 1′ 7.75″, and snap the center of the rectangle to the center of the previous rectangle.
41. Draw a 10′1″ (w) × 10″ (h) rectangle, extrude it by 0.5″, set the Bot Z at 1′ 10.75″, and snap the center of the rectangle to the center of the previous rectangles.
42. Select all 3D forms in the drawing and go to *Model – Add Solids* to join every part of the balustrade into one solid.
43. To view the balustrade, switch to the *Right Isometric* view, select *Normal Perspective* and *Shaded*.
44. To apply texture to the balustrade, select the balustrade.
45. Go to the *Object Info* palette and click on the "Render" tab. Scroll down to Texture and select "Texture" in the dropdown menu.

46. Double-click on the texture icon, a pop-up window (*Resource Manager*) appears. Search for Marble.
47. When the marble icons appear, click on Sone Marble Green 01 RT (or Stone Marble Pink 04 RT), and then on the *Select* button.
48. For a detailed rendering of the form and texture, select *Final Quality Renderworks* in the *Current Render Mode* (teapot) dropdown menu.
49. After texture is rendered on your balustrade, you may adjust the scale and rotation of the marble pattern to your satisfaction by scrolling down the *Object Info* window to make choices.

Project #1: Creating 3D Objects

Objectives

The main purpose of this project is for you to demonstrate your capacity for 3D modeling, rendering, and visualization in a VW working environment. To that end, you will

1. exercise navigation skills.
2. perform appropriate document and page setup.
3. innovatively apply the knowledge and skills of digital modeling, rendering, and visualization that you have acquired to create 3D objects and present them in different views, projections, and render modes.
4. exhibit patience, concentration, attention to details, and professionalism in your work.

Tasks

Through Chapters 1–3, you have learned how to set up the document and navigate in the VW working environment. You have also developed VW skills in drawing, modeling, rendering, and visualization in 2D and 3D forms. Now, it is time for you to explore and discover.

Your main task for this project is to apply the accumulative knowledge and skills that you acquired previously to create two 3D objects that are contrasting in the aspects of form, texture, and color. One object is a stair unit that has predetermined perimeters (see Fig. 3.17 for details); the other is an object with an organic form that does not have predetermined perimeters, but purely comes out of

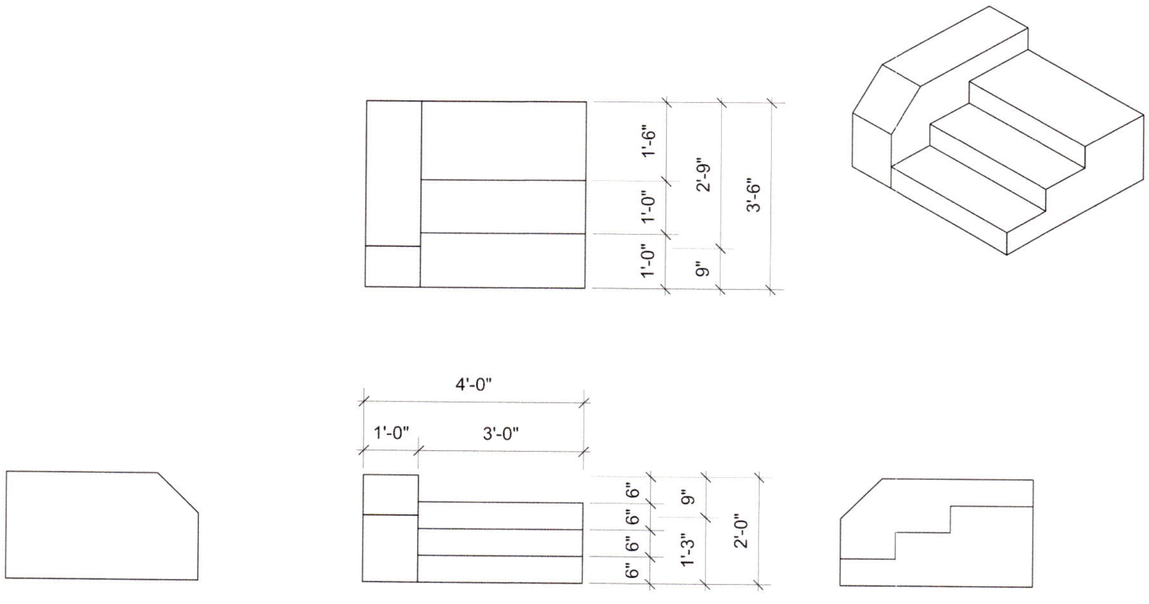

STAIR (SCALE: 1/2" = 1'-0")

Figure 3.17 *Stair Assignment*. This illustration provides detailed information for the construction of a virtual model for the Stair assignment.

your imagination. Please see student work samples in Figs. 3.18–3.29 for reference.

For each of the two objects, you will need to

1. create a digital 3D object using the modeling tools and commands available in VW.
2. apply attributes of color and texture to the surface of the object.
3. render the 3D form in views/projections/rendering modes as specified below:
   a. Image #1: *Top/Plan/Orthogonal/Wireframe*
   b. Image #2: *Front/Narrow Perspective/Shaded*
   c. Image #3: *Right Isometric/Normal Perspective/Final Quality Renderwork*
4. export each image as a separate JPEG file with 300 dpi and save them to your computer.
5. save the original VW files of the two 3D forms (stair and freeform) on your computer.

Required Equipment and Materials

To complete this project, you will need a computer with internet access and Vectorworks Version 2023 installed. Note: It is important that you download VW Version 2023, because this book is based on Version 2023. A different version may cause unpredictable issues during your working processes.

Modeling Scale

½″ = 1′-0″

Procedure

1. Drawing environment setup
   - Set your drawing scale (1/2″)
   - Set the size of your page (US Arch D)
   - Set the workspace preference (designer)
2. For each of your two 3D forms
   - Create your 2D shape in Top/Plan view.
   - Extrude your 2D shape into a 3D form.
   - View the object from various viewing directions and angles.
   - Edit and modify the object to your satisfaction.
   - Render your 3D object in color and texture.
   - Visualize the object in the view/projection/render mode as specified in ***Tasks***.
   - Export each view/projection/render mode into Image files (JPEG) with 300 dpi.
   - Save the Image files on your computer as: Your Last Name_Project Title_Name of the Object_Name of the View (for example: Chen_3D Objects_Stair_Right Isometric)
   - Save your two original objects in VW file format onto your computer as: Your Last Name_Project Title_Name of the Object (for example: Chen_3D Objects_Stair)

Evaluation Criteria

Artistry

1. The organic form is original.
2. The organic form demonstrates sophistication in modeling, rendering, and visualization with exquisite details.
3. The two forms show contrast in form, color, and texture.

Problem-Solving

1. The work has a proper setup of the drawing environment.
2. It shows evidence of navigation skills in a VW environment.
3. It illustrates the use of various modeling, rendering, and visualization tools, commands, and techniques.

Requirements and Presentation

1. The work conforms to the perimeters set in the project guidelines.
2. It is executed with accuracy and professionalism.

Student Work Samples

Figs. 3.18–3.29 are student work samples for Project #1 – Creating 3D Projects.

Figure 3.18 *Speaker*. Created by Mace Gallagher for 3D Objects – Freeform assignment.

Figure 3.19 *Staircase*. Created by Raine Hess for 3D Objects – Stair assignment.

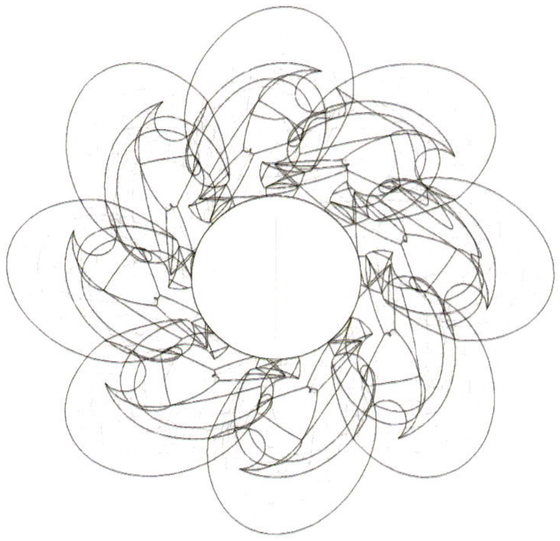

Figure 3.20a *Crystal Ball_Wireframe*. Created by LaTia Cunningham-Moore for 3D Objects – Freeform assignment.

Figure 3.20b *Crystal Ball_Renderworks*. Created by LaTia Cunningham-Moore for 3D Objects – Freeform assignment.

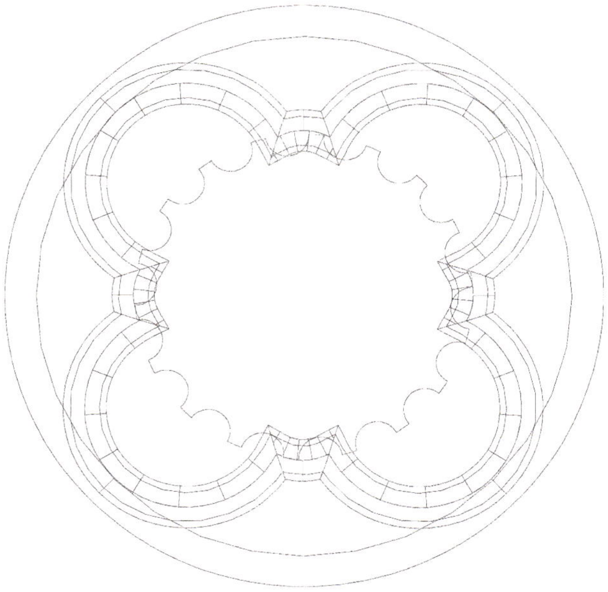

Figure 3.21a *Pedestal_Wireframe*. Created by Ben Holmes for 3D Objects – Freeform assignment.

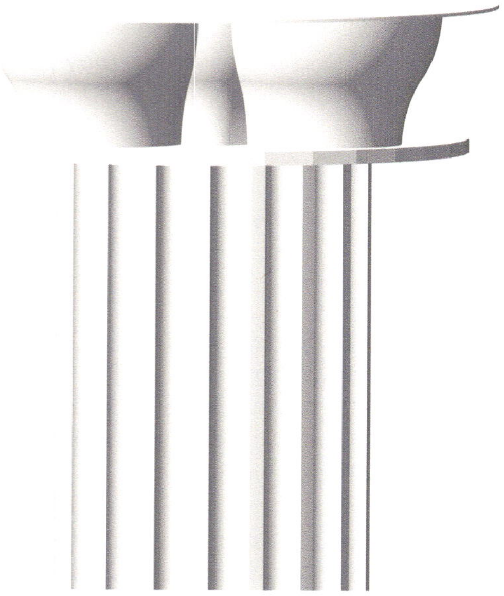

Figure 3.21b *Pedestal_Renderworks*. Created by Ben Holmes for 3D Objects – Freeform assignment.

Figure 3.22 *Wishing Well*. Created by Michelle Lee for 3D Objects – Freeform assignment.

Figure 3.23 *Cat Tower*. Created by Cristine Giacomo for 3D Objects – Freeform assignment.

Figure 3.24 *Pipe and Basket*. Created by Liam Irwin for 3D Objects – Freeform assignment.

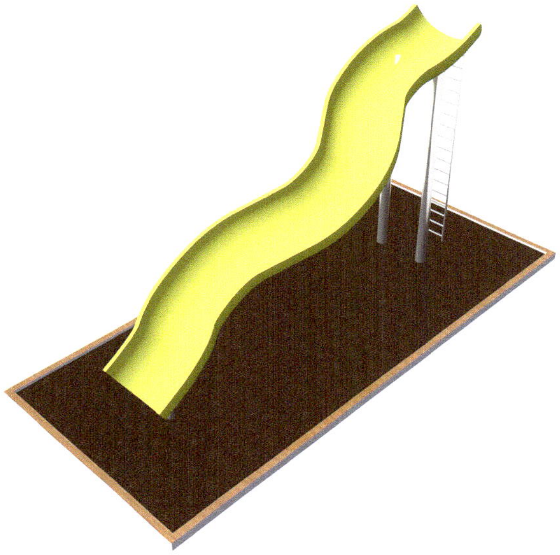

Figure 3.25 *Slide*. Created by Nathan Peters for 3D Objects – Freeform assignment.

Figure 3.26 *Hairspray Bottle*. Created by Eliza Craft for 3D Objects – Freeform assignment.

Figure 3.27 *Crystal Ball Music Box*. Created by Emily Sinatra for 3D Objects – Freeform assignment.

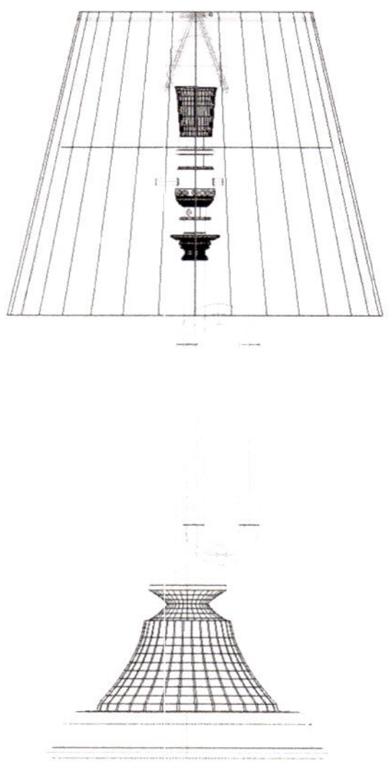

Figure 3.29a *Lamp_Wireframe*. Created by Micah Martin for 3D Objects – Freeform assignment.

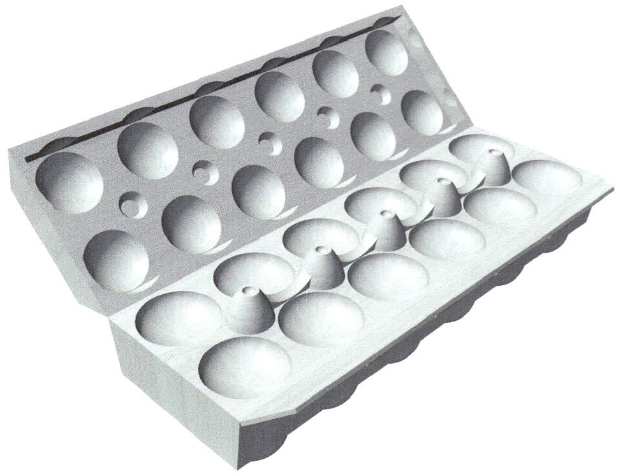

Figure 3.28 *Egg Carton Box*. Created by Mackenzie Scales for 3D Objects – Freeform assignment.

Figure 3.29b *Lamp_Renderworks*. Created by Micah Martin for 3D Objects – Freeform assignment.

Bibliography

Andri, Omelchenko. Fig. 3.6 *Imported Images: Broken Glass*. iStock by Getty Images. 2019.

Craft, Eliza. Fig. 3.26 *Hairspray Bottle*. Design Skill class project. 2022.

Cunningham-Moore, LaTia. Fig. 3.20a *Crystal Ball_Wireframe*. Design Skills class project. 2021.

Cunningham-Moore, LaTia. Fig. 3.20b *Crystal Ball_Renderworks*. Design Skills class project. 2021.

Gallagher, Mace. Fig. 3.18 *Speaker*. Design Skills class project. 2021.

Giacomo, Cristine. Fig. 3.23 *Cat Tower*. Design Skills class project. 2021.

Hess, Raine. Fig. 3.19 *Staircase*. Design Skills class project. 2019.

Holmes, Ben. Fig. 3.21a *Pedestal_Wireframe*. Design Skills class project. 2021.

Holmes, Ben. Fig. 3.21b *Pedestal_Renderworks*. Design Skills class project. 2021.

Irarrázabal, Mario. Fig. 3.6 *Imported Images: a Mano (The Hand)*. 2022. https://luxurypunta.com
Irwin, Liam. Fig. 3.24 *Pipe and Basket*. Design Skills class project. 2019.
Lee, Michelle. Fig. 3.22 *Wishing Well*. Design Skills class project. 2021.
Martin, Micah. Fig. 3.29a *Lamp_Wireframe*. Design Skills class project. 2022.
Martin, Micah. Fig. 3.29b *Lamp_Renderworks*. Design Skills class project. 2022.
Peters, Nathan. Fig. 3.25 *Slide*. Design Skills class project. 2019.
Scales, Mackenzie. Fig. 3.28 *Egg Carton Box*. Design Skills class project. 2022.
Sinatra, Emily. Fig. 3.27 *Crystal Ball Music Box*. Design Skills class project. 2022.
Szopa, Łukasz. Fig. 3.6 *Imported Images: PC Mouse DM1 PRO*. cgtrader. 1 Mar. 2019. https://www.cgtrader.com/3d-models/electronics/computer/pc-mouse-dm1-pro
Unknown. Fig. 3.6 *Imported Images: Broken glass isolated on transparent background*. Adobe Stock. https://stock.adobe.com/images/broken-glass-isolated-on-transparent-background/302938611?prev_url=detail
Unknown. Fig. 3.6 *Imported Images: People of Futuristic Mechanism*. Vector Stock. https://www.vectorstock.com/royalty-free-vector/people-of-the-future-futuristic-mechanism-vector-20950390
Unknown. Fig. 3.6 *Imported Images: Modern robots cartoon friendly mascots personal*. Vector Stock. https://www.vectorstock.com/royalty-free-vector/modern-robots-cartoon-friendly-mascots-personal-vector-35079294
VSG TechPowerUp. Fig. 3.6 *Imported Images: Disassembly-12*. TechPowerUp. 22 Mar. 2018. https://www.techpowerup.com/review/corsair-k63-wireless/4.html

CHAPTER 4

Seating Layout and Stage Masking

Vocabulary

Vector File
Raster File
Theatre Space Arrangement
Stage Space Arrangement
Staging Format
Proscenium Staging Format
Thrust Staging Format
Arena Staging Format
Virtual Volume
Sightline
Masking
C Value
Critical Seats
Leg
Border
Cyc
Groundrow
Portal
Backdrop
Onstage
Offstage
Batten
Upstage

Learning Objectives

- Identify technical terms with corresponding physical components of theatre.
- Show your ability to import a PDF floor plan, trace the plan with accuracy, and scale the plan to prepare for seating layout and scenic design in the VW working environment.
- Utilize tools and commands available in the VW program to create walls, insert doors, reserve aisles, and provide levels and seats in a black box theatre, as well as label the seating sections.
- Create seating layouts in a black box theatre that conform to the venue's safety guidelines, seating requirements, and C value calculations for sightline clearance.
- Demonstrate your mastery of using VW tools and commands to check horizontal and vertical sightlines and install appropriate masking devices to block the audience's view of the offstage space in a proscenium theatre.

Seating Layout

While most theatre venues in the U.S. nowadays still assume the traditional formats, such as proscenium, thrust, and arena, Avant-garde theatre artists of the early 20th century started to explore alternative venue spaces. They converted large rooms into black box theatres and performed in found spaces, from parks to parking lots and from warehouses to train stations. Without predetermined seating areas in a theatre, scenic designers are set free to create audience-performer spatial relationships tailored to specific productions.

DOI: 10.4324/9781003266242-4

Freedom comes with new issues: How could a set designer arrange the spatial relationship between audience and performers in a configuration that best serves the play in question? How could he/she make certain that the theatre space arrangement meets the seating capacity requirement for the venue? How could he/she design a space that conforms to the safety code of the venue? How could he/she arrange the seats with easy access for the audience? How could he/she be sure that all the audience members sitting in the space can see what he/she wants them to see without physical obstacles? The following sections describe the application of the VW program in the seating layout process for a Black Box theatre.

Get to Know the Perimeters for Your Seating Layout

As a set designer, one cannot start designing for a theatre production without knowing the specifications of the venue. These include 1) the dimensions of the venue, 2) the layout of the venue, such as the spatial relationships among entrances/exits, the performance space, the backstage area, and the theatre lobby, 3) the seating capacity requirement of the venue, 4) the venue's safety code for aisle width, and 5) the dimensions of the existing risers for the space, to name a few.

Acquire and Import a Floor Plan of the Venue

Imagine that you are hired to design a set for a theatrical or film production. Aside from reading the script and brainstorming ideas with the director and other collaborators and conducting research, you will start your design process with acquiring a floor plan and a section plan (or specifications with height information) for the venue. Of course, if available, a digital model of the venue will be even better. VW offers options to import a floor plan (or a theatre model) in a variety of formats. Some floor plans are vector graphics, which is native to the VW program; some are raster graphics. The differences between ***Vector File*** and ***Raster File*** are explained in Fig. 4.1.

It is useful to know that, if the original floor plan was a vector file, even though it might be later converted to a PDF file, you can still convert it back to a vector file in the VW environment during the import process.

In the VW program, the workspace that you want to use for your seating layout is the Spotlight workspace,

Vector vs Raster	Vector	Raster
Made Up of	Reference points and Curves	Pixels
Scalability	Scalable without losing quality	Scalable with quality loss
Convertibility	Convertible to Raster	Not convertible to vector
File Size	Smaller with the same quality appearance	Larger with the same quality appearance
File formats	AI, CDR, PDF, SVG, DXF, and EPS	BMP, GIF, JPEG, JPG, PNG, PSD, and TIF

Figure 4.1 *Vector vs Raster*. A chart comparing vector files with raster files.

as this workspace provides tools and commands specifically designed for seating arrangements that are not available in other workspaces. That said, it is more convenient though to first set up your document in a workspace such as Architect, Design Suite, or Landmark, because in these workspaces, if you go to Top Menu – File -Document Settings… – Document Setup, you can set Drawing Units, Scale, Area (size), etc. all in one setting (Document Setup window). This route is not available in the Spotlight workspace. For more explanation on Workspaces, please refer to "*Set Design Application of Tools Found in Different Workspaces*" in Chapter 5.

Scale and Trace the Venue Plan

After the floor plan is imported as a vector graphics file in your drawing, you want to scale the floor plan to meet the needs of your design. You also need to create a new Design Layer to separate the floor plan of your design from the floor plan of the venue. On the new Design Layer, with "Show/Snap Others" selected in Layer Option dropdown menu, you can then take advantage of the snapping function inherited in the vector file to trace the floor plan of the venue onto the new Design Layer with precision and efficiency.

Determine a Staging Format

Theatre Space Arrangement and ***Stage Space Arrangement*** deal with different sets of issues. While Theatre Space Arrangement refers to the arrangement of spatial relationships between audience and performers, Stage Space Arrangement focuses on the organization of the

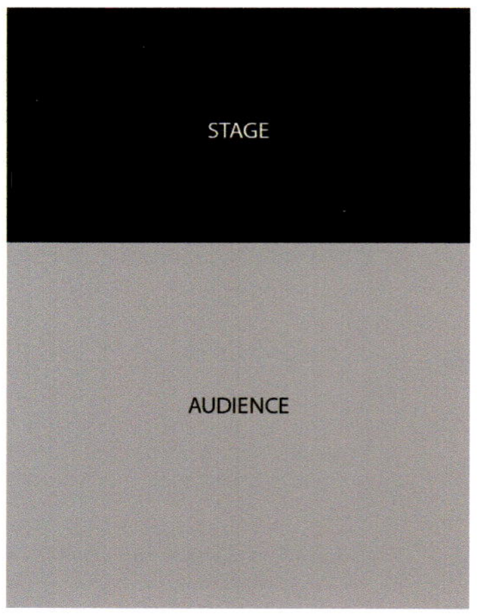

Figure 4.2 *Proscenium Staging Format*. This diagram illustrates the spatial relationship between audience and performers in a ***Proscenium Staging Format***.

space for performers. It solves problems such as dividing acting areas, setting entrances/exits and levels for actors' positions and movements on stage, as well as changing sceneries. As a set designer in a flexible seating space such as a Black Box theatre, before dealing with stage space issues, you will need to address issues regarding audience-performer spatial relationships. In other words, you will need to configure a ***Staging Format*** for the show. You want to ask yourself questions, such as

"Will the audiences sit on one side and the performers perform on the other side of the theatre?" (see Fig. 4.2)

"Will the performance area thrust into the audience area, with the audience surrounded on three sides of the performance space?" (see Fig. 4.3).

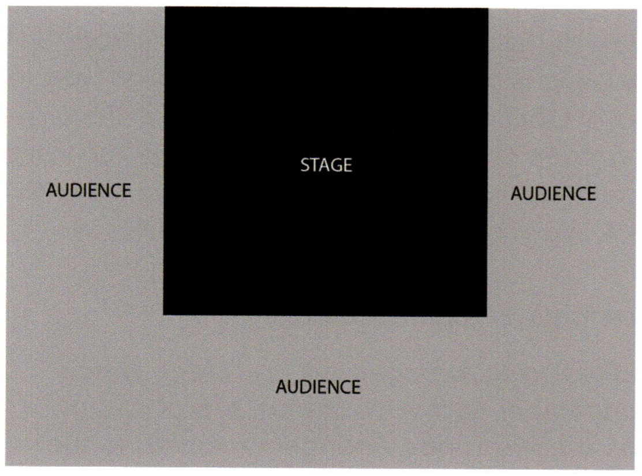

Figure 4.3 *Thrust Staging Format*. This diagram illustrates the spatial relationship between audience and performers in a ***Thrust Staging Format***.

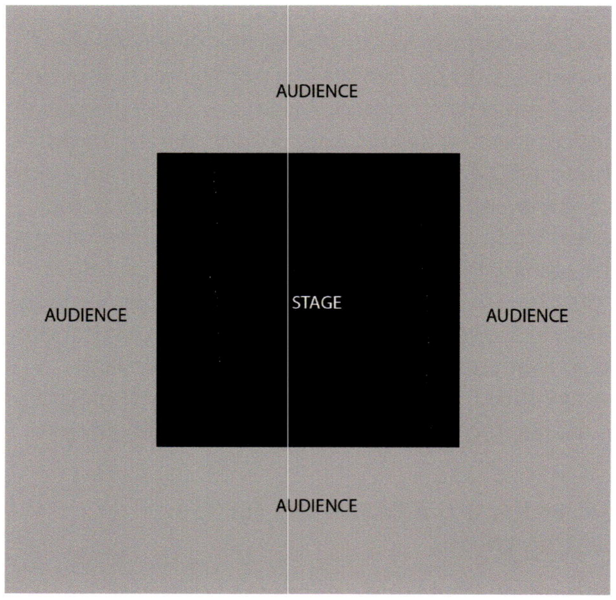

Figure 4.4 *Arena Staging Format*. This diagram illustrates the spatial relationship between audience and performers in an ***Arena Staging Format***.

"Will the performers perform in the middle of the theatre, and the audience surround the performance from all sides?" (see Fig. 4.4).

"Will the performers and audiences mingle seamlessly in a shared space?" (see Fig. 4.5).

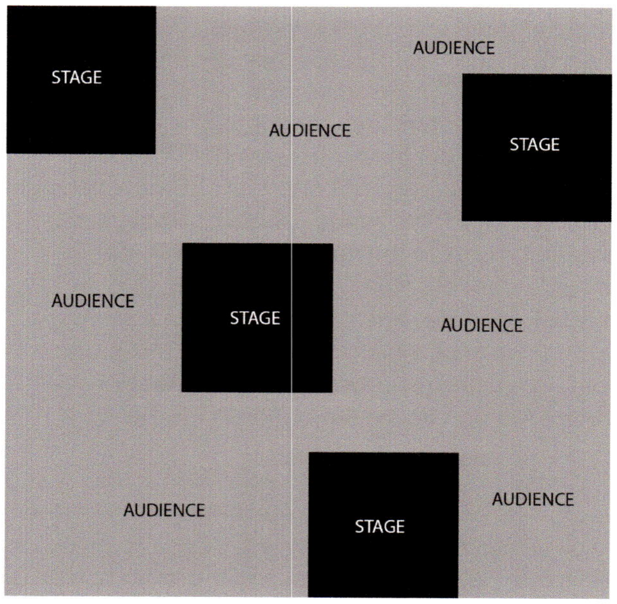

Figure 4.5 *Alternative Staging Format*. This diagram illustrates a possible spatial relationship between audience and performers in an alternative staging format.

What is the best audience-performer spatial arrangement for the show, and why?

Each theatre configuration comes with a unique set of advantages/disadvantages in terms of its

- physical and psychological intimacy between audience and performers/characters (with the same audience capacity in the house),
- ability to create the illusion of real life on stage,
- vantage point(s) from which the audiences view the performance,
- presentational or representational natural of the space,
- pictorial or spatial emphasis in the space.

The uniqueness of various theatre space configurations begs your careful consideration in your decision-making process, aiming for a suitable theatre format (seating layout).

Reserve Performing Space

After you come up with the idea for a staging format, you may start asking yourself: "What is the size of the space needed for the actors to tell the story?" The considerations for the dimensions and shape(s) of this space include 1) the number of actors, especially when they are together on stage, 2) the set requirements, and 3) the ***Virtual Volume*** of the actors' movement patterns (see Fig. 4.6). The term Virtual Volume refers to the space occupancy of the actors in their required physical action.

Figure 4.6 *Virtual Volume*. This image shows that the virtual volume of a person dancing is much larger than that of a person standing.

On your VW file, within the venue floor plan, draw a shape or shapes to reserve space for the performance, knowing that you will try your best to work out seating sections and aisles in the remaining of the given space before coming back to negotiate the space between the audience and performers. Occasionally, the negotiation between performance space and the requirements for the venue's seating capacity and safety code for aisles can be challenging.

Define Seating Areas

Within the venue floor plan and beyond the space reserved for performance, create shape(s) to define the seating area(s). In this step, you want to maximize the audience capacity to at least meet the venue's seating capacity requirement.

Install Seats

The physical installation of the seats in the VW environment is a piece of cake, as the action is done automatically. Nonetheless, you need to provide information, such as the height of the riser, the leg room, the alignment of rows, etc. in a dialog window to customize the seating arrangement for your space.

Create Aisles

Aisles in theatre denote the walkable space between the audience area and the performance area and between seating sections, leading from rows of seats to entrances/exits of the house. Your role as a set designer is to follow the venue's safety guidelines and ensure that the aisle spaces are reserved for the easy access of actors, audience (including wheelchair), and the set units during the performance and at the events of unexpected situations, including fire eruptions and attacks by terrorists. In Vectorworks, the Aisle command allows you to override seating areas and take the seats away if they are in the way of the aisles.

Provide Levels and Stagger Seats

The most used strategies to ensure good seats for every audience member in the house are to provide risers in seating sections and to alternate seats for different rows so that the audience can see the performance between or above the head of the audience in front. Creating platforms for performers can further increase visibility.

In VW, you can extrude 2D shape(s) to create levels, or customize a tool to build platforms, stairs, and risers to meet your needs for audience visibility clearance. Most of the established theatres with a Black Box facility will have a set of risers in stock. It is always a good idea to ask people at the venue for the dimensions and number of risers in their stock before you start to create your seating layout, should the information not already available to you in the theatre specifications.

Attach Data Tags to Seating Sections

Instead of counting the number of seats you installed in the seating sections one by one, which is quite tedious, the VW program makes the counting effortless; you can activate a Data Tag tool in the Tool Sets – Dims/Notes to attach a Data Tag to a seating section, which reveals the seating section information, including the number of seats, seat spacing, row spacing, etc.

Erect a Virtual Model of the Venue

To complete your seating layout model for the space, you need to erect a virtual model of the theatre to define the boundaries of your seating sections.

To do so, you want to make the current design Layer invisible but the venue floor plan Layer active. VW offers two efficient ways to build an encircled space in a few mouse-clicks. One way is to trace the shape of the venue (theatre) floor and use the "Create Room" command to build a 3D model of the venue. The other way is to use the Wall tool to create 3D walls along the shape of the venue floor. After the walls are in place, you can then use the Door tool to insert doors into the walls at the places shown on the venue floor plan.

Present Your Model of Seating Layout

To best present your seating layout, you want to create a few new classes and assign the various 2D and 3D elements in your document to appropriate classes, a topic further discussed in the next chapter named "Layers, Classes, and Build-in Objects."

Below are examples of class names and associated elements in your seating layout.

- Venue Model (a 3D model with theatre walls and doors)
- Seating Layout (a 2D floor plan of the venue that you traced off from the venue plan, shapes of the aisles, and seating sections if they are still outlined)
- Seating Layout Model (a 3D model with platform, stairs, risers, and seats)
- Data Tag (2D texts with information regarding the seating sections)

In this way, you can make 2D elements invisible while showing the 3D model of the space, and vice versa. In addition, as an alternative to solid walls, you can also use a glass texture for the walls to display the relationship of the walls with seating sections without blocking the audience's view of the seating layout in the 3D space, or in navigation palette, turn theatre layer gray.

Sightline Check and Stage Masking

What is a "sightline"?

By definition, a ***Sightline*** is a hypothetical line drawn between an observation point (an audience's eye) and what is seen. In theatre, sightlines are referential lines used to check visibility of the audience.

To better understand the issues with sightline check, it is helpful to become familiar with the terms used to describe the various elements comprising a physical theatre. Fig. 4.7 is a diagram of a proscenium theatre with a set of commonly equipped inventory.

Why Sightline Check?

The main purpose of a sightline check is for you, the designer, to know what the audience can see and cannot see, to validate that the audience can see what you want them to see, and to prevent the audience from seeing what you do not want them to see. The implications of sightline issues can be both technical and aesthetic. Technically, if an audience's view of the stage center is mostly blocked by the head of the person sitting in front, this audience's experience of the show can be severely compromised. Aesthetically, a production team's effort to create a lifelike performance in a

Figure 4.7 *Components of a Proscenium Theatre*. An illustration by Darwin Reid Payne showing the components of a proscenium theatre, with a list of terms keyed to the 19 components (Box 4.2). From the Scenographic Imagination, Third Edition, by Darwin Reid Payne (Southern Illinois University Press, 1993). Copyright © 1974, 1981, 1993 by the Board of Trustees, Southern Illinois University.

1. Proscenium arch
2. Stage floor – (A) Trap in stage floor (Opened here, closed when not in use.)
3. Apron
4. Offstage space (Wings)
5. Orchestra pit (In some theatres, it is slightly recessed under stage.)
6. Back wall of theatre (Usually contains loading doors)
7. Grand drape (Often decorative and used to cut down arch openings)
8. Main curtain (In many theatres, this curtain can be either lowered from above or opened laterally from a draw line at the side of the arch.)
9. Second portal (This arch, usually black velvet or some light absorbing fabric, comes after the main curtain; its purpose is to help mask off backstage and side-lighting arrangements.)
10. Gridiron (A number of supports suspended from the ceiling of the stage house that allow scenery to be flown up and out of sight.)
11. Fly gallery (Usually suspended some distance from the stage floor and where the lines attached to the flown scenery are manipulated after it has been counterweighted.)
12. A cloth drop suspended from the gridiron (These drips have a rigid batten at top and bottom, sometimes wooden, often pipe.)
13. A cut drop suspended from the gridiron (These drops have a rigid batten at the top but are free at the bottom.)
14. Cyclorama (Horizontal – surrounds most of the stage area, unlike a sky drop, which is flat)
15. Scenic unit (Composed of flats, platforms, and steps, all built on a movable wagon.)

16. Ground row (Cut and painted to simulate a distant view: hills, houses, etc. Sometimes these ground rows are built as cycloramas, semicircular rather than flat.)
17. Footlights (Not found in many recent theatres but a feature of most theatres built in the last two hundred years. When they are included in modern-day theatres, they are usually recessed and are able to be covered over when not in use).
18. Light batten suspended from gridiron (These battens most often have attached to them permanent lighting connections that feed into known circuits and are not used for anything else but lighting equipment.)
19. Front of house lighting portals (Usually built into the theatre ceiling, although older theatres do not have them). They are, in most cases, self-made and have wire mesh over the front openings to ensure the safety of the audience seated below. Generally, there is more than one portal.

proscenium theatre can be instantly ruined by a poorly masked stage, because insufficient ***Masking*** (a piece of scenery used to block the view of the audience from seeing the offstage space to complete the stage picture) will allow the audience to sit in the side seats to see actors' changing costumes in the wings!

Building codes for a theatre architecture include a mathematically calculated ***C Value*** (the vertical distance between an audience member's line of sight and the eyes of the person in front), which determines the degree of rake for an auditorium floor. The calculation is to ensure good sightlines for the audience to see the performance. For instance, in 1838, John Scott Russel defined "isacoustic curve" and applied it to the Auditorium Building in Chicago and the Emery Theatre in Cincinnati. While Black Box theatres usually come with a flat floor and the regulations for sightline requirements in these theatres are less well defined, it is important for set designers to be aware of the impact "a bad seat" can have on the audience's experience of the performance and thus carefully consider the use of levels to minimize sightline issues when designing for a Black Box theatre.

Types of Sightline Check and Stage Masking

Two types of sightline check and masking are at issue in theatre: horizontal sightline check/masking and vertical sightline check/masking. Fig. 4.8 is a screenshot of the starting point in a horizontal sightline checking/masking process.

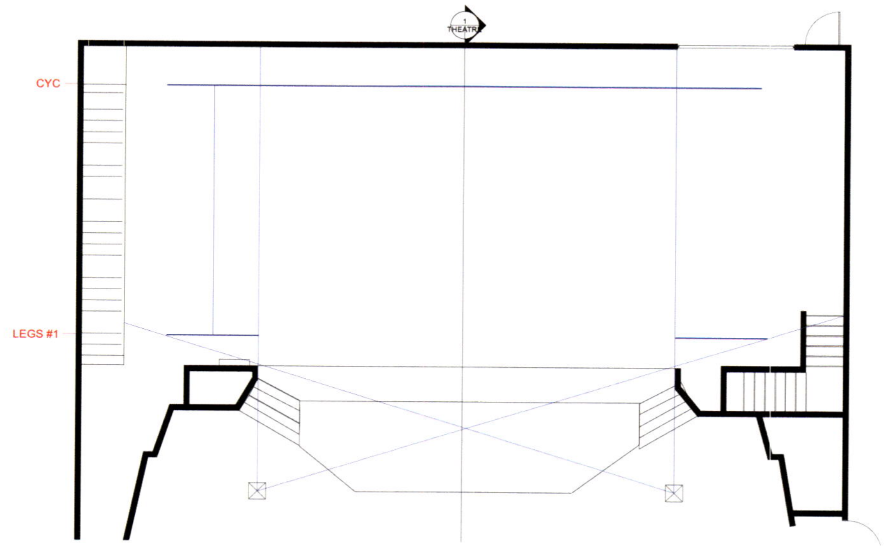

Figure 4.8 *Horizontal Masking Start*. A screenshot showing the beginning process of horizontal masking.

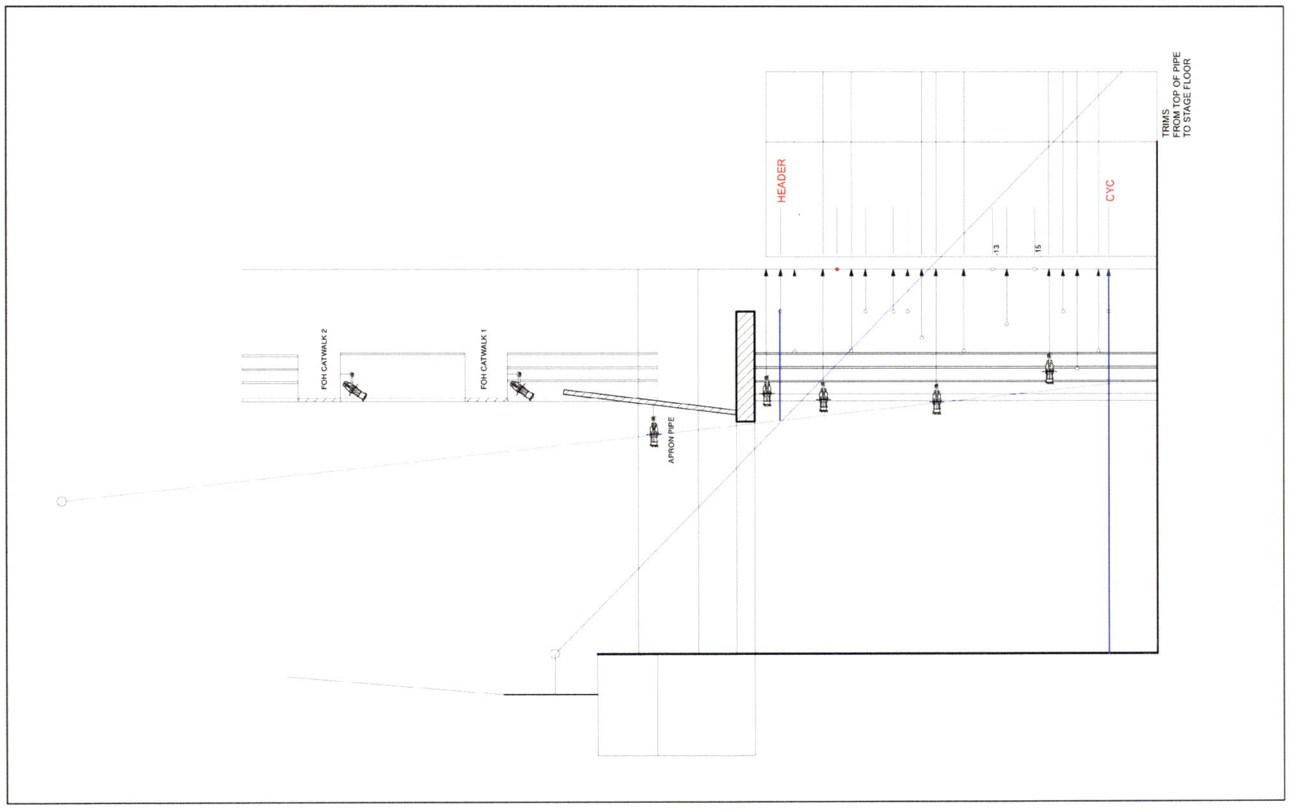

Figure 4.9 *Vertical Masking Start*. A screenshot showing the beginning process of vertical masking.

Fig. 4.9 is a screenshot of the starting point in a vertical sightline checking/masking process.

Sightline Check and Masking Requirements

Critical Seats

It is impractical to check sightlines for individual audience members; therefore, a method of sightline checks for the audience sitting at seats with the steepest viewing angles, namely ***Critical Seats***, in the auditorium has been developed. For horizontal sightline check, the Critical Seats are the two seats on both the left and right sides of the first row that are furthest away from the centerline of the auditorium (see Fig. 4.8). For vertical sightline check, the Critical Seats are the two seats, one located in the middle of the first row and the other located in the middle of the last row of the auditorium (see Fig. 4.9).

Dimensions and Numbers of Masking Devices

To mask the offstage space, you need to know the dimensions and numbers of the masking devises, such as ***Legs***, ***Borders***, and a ***Cyc*** (#12 or #14 on Fig. 4.7), in the theatre inventory.

That said, masking offstage (wing) space with legs, boarders, and a Cyc, though most used, is not the only type of masking device you could consider. Depending on the type of scenery you design, masking can take the form of a ***Ground Row*** (#16 on Fig. 4.7), a ***Portal*** (#9 on Fig. 4.7), or a scenic flat or a cut drop (#13 on Fig. 4.7) with a painting treatment of some sort (e.g., a wall, a cityscape, or foliage).

The Principles and Procedures of Sightline Check and Stage Masking

The video associated with this chapter demonstrates, step-by-step, a standard stage masking process for a proscenium theatre. Though every theatre space is unique, the principles and procedures of both sightline check and stage masking can be applied to other types of theatres.

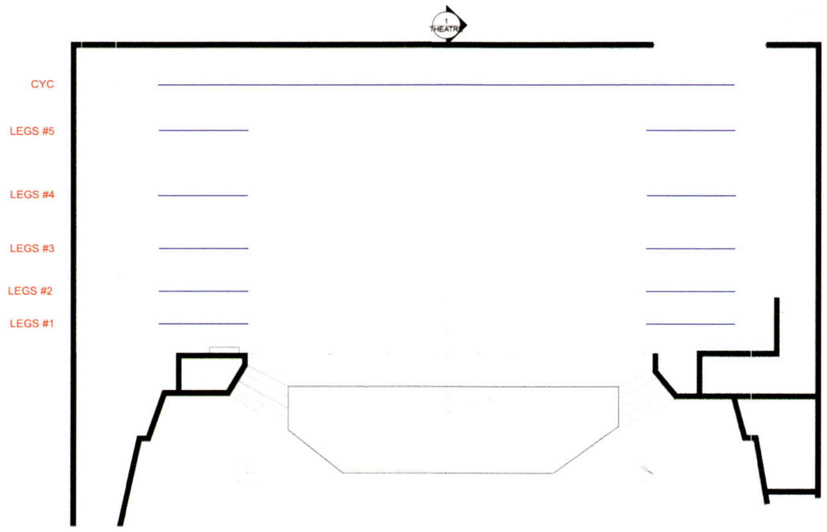

Figure 4.10 *Horizontal Masking Finish*. A screenshot showing horizontal masking at its finished stage.

Horizontal Sightline Check and Masking

To check horizontal sightlines and install conventional masking devises, the following principles are at play. Remember, the goal is to mask everything offstage yet allow for the scenery and actors to move in and out of the stage space fluidly (refer to Fig. 4.10 for an example of these principles applied in a horizontal masking process).

- Use critical seats as the starting point to draw all sightlines.
- Draw the ***Backdrop*** to narrow down the perimeter of your sightline check before drawing the legs.
- Use the proscenium opening line as the ***Onstage*** limit of the legs, as this will keep the audience's view of the stage picture consistent while leaving ample room in the wings for the ***Offstage*** traffic.
- All sightlines from Critical Seats should hit the onstage side of the Legs.
- Each Leg should align with a ***Batten*** position because Legs need to be hung on available battens.
- Place the Legs as far ***Upstage*** as possible, granted that the Legs block the view of the offstage space from the audience sitting in the critical seats. This will maximize the space in between the Legs for stage traffic and, at the same time, save on the use of Legs.

Vertical Sightline Check and Masking

Vertical Sightline Check in a proscenium theatre involves borders as a masking devise. The main goal is to block the views of the audience from seeing what is not intended to be seen, such as lighting instruments, battens, and the bottom of the hanging scenery to be used in other acts/ scenes. For vertical sightline check and masking device installation, a similar set of principles corresponding to the vertical sightline problems should be followed. (Refer to Fig. 4.11 for an example of these principles applied in a vertical masking process.)

- Use critical seats as the starting point to draw all sightlines.
- Draw the backdrop to narrow the perimeter of your sightline check before drawing the borders.
- Use the sightline from the back row Critical Seat of the auditorium as the onstage limit of the borders.
- All sightlines drawn from front row Critical Seats should hit the onstage side of the boarder.
- Each border should align with a batten position because borders need to be hung on available battens. To reserve battens for other uses, it is often possible to hang a pair of legs and a border on a single batten.
- Place the borders as far Upstage as possible, granted that the borders block the view of the offstage space from the audience sitting in the critical seats. This will maximize the space in between the borders for the traffic of scenery flight in and out of stage space and, at the same time, save on the use of borders.

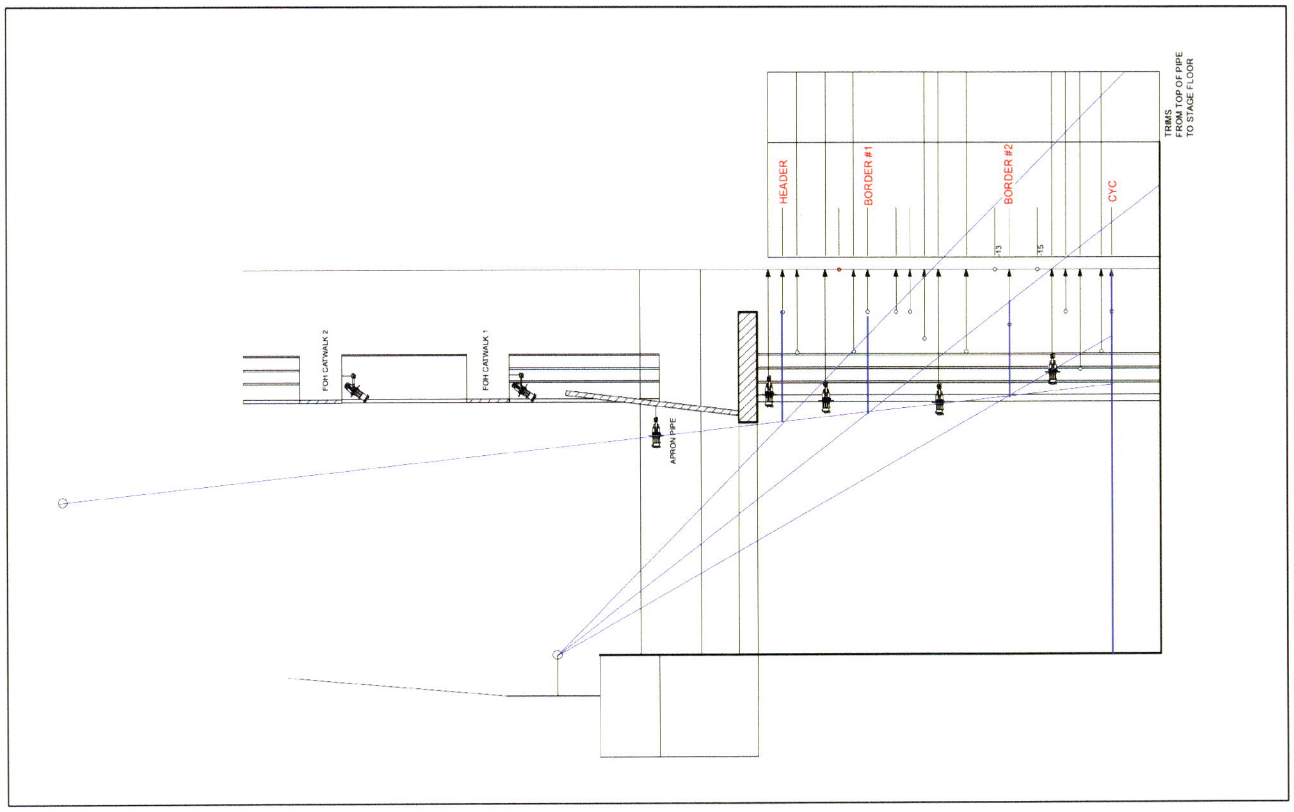

Figure 4.11 *Vertical Masking Finish*. A screenshot showing vertical masking at its finished stage.

Technique 4 – Seating Layout and Stage Masking (Episode One)

In Technique 4, you will practice the basic tools, commands, methods, techniques, and processes involved in seating layout and stage masking. While Episode One emphasizes the technique of creating Seating Layouts in a Black Box theatre, Episode Two focuses on the technique of Stage Masking, both horizontally and vertically, for a Proscenium Theatre.

Mechanics of Seating Layout and Stage Masking

Before diving into the processes of seating layout and stage masking, let us explore the tools, comments, and method options available in the VW program that can benefit us during these processes.

Walls

Activate the Wall Tool

To activate the Wall tool, go to Building Shell in Tool Sets (house icon) – Wall.

Insert Walls

To insert walls, select the Wall tool in Building Shell. There are also Mode choices for wall insertion.

Resize Walls

After you draw the walls, go to the Selection tool to select the wall you want to resize. You can then resize the walls in the Object Info palette.

Join Walls

The individual walls can be joined using the "Wall Join" command in Tool Sets (wall corner icon) or the "Join" command in the Modify menu.

Remove Walls

Remove wall icon is also located on the Tool Sets (a horizontal bar with a cross).

Restore Caps

To restore caps in walls, go to Object Info palette – Caps, then select "start," "end," or "both."

Doors

Insert Doors

1. To insert a door into a wall, select the Door tool in the Tool Sets – Building Shell.
2. Hove your cursor over the section of the wall where you intend to place the door. When the wall is lit in RED, click once on the wall to place the door.
3. Pivot your cursor to determine the swing direction of the door and click the second time to finish the insertion.

Edit Doors

1. After the door is inserted into the wall, you can adjust its placement by dragging the door along the track in the wall.
2. You can adjust other aspects of the door, such as the size, style, orientation of the door swing, and the angle of the door opening, in the Object Info palette.

Levels

You can create levels in space from scratch or use tools and symbols available in Tool Sets and in VW Libraries.

Platforms

Insert a Stage Platform Symbol

1. To insert a stage platform symbol, go to Recourse Manager and search Stage Platform while "All Resources" is selected in the search browser.
2. When the Platform icon(s) appears in the window, double-click on the symbol named "Furn Rect Stage – Platform 144 × 24 × 96in."
3. Click once in your drawing area where you want to place the symbol.
4. Pivot the symbol to your desired angle and click the second time to insert the symbol.

Edit a Stage Platform Symbol

1. To edit a stage platform symbol, double-click on the symbol. This will bring you to a window in which you can edit the symbol.
2. Press the "Exit Symbol" button after you complete the editing.

Note: If some parts of the symbol are grouped, they need to be ungrouped before editing. As an alternative, you can also double-click on the group to enter the second level of the editing window. You need to edit both 2D components and 3D components to make the symbol consistent throughout.

As an alternative to the Stage Platform symbol located in VW symbol libraries, you can also use the Stage Deck tool, which resides in Tool Sets.

1. Go to Tool Sets – Event Design and click on the Stage Deck tool.
2. Click once on your drawing to place the deck where you want the deck to be.
3. Pivot your cursor to set the angle of the deck and click the second time to insert the deck.
4. If the Object Preference window opens, click "OK." You can then customize the stairs in the Object Info palette.

Risers

Insert a Riser Symbol

1. To insert a riser symbol, go to Resource Manager and search Riser while "All Resources" is selected in the search browser.
2. When the Riser icons appear in the window, double-click on the symbol named "Stage Seated Riser 3."
3. Click once in your drawing area where you want to place the symbol.
4. Pivot the symbol to your desired angle and click the second time to insert the symbol.

Edit a Riser Symbol

1. To edit a riser symbol, double-click on the symbol. This will bring you to a window, in which you can edit the symbol.
2. Press the "Exit Symbol" button after you complete the editing.

Stairs

Insert a Stair Unit

1. To insert a stair unit, go to Tool Sets – Building Shell and click on the Simple Stair tool.
2. Click on a point in your drawing, where you want to situate your stair symbol.
3. Pivot the symbol to your desired angle and make the second click to place the symbol.
4. If the Object Preference window opens, click "OK." You can then customize the stair in Object Info palette.

As an alternative to the Simple Stair tool in Building Shell, you can insert a stair unit by using a tool in Event Design.

1. Go to Tool Sets – Event Design, click on Stage Steps, and insert the steps the same way as you insert a stair unit using the Simple Stair tool.
2. If the Object Preference window opens, click "OK." You can then customize the stairs in the Object Info palette.

Legs and Borders (for stage masking)

For stage masking, you can either create simple flats or use VW symbols for legs and borders. There are advantages and disadvantages to either of these two methods. While most theatre legs and borders are made of black fabric, which means that the symbols are true to the visualization of the legs and borders on stage, they are less flexible in terms of color, texture, and image variations compared to the flats that you make from scratch.

Black Box Theatre

Import Theatre Plans

Note: *02 Onyx Theatre Plan.PDF* file is available for you to use. You can find the file on resourcecentre.routledge.com/books/9781032209890 (under a folder named "Appendices"). You must save the folder on your computer before starting to import the Plan.

To import an existing theatre plan in PDF format, do the following:

1. In Architect Workspace, create a blank document.
2. Go to File – Document Settings – Document Setup… and set the document in ¼" scale and use the US Arch D as your document size.
3. Select Spotlight as your workspace.
4. Go to the Top Menu bar and select File – Import – Import PDF…
5. Select the PDF file named Onyx Theatre Plan located on your computer.
6. When a dialog box opens, check the "Snap to Geometry" box, as this will allow you to take advantage of a Vector file while tracing the floor plan onto your working layer.

Scale a Theatre Plan

Note: You must know the actual dimensions of at least one item in the plan to restore the dimensions of the theatre in a scaled drawing. In the case of the Onyx Theatre Plan, the width of the doors and door openings are known factors. They are 4′ each.

To scale the Onyx Theatre plan, do the following:

1. Go to the Tool Sets – Dims/Notes tool and click on the Unconstrained Linear Dimension Tool.
2. Take the measurement for the width of a door opening.
3. Go to the Top Menu bar – Modify – Scale Objects…
4. When the Scale Objects dialog box opens, check the "Symmetric by distance" box.
5. For Current Distance, type in the current measurement of the door opening; for New Distance, type in the desired measurement of the door opening, which is 4′.
6. Check "Entire drawing" box and click "OK."
7. The Onyx Theatre plan is now both to scale and in correct dimensions.

Build a 3D Room

VW offers tools to let you establish a 3D virtual room with only a few mouse clicks. To build a 3D room, follow the steps listed below.

1. Use a polyline or polygon tool to outline the shape of the floor in a room.
2. Then, go to the Top Menu bar – Event Design – Create Room.
3. A popup window appears to let you make a few choices, such as wall height, wall thickness, material, and color.
4. After you click the "OK" button, poof – the room is there!
5. View it yourself in an isometric view.

Instead of using the polyline or polygon tool, you can also apply the Wall tool to accomplish the same task. Here are the alternative steps to building a 3D virtual room.

1. Use the Wall Tool located on the Tool Sets – Building Shell to trace the outline of the floor to define the boundary of the room.
2. Adjust the height, thickness, and attributes of the walls in the Object Info palette.

Seating Layout

Create Seating Sections from Shapes

In the Vectorworks drawing environment, you can create seating sections based on shapes. You can define audience's viewing direction. You can also produce aisles for easy access from the entrances to the seats or from seats to the exits. Furthermore, Vectorworks lets you set other perimeters regarding the seating section and attach a label that reveals specific info about each seating section. Below are a few examples.

1. Open a blank document.
2. In Architecture Workspace, set the document to ¼″ scale.
3. Set the size of your drawing area to US Arch D.
4. Go to the Top Menu bar and click on Tools – Workspace – Spotlight.
5. Draw a rectangle, 40′(W) × 60′(L).
6. Click on Event Design – Seating Section located on Tool Sets. Four drawing modes appear on the mode bar.

   Note: The first mode lets you create a seating section based on a shape you created previously. The rest of the modes let you create a shape and a seating section based on that shape. The shapes available on the mode bar are oval, rectangle, and polygon, created by using polylines.

7. While the rectangle is selected, click on the first mode (Create from Shape Mode).
8. Move your cursor towards the center of the rectangle. The rectangle is lit in RED.
9. Click once on the center point of the rectangle. Move your cursor out of the rectangle towards the direction you would like the seats to face.
10. A ghost image of the rows of seats appears.
11. If the direction is correct, double-click your mouse to evoke the Seating Section Settings dialog box.
12. Click on Arrangement located in the left column of the window, and make sure that the Standard choice in the upper left corner is selected.
13. Make sure the following choices are selected if they are not there as the default settings.
    a. Seating Spacing: 0″
    b. Row spacing: 2′0″
    c. Distance Measurement: Back Leg to Front Leg
    d. Allowable Distance Past Boundary: 0″
    e. Primary Fill Direction: Left to Right
    f. Secondary Fill Direction: Top to Bottom
    g. Rise: Total; 0″
    h. Symbol: Event Chair 1
14. Check the "Use actual symbols" box and click "OK."
15. You may adjust the angle of the seating subsequently either in the Object Info palette or simply drag the Angle Handles in the drawing.
16. See the result in an isometric view.

To try a different mode, go back to Top Plan View.

1. Click on the Seating Section located on Tool Sets – Event Design.
2. Click on the Polyline Mode.
3. Draw a polygon enclosed by polylines. The rows of seats are in their default positions, and the circular angle tool replaces the cursor.
4. To change the default position, use the angle tool by clicking the mouse once in the center of the seating section, then making your second click on the direction you want your seats to face toward. A Seating Section Settings dialog window appears.
5. In the Arrangement located on the left column of the window, switch "Standard" to "Curved."
6. Then click "OK" to accept the default.
7. You may adjust the angle and degree of curve of the seating either in the Object Info palette or simply drag the Angle Handles in the drawing.
8. See the result in an isometric view.

Create Aisles

To create aisles that divide a large seating section into smaller ones, do the following:

1. Click on the "Aisle" tool located on Tool Sets – Event Design. Three modes appear on the mode bar.
2. Select Rectangle Mode.
3. Create a rectangle that cuts across the seating section. An aisle is created.
4. You can now move it about to change its position and rotate its angle. You can also create as many aisles as you wish.
5. To hide the rectangle but retain the aisle, go to the Fill dropdown menu located on the Attributes palette and select none.
6. Then, go to the Pen dropdown menu located on the Attributes palette and select none. The rectangle has disappeared, but the aisle is still there.

Label a Seating Section

1. To set the Data Tag default style, go to Resource Manager – Vectorworks Library – Object Style – Data Tag – Entertainment – Seating Section.vwx – Seating Section Info (right side only), which is the third choice in this group of choices.
2. Go to Tool Sets – Dims/Notes – Data Tag. An information tag is thus generated.
3. Click once on a convenient location for the tag near the seating section.
4. Move your cursor towards the seating section; the section is lit in RED. Click the second time inside the seating section. A Data Tag appears near the seating section (displaying the information you gave previously).

Process of Seating Layout

Now let us practice how to create a seating layout in a black box theatre.

Set Up Drawing Environment

1. Open *03 Onyx for Seating Layout Project_Student Copy.vwx* (available on resourcecentre.routledge.com/books/9781032209890, under a folder named "Appendices.")
2. Make sure that Spotlight workspace is selected. If not, go to Top Menu – Tool – Workspace – Spotlight.
3. Select New Design Layer in the Layer dropdown menu, and type *Onyx Seating Layout-Arena* as the name for the new layer.
4. Validate that your Active Layer Scale is ¼″ scale. If not, Right-click for PC (or Ctrl+Click for Mac) to select Active Layer Scale and then, in the popup window, select ¼″ scale.
5. Go to the Navigation palette. Make the original design layer "Design Layer 1" visible (or gray) and your new layer "Onyx Seating Layout-Arena" both visible and active.

Create Bases for Seating Sections

1. To start with your seating layout, click on the Rectangle tool in the Basic palette, choose second mode (center to center), and draw a 20′ × 9′ rectangle that aligns with the centerlines of the theatre (You will need to type in 10′ × 4.5′ because the measurements are counted from the center point).
2. In the OIP, click on the top-center box position of the rectangle.
3. Select the rectangle you just drew and drag and snap the top-center handle of the rectangle to the center of the wall located on top of the drawing. This is the base for your Seating Layout, Section A.
4. While the rectangle that you just moved is still selected, use the Mirror tool in the Basic palette to draw a horizontal line along the horizontal centerline to create a section base on the opposite side of the space.
5. While the new base you just created is still selected, click on the bottom-center box position of the rectangle in OIP.
6. Select the new rectangle. Drag and snap the bottom-center handle of the rectangle to the center of the wall located at the bottom of the drawing. This is the base for your Seating Layout, Section C.
7. Select and duplicate the rectangle you just created.
8. Rotate the newest rectangle to a 90-degree angle.
9. Click on the left-center box position of the rectangle in OIP and snap the left-center handle of the rectangle to the center of the wall located on the left side of the drawing. This is the base for your Seating Layout, Section D.
10. While the rectangle you just created is still selected, use the Mirror tool in the Basic palette to draw a vertical line along the vertical centerline to create a section base on the opposite side of the space.
11. While the rectangle you just created is still selected, click on the right-center box position of the rectangle in OIP.
12. Select and drag the rectangle to snap the right-center handle of the rectangle to the center of the wall located on the right side of the drawing. This is the base for your Seating Layout, Section B.

Create Shapes for Seating Sections

1. To create aisles in the space
   a. Click on the Rectangle tool in the Basic palette, choose the first drawing mode (corner to corner mode), and draw a 3′(W) × 16′(long) rectangle. Rotate the rectangle to a 45-degree angle and align the top of the rectangle with the door opening located on the top left side of the space to create an aisle.
   b. Mirror the first aisle by selecting it. Use the Mirror Tool in the Basic palette and draw a line along with the vertical centerline. A mirror image of the first aisle has been created. Align the top of the new rectangle with the

door opening located on the top right side of the space to create an aisle leading on the opening at the top-right side of the space.
   c. Select both aisles that you just created. Use the Mirror Tool to draw a line along with the horizontal centerline to create two aisles leading to the opposite openings at the bottom-right side and bottom-left side of the space. Bring each newly created aisle to its nearby opening as closely as you can.
2. Select all eight shapes you have created so far. Go to Top Menu – Modify – Clip Surface.
3. Select all the four shapes defining aisles and delete them. The Shapes for four seating sections are now created.

Insert Seats

1. Select the shape of Seating Section A.
2. Click on the Event Design button located in Tool Sets on the lower left side of your screen, then double-click the "Seating Section Tool" icon in the Tool Sets. A popup window appears.
3. You need to make the following selections in the first category, Arrangement, which is located on the upper left side of the popup window:
   a. Alignment Type: Shift Rows
   b. Seat Spacing: 2″
   c. Row Spacing: 1′-0″
   d. Distance Measurement: Back Leg to Front Leg
   e. Primary Fill Direction: Center Out
   f. Secondary Fill Direction: Top to Bottom
   g. Rise: Per Row; 8″
   h. Click on Event Chair.
   i. Click on the arrow located on the right side of the symbol display box, select Event Chair 1, and click "OK." The popup window disappears.
   j. This is the time for you to pick a focal point for Seating Section A. Draw a vertical line starting from the center of Seating Section A, which will turn RED, to the intersection of the centerlines (of the theatre).
   k. After you pick the focal point for Seating Section A, the popup window returns.
   l. Check the box for Use Actual Symbol to preview the result.
4. Switch to the second category, Section Information, located on the upper left side of the popup window, and do the following:
   a. Give a name to Section info: Onyx Seating Section A.
   b. Check the box: Number of Seats
   c. Number Direction: Left to Right
   d. Check the box: Restart on the next row (if you are assigning the seats). Leave it unchecked (if you are counting the total number of seats in this section).
   e. Start at: 1
   f. Increment: 1
   g. Check the box: Number Rows
   h. Number Direction: Top to Bottom.
   i. Start at: A
   j. Increment: 1 (if you are assigning the seats). 0 (if you are counting the total number of seats in this section).
   k. Display Row Number: On Every Symbol.
5. Switch to the third category, Angle, located on the upper left side of the popup window. Check the Angle Seating box and make sure that the angle is 180 degrees and the angle base is on the Left. Click OK. All the seats are automatically populated, and seating numbers are assigned.
6. Check to see the result in the preview window.
7. Repeat Step 4 for Seating Sections B, C, and D.

   Note: you may have to make adjustments to the number directions (left to right/right to left; top to bottom/bottom to top) in the Section Info category and the seating angles in the Angle category to ensure that the backs of the seats are facing the wall and the seating numbers are arranged in the way you wanted.

Level the Floor

1. To level the floor, use the Rectangle tool and Extrude command to draw a platform that is 20′-0″ (W) × 2′-9″ (D) × 16″ (H).
2. Then use the Rectangle tool and Extrude command to draw another platform that is 20′-0″ (W) × 2′-9″ (D) × 8″ (H).
3. Position the second platform right below the first platform.
4. Select both platforms and go to Model at the top menu bar. Select Add Solids to combine the two platforms into one leveled platform. You need to do this for all four seating sections.
5. Select this leveled platform and align it with the wall on top of the drawing.
6. To see the result of your drawing, select from the View bar "Left Isometric" and "Normal Perspective" views, and "Shaded" rendering mode.

Adjust Seats

1. To allow the audience to reach the back seats, you need to get rid of two end seats on the second row. You can do it by creating small aisles at the ends of the platform.

Label Seating Sections

1. To label the seating sections you created with Data Tags, please refer to previous instructions on "Label a Seating Section."
2. Repeat Steps 5 and 6 for Seating Sections B, C, and D.

Build Walls

1. Select Building Shell in your Tool Set.
2. Double-click on the Wall tool located in the Building Shell tool set. (The icon of the Building looks like a house.) A popup window appears.
3. Set the thickness of the wall to 6″ and the height of the wall to 24′-0″, then click OK.
4. Select the first mode in the mode bar and trace off the walls along the original drawing. You will need a double-click to end this series of walls.

Insert a Door and Door Openings

1. Select the Symbol Insertion Tool.
2. Go to Resource Manager to find Door Flush (DIN).
3. Double-click the symbol to select that symbol.
4. Go to the wall where the front door is located. When the wall is lit in RED, click on the place for insertion, and your symbol will be snapped onto the wall.
5. The second click will allow you to define the direction of the door opening.
6. After you made the second click, if this door doesn't open in the direction you wanted, go to the Object Info palette to Flip the doors.

   Note: If you insert the symbol when it is lit in RED, it will always be hooked on the wall until you force-drag it to another place. When the symbol is Snapped into place, you may still move its position along the wall.

7. When the door is still selected, go to the Object Info palette (Door in Wall). Under "General," change the width of the door to 4′–0″ and the height of the door to 8′–0″.
8. While the Symbol Insertion Tool is still selected, go to Resource Manager to find Door Opening (BSI).
9. Double-click the symbol to select that symbol.
10. Insert the Door Opening three times into the three walls located at the rest of the three corners of the space.
11. Select the three Door Openings. Go to the Object Info palette (3 Door Objects in Walls), under "General," change the width of the door opening to 4′–0″, and the height of the door opening to 8′–0″.
12. To check the result of your drawing, select Left Isometric View and render your drawing in Shaded rendering mode.
13. You can customize your view by using the Flyover Tool located in the Basic palette.

Technique 4 – Seating Layout and Stage Masking (Episode Two)

Stage Masking

Note: *04 Stillwell Theatre_Floor Plan.vwx* and *05 Stillwell Theatre_Centerline Vertical Section.vwx* files are available on resourcecentre.routledge.com/books/9781032209890 (under a folder named "Appendices"). You must save the folder on your computer before starting the exercises below.

Imagine that KSU Stillwell Theatre (see Fig. 4.12), a type of proscenium theatre, is equipped with a cyclorama (Cyc) of 52′ (W) × 28′ (H), four pairs of legs each measuring 8′ (W) × 24′ (H) and pivoting around a center core, and four borders each measuring 52′ (W) × 7′ (H). These masking devices are used to block the audience's view of offstage space. The following procedure lets you practice checking the audience's sightlines and install the Cyc, the legs, and the borders in appropriate positions and angles so that the masking devices will serve their primary function.

Horizontal Masking

Install a Cyc

1. Open the file named *Stillwell Theatre_Floor Plan* (available on resourcecentre.routledge.com/books/9781032209890 (under a folder named "Appendices")
2. Create a New Layer and name the layer "Horizontal Masking."
3. In the Layer Options dropdown menu located in the Navigation palette, select Gray/Snap Others.

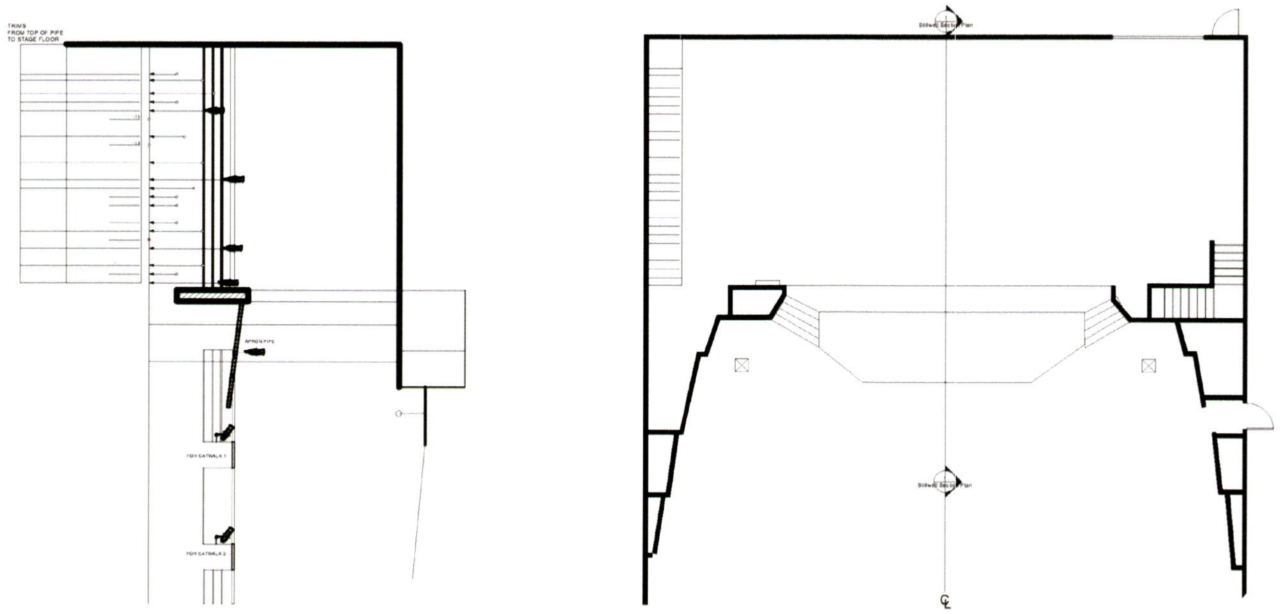

Figure 4.12 Proscenium Theatre Plans. A floor plan and a centerline vertical section plan of the Stillwell Theatre, Kennesaw State University.

4. Select the line tool in the Basic palette and click on the Center mode located on the Mode bar.
5. From the centerline of the theatre, draw a 52′ (W) line that aligns with the last batten position (Line #20).
6. This is the Cyc that blocks the audience's view of the backstage wall.

Before installing the legs, you need to draw a couple of reference lines.

Draw a Reference Sightline

Note: The horizontal critical seats refer to the two seats that are located at the furthest left and right (from the centerline of the theatre) on the first row in the house. They must be marked on the theatre floor plan before the audience's sightline can be checked.

1. Draw a diagonal line, starting at the "critical seat box" located on the right side of the audience.
2. Run the line through the left corner of the proscenium arch all the way to the stage-right side of the offstage space and make the second click. This is the first referential sightline.

   Note: The audience cannot see the offstage space on the left side of this sightline because the sightline is blocked by the wall of the proscenium arch. However, the audience can still see the offstage space on the right side of the sightline until it meets the left edge of the Cyc.

Draw a Reference Line to Mark the Onstage Border of the Legs

1. Draw a vertical reference line starting at the corner of the proscenium arch located on Stage Right (SR).
2. Extend the line to the Cyc and make the second click. This is a line marking the onstage border of all the legs located on SR.

Install Legs

You are now ready to install the legs on SR.

1. To install the first leg, draw an 8′ (W) horizontal line to represent a leg.
2. Rotate the leg to a 20-degree angle (to block a wider sightline area).
3. Click and drag the middle point of the line to align it with Line #3 of the batten position. The onstage side of the leg needs to hit the proscenium reference line.
4. Drop the leg in its position.
5. When the leg is still selected, go to Edit located on the Top Menu bar. In the Edit dropdown menu, select Duplicate Array.

6. When a dialog window appears, make the following selections:
   a. Shape: Linear Array
   b. Number of Duplicates: 3
   c. Cartesian Offset:
      i. X: 0″
      ii. Y: 3′
   d. Uncheck Rotate Duplicates.
   e. Original Object: Check "Retain."
7. Check "OK" to close the Duplicate Array dialog box. Now you can see that you have just created three more legs ready to be installed in the correct positions.
8. Draw another vertical reference line that starts from the center of the first leg, goes upward, and ends near the Cyc.
9. Draw a second sightline that starts at the critical seats on the right side of the audience. Lead the line towards the offstage space on SR. This line must hit the onstage side of the first leg.
10. Now, it is the time to install the second leg.
11. Click on a new leg you created.
12. Drag the middle point of the leg and put it in a position so that the offstage side of the leg meets (or intersects) the second sightline and the middle point of the curtain meets both the second vertical referential line and one of the batten positions.

    Note: To ensure ample space for actors' entrance to the stage, you need to push the leg as upstage as you can but still block the second audience's sightline.

13. Continue to check the sightline and place the rest of the two legs in places so that they will block all the offstage space on SR.
14. After you have installed all four legs, select all the legs.
15. Click on the Mirror tool located on the Basic palette.
16. Draw a vertical line to install the four legs on the stage left side of the theatre.
17. Delete the two vertical reference lines.
18. Save your vwx file as: Your last name_Horizontal Masking

Note: If you are working in a 3D environment, which you are currently not, you can either extrude the first leg 24′ (before duplicating it) or install a 3D stock leg (before duplicating it).

To install a 3D stock leg, do the following:

1. Go to the Top Menu bar to select Tool – Workspaces – Spotlight.
2. Click on the Event Design icon located on Tools Sets.
3. Click on Soft Goods.
4. Draw a horizontal line (8′) and double-click to end the line.
5. Go to the Object Info palette to change the Height to 24′.
6. See the result in Front view.

Vertical Masking

Install a Cyc

1. Open the file named *Stillwell Theatre_Centerline* (available on resourcecentre.routledge.com/books/9781032209890 (under a folder named "Appendices").
2. Create a New Layer and name the layer "Vertical Masking."
3. In the Layer Options dropdown menu located in the Navigation palette, select Gray/Snap Others.
4. Select the line tool in the Basic palette and click on the Vertex mode located on the Mode bar.
5. Draw a vertical line (28′ high) that aligns with the last batten position (Line #20), starting from the floor of the stage. This is the Cyc that blocks the backstage wall of the theatre.

Before installing the borders, you need to draw a couple of reference lines.

Draw a Reference Sightline

Note: The two critical seats for checking vertical sightlines are located on the first row and the last row of the theatre. They are indicated in the Centerline Vertical Section by two small circles in the house.

1. Draw a diagonal line, starting at the critical seat located on the first row of the house.
2. Run the line through the right corner of the proscenium arch all the way to the offstage space and make the second click. This is the first referential sightline.

   Note: The audience cannot see the offstage space on the left side of this sightline because the sightline is blocked by the wall of the proscenium arch. However, the audience can still see the offstage space on the right side of the sightline until it meets the top edge of the Cyc.

Draw a Reference Line to Mark the Onstage Limit of the Borders

1. Draw a diagonal reference line, starting at the critical seat located on the last row of the house.
2. Extend the line through the right corner of the proscenium arch all the way to the Cyc and make the second click. This is a line marking the onstage side of all the borders.

Install Borders

You are now ready to install the borders.

1. Draw a 7′ high vertical line. This is your first border.
2. Align the border with one of the batten positions; in the meanwhile, block the first sightline and meet the reference line that marks the onstage limit of the borders. You need to push the border to a batten position as further upstage as possible to save unnecessary borders while still blocking the first sightline.
3. Draw a second sightline, starting from the critical seat located on the first row of the house.
4. Run the line through the onstage side of the first border all the way to the offstage space and make the second click. This is the second referential sightline.
5. Draw a 7′ high vertical line. This is your second border.
6. Align the border with one of the batten positions; in the meanwhile, block the second sightline and meet the reference line that marks the onstage limit of the borders. You need to push the border to a batten position as further upstage as possible to save unnecessary borders while still blocking the second sightline.
7. Repeat the previous two steps as many times as needed until the borders block all the audience sightline to the offstage space.
8. Save your vwx file as: Your last name_Vertical Masking.

Note: If you are working in a 3D environment, which you are currently not, you can extrude the first Boarder 52′ and change the Bottom Z to 17′ (before duplicating it).

Experiment and Practice

Sightline Check and Stage Masking

1. Import a ground plan and a centerline vertical section plan of a proscenium theatre into the VW drawing environment (see Fig. 4.12).
2. Scale the plans if they are PDF files.
3. Use the plans as a base and follow the procedures of sightline check and stage masking discussed in this chapter to complete the installation of masking devises (both horizontally and vertically) for the proscenium theatre.

Project #2: Planning Seating Layout

Objectives

The purpose of this project is for you to

- exhibit your capability of using appropriate commands, tools, and symbols available in the VW program to create two different seating layouts in a Black Box Theatre.
- create seating layouts within the perimeters of 1) safety guidelines, 2) required seating capacity, and 3) sightline consideration (levels in space).
- Label the seating sections to provide information, such as the number of seats, in the section.
- develop patience, concentration, attention to details, and professionalism.

Tasks

Your task for this project is to create 3D digital models of two different seating layouts in the KSU Onyx Theatre. Each seating layout must conform to the theatre safety code for emergency exits (three-foot-wide aisles) and meet a minimum seating capacity of 75. In addition, each seating section needs to be labeled using the Data Tag available in VW Libraries in a style named "Seating Section Info (right side only)."

Required Equipment and Materials

To complete this project, you will need a computer with internet access and the Vectorworks 2023 version installed. A floor plan of a Black Box Theatre in vector format or PDF format (see Fig. 4.13). *02 Onyx Theatre Plan.PDF* file is available in a folder named Appendices that comes with your book.

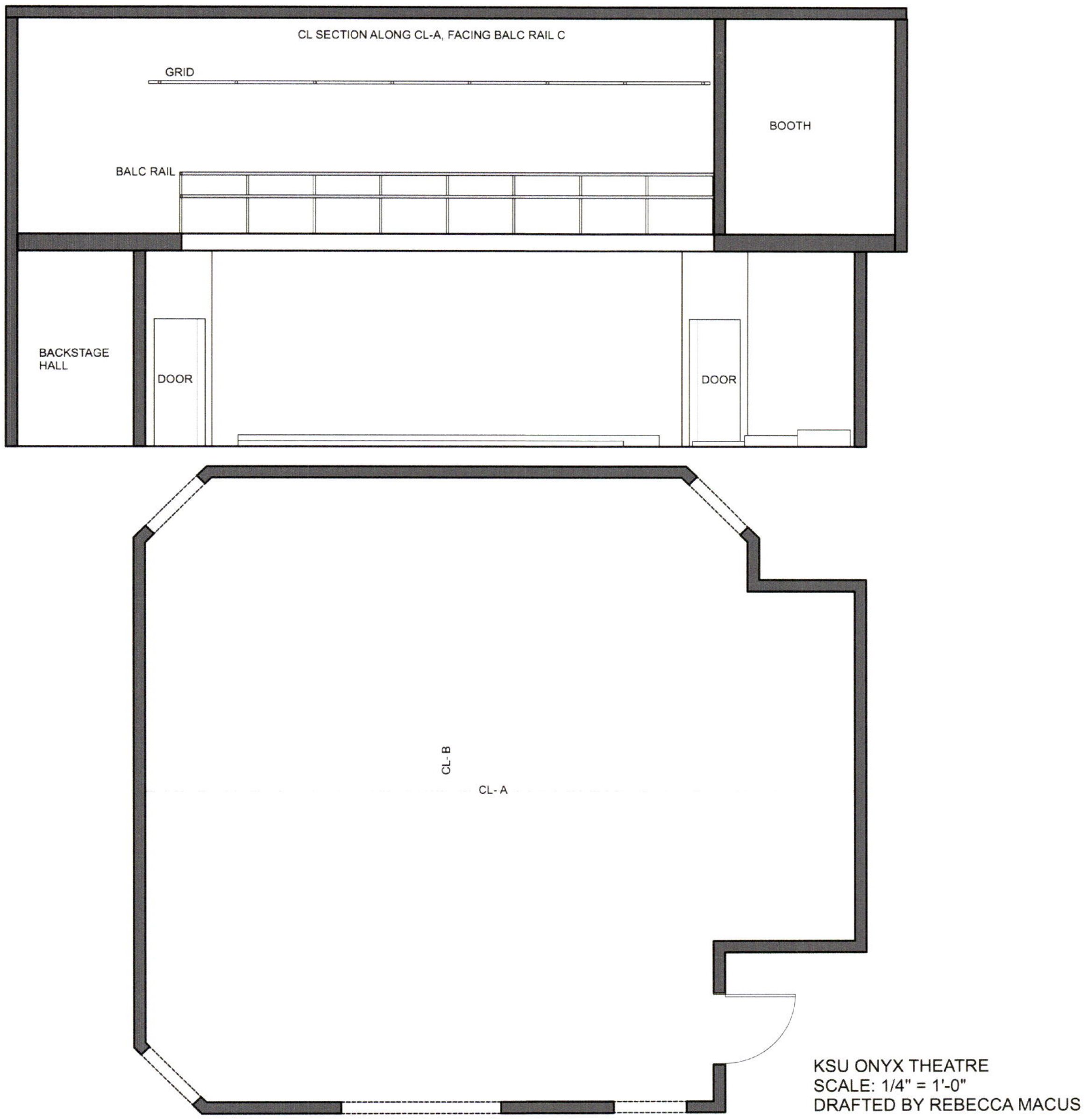

Figure 4.13 Black Box Theatre Plans. A floor plan and a centerline vertical section plan of the Onyx Theatre, Kennesaw State University.

Modeling Scale

(¼″ = 1′ – 0″)

Procedure

For each of your seating layouts, follow the steps suggested in this chapter (Technique 4 – Seating Layout – Process of Seating Layout) and the associated instructional video.

- Save the drawing (vwx file) to your computer as: your last name_name of the staging format.
- Export the Top/Plan view to an image file (JPEG, 300 dpi) and save it on your computer as: your last name_name of the staging format_name of the view.

- Switch from Top/Plan View to an Isometric View in your drawing environment and render it in Final Quality Renderworks.
- Export the Isometric View to an image file (JPEG, 300 dpi) and save it on your computer as: your last name_name of the staging format_name of the view.

Evaluation Criteria

Artistry

1. The work includes seating layouts for two different staging formats.
2. It exhibits the application of appropriate drawing, modeling, and rendering tools, commands, and techniques.
3. It showcases a mastery of acquiring and editing symbols.

Problem-Solving

1. The work follows the safety guidelines.
2. It meets the required seating capacity.
3. It provides levels in the space to solve the sightline problems.

Requirements and Presentation

1. The work is complete and meets the required components and formats.
2. It was executed with accuracy and professionalism.

Student Work Samples

Figs. 4.14–4.19 are samples of student work on Project #2 – Planning Seating Layout

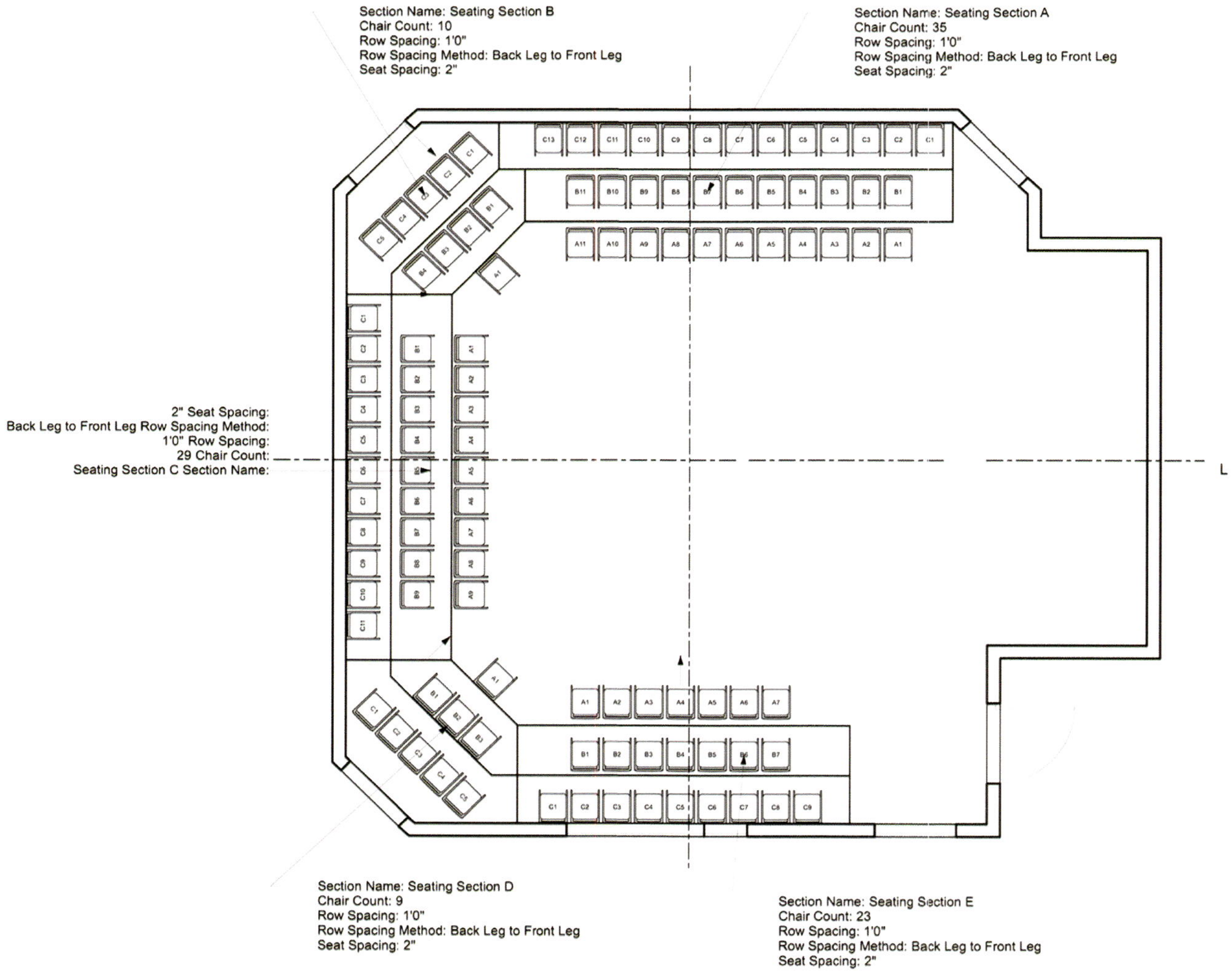

Figure 4.14 *Thrust Staging Format – Top/Plan View*. Created by Mackenzie Scales for the Seating Layout project.

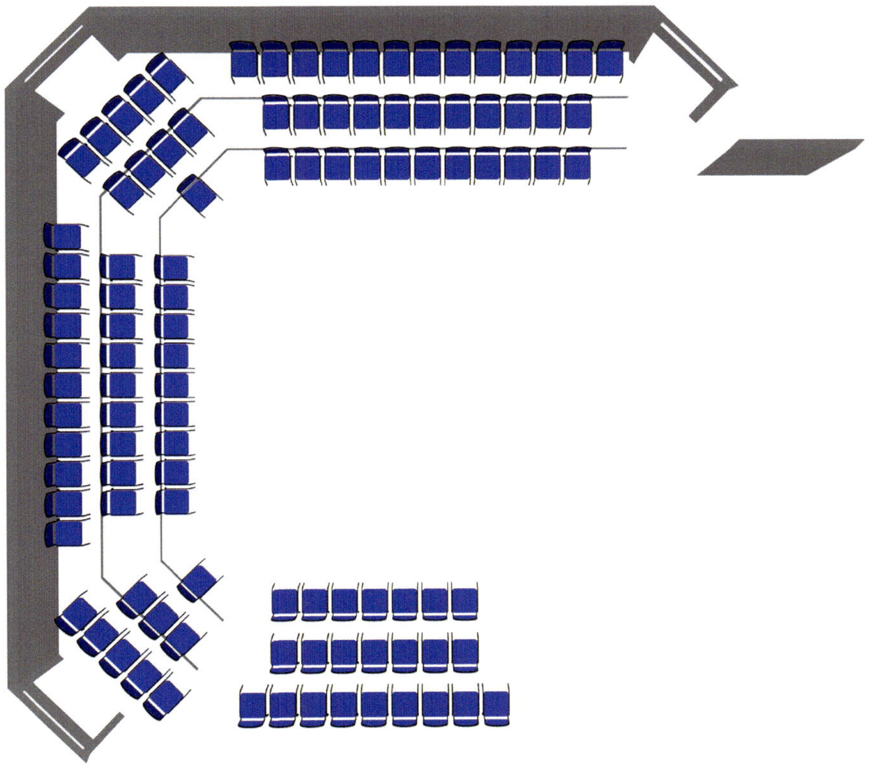

Figure 4.15 *Thrust Staging Format – Top View*. Created by Mackenzie Scales for the Seating Layout project.

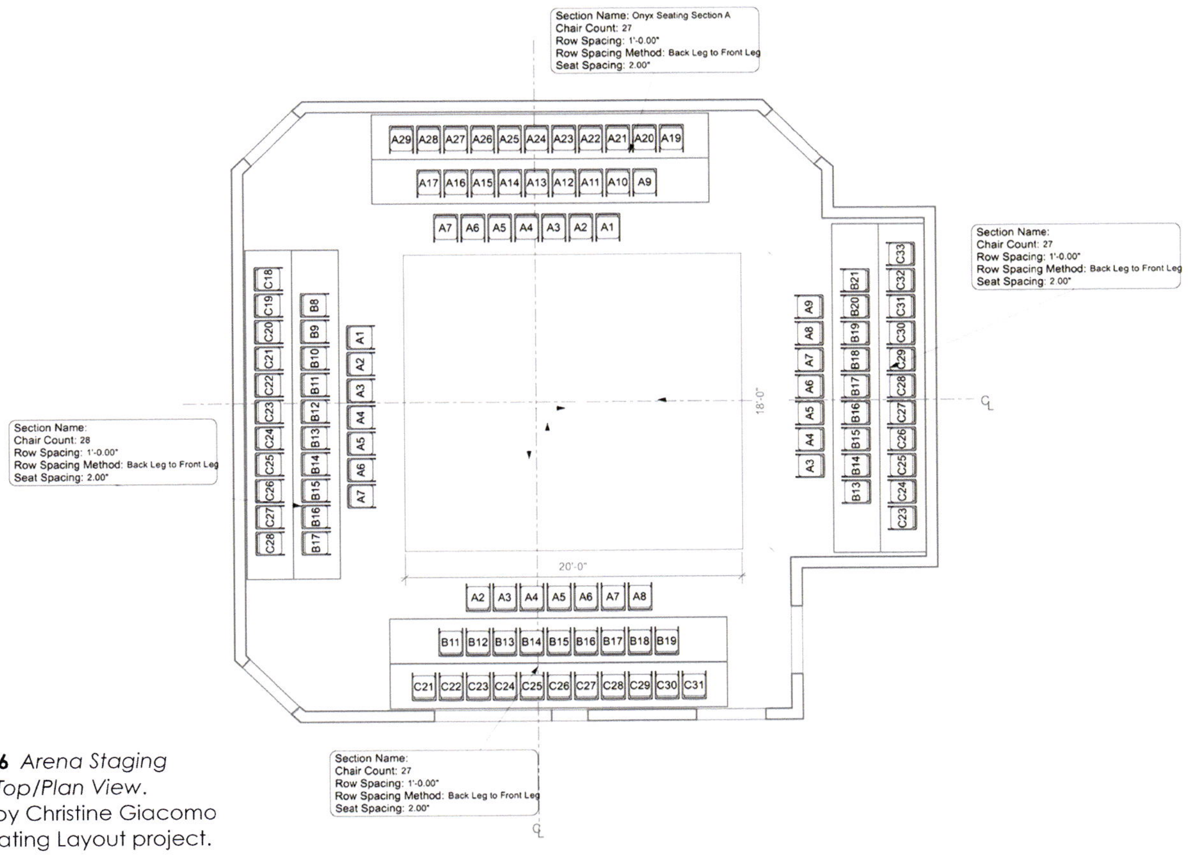

Figure 4.16 *Arena Staging Format – Top/Plan View*. Created by Christine Giacomo for the Seating Layout project.

Figure 4.17 *Arena Staging Format – Right Isometric View*. Created by Christine Giacomo for the Seating Layout project.

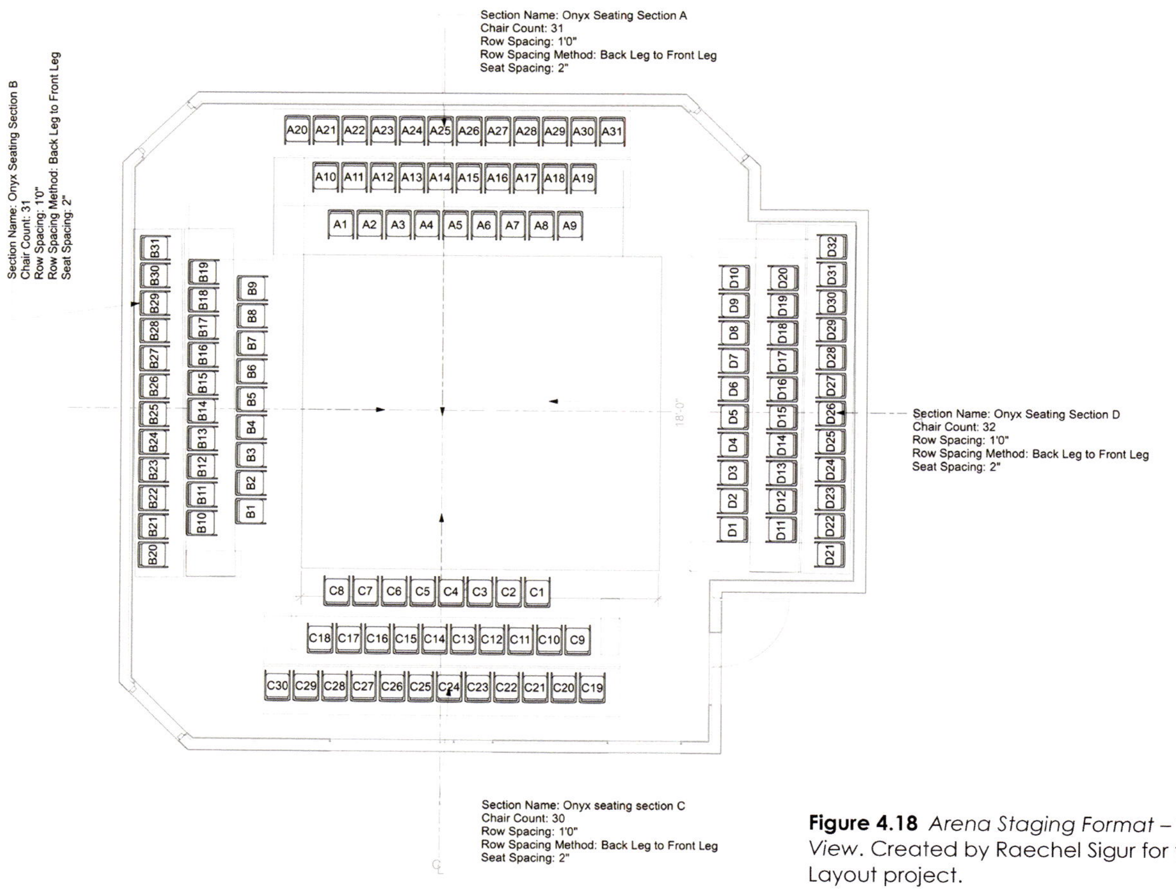

Figure 4.18 *Arena Staging Format – Top/Plan View*. Created by Raechel Sigur for the Seating Layout project.

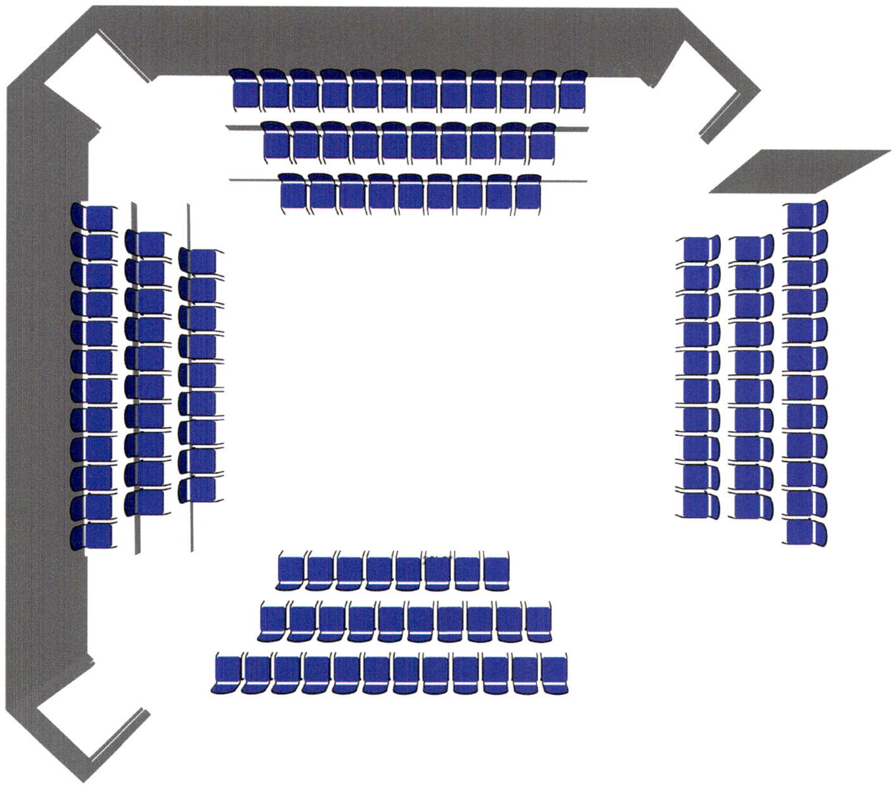

Figure 4.19 *Arena Staging Format – Right Isometric View*. Created by Raechel Sigur for the Seating Layout project.

Bibliography

Barranger, Milly S. *Theatre: A Way of Seeing* (7th Edition). Cengage Learning, NYC, 1st Jan. 2014.

Birkmire, William H. *The Planning and Construction of American Theatres*. John Wiley & Sons, New York, 1907.

Deborah M., Sweet, Harvey. *The Complete Book of Drawing for the Theatre*. Allyn and Bacon, Boston, 1995.

Giacomo, Christine. Fig. 4.16 *Arena Staging Format – Top/Plan View*. Design Skills class project. 2021.

Giacomo, Christine. Fig. 4.17 *Arena Staging Format – Right Isometric View*. Design Skills class project. 2021.

Payne, Darwin Reid, Fig. 4.7 *Components of a Proscenium Theatre. The Scenographic Imagination* (Third Edition). Southern Illinois University Press, Carbondale and Edwardsville, 1993.

Russell, John Scott. *Treatise on Sightlines.* Edinburgh new philosophical Journal 27, 1838.

Rose, Rich. *Drafting Scenery*. Betterway Publications, Inc., Virginia, 1990.

Rose, Rich. *AutoCad Onstage: A Computer-Aided Design handbook for Theatre, Film, and Television*. Betterway Publication, Inc., Virginia, 1990.

Scales, Mackenzie. Fig. 4.14 *Thrust Staging Format - Top/Plan View*. Design Skills class project. 2022.

Scales, Mackenzie. Fig. 4.15 *Thrust Staging Format - Top View*. Design Skills class project. 2022.

Sigur, Raechel. Fig. 4.18 *Arena Staging Format – Top/Plan View*. Design Skills class project. 2022.

Sigur, Raechel. Fig. 4.19 *Arena Staging Format – Top View*. Design Skills class project. 2022.

CHAPTER 5

Layers, Classes, and Build-in Objects

Vocabulary

Layer
Blocking
Light Plot
Shift Plan
Line Weight
Class
Design Layer
Sheet Layer
Levels
Stories
Original Z
Local Z
3D Build-in Objects
2D Symbols
3D Symbols
3D Modular Objects
Unstyled
Styled

Learning Objectives

- Explain the similarities and differences between the functions of Layer and Class.
- Memorize Layer icon and Class icon and the various locations to access the commands.
- Distinguish Levels from Layers.
- Distinguish Design Layer from Sheet Layer.
- Apply Classes and Layers in design processes for a systematic approach to document organization.
- Demonstrate the ability to manipulate the visibility of Layers and Classes.
- Display ways to activate, apply, and edit 3D Build-in Objects.

In Vectorworks, both *Layer* and Class are tools for you to organize the various components in your design. With a well-organized file, you can easily manipulate the visibility and location of each component as well as the interactive relationships among them. These tools have the potential to significantly increase the efficiency of your work during the design composition, components organization, presentation, and printing processes. In a VW document, you can create as many Layers and Classes as needed. The main difference between the two is that the ***Layer*** command can *determine* the components' physical location (elevation), because each Layer can be assigned a different height and the components created on a Layer will be automatically situated on the Layer elevation, whereas the ***Class*** command can determine the appearance (attributes) of the components, thus helping you to categorize the components of your design in a systematic fashion. While the Layer command does not influence the appearance of individual components, the Class command cannot decide the elevations of the components. Nevertheless, a Class can be assigned to components located in all Layers.

DOI: 10.4324/9781003266242-5

Classes

Class Icon and Location

The Class icon looks like a hierarchy of squares (see Fig. 5.1). You can access the Class command from the Top Menu bar (Tools – Organization… - Class), from View bar (Class Icon or Class Dropdown menu), from Object Info palette (Class dropdown menu), or from Navigation palette (Class Icon).

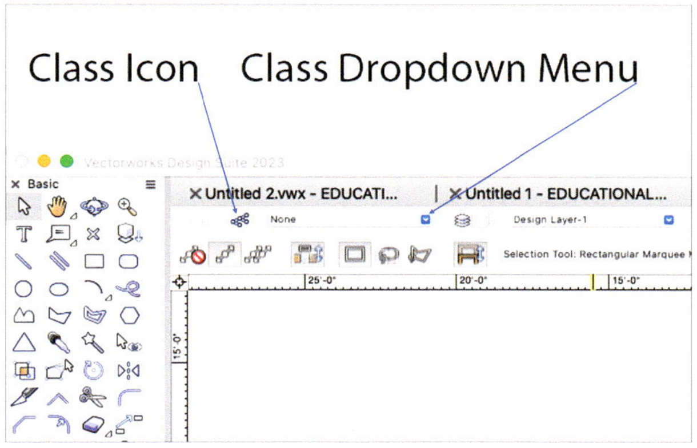

Figure 5.1 *Class Access*. A screenshot showing what the Class icon and Class dropdown menu look like in the VW application window.

Default Class

If you start a new document for a project, the default Class is called "None." There is also a Class named "dimension," which comes with the program. Still, unless you intentionally select the Dimension Class or create a new Class and give it a different name, everything you produce on your drawing area will be automatically assigned to the Class named "None."

Creating a New Class

To create a new Class, choose one of the following options:

1. You can
   a. Go to the Top Menu bar and click on Tools – Organization…
   b. When a dialog box opens, make sure the "Classes" tab located on the top of the window is selected. Click on the "New…" button located on the lower left corner of the window.
   c. When a (second) dialog box appears, give a name to the Class, check the "Edit properties after creation" box, and click "OK."
   d. When a (third) dialog box appears, make your selections on the attributes of the Class, such as pen style, color, and line thickness, etc., check "Use at Creation" box and click "OK" and "OK" again to establish the new Class. All components assigned to your newly established Class will then assume the attributes you selected for the Class.
2. You can go to the View bar and select "New Class…" located in the Class dropdown menu, then follow the instructions shown above in Section 1 – c and d.
3. You can click on the Class icon located on the View bar. Then follow the instructions shown above in Section 1 – b, c, and d.
4. You can go to Navigation palette and double click on the Class icon. Then, follow the instructions shown above in Section 1 – b, c, and d.
5. If you have an object drawn in your document, you can also select the object and go to the Object Info palette. Press the "Shape" tab. In the "Class" dropdown menu, click on "New Class…" Then, follow the instructions shown above in Section 1 – c and d.

Naming Classes – Division and Subdivision

In the design process, if you use Class to categorize various design components, you can then control the visibility of these components for different purposes. It is important to select a simple and direct name for a Class for easy remembrance and keep the Classes in a hierarchical order when applicable. For instance, imagine that you are designing a set consisting of a house façade and a front yard filled with trees and bushes. For such a design, you may want to create a Class for the house façade and name it "HOUSE." In addition, you may also want to create a Class for your plants, but subdivide the plants into bushes and trees. In this case, you would name the bushes "PLANTS-BUSHES" and the trees "PLANTS-TREES." Here, the hyphen in between the words stands for subdivision. With the hyphen in place, VW will put the BUSHES and TRESS under a Class named PLANTS (see Fig. 5.2).

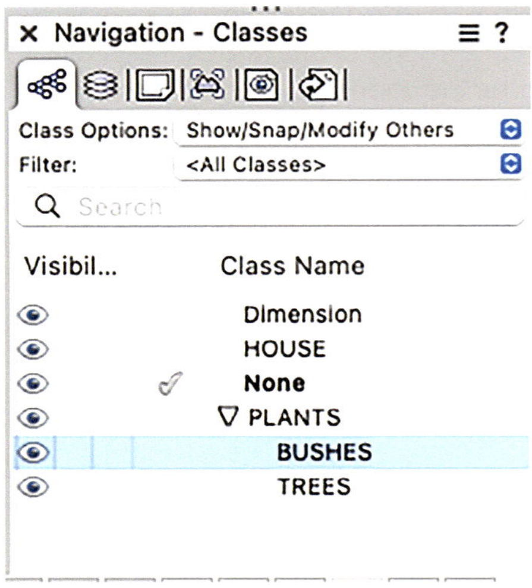

Figure 5.2 *Class Division and Subdivision*. A screenshot providing an example of hierarchical order in Class.

Assigning Components to a Named Class

For a simple design project, designers who are experienced in VW software may prefer to create Classes before the drawing starts and then select an appropriate Class to draw the components within. With this method, when a Class is selected, the components you create in the drawing area will automatically belong to this Class until you switch to a different Class. For more complex designs, however, a designer often creates Classes as the design progresses. The good news for the designers choosing this method of Class assignment is that VW offers the flexibility to assign and reassign Classes as well as edit their names and attributes whenever needed.

To assign a component or components of your design to a named Class, select the component(s). Go to the View bar or Object Info palette and click on the Class dropdown menu to select the name of your desired Class. The component(s) that you selected is/are then assigned to the Class and assume(s) the attributes associated with this Class.

If you want to check which Class a specific component is currently assigned to, select the component and see its name displayed in the Object Info palette – Class.

Reassigning Classes to a Component

To change the Class assignment for a component, the process is equally simple. Select the component. Go to the View bar or Object Info palette and click on the Class Dropdown menu to select the name of your desired Class. The component(s) that you selected is/are thus switched to your newly assigned Class and assume(s) the attributes associated with this Class.

Editing Class Attributes

If you want to edit the attribute(s) of a Class, double-click on the Class icon located either in the Navigation palette or in the View bar. The Organization dialog box appears. Select the name of the Class that you would like to see a change in Class attributes and click on the "Edit" button. This will bring up a new dialog box, in which you can change the attributes originally set for this Class. As soon as you click on the "OK" buttons to close the dialog boxes, all the components that you previously assigned to this Class will now assume the new attributes that you just selected for this Class.

Manipulating Class Visibility

The easiest way to manipulate the visibility of Classes is to use the tools available in the Navigation palette. If you press the Class tab in the Navigation palette, you will see three columns of visibility control. The "eye" icon stands for visible. The "x" sign represents the invisible. The "dimmed eye" icon provides a gray appearance for the Class. This means that you can make a Class visible, invisible, or gray simply by pressing a button in one of the columns associated with that Class. That said, the active Class, which is indicated by a check mark on the right of the columns, is always going to be visible. In other words, no matter what visibility options are displayed on one of the columns, the check mark (active Class) will override the current visibility option of this Class.

Aside from the visibility tools mentioned above, VW lets you manipulate the visibility and interactive relationships among various Classes. If the Class tab in the Navigation palette is on, you can see a variety of choices in the Class Options dropdown menu as follows:

1. Active Only
2. Gray Others
3. Gray/Snap Others
4. Show Others
5. Show/Snap Others
6. Show/Snap/Modify Others

The video associated with Chapter Five illustrates how each visibility option functions.

Class Application in Set Design

In a scene design process, the designer can assign and reassign Classes to all design components at any time for different purposes. Below are some scenarios of Class application in a design process.

Separating 2D Components from 3D Components for the Presentation of a 3D Model

If a designer creates Classes for 2D components (e.g., title blocks, dimensions, and notations) and 3D modeling components separately, he/she can then make the 2D components invisible when presenting a 3D model to the production team (see Figs. 5.3 and 5.4).

Subdividing Components in a Ground Plan

A Ground Plan of a set (represented through a top/plan view of the set in a VW environment) conveys information that interests many members of a production team. The director wants to see the Ground Plan for ***Blocking*** (placement and movement of actors on stage). The lighting designer based his/her ***Light Plot*** (a plan showing the placement, type, size, color, and focus of each lighting instrument being used for a theatre production) on this plan. The stage manager relies on this plan to tape the stage floor for the actors to use in rehearsals. The technical director needs to refer to this plan to situate the set pieces on the stage after they are built, and the stagehands want to see a ***Shift Plan*** (the layout of set/furniture pieces for each act/scene) that can guide them to change the scenery for various acts and scenes during the tech rehearsals and performances.

Since different people in the same production team are looking for different information in the plan, it is wise to divide the Ground Plan Class into a variety of subdivisions, such as labels, levels, set placement dimensions, permanent set structures, moveable set props, etc., so you can call the elements off and on for different configurations that are relevant to specific individuals. As an alternative, you may want to assign each subdivision of the Class a specific attribute, such as a color. So, even if all the Class subdivisions are visible simultaneously, people can still distinguish information relevant or irrelevant to them immediately (see Fig. 5.5).

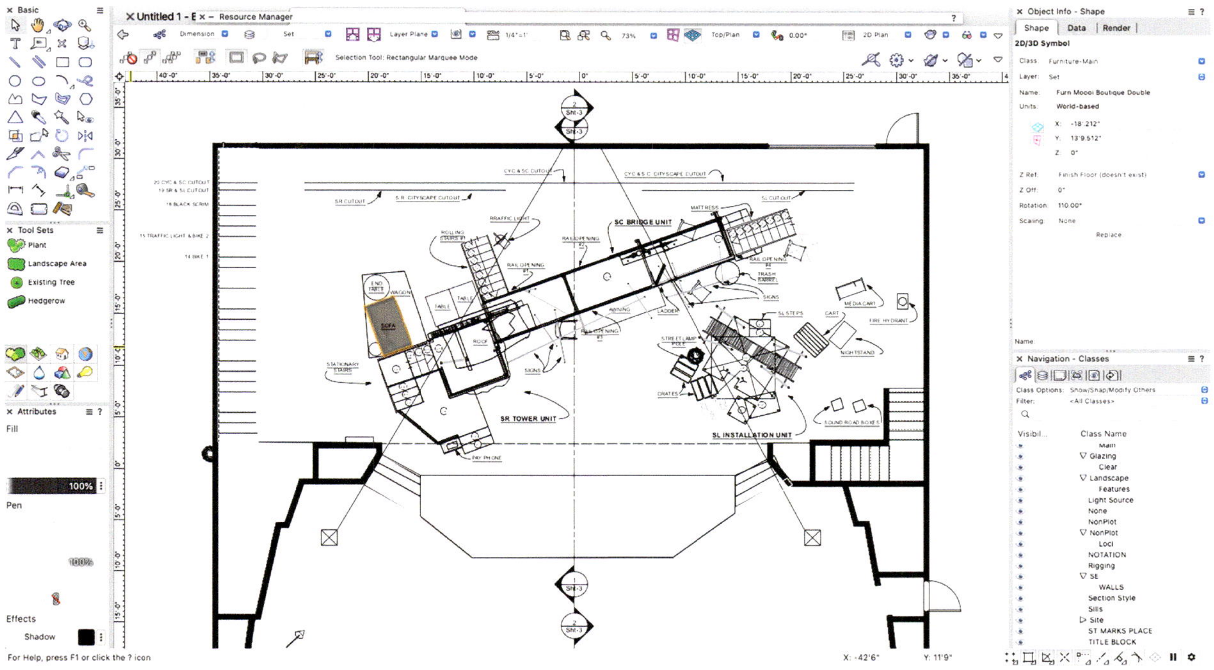

Figure 5.3 *Floor Plan for Rent*. Compared to Fig. 5.4, in this rendition of the set design for *Rent*, all the classes are visible.

Figure 5.4 A Virtual Set Model for *Rent*. In comparison to Fig. 5.3, in this rendition of the set design for *Rent*, all classes for 2D components, such as NOTATION, TITLE BLOCK, and DIMENSION, are invisible. The background of the set is a photo by Dan_Prat.

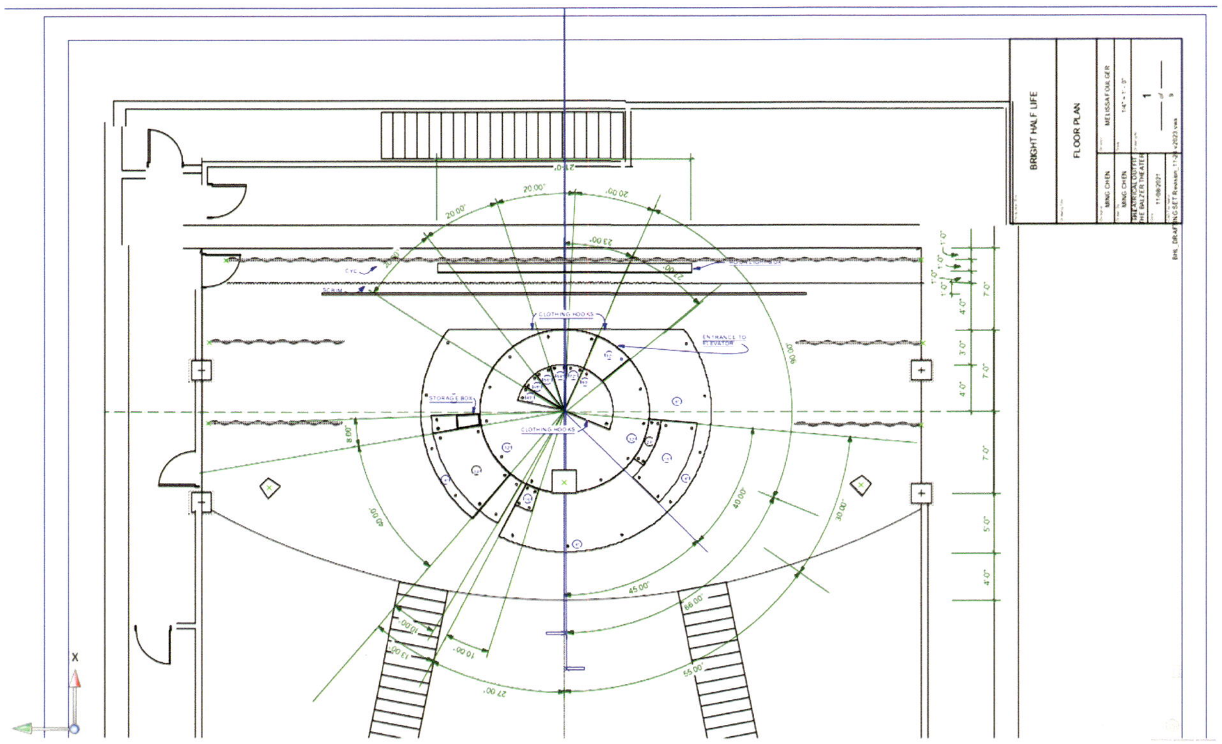

Figure 5.5 *Class Attributes*. This screenshot illustrates the use of colors to subdivide components on a Ground Plan. While the information conveyed in all colors is relevant to the technical director, the information made visible in green is much less relevant, if at all, to the director.

Assigning Different Line Weights for Different Classes

USITT drafting standards suggest that scenic designers use different ***Line Weights*** (the width of the line) to draw different components to achieve clarity in conveying design ideas. For instance, USITT recommends the use of 0.010 in (0.25 mm) light-weight line for dimension lines and extension lines and the use of 0.014 in (0.35 mm) medium-weight line for object lines (USITT, 3). During the design process, designers can create a Class named Dimension or use the default Dimension Class and set the light-weight line in the Edit Class window (under Graphic Attributes) for the Class. All the dimension and extension lines they draw in this Class will assume the appropriate line weight. Likewise, they can create a Class named Set and set the medium-weight line in the Edit Class window (under Graphic Attributes) for the Class. All the set lines they draw in this Class will assume the appropriate line weight for the Class.

These are only a few examples of scenarios in which a designer could apply Class options during a design process.

Layers

There are two types of Layers co-existing in VW. One is called ***Design Layer***; the other is called ***Sheet Layer***.

Design Layer vs. Sheet Layer: Purpose and Scale

As the name implies, the Design Layer is conceived for design purpose, whereas the Sheet Layer is conceived for drafting and printing purposes. While the Design Layer can be assigned to a certain scale, such as 1/2, 1/4, or 1 inch scale, the Sheet Layer is inevitably 1:1 scale. To avoid confusion, since Sheet Layer deals with drafting and printing, which is not relevant to the subject of this chapter, it will be discussed in greater detail in Chapter 8 – Drafting.

Layer Icon and Location

Layer icon looks like a bunch of velum sheets stacking one on top of another (see Fig. 5.6). You can access the Layer command from the Top Menu bar (Tools – Organization… - Design Layer), from View bar, from the Object Info palette, or from the Navigation palette.

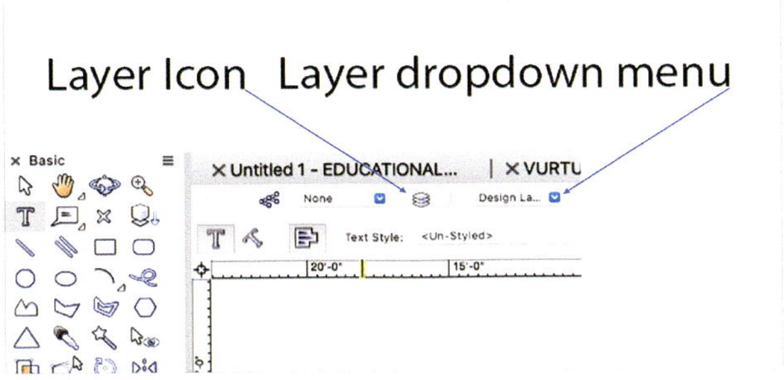

Figure 5.6 *Layer Access*. A screenshot illustrating what the Layer icon and Layer dropdown menu look like.

Default Design Layer

If you start a new document for a project, the default Design Layer is called "Design Layer 1." Unless you intentionally create a new Layer and give it a different name, everything you produce on your drawing area will be automatically assigned to the Layer named "Design Layer 1."

Levels and Layers: Similarities and Differences

In VW environment, ***Levels***, Layers, and ***Stories*** are all organizational tools to establish the elevations of 3D objects. While Stories and Levels, such as slabs, are specifically intended for the designs of residential and commercial buildings, Layers and Levels, such as platforms and staircases, are frequently used tools for scenic designers.

Levels are horizontal planes that are offset vertically from a story or a Layer that contains them. Their heights are measured from local zero, meaning from the bottom of a Story or a Layer. However, if the elevation of the Story or Layer changes, the Level elevation changes accordingly. That said, it is important to understand that the Z value of an object depends on the layer elevation the object is measured from. For example, if Design Layer 1 stays on its default elevation 0" (the origin) and Design Layer 2 is set 10′ above the origin, when you create a chair on Design Layer 2, the Z value of the chair measured from Design Layer 2 is 0", while the Z value measured from the origin is 10′. Remember, the Z value of an object shown in the Object Info palette is always measured from the bottom of the active Layer. In the case of the chair, this means that, if you make Design Layer 1 as the active Layer, the Z value of the chair shown in the Object info palette is 10′ (see Fig. 5.7), but if you make Design Layer 2 as the

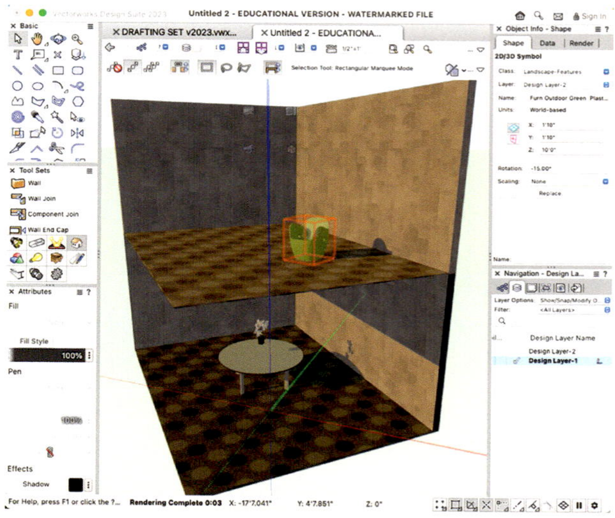

Figure 5.7 *Chair Upstairs*. This screenshot shows that, when the active layer is Design Layer 1, the Z value of a chair located upstairs (on Design Layer 2) is 10′, because it is measured from Design Layer 1.

active Layer, the Z value of the chair shown in the Object info palette is 0″ (see Fig. 5.8).

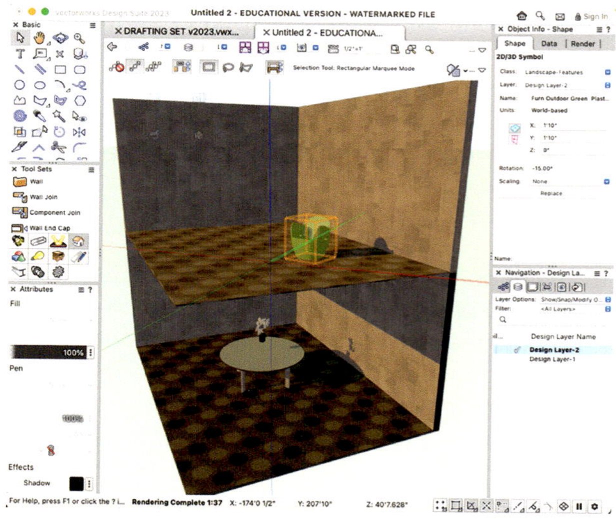

Figure 5.8 *Chair on the Floor*. This screenshot shows that, when the active layer is Design Layer 2 (upstairs), the Z value of a chair set on the same floor is 0″, because it is measured from Design Layer 2.

Likewise, if you place a table on Design Layer 1, when Design Layer 1 is active, the Z value of the table shown in the Object Info palette is 0″ (see Fig. 5.9).

However, if you switch the active Layer to Design Layer 2, the Z value of the table shown in the Object Info palette is −10′ (see Fig. 5.10).

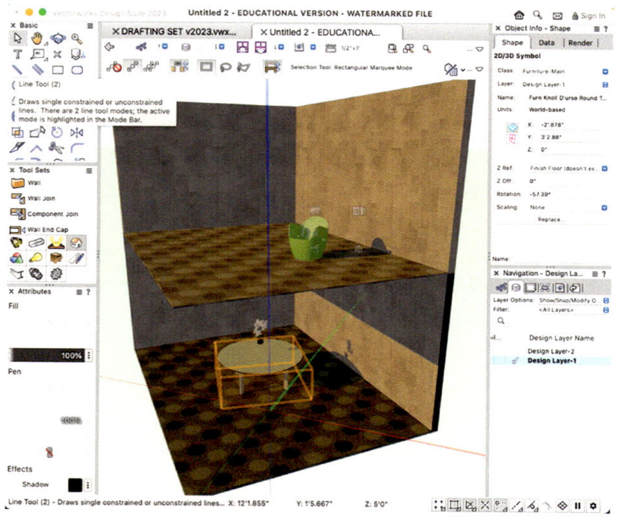

Figure 5.9 *Table on the Floor*. This screenshot reveals that, when the active layer is Design Layer 1, the Z value of a table set on the same floor is 0″, because it is measured from Design Layer 1.

In addition, Layer Z height and Bottom Z (Bot Z) are different concepts. While layer Z height is the default Z height for all objects created on that layer until a bottom Z height (Bot Z) is defined for an individual object, Bot Z reflects the bottom elevation for a particular object. (Note: you may open the file named *06 Layers.vwx* available in the Appendices folder (resourcecentre.routledge.com/books/9781032209890) to get a better understanding of these concepts.)

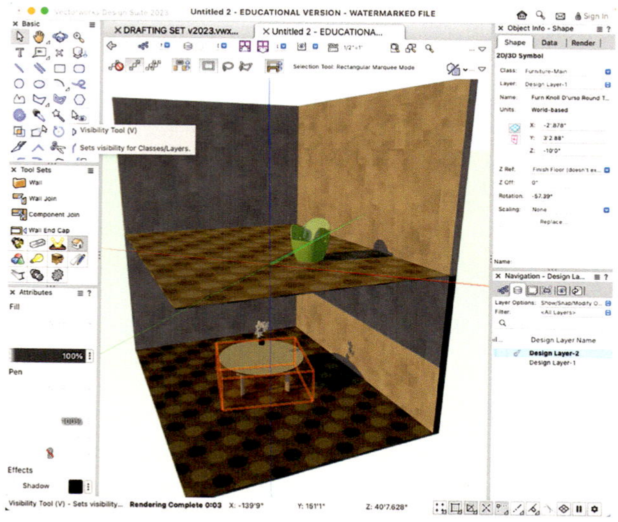

Figure 5.10 *Table Downstairs*. This screenshot demonstrates that, when the active layer is Design Layer 2, the Z value of a table downstairs is −10′, because it is measured from Design Layer 2.

Creating a New Layer

To create a new Layer, choose one of the following options:

1. You can
   a. Go to the Top Menu bar and click on Tools – Organization…
   b. When a dialog box opens, make sure the "Design Layers" tab located on the top of the window is selected. Click on the "New…" button located on the lower left corner of the window.
   c. When a (second) dialog box appears, give a name to the Layer, check "Edit properties after creation" box, and click "OK."
   d. When a (third) dialog box appears, make your selections, such as scale, elevation, etc., for the Layer and click "OK" and "OK again to establish the new Layer. The object you create on this Layer will then assume the scale and elevation you set for this Layer.
2. You can go to the View bar and select "New Design Layer…" located in the Design Layers dropdown menu, then follow the instructions shown above in Section 1 – c, and d.
3. You can click on the Layer icon located on the View bar. Then follow the instructions shown above in Section 1 – b, c, and d.
4. You can go to the Navigation palette and double-click on Layer icon. Then, follow the instructions shown above in Section 1 – b, c, and d.
5. If you have an object drawn in your document, you can also select the object and go to the Object Info palette, and then press "Shape" tab. In the "Layer" dropdown menu, select "New Design Layer…" Then, follow the instructions shown above in Section 1 – c, and d.

Reassigning Layer to a Component

To move a 3D component from one Layer to another, select the component, go to the View bar or Object Info palette, and choose the name of your desired Layer located on the Layer dropdown menu. The component that you selected is thus switched to your newly assigned Layer and assumes the perimeters you set for that Layer. When working with Layers, you should remember not to move 3D components by dragging them from one Layer to another in a 3D view if the Layers were set at different elevations, but to move them through Layer options located on the View bar or on the Object Info palette, as explained.

Editing Layer Settings

If you want to edit the settings of a Layer, double-click on the Layer icon located either in the Navigation palette or in the View bar. The Organization dialog box appears. Select the name of the Layer that you would like to see a change in Layer setting and click on the "Edit" button. This will bring up a new dialog box, in which you can change the settings for this Layer. As soon as you click on the "OK" buttons to close the dialog boxes, the components that were previously assigned to this Layer will assume the new setting that you have just selected for this Layer.

Manipulating Layer Visibility

The ways to exercise control over Layer visibility are the same as those to manipulate the visibility of Classes. The only difference is to make sure that you press the Layer tab (as opposed to the Class tab) in the Navigation palette before making your choices. Refer to previous section named ***Manipulating Class Visibility*** for details.

Layer Application in Scene Design

In a scene design process, the designer can create Layers for different purposes. Below are a few scenarios in which Layer options can be very helpful.

Separating the Floor Plan of the Set Design from the Venue Floor Plan

In theatre, a freelance scenic designer can expect to receive a scaled floor plan of the venue upon hiring. It is based on this floor plan that the designer starts to create a set for a specific production. Working in a VW environment, you want to import the venue plan into one Layer but trace the venue plan and create your own floor plan for the set in another Layer. You can do this by creating a new document, naming it "(Title of the Show) Floor Plan," and choosing "Show/Snap Others" in the Class Option dropdown menu (Navigation palette) in this Layer. In this way, when you trace the venue plan and erect your model stage and the 3D set model, your original venue plan is preserved.

Setting a New Layer for Each Set Unit

Another way to use Layer in a scene design process is to create a new Layer for each of the set units you design in addition to the Floor Plan. By doing so, you can 1) select "Active Only" in Layer Option dropdown menu while working on an individual set unit (Fig. 5.11), 2) make the unit's Front View facing parallel with the picture plane for an easy 3D modeling process, and 3) make the unit's Front View facing parallel with the picture plane to meet the requirement for drafting multiple views on Sheet Layers and Viewports, which is a later step in the design process described in Chapter 8 – Drafting.

Theoretically, you can also use Classes to fulfill these functions. Nevertheless, since you may have much more Classes than you have Layers in a document to keep track of, utilizing Layer command might be a wise choice.

Establishing a New Elevation Base

A third instance in which you will want to create a new Layer is when a new horizonal plane is needed to contain many objects. For example, you want to place furniture pieces and pot plants on a second floor or on a platform. Instead of raising the Bot Z height for each set prop, you could bound the floor

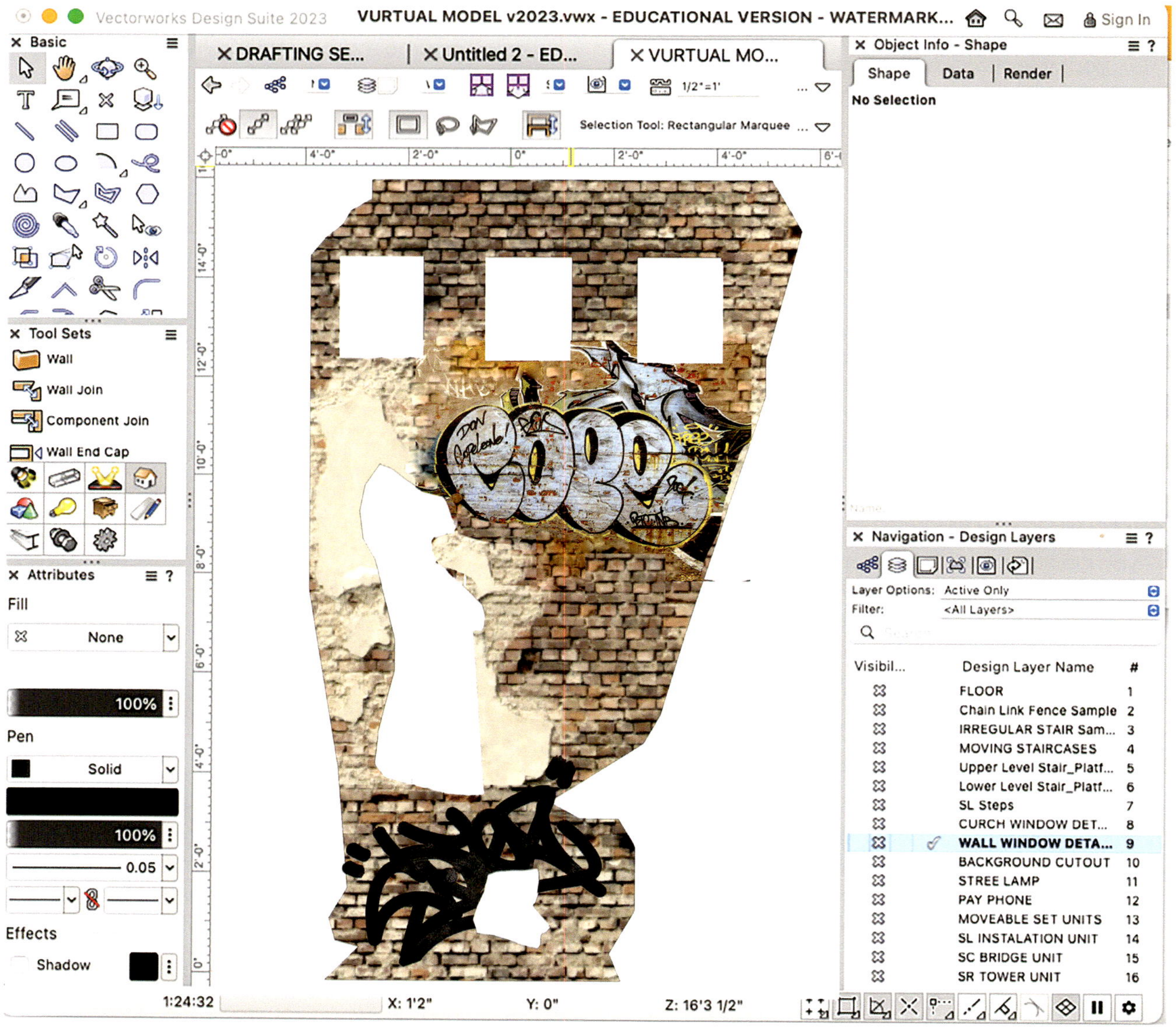

Figure 5.11 *Wall Unit for Rent*. Taken during the design process of modeling and rendering a wall unit, this screenshot provides an example of making each set unit a separate Layer for the convenience of detailed work on individual units.

of the second level or platform landing with a new Layer and set the Layer height for these pieces to be placed upon.

3D Build-in Objects

Build-in or plug-in components in VW refer to 2D and 3D Symbols, geometric shapes, and readymade objects that you can use in your designs. With those build-in components at hand, you can produce a wall and insert a door or a window in the blink of an eye – the building of a residential house is only a few clicks away. In the VW program, you can find thousands of built-in components, either in various Tool Sets or in Resource Manager – VW Libraries. To assist you in making 3D set models, this section will introduce methods, techniques, and processes to access, edit, and customize ***3D Build-in Objects***.

Types of 3D Build-in Objects

3D build-in objects can be categorized by the nature of their application. Most readymade objects that you find in Tool Sets are of a modular nature. They are made for you to customize the objects to your liking for repeated use in your document. Some of the readymade objects or symbols you find in VW libraries are editable; others are not.

3D Modular Objects

Access and Customize 3D Modular Objects

You can access frequently used tools for 3D objects, such as Door, Window, Stair, Plant, etc. from various Tool Sets. They are called tools because they come in as prototypes and are of a modular nature. For instance, if you click on the Wall tool, you can "click" and "click" your computer mouse to define the length and orientation of an ***Unstyled*** wall that has a default preset of wall elements, such as wall thickness and wall height. Due to these presets, by making two mouse-clicks, you can instantly build a wall and put the wall in a certain location and orientation. If you want to change the setting of this specific wall, you can select the wall, and then go to the Object Info palette. In this palette, you can not only change the thickness, height, and other elements of the wall but also replace the Unstyled wall with any Styled wall available in VW Libraries. Experienced VW users know that this editable capability does not belong to ***3D Modular Objects*** only; it is observable in many 3D objects taken from the VW library.

What is unique about 3D Modular Objects, however, is that they come with a preference setting option accessible by clicking on the Preferences button located in the Mode bar (see Fig. 5.12).

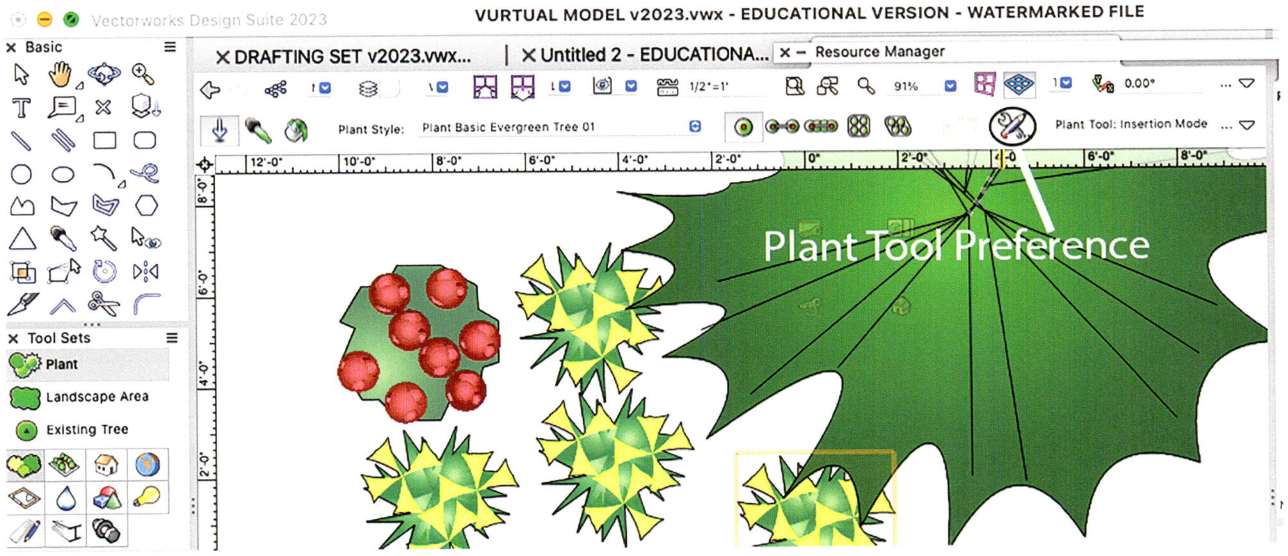

Figure 5.12 *Tool Preference Access.* A screenshot displaying the look of Tool Preference icon.

For example, if you draw a wall with the Wall tool, then click on the Preferences icon, you can make choices on the wall thickness (under Definition tab), wall height (under Insertion Options tab), and even replace the Unstyled wall with any Styled wall available in VW Libraries. One major difference between changing the values of the wall in the Object Info palette and changing them in the Wall Preferences window is that the former changes the setting only relevant to the specific object that you selected, but the latter changes the setting for all the walls you produce thereafter in the document. In other words, it becomes a new default setting for the Wall tool, even after you close and reopen the same document. This setting will not change until you adjust the setting again in Wall Preferences window to set a new default for the modular object. The working method for the use of Wall tool discussed above applies to all modular tools for 3D objects.

Set Design Application of Tools Found in Different Workspaces

As mentioned in Chapter Four, in VW, there are different sets of tools available in Tool Sets for various workspaces. These Tool Sets are intended for designers in various disciplines. For example, the Tool Sets in the "Architect" workspace are primarily designed for architects, "Landmark" workspace for landscaping designers, and "spotlight" workspace for lighting designers in the entertainment industry. Currently, there is no default workspace customized for scenic designers. Nevertheless, the good news is that there are no boundaries set among various workspaces in VW; during an entire design process, you can switch from one workspace to another and use the tools available in any Tool Sets without a trace. By the nature of scene design, this borderless setup is certainly an advantage because, to design scenery, you will need tools available in all areas, including architecture, interior design, landscaping design, and lighting design. The freedom of switching between workspaces affords you the freedom to take whatever is needed for the project at hand to fulfill your dream.

3D Symbol Objects

There are numerous ***2D Symbols*** and ***3D Symbols*** available in VW Libraries. This section will only cover the application of 3D Symbols or objects for the purpose of creating set models in the VW environment.

Find a Symbol Object

VW Library resides in Resource Manager. Unless you know the name/code of a specific 3D object and the category in which the object is placed, the most efficient way to find a 3D object in the library is to type its generic name (chair, cabinet, sofa, etc.) in the resource browser to conduct a search. It can never be overemphasized that "All Resources" needs to be selected in the top bar dropdown menu in Resource Manage before you start the search, because if you ignore this tip, you may not find the object that is actually available in the VW Libraries. By searching for an object in the resource browser, an array of object icons associated with the generic name will show up in the resource window. You can then select a specific object and insert it into your drawing.

Edit a Symbol Object

Some of the Symbol Objects allow you to edit its dimensions after being placed on the drawing; others do not. Some allow you to change certain dimensions, but not other dimensions. For some objects, you can change their dimensions in the Object Info palette; for other objects, you need to double-click the object to enter the symbol Edit window to do so. The example provided in Technique 5 - Symbol Objects - Edit a Symbol Object and the video associated with this section demonstrate the steps taken to edit a Symbol Object.

Convert a 3D Object into a Symbol

You may have created a 3D object from scratch, by editing an existing symbol, or by using a modular tool. No matter what method you use to arrive at a 3D object, you can convert it into a Symbol Object for repeated use in the document or even in future projects.

Some of the objects you created using modular tools, such as Stair, give you options to save the object as a symbol after you have changed the perimeters of the object. For other objects, you may need to go through several steps to save the objects as symbols. The video associated with Chapter Five – Convert a 3D Object into a Symbol explains this process.

Technique 5 – Episode One: 3D Build-in Objects, Layers, and Classes

This Episode covers topics relevant to 3D Build-in Object Layers and Classes.

3D Build-in Objects

In the VW program, you can access 3D build-in Objects either by activating the 3D Object Tool in a Tool Sets or by acquiring objects from VW Libraries. For clarity, let us call the objects created by using one of the tools in the Tool Sets "Modular Objects" and those created by inserting objects from VW Libraries "Symbol Objects."

Modular Objects

Command: One of the Workspaces – Tool Sets – One of the Build-in 3D Objects

Insert a Modular Object

To insert a Modular Object, a staircase, for instance, do the following:

1. Create a new blank document.
2. Go to the Top Menu bar – File – Document Settings – Document Setup…
3. In the Document Setup window, change the Layer Scale to ½″ scale and the Drawing Area to US Arch D.
4. Go to Tool – Workspaces – Architect.
5. In Top/Plan view, click on the Building Shell icon.
6. Select "Stair" to activate the Stair tool.
7. Click once on the Drawing Area to set the location for the stair.
8. Rotate your cursor to determine the angle for the stair and click the second time to drop the stair in the drawing. See the result in an isometric view.

Edit a Modular Object

To edit the stair that you have just inserted, select the stair and make a duplicate.

1. Go to the Object Info palette and click on "Settings."
2. When a dialog window opens, make the following changes:
    a. Click on the "General" tap located on the top menu bar of the Stair Settings.
    b. Change Stair Width to a new value. For example, change it from 3′ to 2′-6″.
    c. Click on the "Railings" tap located on the top menu bar of the Stair Settings.
    d. Under "Accept Setting for," uncheck "Both Sides," and check "Right Railing."
    e. Under "Parameter," select "Handrail," and uncheck the "Show Handrail" box.
    f. Still under "Parameter," select "Guardrail," and uncheck the "Show Guardrail" box.
    g. Click "OK" to exit the window.
    h. In the Object Info palette, under guardrail, uncheck "Show right guardrail," and check "Show left guardrail" to finish the editing.
3. See the change you have just made in an isometric view.

Save a 3D Object as a Symbol

To save a 3D object as a symbol, do the following:

1. While the object is still selected, go to the Top Menu bar – Modify – Create Symbol. A dialogue box appears.
2. Select "Next mouse click for insertion point" and click "OK."
3. Click a place on the symbol for the insertion point. A dialogue box appears to show you where (in which folder) your symbol is located. Click "OK."
4. Now you can see and retrieve the symbol by going to the folder in which you saved the symbol.
5. Then, you can either double-click or drag and drop the symbol to your drawing as needed.

Symbol Objects

Command: Resource Manager – Search in the browser by the generic name of the object.

Insert a Symbol Object

1. In Top/Plan view, go to Resource Manager to search for "event table." Make sure "All Resources" is selected in the dropdown menu on the top of the window before making the search.
2. Double-click on Event Table – 72-in Round. This will both select the table and activate the Symbol Insertion Tool in the Basic palette.
3. Click once on the drawing area to place the table at a specific location in the drawing.
4. Rotate the table to choose an appropriate orientation/angle for the table, then make the second click to drop the table on the drawing.

Edit a Symbol Object

Some Symbol Objects are editable; others are not. Some symbols allow you to edit them in the Object Info palette when they are selected; others will require you to enter an edit Symbol window to do so. To edit a symbol that you cannot edit when the symbol is selected, do the following:

1. Double-click on the table you just inserted. This will bring up a dialogue box, asking which component you would like to edit. You would want to edit both 2D component and 3D component one at a time.
2. After you select "2D Component" and click "Edit," you will be inside a Symbol edit window.
3. Select the object. In the Object Info palette, change the diameter of the table from 6′ to 4′ and press the Exit Symbol button to come back to the drawing board.
4. Repeat the above steps to change the dimension(s) for the 3D component of the table. In the Top/Plan view, the new diameter of the table in 3D Symbol edit window should coincide with the new diameter for the 2D component. Now you have a table with a new dimension(s). Check the result of your editing in an isometric view.

   Note: For some objects, after you have entered the edit Symbol window, you will need to ungroup the object and double-click one of the components to edit it in a second level of the edit Symbol window. That said, some symbols will never allow you to edit, no matter what.

Layers and Classes

In Vectorworks, both Layer and Class are tools to help you organize the components and their visibility, as well as interactive relationships in a drawing. The Layer icon looks like a bunch of velum sheets stacking one on top of another, while the Class icon looks like a hierarchy of squares. The main difference between the two is that the Layer command determines an object's "physical" location, because each layer can be assigned a different height, whereas the Class command helps you categorize elements in a drawing. It applies to objects in all layers.

Everything that exists in a drawing is both in a class and on a layer by default. If you do not assign them a name, the default Layer is called "Design Layer 1" and the default Class is called "None." There is no limit on the number of design layer and class you can create. However, it is said that you will usually have more classes than layers in a set of drawings.

Classes

Create a New Class

1. To create a new class, first create a blank document and set the scale of the document to ¼″ scale and the size of the document to US Arch D.
2. Double click on the Class icon located either in the Navigation palette or on the View bar. A dialog window appears.
3. Click on the "New…" button located on the lower left corner of the window. Another dialog window appears.
4. Give a name to the class, check the "Edit properties after creation" box, and click "OK." A third dialog window appears.
5. In this window, if you check "Use at Creation" box, you can make choices on Graphic Attributes, Textures, and Visibilities for the class. This means, in the future, if you assign an object(s) to this class, the object will assume the attribute, texture, and visibility that you selected for this class.
6. Click "OK" to close the window.

Assign Objects to a Class

1. To assign an object or a group of objects to the class that you newly created, draw a shape or group of shapes and select the object(s).
2. Go to the Object Info palette.
3. In the class dropdown menu, look for the name of the new class you created and select it. A dialog window appears.
4. Click "Yes." The object(s) you selected are now in the new class, which assumes the choices you made for the class.

Manipulate the Visibility of Classes

Note: You can make any object you draw either visible, invisible, or gray using the icons in the three narrow columns located on the Navigation palette. The icons in the first column (the EYE signs) stand for "visible." The icons in the second column (the CROSS-DIAGONAL signs) stand for "invisible." The icons in the third column (the DIMMED EYE sign) represent "gray," and the active class, which is identified by a CHECK MARK, is always "visible," no matter what.

To find out how you can manipulate the visibility of classes, do the following:

1. Double-click on the Class icon and create the following new classes and name them:
   a. Circle
   b. Triangle
   c. Rectangle
   d. Purple
   e. Green
   f. Orange
2. In the Edit Class(es) window, uncheck the "Use at Creation" box, and click "OK."
3. With tools in the Basic palette, draw three circles, three triangles, and three rectangles.
4. Make one circle, one triangle, and one rectangle purple.
5. Make one circle, one triangle, and one rectangle green.
6. Make one circle, one triangle, and one rectangle orange.
7. Select all the circles.
8. In the Class dropdown menu located in the Object Info palette, select "Circle."
9. Select all the triangles.
10. In the Class dropdown menu, select "Triangles."
11. Select all the rectangles.
12. In the Class dropdown menu, select "Rectangle."
13. After you assigned shapes to various classes, go to the Navigation palette.
14. When the Class icon is selected, you can now make any of the three groups of shapes visible, invisible, or gray.

Switch Objects' Class Assignment

1. To switch objects' Class assignment from one Class to another, select all the purple shapes.
2. In the Class dropdown menu located in the Object Info palette, select "Purple."
3. Select all the green shapes.
4. In the Class dropdown menu, select "Green."
5. Select all the orange shapes.
6. In the Class dropdown menu, select "Orange."
7. Now you can make any of the three groups of colored shapes visible, invisible, or gray.

Organize the Relationships among Classes

In the Navigation palette, the check mark indicates which class is currently active. That said, you have options to treat other Classes in relation to the active class in a variety of ways by making your selections in the Class Option dropdown menu located in the Navigation palette. Now, you can try it.

1. Go to the Navigation palette and click the Class icon if it is not already selected.
2. Make PURPLE CLASS active.
3. Click on the Class Options dropdown menu and select "Active Only." All the shapes with colors other than purple become invisible.
4. In the Class Options dropdown menu, select "Gray Others." The objects existing in all other classes appear as ghost images. You can see them, but you cannot interact with them; nor can you move or change them.
5. In the Class Options dropdown menu, select "Gray/Snap Others." You can now snap the purple shapes to the gray shapes, but still cannot move or change the gray shapes.
6. In the Class Options dropdown menu, select "Show Others." This selection lets you see the color images but does not interact with them, or move or change them.
7. In the Class Options dropdown menu, select "Show/Snap Others." With this option, you can both see the color images and snap the purple shapes onto those images.
8. In the Class Options dropdown menu, select "Show/Snap/Modify Others." This option lets you not only see the colored images and snap purple shapes onto them, but also make changes to the images in other classes.

Assign Active Class

You can also make a class Active either in the Class dropdown menu located on the View bar or make selection for the active class in the Navigation palette.

Force Select a Class

If a class option is missing, you can right-click the mouse (Ctrl+Click for Mac) and force select it.

Layers

Create a New Layer

1. Create a blank document and set the scale of the document to ¼″ scale and the size of the document to US Arch D.
2. Double-click on the Layer icon located either in the Navigation palette or on the View bar. An Organization dialog window appears.

3. Click on the "New…" button located on the lower left corner of the window. Another dialog window appears.
4. Give a name to the layer, check the "Edit properties after creation" box, and click "OK." A third dialog window appears.
5. In this Edit Design Layer window, input 0″ in the Elevation slot and click "OK" and "OK" again to close the dialog windows.
6. In Top/Plan view, use the Rectangle tool to draw a 20′ (W) × 12′ (H) rectangle.
7. Extrude the rectangle by 1″.
8. Click on Symbol Insertion Tool located on the Basic palette.
9. Go to Resource Manager to search for "Chairs."
10. Double-click on "Event Table 36 and Chairs" to select it.
11. Drop the table and chairs in the middle of the rectangle.
12. See the result in an isometric view.

Assign Height to a Layer

1. To assign height to a layer, double-click on the layer icon located in the Navigation palette. An "Organization" dialog window appears.
2. Click on the "New…" button located on the lower left corner of the window. Another dialog window appears.
3. Give a name to the layer, check the "Edit properties after creation" box, and click "OK." A third dialog window appears.
4. In this "Edit Design Layer" window, input 10′ in the Elevation slot and click "OK," "OK," and "OK" again to close all the dialog windows.
5. In Top/Plan view, use the Rectangle tool to draw a 20′ (W) × 12′ (H) rectangle on top of the original rectangle.
6. Extrude the rectangle by 1″.
7. Click on the Symbol Insertion Tool located on the Basic palette.
8. Go to Resource Manager to search for "Chairs."
9. Double-click on "Event Table 4ft × 3ft and Chairs" to select it.
10. Drop the table and chairs in the middle of the rectangle.
11. See the result in an isometric view.

Check Layer Elevation

1. If you want to see the elevation of a layer plane, switch to an isometric view.
2. Click on the plane of your interest and look for the Z data on the lower right corner of the screen.

   Note: Layer Z height and Bottom Z height are different. Beware: Do not physically move an object from one layer to another, but go to Object Info palette to do so.

Manage the Visibility and Interactive Relationships among Layers

You can manipulate the visibility of layers and manage the interactive relationships among them the same way as you do with Classes.

Change the Stacking Order of Layers

You can change the stacking order of the Layers by double-clicking on the Layer icon and physically moving the layers to rearrange their stacking order.

Assign Active Layer

You can also make a Layer Active either in the Layer dropdown menu located on the View bar or by making a selection for an active Layer in the Navigation palette.

Note: For easy access to Class and Layer Options, such as active layer scale, layer and class visibility options, force select, and active layer and class choices, you may simply right-click the mouse (Ctrl+Click for Mac) to select them directly.

Technique 5 – Episode Two: Lincoln Memorial

Note: The original exercise of the Lincoln Memorial (see Fig. 5.13) was designed by Donald Ward Jr. The author of this book attended four-day workshops conducted by Mr. Ward in 2016, transcribed the instructions of the exercise from memory and notes, and slightly modified this exercise to suit the content and length of this chapter. For a full version of the original exercise, please visit "Exercise: Colannade" by Donald Ward Jr. at Vectorwoarks University. https://university.vectorworks.net/mod/scorm/player.php?a=24&currentorg=articulate_rise&scoid=48

In this episode, we will practice the making of a model for Lincoln Memorial originally conceived by Mr. Donald Ward for training in Vectorworks to

Figure 5.13 *Lincoln Memorial*. This illustration displays the result of a well-organized modeling process conceived by Donald Ward Jr.

exercise the use of Layer and Class commands during the modeling process.

Document Setup

1. Create a blank document.
2. In the Architect workspace, go to Top Menu – File – Document Settings – Document Setup.
3. In the Document Setup window, change Layer Scale to 1/4″ and Drawing Area to US Arch D (under Choose size unavailable in printer set up) and click "OK."
4. Go to the Navigation palette. Under the Layer Option dropdown menu, select "Show/Snap/Modify Others."

Creating Classes

Let us start our modeling process by creating four classes:

1. In the Class dropdown menu located on the left side of the View bar, select "New Class..."
2. When the New Class window appears, name the class "Steps," check "Edit properties after creation," and click "OK."
3. When another dialog window opens, click "OK" to accept the default.
4. Repeat the above three steps to create three more classes and name them "Columns," "Structures," and "Roof."

Creating Layers

Since the components of the building are landed on different heights, let us create three more Layers, in addition to the default Layer, and set them to various elevations.

1. In the Layer dropdown menu located on the left side of the View bar, select "New Design Layer..."
2. When the "New Design Layer" window appears, name the new Layer "Design Layer-2" and click "OK." An "Edit Design Layer" window appears.

3. In "Elevation" slot, change the Layer elevation to 4′ and click "OK" to exit the window.
4. Repeat Steps 1–3 to create Design Layer-3 (elevation: 14′) and Design Layer-4 (elevation: 18′).

Creating Steps

1. Go to the Navigation palette to make all Layers and Classes visible.
2. On the View bar, in Class dropdown menu, select "Steps."
3. In the Layer dropdown menu, select "Design Layer-1."
4. Use the Rectangle Tool in the Basic palette to Draw a rectangle (70′ wide × 50′ high).
5. While the rectangle is still selected, go to the Basic palette and click on Offset Tool.
6. Click on the Offset Tool Preferences icon. In the Preferences window, check the "Offset by Distance" box and type 2′ in the distance slot. Check the "Duplicate and Offset" box and the "Offset from Center Line" box, and click "OK."
7. Click inside the rectangle three times to create three smaller rectangles.
8. Make sure that the smallest rectangle is selected, and go to Top Menu - AEC and select "Floor…" A dialogue box pops up.
9. Set the Bottom Z to 3′, the Thickness to 1′, and click "OK."
10. Click on the second smallest rectangle. Go to the Top Menu – AEC and select "Floor." In the popup window, set the Bottom Z to 2′, the Thickness to 1′, and click "OK."
11. Click on the second largest rectangle. Go to the Top Menu – AEC and select "Floor." In the popup window, set the Bottom Z to 1′, the Thickness to 1′, and click "OK."
12. Click on the largest rectangle. Go to the Top Menu – AEC and select "Floor." In the popup window, set the Bottom Z to 0, the Thickness to 1′, and click "OK."
13. Reorder the visibility of this stack by pressing the "B" key on the keyboard for selection while using the "Send" command (in Top Menu – Modify) to set the items in order. This means the smallest rectangle is on top; the second smallest one is right below the smallest rectangle; the second largest one is right below the second smallest one; and the largest rectangle is at the bottom of the stack.
14. To view the result of the modeling for the Steps, go to View on the Top Menu bar. In the dropdown menu, select the following:
    a. Standard View – Right Isometric
    b. Projection – Perspective
    c. Rendering – Shaded
15. Go back to Top/Plan view.

Creating Columns

1. Go to the View bar, in the Class dropdown menu, select "Columns."
2. In the Layer dropdown menu, select "Design Layer-2."
3. Go to Tool Sets – Building Shell and double-click on the Column Tool. A "Create Objects" dialog window opens.
4. In this window, make sure that the column Height is set to 10′.
5. In the Arch Comp. Class slot, change Shaft Type to "Oval," Shaft Taper to "Classic Taper," and Base Type to "Oval."
6. Select the column and move it to the upper left corner of the smallest rectangle.
7. Click on the Mirror Tool. Draw a vertical line in alignment with the center of the rectangle to produce another column on the opposite corner of the rectangle.
8. Draw a horizontal line between the centers of columns and delete the second column.
9. Use the "shift" key to select both the column and the line.
10. Go to Top Menu – Edit, and select "Duplicate Along Path…." A popup window appears.
11. Click on "Number of Duplicates." Type 12 and click "Preview" to view the result. Click "OK" to exit the window.
12. Delete the horizontal reference line.
13. Select all the columns. Click on the Mirror Tool and draw a horizontal line in alignment with the center of the rectangle to produce another row of columns on the opposite side of the rectangle.
14. Repeat the steps to draw the row of columns along the left and right sides of the rectangle. Set the column number at 8 for both sides. (Delete the two columns located at the ends of the two horizontal rows of columns before mirroring the columns on the left side to produce the columns on the right side.)
15. See the result in the Right Isometric view.
16. Go back to Top/Plan view.

Creating Structures

1. Go to the View bar. In the Class dropdown menu, select "Structures."
2. Use the Smart Cursor and Rectangle Tool to draw a rectangle inside the smallest rectangle (on its left side) in alignment with the center of the second column (both on the vertical and horizontal axes) and the fifth column (on the horizontal axis).
3. Use the Mirror Tool to create another rectangle of the same size on the right side of the center vertical dividing line.
4. Select both rectangles you have just drawn.
5. Go to Top Menu – Model – Extrude… Set the Extrude to 10′ and click "OK."
6. Go to the View bar. In the Layer dropdown menu, select Design Layer-3.
7. Draw a rectangle that is the same size as the smallest rectangle on the floor, and select it. Go to Model - Extrude… and set the Extrude value to 4′.

Creating a Roof

1. Go to the View bar, in the Class dropdown menu, select "Roof."
2. In the Layer dropdown menu, select "Design Layer-4."
3. Click on Building Shell located in the Tool Sets and select Wall Tool.
4. Select "Linear Path Mode" and "Left Control Line Mode" on the Mode bar.
5. Draw four walls alongside the outer edge of the two rectangle structures combined and double-click to end the drawing of the walls.
6. Select the four walls. Go to the OIP. Under Height, change the wall height to 4′.
7. While the walls are still selected, go to Top Menu – AEC and select "Create Roof."
8. In the popup window, click "OK" to accept the default.
9. Now, the model for the Lincoln Memorial is complete, you can view the result of your virtual model by selecting "Right Isometric" view and "Normal Perspective."
10. To see how the "visibility" function works for components assigned to various classes, press the "Class" tab on the Navigation palette and switch visibility options. This is the same for the Layer visibility options.
11. For presentation, adjust the viewing size, direction, and angle to your satisfaction by using pan, zoom, and flyover tools and select the "Final Quality Renderworks" in the Render dropdown menu.

Experiment and Practice

Loft Apartment

Figs. 5.14 – 5.18 feature the result of the following practice.

Document Setup

1. Start a new document, go to File – New… When the dialogue box opens, check "Create blank document," and click "OK."
2. To set up the document, go to File – Document Settings – Document Setup.
3. In the Document Setup window, set Layer Scale to 1/2″ and set Drawing Area to US Arch D (under Choose size unavailable in printer set up) and click "OK" and "OK" again.
4. Save the document as "Loft Apartment" on your desktop.

Creating Layers

Start your modeling process by creating two Layers:

1. Double-click on the Layer icon located in the Navigation palette. A dialog box appears.
2. When Design Layer 1 is selected, click on the "Edit" button, and a second dialog box opens.
3. Change the name of "Design Layer 1" to "Combo Room" and click "OK" to close the second dialog box.
4. As the first dialog box is still open, click on the "New" button, and another dialog box opens.
5. In the Name slot, type "Bedroom."Check the "Edit Properties After Creation" box and click "OK."
6. When the "Edit Design Layers" dialog box appears, set the Layer Elevation to 10′ and the Wall Height to 8′. Then, click "OK" and "OK" again to close the windows.

Creating floors

1. Go to Top Menu – Tools – Workspaces – Architect, if "Architect" is not already selected.
2. In the Navigation palette, press the Layer tab and make Combo Room the active layer.
3. Create a rectangle (35′ wide × 40′ tall) and extrude it by 0.2″. This is the floor of the downstairs.

Figure 5.14 *Loft Downstairs*. Along with Fig. 5.15, the image featured here provides an example of using the Layer command to organize building components located at different elevations.

Figure 5.15 *Loft Upstairs*. Along with Fig. 5.14, the image featured here provides an example of using the Layer command to organize building components located at different elevations.

4. In the Navigation palette, select "Show/Snap/ Modify Others in the Layer Option dropdown menu and make Bedroom the active layer.
5. Starting from the upper left corner of the rectangle, draw another rectangle (17′-3″ wide × 13″-6″ height) and extrude it by –9″. This is the floor of the upstairs.

Creating a Staircase

1. Switch the active Layer to Combo Room and select "Gray/Snap Others" in the Layer Option dropdown menu.
2. Click on the Circle Tool in the Basic palette and use the lower right corner of the floor upstairs as the center to draw a circle with a diameter of 9″.
3. Extrude the circle by 10′. This is the core (the post) of the winding stairs that bridge the two floors.
4. Go to Tool Sets – Building Shell, click on the Stair Tool, and place the staircase in the drawing area.
5. With the staircase still selected, double-click on "Settings" located in the Object info palette. A Stair Settings dialog box appears.
6. Click on the "General" tab if it is not already selected.
   a. Under "Symbol Selection," click on "Select Standard Configuration." A group of configuration-style icons appears in a new window. Check "Circular Stair" and click "OK."
   b. Under General Geometry, insert the following values. Press the "locker" icon button on the right after you enter the value for the individual item.
      i. By Value: 10′0″
      ii. Tread Depth: 11.424″
      iii. Riser height: 7.059″
      iv. Stair Width: 3′4″
      v. Outside Diameter: 7′5″
      vi. Inside Diameter: 9″
      vii. Sweep: 427.45°
7. Click on the "Railing" tab. A new set of options comes up.
8. Under "Accept Settings for," uncheck "Both sides" and check "Outside railing." Then click "OK" to close the window.
9. Check the result in Right Isometric View. If the guardrail on both sides is still shown, go to the Object Info palette. Under "Guardrail," uncheck "Inner Guardrail."
10. While the stair is still selected, go to Top Menu bar – Modify – Create Symbol… A dialog window shows up.
11. Give the stairs a name.
12. Under "Insertion Point," check "Next mouse click," and click "OK" to close the window.
13. Click on the top-right corner of the highest step indicated by an arrow to set the insertion point, a "Select Folder" window opens.
14. Click "OK" to accept and remember the name of the folder.
15. Go to Resource Manage to locate the stair symbol that you have just created, and double-click to select it.
16. In your drawing area, click once on the point where the bottom edge of the Bedroom floor meets the post of the winding stair, pivot the stair to allow the top of the stair to align with the bottom edge of the Bedroom floor, and then make the second click to place the stair. (See Fig. 5.16)
17. As an alternative to Steps 10–16, on Top/Plan view, snap the center of the staircase onto the center of the post that you previously created and use the Rotation Tool in Basic Palette to pivot the staircase until the Top line of the highest stair coincides with the bottom line of the Bedroom floor (see Fig. 5.16).

Installing the Railings

1. To install the railings upstairs for safety, make the Bedroom active layer again.
2. In Top/Plan view, click on the Symbol Insertion Tool located on the Basic palette.
3. Go to Resource Manager, make sure "All Resources" is selected, and do a search on "railing."
4. Double-click on "Railing Mtl Rnd Top Rail with Panel Metric" to select the symbol.
5. In your drawing, place two sections of the railing along the bottom line of the Bedroom floor, starting from the lower left corner of the floor, and place two sections of the railing along the right-side line of the Bedroom floor, starting from the upper right corner of the floor. Use "click" "click" to place the symbols in the right position and in the right orientation (see Fig. 5.17).

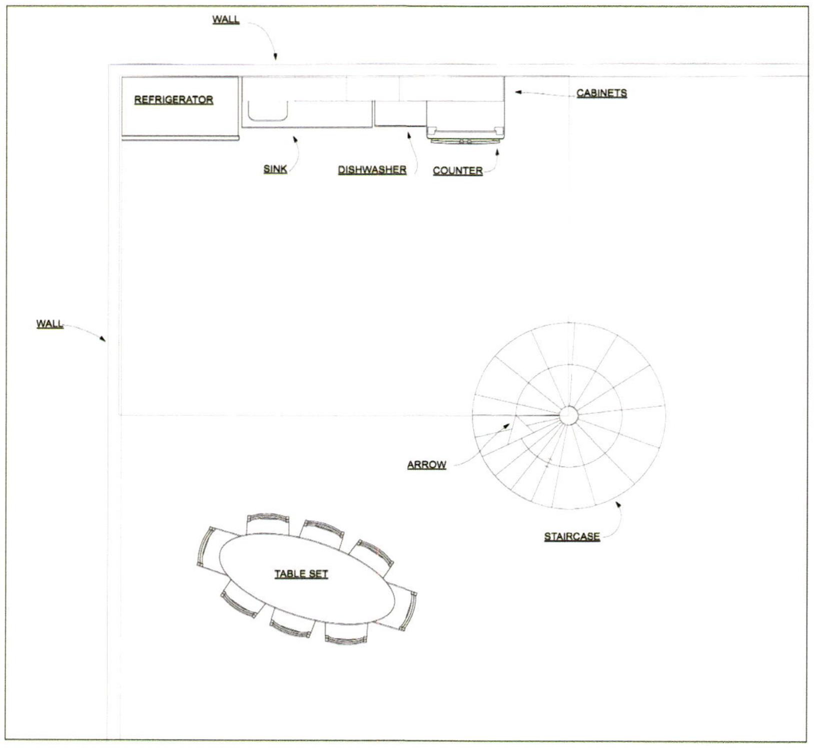

Figure 5.16 *Combo Room Floor Plan*. This illustration shows the placement of the staircase, appliances, and furniture on the Combo Room Layer.

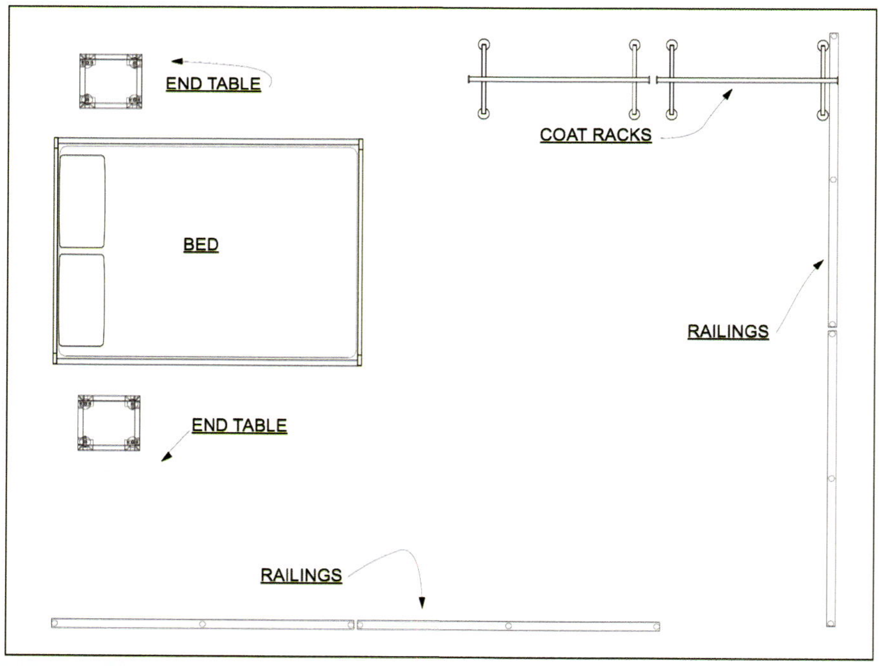

Figure 5.17 *Bedroom Floor Plan*. This illustration shows the placement of the railings and furniture on the Bedroom Layer.

Placing Appliance and Furniture

1. While the Bedroom Layer is still active, use the symbol insertion tool to bring the following furniture pieces to the Bedroom.
   a. Search for "bed" in the Resource Manager browser, select "Ikea Bedframe Askvoll Queen," and place it on the left end of the Bedroom.
   b. Search for "end table" in the Resource Manager browser, select "zNested SiteScapes QuarryView Bench...," and place two of them on both sides of the bed.
   c. Search for "coat rack" in the Resource Manager browser, select "Event Coat Rack Mobile 24 Garment," and place two of them against the upper edge towards the right end of the Bedroom floor.
2. Make Combo Room the active Layer and choose "Active Only" in the Layer Options dropdown menu. Use the Symbol Insertion Tool to bring the next appliance to the kitchen area, underneath the bedroom.
   a. Search for "refrigerator" in the Resource Manager browser, select "Equip Reach-in Refrigerator Dbl54in," and place it on the left corner of the kitchen area.
   b. Search for "Sink" in the Resource Manager browser, select "Equip Food Prep Sink 60in," and place it on the right side of the refrigerator."
   c. Search for "dishwasher" in the Resource Manager browser, select "Equip Under-the-Counter Dishwasher 24in," and place it on the right side of the sink."
   d. Search for "counter" in the Resource Manager browser, select "Appliance Refrig French Door Counter Depth 22.1 Cu. Ft.," and place it on the right side of the dishwasher."
   e. Search for "cabinet" in Resource Manager browser, select "Merillat Wall Cabinet Style," and place five sections of cabinet above the Sink–Dishwasher–Counter combined.
   f. Select all cabinets, adjust the Z height of the cabinets to 9" to make its top even with the refrigerator.
   g. Search for "table in Resource Manager browser, select "Furn Table w Chairs Dining Oval 36x84in," and place the group in the middle of the room (closer to the left wall).

Erecting Walls

1. Go to Tool Sets – Building Shell and select Wall Tool.
2. Select the first mode of the tool on the Mode bar.
3. Starting from the upper right corner of the Combo Room floor, draw walls along the top and left edges of the Combo Room floor, and double-click to finish drawing the walls.
4. While the walls are still selected, go to the Object Info palette to change the wall height value to 16′.
5. Now, the model for the Loft Apartment is complete, you can select "Show/Snap/Modify Others" in the Layer Option dropdown menu and view the Result of your modeling in Right Isometric View, as shown in Fig. 5.18.
6. To see how the visibility function works for components assigned to the two layers, press the "Layer" tab on the Navigation palette and select visibility options either in the Navigation window or from the Class Option dropdown menu.
7. For presentation, adjust the viewing size, direction, and angle to your satisfaction by using pan, zoom, and flyover tools, and select "Final Quality Renderworks" in the Render dropdown menu.

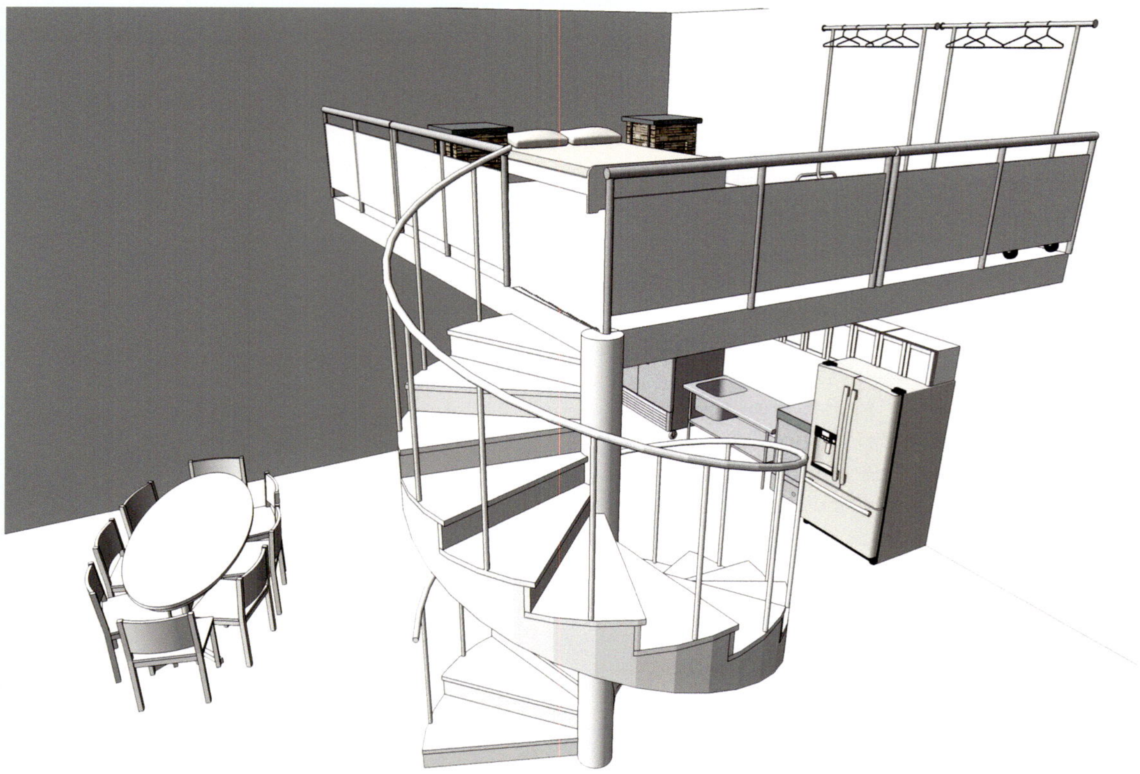

Figure 5.18 *A Shaded Rendition of the Model*. This illustration shows the result of the above modeling process.

Project #3: Building a Set Model

Objectives

The purpose of this project is for you to

1. practice stage space-arrangement techniques, such as dividing acting areas, setting levels, defining entrance/exits, providing physical supports, sightline checking, and masking in VW working environment.
2. exercise the technique of sightline-check and apply masking devices.
3. create a set model with appropriate drawing and editing tools, commands, and techniques.
4. manipulate "Class" and "Layer" commends to exhibit various visibility options.
5. demonstrate your ability to render the set model in color and texture.
6. develop patience, concentration, attention to details, and professionalism, which are much needed assets for designers.

Tasks

Through Chapters 4 and 5, you have learned the techniques of checking audience sightlines, placing the masking devices, and using Class and Layer commands to organize documents for various viewing and presentation purposes. Your task for this project is to apply what you have learned so far to a set design project. To be more specific, you will need to choose a play from a list of plays shown in Box 5.3.

Box 5.3 Play Choices

The Importance of Being Earnest by Oscar Wilde
The Death of a Salesman by Arthur Miller
Romeo and Juliet by William Shakespeare
Piano Lessons by August Wilson
West Side Story (Broadway Musical)

Create a digital set model (on the base of a theatre ground plan) for one of the scenes from the play of your choice. The set model should address the space needs of the scene. Although the locale, period, and genre of the play are not requirements of this model, you are encouraged to suggest them in your choices of colors and textures for the rendering of the model.

Required Equipment and Materials

To complete this project, you will need a computer with access to internet, the Vectorworks 2023 version installed, and a model of a proscenium theatre. *07 Stillwell Theatre 3D Model.vwx* is available for you to use. It is on resourcecentre.routledge.com/books/9781032209890 (under a folder named "Appendices").

Drawing Scale

¼″ = 1′ – 0″

Procedure

The following steps will guide you to accomplish your task for this project.

1. Select a play from the play list shown in Box 5.3.
2. Read the play.
3. Select a scene from the play.
4. Conduct visual research.
5. In Top/Plan view of Stillwell Theatre 3D Model, check the horizontal audience sightlines and install appropriate masking devices (backdrop and legs) to mask off stage space.
6. In a different Design Layer, sketch a floor plan. This floor plan needs to include the necessary elements for the scene and solve the problem of stage space arrangement, such as dividing acting areas, setting levels, defining entrance/exits, providing physical supports for the actors. For example, something to sit on, lean to, and/or climb up.
7. Extrude all the set elements into a 3D model, using the Layer and Class options in your process.
8. Apply texture and color attributes to bring your model to life.
9. Install additional masking device(s) if needed in the case of set openings, such as doors and windows.
10. Apply modeling, rendering, and presentational techniques to showcase the virtual model and save the views using the Save View command located on the View bar (the "eye" icon dropdown menu).
11. Save your vwx file to your computer.
12. Export the Top/Plan view of your model to an Image file (300 dpi) and save it to your computer as: your last name_the project_the name of the view.
13. Switch from the Top/Plan View to an Isometric view, render it in Final Quality Renderworks, export it to Image file (300 dpi) and save it to your computer as: your last name_the project_the name of the view.
14. Switch to a layer or class option to reveal a specific group of objects (e.g. masking or furnishing) and save it to your computer as: your last name_the project_the name of the class (for example, masking or furnishing).

Evaluation Criteria

Artistry

1. The set model showcases the application of various drawing and editing tools, commands, and techniques.
2. It demonstrates the designer's ability to render the model in colors and textures.
3. It involves the use of "Class" and "Layer" commends that possess various visibility options.

Problem-Solving

1. The set model has a sound stage space arrangement.
2. It solves the problem of audience sightlines check.
3. It successfully installs appropriate horizontal masking devices to mask offstage space.

Requirements and Presentation

1. The work conforms with the perimeters set in the project guidelines.
2. It is executed with accuracy and professionalism.

Student Work Samples

Figs. 5.19–5.23 showcase the student work samples for Project #3 – Building a Set Model.

Figure 5.19 *The Importance of Being Earnest* (Act 2). A virtual model created by Mackenzie Scales for the class project titled *Building a Set Model*.

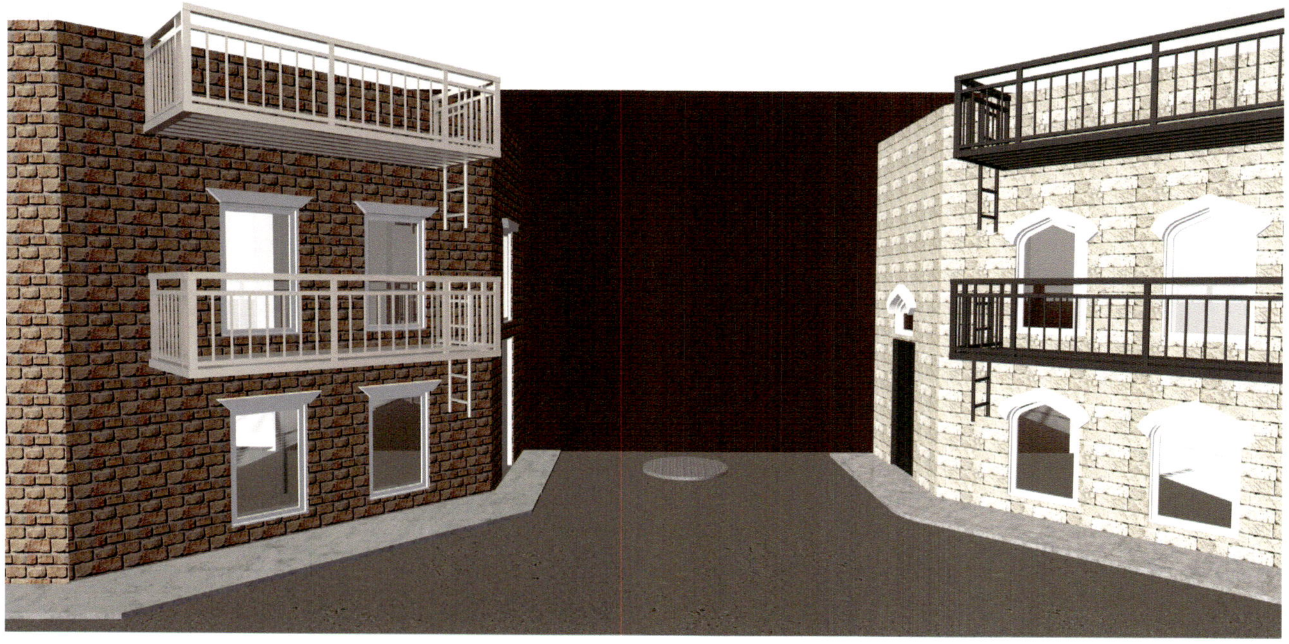

Figure 5.20 *West Side Story*. A virtual model created by LaTia Cunningham-Moore for the class project titled *Building a Set Model*.

Figure 5.21 *The Importance of Being Earnest* (Act 1). A virtual model created by Mariah Johnson for the class project titled *Building a Set Model*.

Figure 5.22 *The Importance of Being Earnest* (Act 2). A virtual model created by Micah Martin for the class project titled *Building a Set Model*.

Figure 5.23 *The Importance of Being Earnest* (Act 3). A virtual model created by Emily Sinatra for the class project titled *Building a Set Model*.

Bibliography

Cunningham-Moore, Latia. Fig. 5.20 *West Side Story*. Design Skills class project. 2021.

Dan_Prat, Fig. 5.4 *Virtual Set Model for Rent* (background photo). iStock by Getty Images. 2011.

Johnson, Mariah. Fig. 5.21 *The Importance of Being Earnest* (Act 1). Design Skills class project. 2022.

Martin, Micah. Fig. 5.22 *The Importance of Being Earnest* (Act 2). Design Skills class project. 2022.

Nemetschek Group. Fig. 7.12 Details (a Corinthian column obtained from VW Libraries). Vectorworks. 2023.

Scales, Mackenzie. Fig. 5.19 *The Importance of Being Earnest* (Act 2). Design Skills class project. 2022.

Sinatra, Emily. Fig. 5.23 *The Importance of Being Earnest* (Act 3). Design Skills class project. 2022.

USITT. "USITT Graphic Recommended Best Practices_ Proposed." *USITT*, 13 Mar. 2019, https://www.usitt.org/graphicrbp

United States Department of the Interior, National Park Service. "Lincoln Memorial Restoration." *National Capital Planning Commission*, 13 July 2017, https://www.ncpc.gov/docs/actions/2017July/7866_Staff_Report_Jul2017.pdf

Vectorworks. "Levels, Layers & Stories: A Tutorial." 21 Apr. 2015. *Nemetschek*, chrome-extension://efaidnbmnnnibpcajpcglclefindmkaj/https://www.vectorworks.net/assets/files/design_summit/1437496508xVpClLn3s6.pdf

Ward, Donald. "Exercise: Colannade." *Vectorwoarks University*, https://university.vectorworks.net/mod/scorm/player.php?a=24&currentorg=articulate_rise&scoid=48

Ward, Donald. Fig. 5.13 *Lincoln Memorial*. (Author's rendition of the exercise conceived by Donald Ward Jr.). Vectorwroks Workshop. May 2016.

CHAPTER 6

The Mechanics of Drafting

Vocabulary

Drafting Conventions
Line weight
Symbol
Scale
Sound Stage
Extension Line
Dimension Line
Dimension Mark
Numeral
Baseline Dimensioning
Continuous-line Dimensioning
Parallel Dimensioning
Break Lines
Notation
General Note
Local Note
Label
Title Block

Learning Objectives

- Gain knowledge of scenic drafting conventions, including the terminologies, roots, historical development, and current practices of these conventions.
- Demonstrate the ability to apply drafting conventions in digital drawing practice. This includes, but is not limited to:
  a. utilizing Sheet Layer and View Port to generate technical drawings for printing;
  b. providing dimensions, labels, and notations to drawings when they are due;
  c. creating a title block with all required information included.
- This should be included in the upper level. It should be on the bullet point level.

Designer's Drafting

A scenic designer's drafting refers to a set of technical drawings intended to communicate design ideas to other members of the production team through a concrete and coded language comprised of lines, symbols, dimensions, labels, and notations.

If you were a director of the production, can you imagine blocking a show without knowing where the entrance and exits are, how the actors can ascend to or descend from a platform that is taller than themselves, and if there is enough space for a cast of 30 to dance around the set simultaneously in the performance space? If you were a lighting designer, can you imagine planning the positions of lighting instruments for a show without knowing the geography of the scenery in space? If you were a prop master, do you want to know the width and height of the doors on the set leading to an interior room before constructing a gigantic cake for a surprising birthday party in the space, which is called for by the script of the play? If you were a costume designer conceiving the shoes for the actors, could

DOI: 10.4324/9781003266242-6

you ignore the material that the set designer uses for the construction and painting of the stage floor as well as the stairs and platforms the actors will walk on? If you were a stage manager, could you tape the floor for rehearsal without consulting the set designer's drafting of the floor plan? Do you want to see shift plans for a set design with 25 scene changes? If you were a technical director, could you start constructing a set without knowing the dimensions of the set units and the placement of the set on stage? The answer to these questions is obviously "no," because this is what the scenic designer's drafting is for.

In *Design and Painting for the Theatre*, Lynn Pecktal stresses the importance of drafting as a means of communication during the production process: "Whether the designer chooses to do sketches or a painted model for his production, the drafting is an absolute must, for it is his translation of the technical aspects of the scenery – how it is built, how it is placed on stage, how it hangs, how it moves, and how it is stored" (Pecktal, 136).

The most efficient way to learn drafting is to get familiar with the drafting conventions and apply them in practice. The best drafting practices often exhibit the characteristics of informativeness, clarity, concision, and accuracy.

Drafting Conventions

Drafting Conventions are a set of rules or standards agreed upon by both the maker and the reader of the drafting for efficient communication among members of any production team. Before 1982, scenic designers and technicians in the US and Canada had practiced drafting with graphic language adopted from other professions, such as architecture and engineering. In 1982, the USITT Graphic Standards Board published an article titled "Recommendations for Standard Graphic Language in Scene Design and Technical Production" through *Theatre Design & Technology*, a peer reviewed publication by USITT. The main reasons for the recommendations are 1) to "achieve effective communication" among members of production who traveled from place to place in production processes and could not afford to be with the production team all the time, and 2) to train the incoming scenic designers and technicians in drafting standards aligned with professional standards (Wolff, 8). Since drafting with CAD had still been in its infancy in 1982 and the standards had been set with hand drafting in mind, the USITT revision of the drafting standards in 1992 acknowledged the rising attraction of CAD drafting in the industry. Still, the authors of the 1992 revision encouraged the CAD drafters to "work to produce images which follow this standard as closely as practicable" (USITT Education Commission Graphic Standards Board). Later, as CAD programs became more and more widely used in the entertainment world, some of the drafting standards set in the 1992 revision came to be irrelevant or even burdensome for CAD users. For example, producing legible letters, numbers, crisp and consistent lines, and using guidelines for the alignment of the text in notations used to be a part of hand-drafting training. With CAD, these standards are all imbedded in the program by default. Furthermore, designers have more choices, such as colors, symbols, line weights, and line types, to express their design ideas clearly and fully, as opposed to working with limited means of hand-drafting. In 2019, USITT proposed a new revision in its article titled "USITT Graphic Recommended Best Practices – Proposed (www.usitt.org/graphicrbp)." The authors of the new revision state, "At this time USITT no longer creates standards and has determined that future documents should be referenced as 'recommended best practices' rather than as an actual standard. In this document which services both hand and CAD drafting, it is left to the user to determine what is applicable, or not." (dld & sn, 1) Despite the flexibility in the application of the drafting conventions as suggested in the 2019 proposal, the authors of this revision maintained: "…many aspects overlap, and graphic communication remains the same whether done by pencil or computer." (USITT Education Commission Graphic Standards Board, 1)

The following passages introduce the drafting conventions in a way that is meaningful to the audience of this book. For "USITT Graphic Recommended Best Practices – Proposed" (USITT GRBP), a more detailed and comprehensive document on the subject, visit https://www.usitt.org/graphicrbp. It is important to remember, no matter how complicated scenic drafting conventions or standards may seem to be, they are not meant to drive you crazy, but to help you communicate your design idea more clearly and efficiently.

The Language of Line

Line Weights

Drafting is a special language in which lines, symbols, and numbers all carry meanings. ***Line Weight*** refers to the thickness of a drafted line. In scenic drafting with CAD, it is important to distinguish between the use of three different line-weights. Heavy-weight lines (thick lines) are used for the outline of a section view. Fig. 6.1, Nos. 1 and 5, show examples of heavy-weight lines being used in a section view and cutting plane.

Medium-weight lines (medium thick lines) are used for the outline of an object that is being physically constructed. Outlines of walls, doors, platforms, and furniture pieces fall into this category. Fig. 6.1, No. 2, provides an example of medium-weight lines being used for drawing the outline of an object.

Light-weight lines (thin lines) are used for the drafting of things that do not physically exist. Things like centerlines, dimension lines, extension lines, break lines, crosshatches in section views, and leader lines are such examples (Fig. 6.1, No. 3, 4, 6, 7, 8, and 9).

Appropriate use of line weights in drafting can facilitate a better understanding of a rather complex drawing. Fig. 6.2 is a comparison between drafting with and without the appropriate use of light weights.

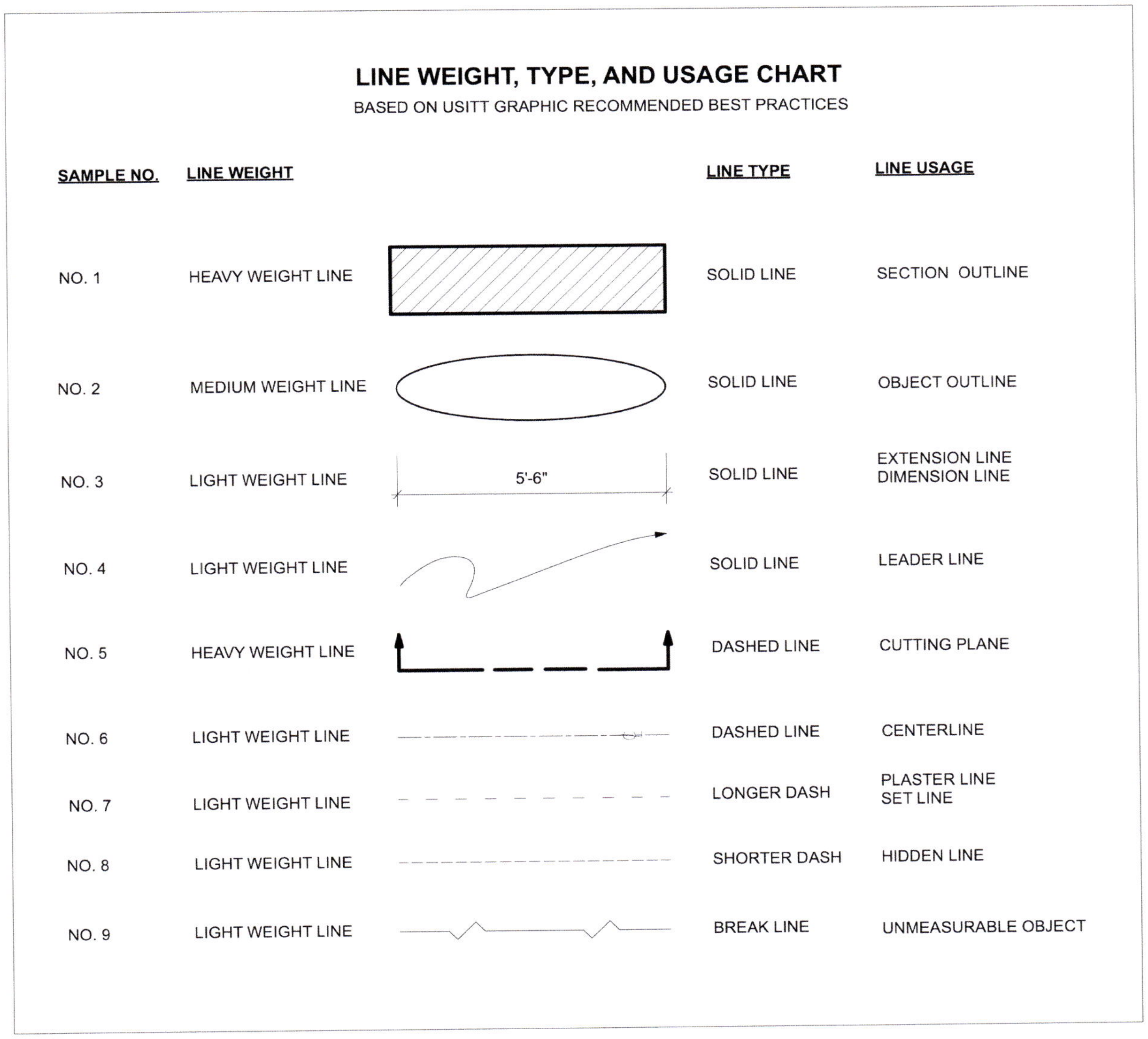

Figure 6.1 *Language of Line*. A chart showing different line weights, line types, and their usage in scenic drafting.

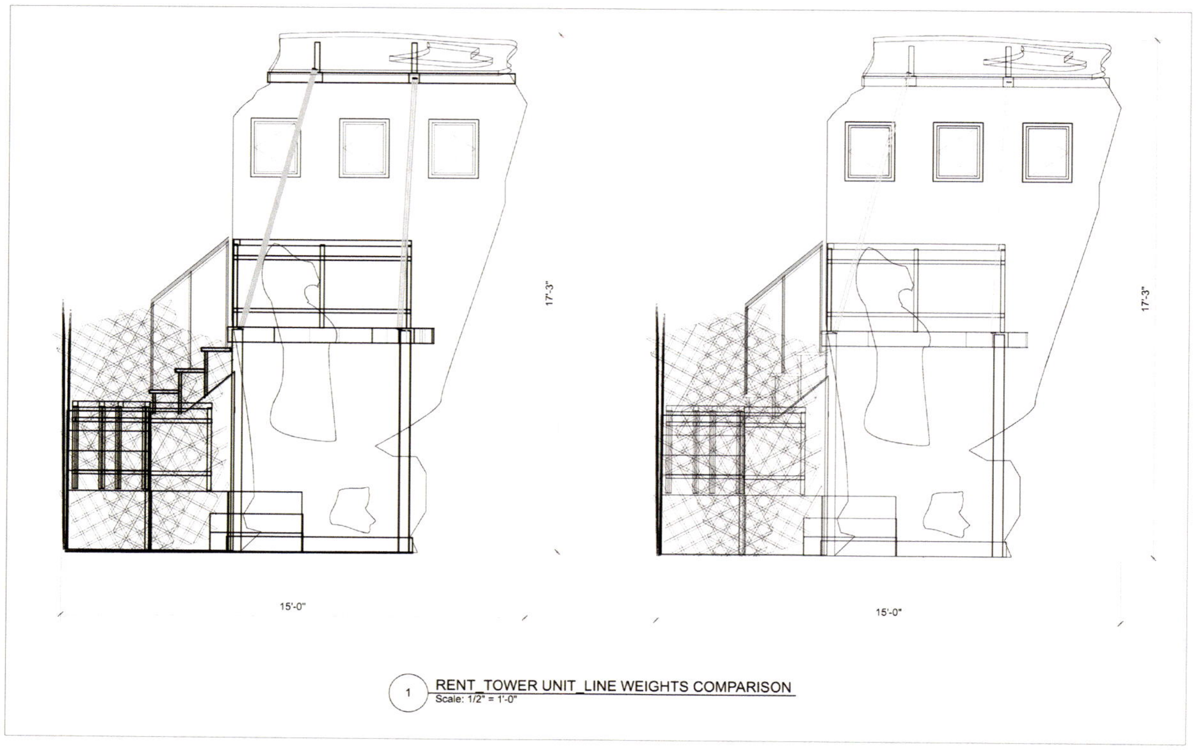

Figure 6.2 *Comparison of Line Weights*. An illustration showing the importance of drafting with appropriate line weights. The image on the right shows that a set unit is drawn with the lines of same weight. This drawing lacks organization because the structure information is not come through clearly. In contrast, the drawing on the left reveals that the appropriate line weights are used to set the elements of the set unit in a hierarchical order of importance. The differentiation of line weights helps to emphasize the structure of the set unit. In this drawing the design ideas are communicated more clearly.

Line Types

Like the use of various line weights, line types are also specifically assigned to draw different things. Fig. 6.1 also features an array of line types commonly used in scenic drafting. For instance, solid lines are used to draw dimension lines and extension lines (Fig. 6.1, No. 3), visible outlines of physical objects (Fig. 6.1, No. 2), section outlines (Fig. 6.1, No. 1), sheet borders, leader lines (Fig. 6.1, No. 4), and crosshatches in section views (Fig. 6.1, No. 1). Dashed lines are used to draw cutting planes (Fig. 6.1, No. 5), centerlines (Fig. 6.1, No. 6), plaster lines (Fig. 6.1, No. 7), hidden construction (Fig. 6.1, No. 8), alternating positions of objects, match lines, and break lines (Fig. 6.1, No. 9). Within the category of dashed lines, there are also subtypes. A centerline, for instance, is uniquely represented by alternating one long dash with one short dash and is emphasized with the letters "CL" placed at the bottom of the centerline.

Symbol

Before CAD came into being, drafting symbols were only 2D and used mostly in floor plans. To make the drawing of the ***Symbols*** less time-consuming, the most commonly used symbols were made into plastic templates for designers to trace off.

CAD programs afford scenic designers an abundant choice of readymade 2D and 3D symbols, from stairs and platforms to appliances and furniture pieces, from trees and bushes to lighting fixtures. You name it, VW likely will have it in its Symbol Libraries.

The major drawback of using readymade symbols from VW symbol libraries on a floor plan is twofold. First, some of the symbols are not dissectible due to their file format, especially in the case of plants, including most of the trees. Therefore, if you use these symbols in a set model, when making a horizontal cut-through of the model to produce a floor plan of the set design, these symbols simply disappear on the sheet layer. Secondly, even though the dissectible symbols can be horizontally cut-through, the symbols shown on the sheet layer only reflect the images below the cutting plane while, traditionally, the part of the symbol above the cutting plane, is supposedly drawn and shown in dashed lines.

Scale

As a rule of thumb, all scenery must be drafted in ***Scale***. To scale in a drawing is to use a specific increment on a scale ruler to represent a measured foot on stage. For example, drafting in ½″ scale means that every ½″ shown on a drafted sheet represents 1 foot on stage, while drafting in ¼″ scale means that every ¼″ on a drafted sheet stands for 1 foot on stage.

Since the size of standard drafting paper (e.g., 24 × 36 inches) is limited, in most cases, it is impossible, impractical, and inconvenient to draw scenery to its life-size. It is possible, however, to fit scenery on a sheet of drafting paper if the size of the scenery is proportionally reduced. This is what "scale" was invented for.

The commonly used scales in scenic drafting for indoor theatre productions are as follows:

- ½″ = 1′-0″
- ¼″ = 1′-0″
- 1″ = 1′-0″,
- 3″ = 1′-0″
- 1″ = 1″

Floor Plans and Cross Sections are often drafted in ¼″ scale, because the size of a printed drafting paper can only contain the size of these plans being drafted in ¼″ scale, but not in ½″ scale. Most set units are drafted in ½″ scale. That said, if a set unit has excessive details and the details are important to the designer, 3″ scale and even full scale (1:1) are used. When the scale of a unit is different from the scale of most of the units on a drafted sheet, the scale needs to be noted right below the label of the drawing.

For outdoor theatres, movie productions, and theme park projects, Floor Plan scales vary greatly. 1/8″ scale for a production on a sound stage is not unusual. In the floor plans of theme park designs, designers often apply a map scaling system, either by using a graphic scale (a bar marked off like a ruler with labels outlining the distances the segments represent) or by using a fractional scale. For example, 1:50,000 means that one unit (inch, centimeter, etc.) on the drawing represents 50,000 inch or centimeter in real life. Fig. 6.3 samples

Figure 6.3 *Amusement Park Master Plan*. Master plan of Colorful Yunnan Paradise Park in China. Director of Creative Design: Matthew L McCoy. Kunming NorthStar Group, planning through Sanderson Group China. Park opening date 2018.

a scaled Master Plan for Colorful Yunnan Paradise Park in China. In the U.A., we work in inches and feet (the imperial system of measurements). Unlike the USA, most countries in the world use centimeters and meters (the metric system of measurements). The Master Plan illustrated in Fig. 6.3 uses the metric system, as the "M" on the scale is an abbreviation of meter (1 meter = 3.28084 feet).

Letter

All letters on a sheet of drafting must be uppercase letters. This rule was originally set for hand drafting to address the problem of eligible lettering. Although eligible lettering is no longer an issue in CAD drafting, since it only takes a click on the keyboard to keep the letters all capital letters, most CAD drafters have continued this convention. USITT GRBP recommends the use of either Sans Serif, Calibri, Arial, Romand, or City Blueprint for letters in scenic drafting. It suggests that, if you choose one font to use, keep the use of this font throughout the entire set of drafting. It also discourages the use of italics, underlining, bold, or other highlighting techniques.

Dimension

Components of Dimensioning

A dimension provides a numerical value of an actual distance (not a scaled distance) between two points. To give dimensions to an object, the following four elements are at play (Fig. 6.4).

- ***Extension Lines*** refer to the dimensions of specific points on the object. Extension lines allow dimensions to be placed away from the object in a convenient location (Fig. 6.4). To avoid confusion,
  - do not draw extension lines through the outlines of the object being dimensioned, but to start slightly away from the object lines and extend slightly beyond the dimension line.
  - do not let the extension lines cross dimension lines other than the dimension line that these extension lines lead up to.
  - do not let extension lines cross each other if you can avoid it.
- ***Dimension Lines*** indicate the direction of the measurements. Dimension lines are drawn parallel to the object lines being dimensioned (Fig. 6.4).
- ***Dimension Marks*** emphasize the beginning and ending points of dimensions (Fig. 6.4). Arrows, shot slashes, and dots are all acceptable dimension mark styles in our profession, so long as your choice of style is consistent throughout your drafting set (Fig. 6.5).

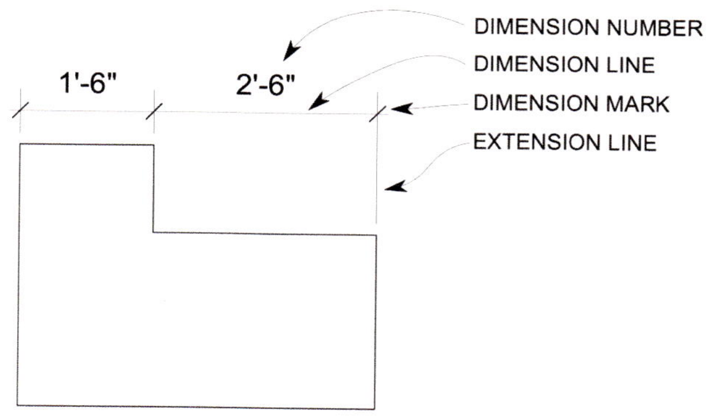

Figure 6.4 *Components of Dimensioning*. An illustration indicates four components of dimensioning. The illustration samples appropriate way of dimensioning.

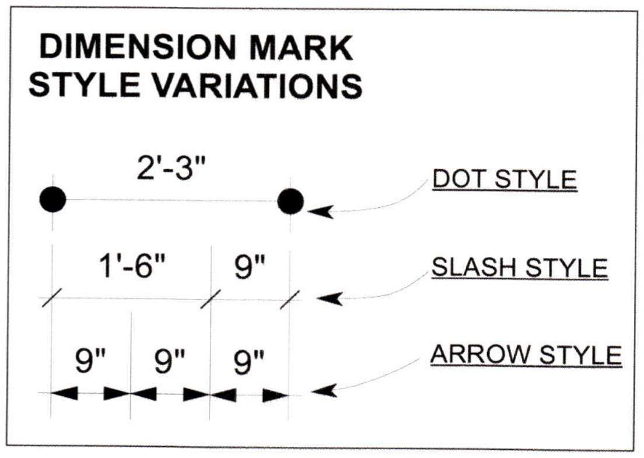

Figure 6.5 *Dimension Mark Styles*. An illustration of three styles of Dimension Mark permissible in the scenic design and production industry.

- ***Numerals*** provide measurement information about the object being dimensioned (Fig. 6.4). In general, dimensions that are less than one foot are given only in inches (e.g., ½", 6", and 9") and dimensions of 1 foot or greater are given in both feet and inches, which are separated by a dash in between, even if the inch dimension is zero (e.g., 1'-6", 2'-0, etc.). However, the heights of any walking surfaces, such as platforms and stairtreads, on a Floor Plan are dimensioned in inches only, even when the dimensions are one foot or greater (Fig. 6.6).

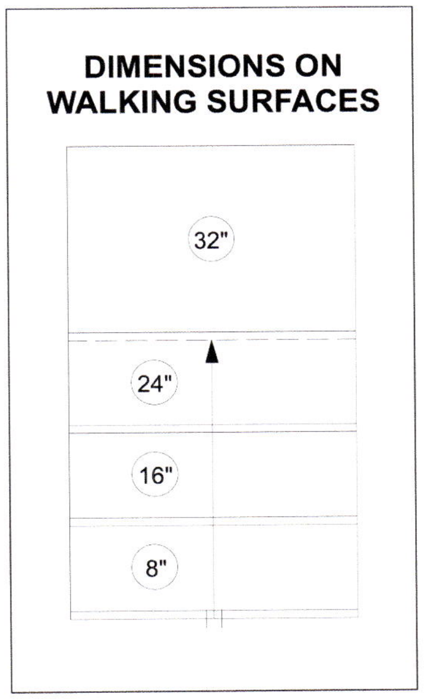

Figure 6.6 *Dimensions on Walking Surfaces*. An illustration of dimensions on walking surfaces in a floor plan.

Dimensioning Modes

There are three dimensioning modes commonly used in scenic drafting: ***Baseline Dimensioning*** mode, ***Continuous-line Dimensioning*** mode, and ***Parallel Dimensioning*** mode. Fig. 6.7 shows three modes of dimensioning and provides examples of situations where each of these modes suits a specific dimensioning scenario.

Basic Dimensioning Tools

Dimension Angles

To dimension angles, you need to invoke the Angular Dimension tool resides in Tool Sets – Dims/Notes. Fig. 6.8 provides examples of angular dimensioning.

Dimension Circles

There are two different ways to dimension circles: dimension by radius and dimension by diameter. Examples can be found in Fig. 6.8. You can find the Radial Dimension Tool in Tool Sets – Dims/Notes.

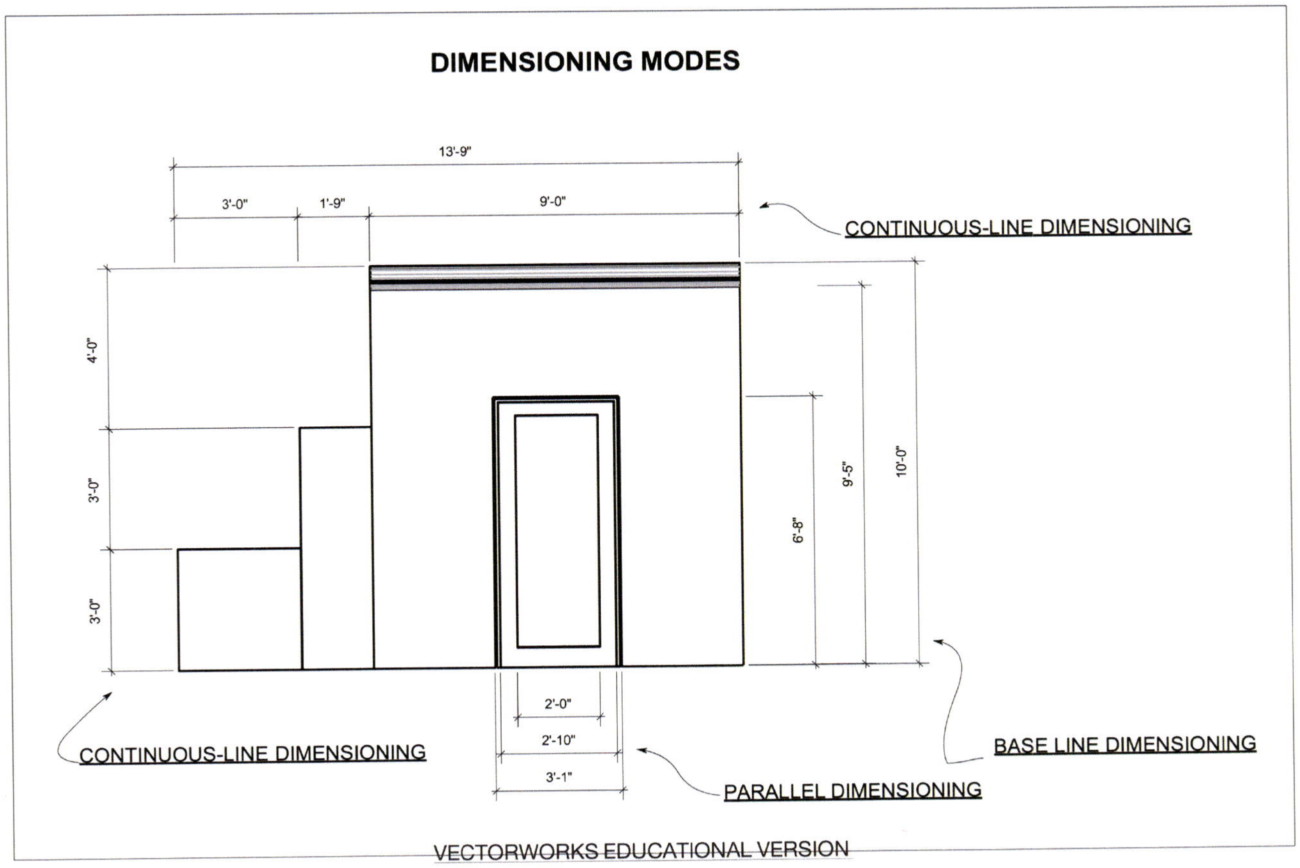

Figure 6.7 *Dimensioning Modes*. An illustration of three dimensioning modes.

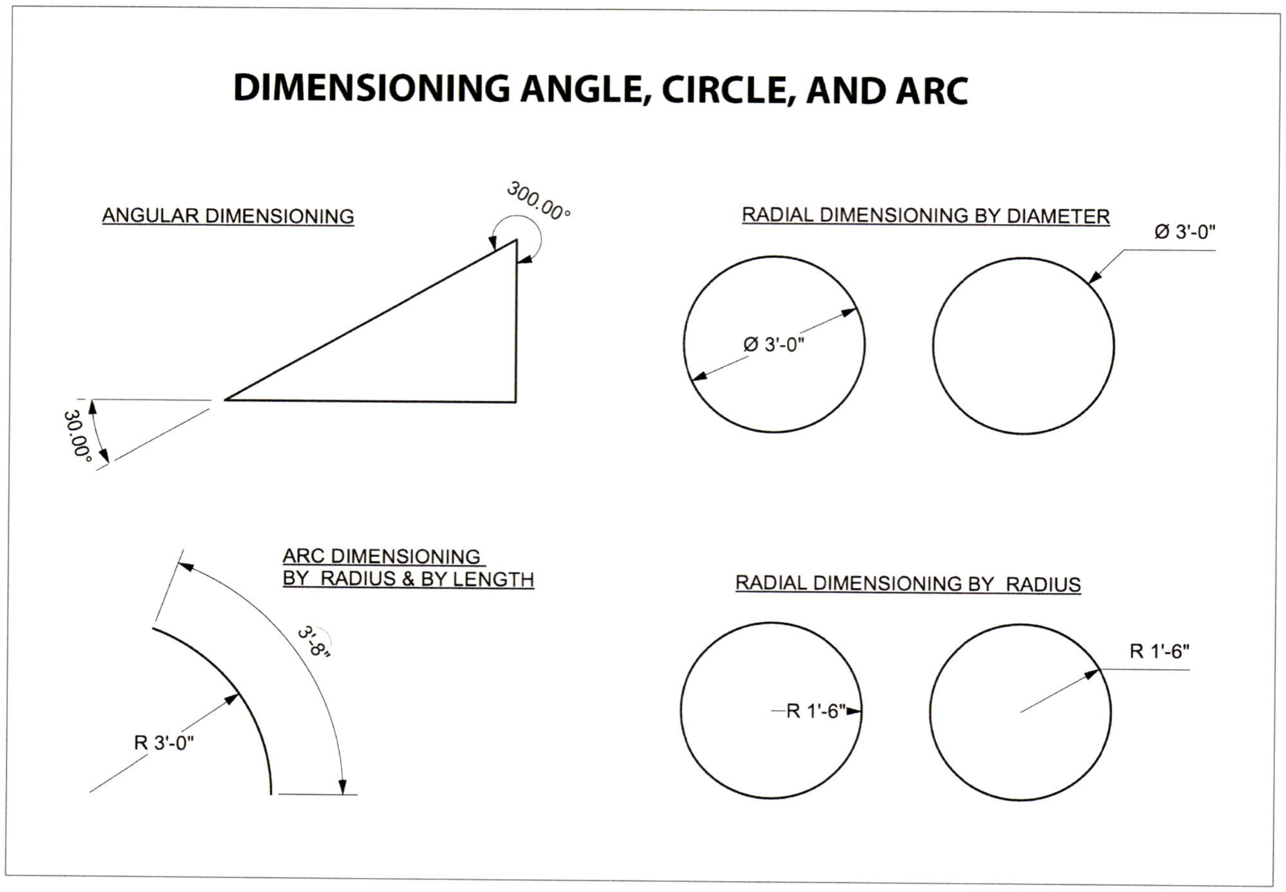

Figure 6.8 *Dimensioning Angle, Circle, and Arc*. A display of dimensioning angle, circle and arc using angular, radial, and arc dimensioning methods.

Dimension Arcs

You can dimension an arc by utilizing the Arc Length Dimension Tool or the Radius Dimension Tool (Fig. 6.8). Like the Radial Dimension Tool, the Arc Length Dimension Tool is also in Tool Sets – Dims/Notes.

Dimensioning Guidelines

To dimension properly, follow the guidelines listed below.

- Provide all dimensions necessary for the fabrication of each set unit.
- Avoid duplicating dimensions in the drawing of any set unit.
- Place shorter dimensions closer to the drawing and overall dimensions of a set unit outside all shorter dimensions (Fig. 6.9).
- Unless it is important to your design, round your dimensions to simple numbers, such as inches or quarters (3 inches), avoiding fractional numerals.
- Numerals can be placed in the middle or on the top of the dimension lines (Fig. 6.9).
- Dimensions are oriented on the drawing to be read from the bottom or right edge of a drafted sheet only (Fig. 6.9).

Dimensioning Technique

Scenic designers often encounter challenging dimensioning situations. Special techniques discussed here can be invoked to meet these challenges.

Dimension Irregular Shapes

To solve the problem of dimensioning irregular shapes, Fig. 6.10 provides two alternative methods.

Dimension Center to Center

Sometimes it is more efficient to provide dimensions from center to center if the items and distances between them are repeated regularly (Fig. 6.11).

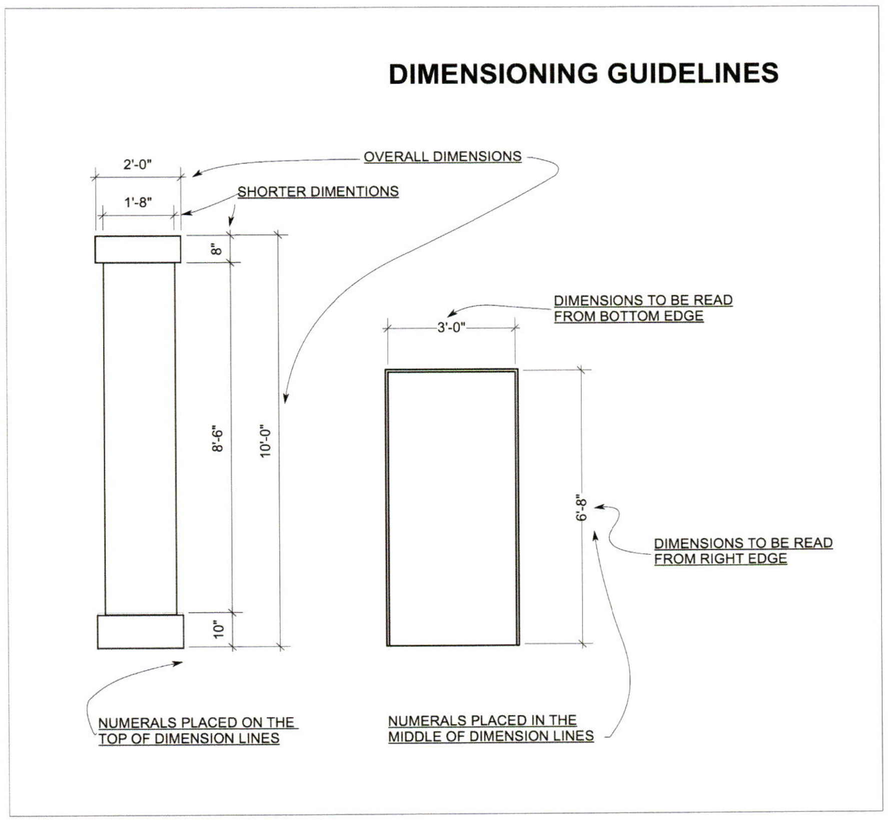

Figure 6.9 *Dimensioning Guidelines*. An image serves as references to the dimensioning guidelines.

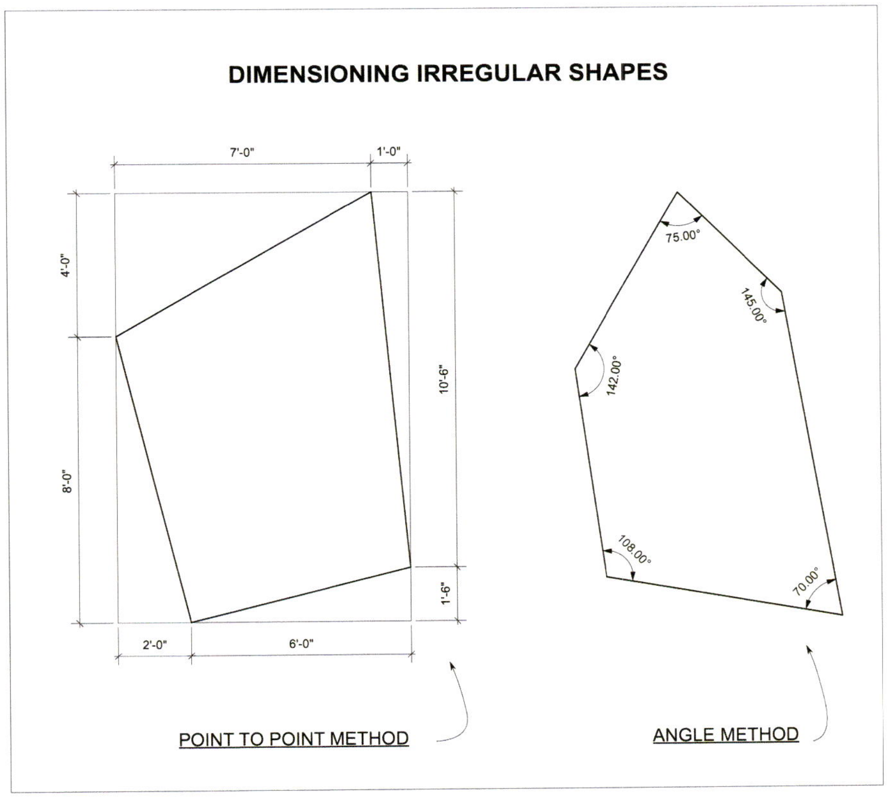

Figure 6.10 *Dimensioning Irregular Shapes*. This illustration shows the use of a Point-to-Point method on the left and an Angle method on the right to dimension irregular shapes.

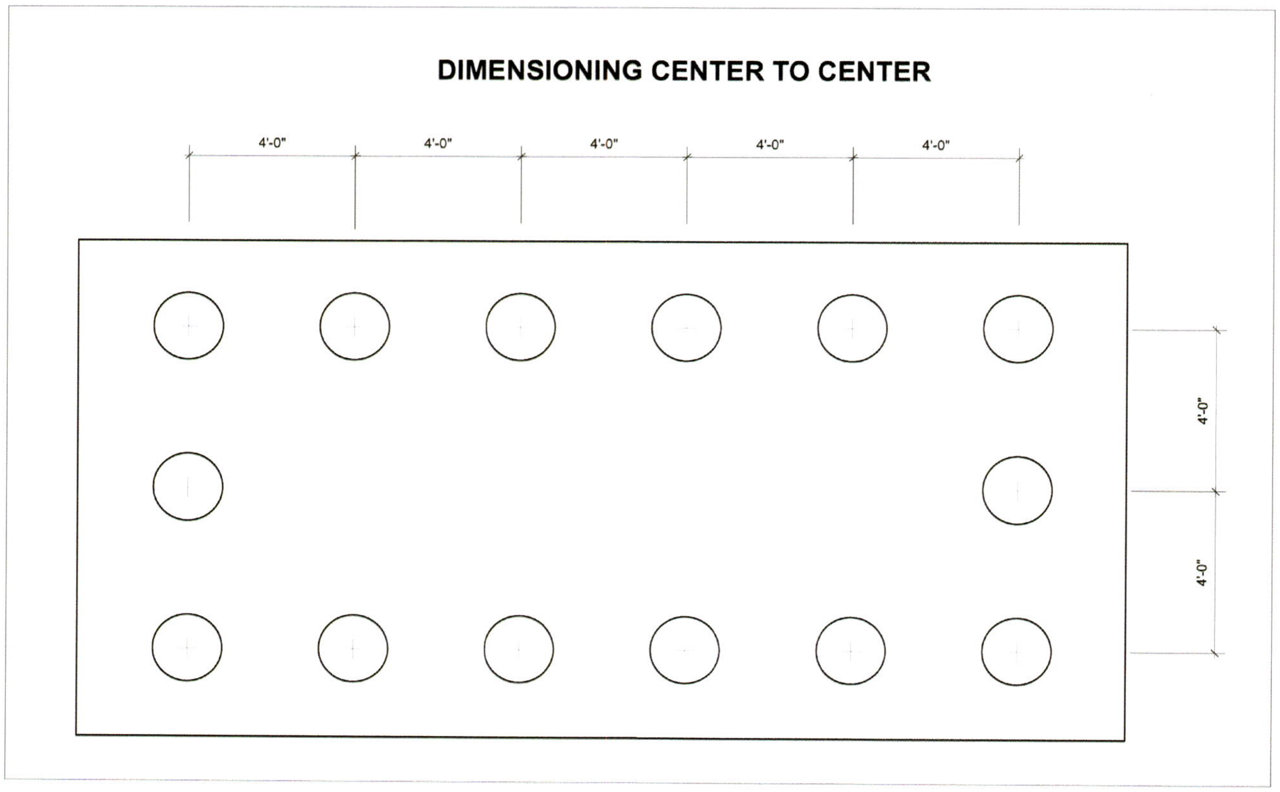

Figure 6.11 *Dimensioning Center to Center*. An illustration of center-to-center method of dimensioning.

Dimension Disproportionate Objects

In Fig. 6.12, ***Break Lines*** (available in Tool Sets – Dims/Notes) were applied to draw and dimension the width of a fence that cannot fit into a drafted sheet using normal drawing scales for set units. In a case such as this, the designer must provide actual width measurements of the fence in the drawing, despite the discrepancy between the dimension given and the width of the fence on the drawing.

Dimensioning Organic Shapes

In hand drafting, a designer would use a gridded velum sheet for the drafting of an organic shape,

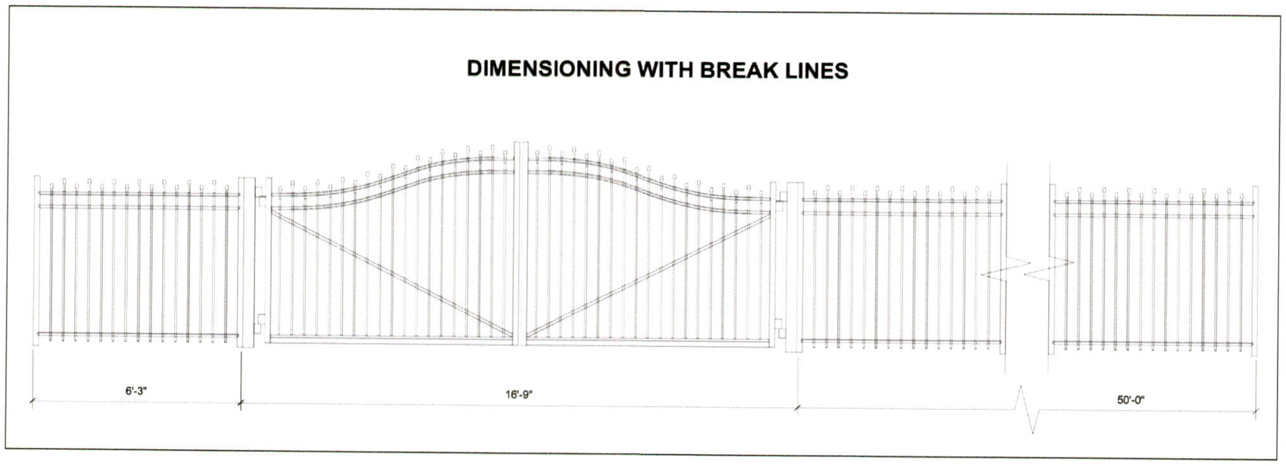

Figure 6.12 *Dimensioning with Break Lines*. This is an instance of using Break Lines to dimension an unproportionate object. The fence in real life is 50 feet long, but the width of the fence in the drawing is not scaled to 50 feet.

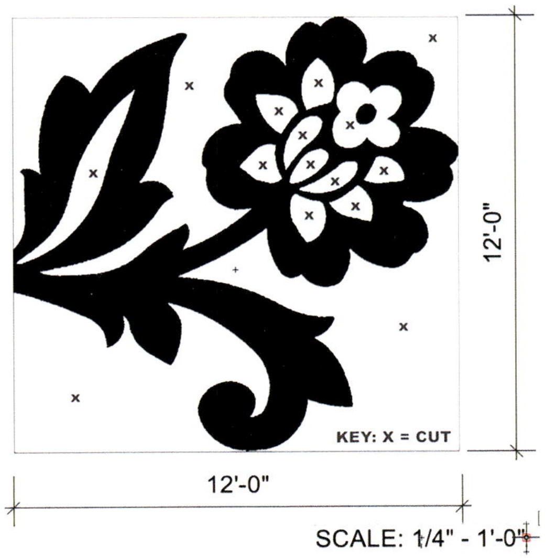

Figure 6.13 *Dimensioning Organic Shapes*. This image explains the method of dimensioning an organic shape with the reference grid on in VW program. "Floral Pattern" by HomeSpot HQ is licensed under CC BY 2.0.

as this will help the construction crew to transfer the shapes onto the construction material. In a CAD environment, a designer or construction crew can simply turn the grid on in a VW to get the same benefit (Fig. 6.13).

Notation

Notations are an important part of drafting, for they can provide information about a designer's choices of construction material, molding, hardware, assembly procedures, fastening techniques, and desired finishes for the set units, to name a few.

There are two types of notations in scenic drafting. ***General Notes*** concern issues related to the various drawings on a sheet of drafting, while ***Local Notes*** apply only to a particular part or parts of a drawing. Place general notes on the upper right-hand corner of a drafted sheet or directly above the Title Block. Place a local note near the part being noted, with a leader line and an arrowhead point toward that part (Fig. 6.14).

As noted in the USITT GRBP proposal, "Developments in drafting technology and CAD systems have made the preparation of notes less burdensome but have also made it easier to create overly long notes—diluting efficient communication." The proposal recommends "streamlining" the notes, use "active voice," "imperative mood," and "complete

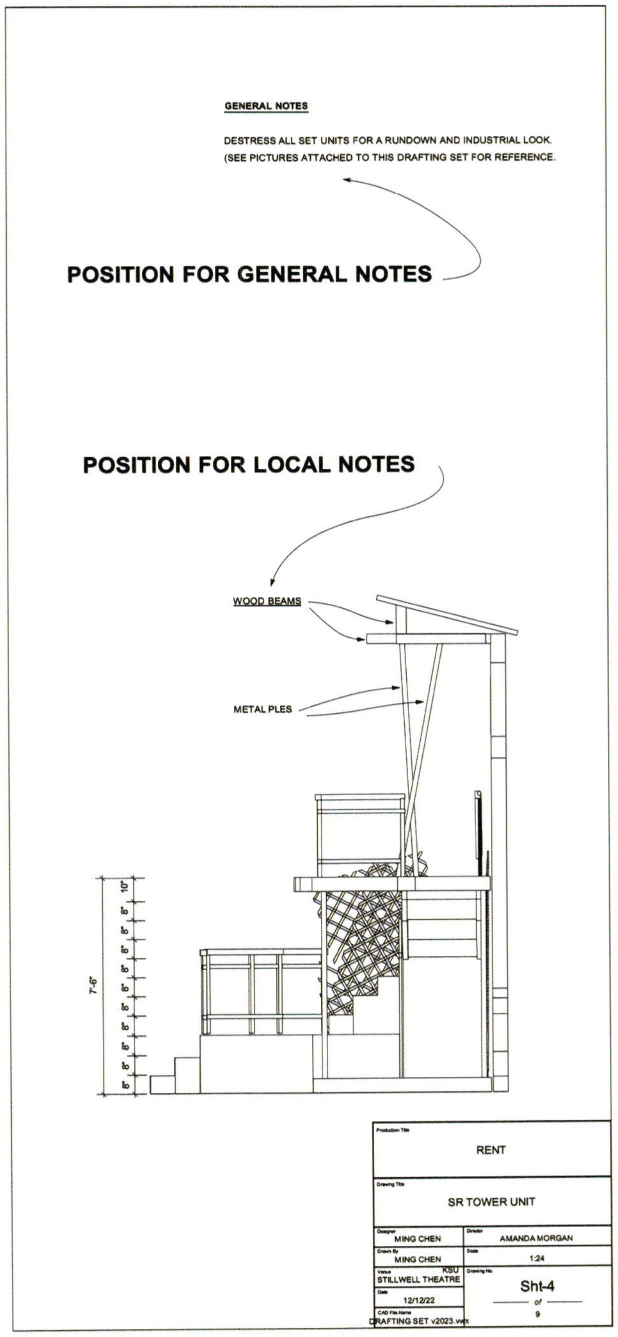

Figure 6.14 *Notation*. An illustration indicating the conventional location for general notes and local notes on a sheet of scenic drafting.

terminology" for more efficient communication. "Where an abbreviation is essential, be consistent and use recognized abbreviations." For a list of recognized abbreviations in our profession, refer to the USITT GRBP proposal (USITT Education Commission Graphic Standards Board, 5).

Label and Drawing Title

Scenic designers utilize labels and drawing titles to tag, reference, summarize, indicate, or explain the drawings. Below are important conventions to remember.

- Every drawing needs to be labelled.
- Place the title of a set unit below its projections combined (Fig. 6.15).
- Use standard labels available in Tool Sets and VW Symbol Libraries when appropriate. Fig. 6.16 displays a few examples of those readymade labels.

Note: The "texts" on the VW existing labels are not written consistently in capital letters, and they are not changeable by individual designers. This is another example of the shift in drafting rules due to the emergence of new technology, since drafting with CAD does not have lettering "legibility" issues as hand drafting has.

Title Block

Title Block refers to a clear and concise directory comprised of key information on a drafted sheet. It is a stripe or block located on the lower right-hand corner of the sheet. In the VW program, designers can choose a readymade Title Block template and fill in the information for the design being drafted. The key components of a Title Block are listed below.

1. Title of the production
2. Name of the producing organization
3. Name of the production site
4. Name of the director
5. Name of the scenic designer
6. Name of the drafter (if different than the designer)
7. Name of the technical director
8. Title of the drawing
9. Drawing (sheet or plate) number

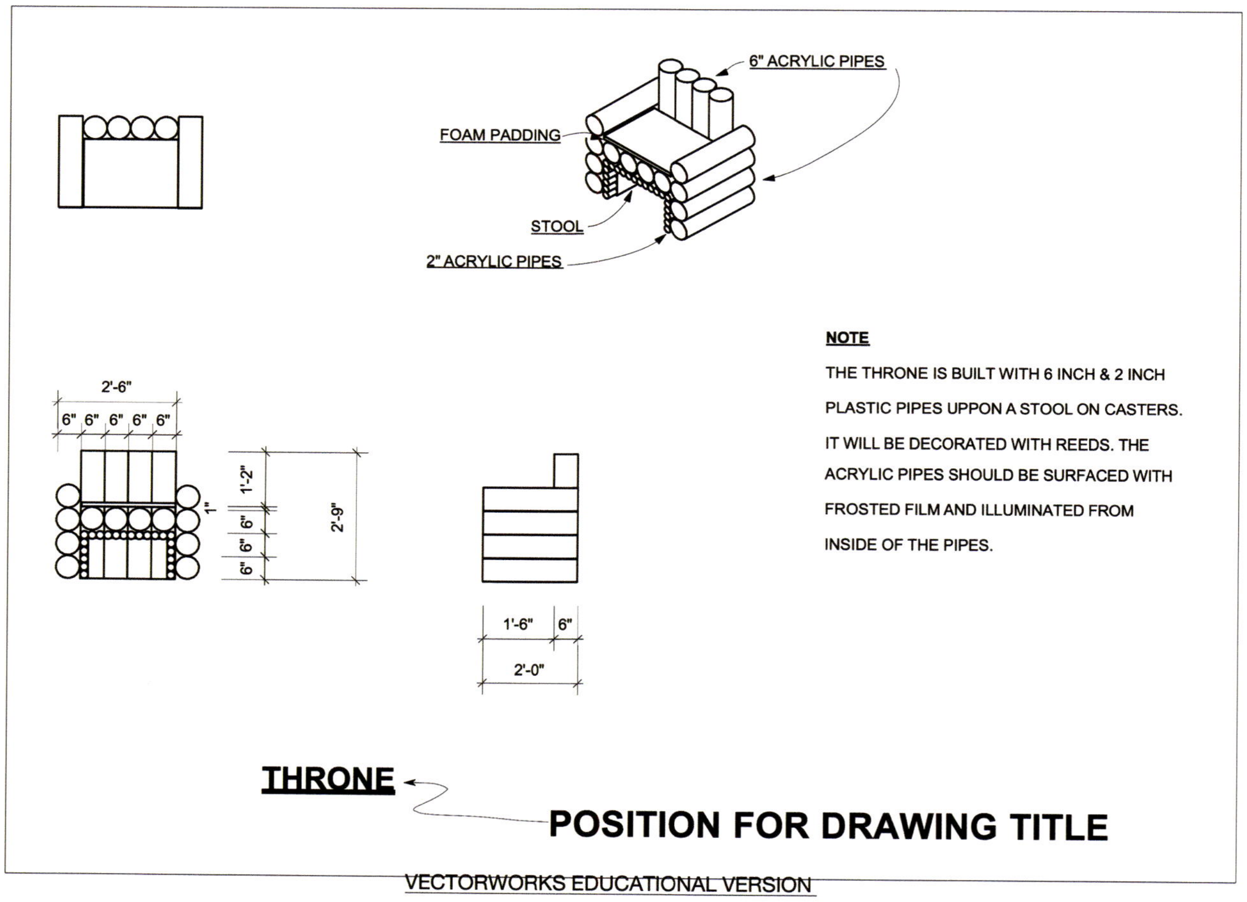

Figure 6.15 *Position for Drawing Title*. An orthographic projection drawing of a "throne" for *The SpongeBob Musical*. Note the position of the drawing title, which is below the various projection views of the set unit combined.

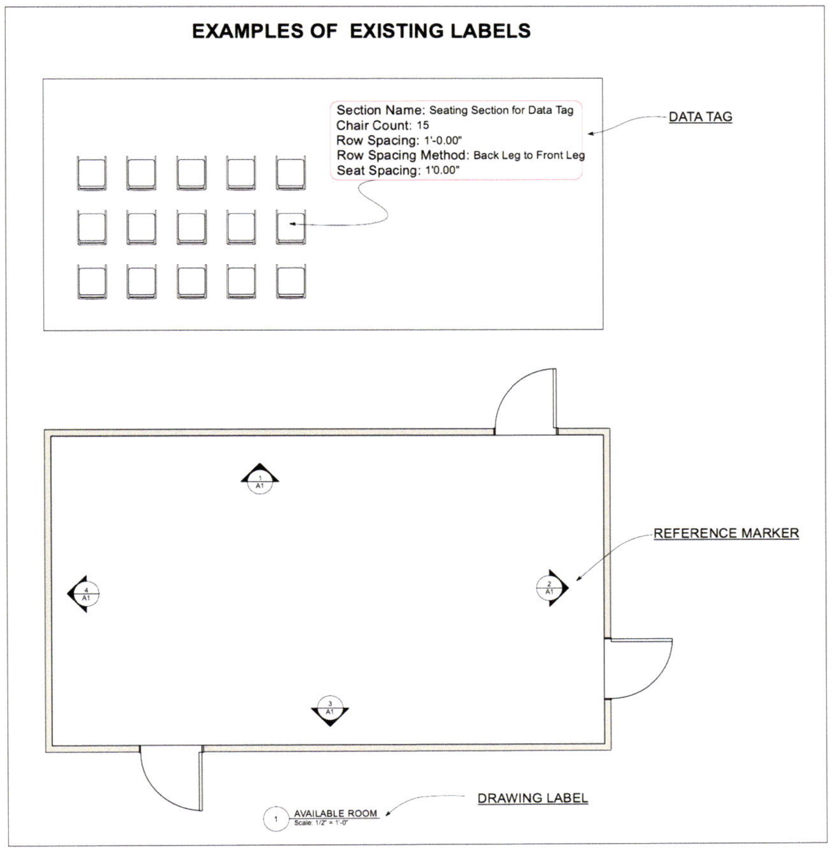

Figure 6.16 *Labels*. This illustration features the use of Data Tag, Drawing Label, and Reference Marker in their appropriate context.

10. Scale of the drawings on the sheet (If different scales are used, state "scale as noted" on the scale slot and note the scale right below the title of each drawing on the sheet.)
11. Date of the drawing

Technique 6 – The Mechanics of Drafting

In this section, you will practice the use of VW tools to build a simple ***Box Set***, a set with three walls placed on a proscenium theatre, aiming to create the illusion of an interior room on stage (Fig. 6.17).

You will also learn the method, process, and technique to use VW Sheet Layer and Viewport functions to create a technical drawing of the Box Set that conforms with the drafting conventions recommended by USITT. This includes the proper application of lines, symbols, dimensions, notations, and labels. In addition, you will go through the process of creating a Title Block for your technical drawing using a template available in VW Libraries.

Without further ado, let's get started.

Create a Box Set

Get Ready

1. Open the file titled Your Name_Horizontal Masking that you created in Technique 4-2 and use it as a base for the Box Set.
2. Go to the Navigation palette, make the Horizontal Masking layer the active layer, and select Gray/Snap Others.
3. Delete the five sightlines previously drawn for masking purposes and draw two sightlines from each of the two critical seats marked on the plan.
4. Create a new Design Layer and name it Set, and set the scale to ¼″ scale.

Figure 6.17 *Box Set*. A rough digital model for *School Girls*, a production of Kenny Leon's True Colors Theatre Company. The set design is created in a Box Set style. The two gray theatre walls on both side of the image were shortened for this illustration to reveal the set structure.

5. On this Layer, create five Classes and name them: SET STRUCTURE, FURNITURE/DECOR, ADDITIONAL MASKING SIGHTLINES, ADDITIONAL MASKING, and LABLES.
6. Save the drawing as "Your Name_Mock Box Set" on your computer desktop for easy access later.
7. Go to Top Menu bar – Tools – Workspaces and select "Spotlight."

Establish a Set Structure

1. Draw Walls at optimal angles with audience sightlines in mind.
   a. Go to the View bar. In the Class Dropdown menu, select "SET STRUCTURE."
   b. In Top/Plan view, click on the Wall Tool located in Tool Sets – Building Shell.
   c. Double click on the Wall Tool Preferences. When a dialog window opens, click on the "Insertion Options" tab. Set the height of the wall to 12′ and click "OK."
   d. Draw a wall, starting from the point where the proscenium wall on SR and the plaster line join, going toward the upstage center (Length: 18′; Angle: 50) and make a click to confirm the wall.
   e. Continue to draw a wall toward SL (Length: 14′; Angle: 0) and click to confirm the wall.
   f. Continue to draw a wall toward downstage left (Length: 6′; Angle: -60) and click to confirm the wall.
   g. Continue to draw a wall toward SL (length: 3′; angle: 0) and click to confirm the wall.
   h. Continue to draw a wall toward downstage left (length: 10′; angle: -60) and make a double click to end the wall drawing.
2. Draw two platforms behind the upstage wall to provide levels in the space.

Draw a Short Platform

a. Activate the rectangle tool, draw a rectangle (Width: 30′; Height: 8′; Extrusion: 8″), center it on the centerline of the theatre, and place it right against the upstage wall.

Draw a Tall Platform

a. Draw another rectangle aligned with the upper right corner of the first rectangle (width: 6′; Height: 3′).
b. Go to Top Menu – Event Design – Create Stage… A dialog widow opens.

   c. In this window, make the following selections.
      - Stage height: 56″
      - Standard Stage Deck Width: 6′
      - Standard Stage Deck Depth: 3′
      - Structure: Border
      - Fill Color: White
   d. Click "OK" to close the window.
   e. While the object is still selected, go to the Object Info palette and change the Z value to 8″.
   f. Under Railing Details (Front), select straight in the dropdown menu and input the number "6" in Add'l L/R Uprights.
3. Draw two stairs leading to the tall platform.

   Draw a Stair on the Left Side
   a. While the tall platform is still selected, go to Top Menu – Event Design – Create Stair… A dialog window opens.
   b. Ensure that the width is 3′ and the fill is White, and click "OK."
   c. On your drawing window, draw the stairs against the left side of the tall platform.
   d. Go to the Object Info palette and change the Z value to 8″.
   e. In "Draw Arrow" dropdown menu, select "Up."
   f. Under Railing Details, check "Show Right."
   g. In Add'l Uprights, insert the number "6."

   Draw a Stair on the Right
   a. Select the tall platform again and go to Top Menu – Event Design – Create Stair… A dialog window opens.
   b. Ensure that the width is 3′ and the fill is White and click "OK."
   c. Go to the Object Info palette, change the Z value to 0″ if it is not already at 0″.
   d. Under Step Details, change the Stage Height to 64″.
   e. In "Draw Arrow" dropdown menu, select "Up."
   f. Change the Number of Steps to 7.
   g. Under Railing Details, check "Show Left."
   h. In Add'l Uprights, insert the number "7."
4. Setting Entrances/Exits
   a. Conduct a search for "Door Opening" in Resource Manager and double click "Door Opening (BSI)" to select it from the list.
   b. Hove over your mouse to the upstage wall. When the wall is lit in RED, insert the Door Opening symbol in the center of the wall for access to upstairs.
   c. Click on the Door Opening to select it and adjust the width of the opening in the Object Info palette (width: 10′).
   d. Click on Door Tool in Tool Sets – Building Shell to select the door.
   e. Insert a door into the wall on the downstage right when the wall is lit in RED.
   f. Go to the Object Info palette, click on Visualization – Show 3D open, and change the opening angle to 45.
   g. Click on Door Tool again to select it.
   h. Insert a door into the wall on upstage left when the wall is lit in RED.
   i. In Object Info palette, click on Visualization – Show 3D open, and change the opening angle to 20.
   j. Click on Window Tool in Tool Sets – Building Shell to select the window.
   k. Insert two windows into the wall on downstage left.

Import Furniture and Décor

1. Go to the View bar and in the Class dropdown menu, select "FURNITURE/DECOR."
2. Conduct a search in Resource Manager for the following items and place them inside the room.
   a. Furn Knoll Pfister Sofa (a sofa)
   b. Furn Living-Side Table 04A (a side table)
   c. Furn Knoll Mies Krefeld Coffee Table (a coffee table)
   d. Furn Furn Table w Chairs Dining RD 1100mm (a table and four chairs)
   e. Light Fixt Moooi, Dear Ingo (a chandelier)
3. Select the chandelier and change its Z height to 12′ in the Object Info palette.

Re-Check Audience's Horizontal Sightlines

1. Go to the View bar, and in the Class dropdown menu, select "ADDITIONAL MASKING SIGHTLINES."
2. Check the Audience's sightline again to see what additional masking devises are needed to prevent the audience from seeing offstage space through the following openings.
   a. the doors (when open)
   b. the door-opening
   c. the window.

Install Additional Masking Devices (Using the Wall Tool)

1. Go to the View bar, and in the Class dropdown menu, select "ADDITIONAL MASKING."
2. Install a painted flat behind the short platform (30′ wide × 1″ thick).
3. Install two painted flats behind the SR door, one parallel to the SR door (6′3″ wide × 1″ thick) and one perpendicular to the SR door (5′ wide × 1″ thick).
4. Install two painted flats behind the SL door, one parallel to the SL door (3′3″ wide × 1″ thick) and one perpendicular to the SL door (4′6″ wide × 1″ thick).
5. Install a painted flat behind the two window openings combined (6′ wide × 1″ thick).

Label the Set

Label the Walls

1. Go to the View bar, in the Class dropdown menu, select "LABLES."
2. Go to Tool Sets – Dims/Notes and double-click on the Reference Marker tool. A dialog box opens.
3. In Style dropdown menu, select "Replace…"
4. Click on the arrows next to the label icon and double-click on the "Ref Marker – Dwg No Sht No Lrg Arrow" icon to select it.
5. Place the markers near each of the five individual walls.

   Note: you will need to label the walls, starting from the wall located furthest downstage right to the wall in the upstage center, and end the labeling on the wall located furthest downstage left. You will number the walls in this order. Let's try to do two of them.

6. Select the marker for the wall located furthest downstage right.
7. Go to the Object Info palette, leave the Drawing Number as 1, change the Sheet Number to WALL, and the Arrow Angle to 130.
8. Select the marker for the upstage wall, change the Drawing Number to 2, Sheet Number to WALL, and the Arrow Angle to 120. Continue until all the walls are labelled correctly.

Label the Flats

1. Place the Reference Markers near each of the six individual flats (for additional masking).
2. Select the marker for the flat located furthest downstage right.
3. Go to the Object Info Palette, leave the Drawing number as 1, change the Sheet Number to FLAT, and Arrow Angle to -60.
4. Select the marker for the next flat.
5. Go to the Object Info Palette, change the Drawing Number to 2, Sheet number to FLAT, and Arrow Angle to 110. Continue until all the flats are labelled correctly.

Note: You can use the Text Tool and Freehand Tool available in the Basic palette, along with an arrow mark, to label the rest of the set, including platforms, furniture/decor pieces, exits, and soft goods.

Label the Platforms

1. Shot Platform
2. Tall Platform

Label the Furniture/Decor Pieces

1. Coffee Table
2. Sofa
3. Side Table
4. Chandelier
5. Table/Chair Set

Label the Entrances/Exits

1. Exit to Kitchen (SR door)
2. Exit to Backyard (SL door)
3. Exit to Upstairs and Other Rooms (Door Opening)

Label the Soft Goods

1. Cyc
2. Legs

Dimension the Set

Note: Dimension Class is one of the default classes. Therefore, even if we didn't create this class, it is available in the Class dropdown menu.

Dimension the Walking Surfaces

1. Go to the View bar, in the Class dropdown menu, select "Dimension."
2. Give height dimension to the platforms, (Short Platform: 8″; Tall Platform: 64″) using a circle (11″) and texts (9 pt.)
3. Give height dimensions to the stairs.

Dimensioning the Set Positions

Note: For this set, the positions of the beginning and ending points of the upstage wall and the swing angle for the SR and SL walls are crucial. Based on these positions, all other set pieces will fall into place.

1. Give horizontal dimensions from the centerline to the beginning and ending of the upstage wall.
2. Give a vertical dimension from the upstage wall to the plaster line.
3. Give an angular dimension for the swing of the SR Wall (from the upstage wall).
4. Give an angular dimension for the swing of the SL Wall (from the upstage wall).

Designate Hanging Positions

Make the layer named "Theatre" the active layer and allocate the following items to the batten positions located at the Flying Gallery.

1. Cyc (Line #20)
2. Legs and Borders #4 (Line #15)
3. Legs and Borders #3 (Line #11)
4. Legs and Borders #2 (Line #7)
5. Legs and Borders #1 (Line #3)
6. Chandelier (Line #6)

Generate a Top/Plan View on Sheet Layer and Viewport

Note: before generating a view on Sheet Layer and Viewport for printing. You want to organize what you want to see or not see in your drawing area.

Get Ready

1. Make Set Layer as the active layer.
2. Go to Navigation palette. In the Layer Option dropdown menu, select "show Others."
3. Make all Layers visible, except for the SECTION Layer.
4. Click on the Class icon in the Navigation palette.
5. Make all Classes visible, except for the ADDITIONAL MASKING SIGHTLINES Class.

Note: You can now adjust line weights for various classes based on the conventions of line weights recommended by USITT or simply categorize them into Lightweight Line, Medium-weight Line, or Heavy-weight Line, as discussed previously for the final printing of this drawing.

Let's try it.

1. In Navigation – Classes, make SET STRUCTURE Class the active Class and ADDITIONAL MASKING SIGHTLINES, Dimension, and LABLES invisible.
2. Click on the Layer icon, make the SET layer active, and select "active only" in the Layer Options dropdown menu.
3. Select all the items in the drawing area.
4. Go to the Attributes palette and change the line weight to 0.5.
5. In your drawing area, deselect everything to see the result.

As an alternative, you might want to gray some of the classes to give priority to the Set Structure and Furniture/Decor pieces for printing.

Generate a Top/Plan View on the Sheet Layer and Viewport

1. Go to Top Menu – View – Create Viewport… A dialog window appears.
2. In Create on Layer dropdown menu, select "New Sheet Layer…" Another dialog window appears.
3. In Sheet Title slot, type "Box Set-Top/Plan," check the "Edit Properties After Creation" box, and click "OK." A third dialog box opens.
4. Change Raster Rendering DPI to 150, click on Page Setup to make sure that "US Arch D" is selected as the size of the sheet, and click "OK" to close the window.
5. In "Create Viewport" window, check "Create drawing label," type "Box Set-Top/Plan view" in the Drawing title slot, and click "OK" to close the window.
6. The Top/Plan view of your drawing is now on a Sheet Layer.

Create a Title Block for the Drawing

Invoke a Title Block Template

1. Go to Dims/Notes located in the Tool Sets. Double-click on the Title Block Border tool. A Title Block Preferences window appears.
2. Click on the Use Style dropdown menu, a plug-in window appears.

3. In the left column, go to Vectorworks Libraries – Annotations – Title Block Border (styles), select "Spotlight Title Blocks.vwx"
4. Double-click on "Spotlight Title Block."
5. Click "OK" to close the Title Block Border Preferences window.
6. Click on the drawing sheet to insert the Title Block Border.

Insert Information into the Title Block Template

1. With the Select Tool activated, double click on the Title Block. A "Title Block Border Setting" dialogue box appears.
2. In the Title Block Border Settings window, click on the item named "Project Data" located on the left column of the window, and input the following information:
   a. Project Date: Current Date (e.g., 06-12-2023)
   b. Project Name 1: Title of a Play (e.g., Mock Box Set)
   c. Venue: The Name of the Production Site (e.g., KSU Stillwell Theatre)
3. Switch to "Sheet Data" also located on the left column of the window, and input the following:
   a. Sheet Title: Name of the Sheet (e.g., Box Set Top/Plan View)
   b. Sheet Number: The actual sheet number of the total number of sheets in this set (e.g., Sht-1)
   c. Sheet Scale: ¼″ = 1′-0″
   d. Design by: Your name (e.g., Helen Chang)
   e. Direct by: Director's name (e.g., Helen Chang)
   f. (Click on "Next.")
   g. Drawn by: Your name if you are the drafter (e.g., Helen Chang)
4. Under the Preview window located on the right column of the window, check the "Zoom in on the Title Block" box. If everything looks good, click "OK" to close the window. You can now see a customized title block located on the lower right corner of your drawing.
5. Save your drawing to complete this exercise.

Experiment and Practice

In this chapter, we have discussed many drafting conventions. Do you know what you've learned and retained about these conventions? You can try to do the following activities to find out for yourself. The correct answers are at the end of this Experiment and Practice.

True or False

1. USITT drafting convention requires all scenery to be drafted in scale.
   a. True
   b. False
2. SL is the abbreviation for Stage Left, which refers to the part of the stage on the left side of the audience.
   a. True
   b. False
3. Extension lines should not be drawn through the lines of an object being dimensioned.
   a. True
   b. False
4. In Vectorworks, the standard sheet size for scenic drafting is US ARCH D, which is 30″ × 18″.
   a. True
   b. False
5. Dimensions are located on a drawing to be read from the bottom or right edge of the paper only.
   a. True
   b. False
6. The outline of a cut-through view of an object should be drawn in a medium-weight line.
   a. True
   b. False
7. The drawing title of a set unit should be placed above the projection views of the set unit combined.
   a. True
   b. False
8. A Title Block should be placed in the lower-right corner of a drafted sheet.
   a. True
   b. False

Multiple Choice

1. which of the following is ***not*** a necessary element included in a title block?
   a. Drawing scale
   b. Production site
   c. Drawing title
   d. Sheet number
   e. None of the above
2. Which of the following is the most common scale of a floor plan for indoor theatre productions?
   a. 3″ scale
   b. 1 inch scale
   c. ½ inch scale
   d. ¼ inch scale
   e. None of the above
3. Which of the following is/are the standard way(s) of dimensioning a 4-foot-high platform in a ground plan?
   a. 4′ (with a circle around it)
   b. 48″ (with a circle around it)
   c. 4′-0″
   d. All the above
   e. None of the above
4. Which of the following is the standard line type for a plaster line on a drafted sheet?
   a. Dashed line
   b. Solid Line
   c. Break Line
   d. None of the above
5. Which of the following information will be most unlikely found in a standard floor plan?
   a. The labels of set units
   b. A Title Block
   c. The height of a platform
   d. The length of a platform
6. The overall dimensions of an object should be drawn
   a. closest to the object being dimensioned.
   b. second closest to the object being dimensioned.
   c. furthest away from the object being dimensioned.
   d. second furthest away from the object being dimensioned.
   e. all the above.
7. Local notes should be situated
   a. on the upper left corner of a drafted sheet.
   b. on the upper right corner of a drafted sheet.
   c. above the title block
   d. below the projection views combined of the relevant set unit.
   e. None of the above.
8. On the following list, which is a lettering convention in drafting.
   a. Uppercase letters
   b. Lowercase letters
   c. A combination of uppercase and lowercase letters
   d. None of the above

Treasure Hunt

Instruction: Open the floor plan you created in Technique 6 in Vectorworks. Turn on all layers but the layer named "SECTION." Turn on all classes, but the class named "Additional Masking Sightlines." Fill in the blanks below based on your reading of the plan, as seen.

1. What is the dimension of the highest walking surface on this floor plan? ____
2. How many openings (door opening, window, door) can the audience member sitting in the critical seat located in the house right see? ____
3. On which batten/line does the Chandelier hang? ____
4. Is Wall 1 located on upstage left, upstage right, downstage right, or down stage left? ____
5. How many individual pieces of flats are used to mask the opening of the walls? ____
6. How many legs are used to mask the off-stage wing space? ____
7. What is the dimension from the plaster line to the back of the upstage wall. ____
8. What is the swing angle of the SR Wall? ____
   What is the swing angle of the SL Wall? ____

Correct Answers (key to the questions in this Experiment and Practice)

True or False: 1) a; 2) b; 3) a; 4) b; 5) a; 6) b; 7) b; 8) a

Multiple Choice: 1) e; 2) d; 3) b; 4) a; 5) d; 6) c; 7) e; 8) a

Treasure Hunt: 1) 64″; 2) 2; 3) Line #6; 4) downstage right; 5) 6; 6) 8; 7) 14′-4″; 8) SR 130 and SL 120

Bibliography

Aronson, Arnold, editor. "Recommendations for Standard Graphic Language in Scenic Design and Technical Production by USITT Graphic Standards Board." *TD&T*, XVIII, no. 1, Spring 1982, pp. 8–9.

dld & sn. "USITT Graphic Recommended Best Practices - Proposed." *United States Institute for Theatre Technology*, 13 Mar. 2019, www.usitt.org/graphicrbp.

Dorn, Dennis, and Mark Shanda. *Drafting for the Theatre*. Southern Illinois University Press, 2012.

McCoy, Matthew L. Fig. 6.3. *Amusement Park Master Plan*. Master plan of Colorful Yunnan Paradise Park in China, 2018.

Pecktal, Lynn. *Designing and Painting for the Theatre*. Holt, Rinehart and Winston, 1975.

Rose, Rich. *Drafting Scenery for Theatre, Film, and Television*. Betterway Publications, Inc, 1990.

O'Skea, Sean. "Drafting Conventions for Theatre." *YouTube*, 8 Sept. 2019, www.youtube.com/watch?v=227A07BSVcI.

Sweet, Harvey. *The Complete Book of Drawing for the Theatre*. Allyn and Bacon, 1995.

USITT. "USITT Scenic Design and Technical Production Graphic Standard." USITT Education Commission Graphic Standards Board, 18 Mar. 1992, https://ulife.vpul.upenn.edu/dolphin/pacshop/usitt92.pdf.

Wolff, Fred M. "Recommendations for Standard Graphic Language in Scene Design and Technical Production by USITT Graphic Standards Board." *Theatre Design & Technology*, vol. 18, no. 1, 1982, pp. 8–9.

Woodbridge, Patricia. *Designer Drafting for the Entertainment World: Theatre, Motion Pictures, Television, Trade Shows, Amusement Park Scenery, Computer-Drafted Scenery, Virtual Scenery*. Focal Press, 2000.

CHAPTER 7

Types of Drafting

Vocabulary

Elevation
Flat
Reference Marker
Orthographic Projection
Auxiliary View
Section
Revolved Section
Detail
Floor Plan/Ground Plan/Plan/Staging Plan
Composite Floor Plan
Shift Plan
Centerline Vertical Sections/Cross section/Section Plan
Hanging Section

Learning Objectives

- Gain knowledge of scenic drafting conventions and the current practices of these conventions.
- Show capacity for reading and interpreting various types of drafting, including Elevation, Orthographic Projection, Section, Detail, Floor Plan, Cross Section, Hanging Section, and Shift Plan.
- Demonstrate the ability to create the various types of drafting mentioned above, using a digital model of a scenic design as the base.
- Display patience, attention to details, and thoroughness in drafting work.

Types of Scenic Designers' Drafting

This chapter introduces drafting conventions with regard to the production of various types of scenic drafting. A designer's drafting set may include some or all of the following:

1. Elevations or orthographic projections of various set units
2. Section(s) of set units (if applicable)
3. Details of set units or part of set units (if applicable)
4. A floor plan or floor plans
5. Cross sections
6. A hanging section (if applicable)
7. Shift plans (if applicable)
8. Isometric views (optional)

Elevation

In scenic drafting, an ***Elevation*** depicts a view of a shape in a "straight on, flattened out, full face, no perspective" manner. (Rose, 76). An elevation view of a shape is different from a perspective view of that shape. A shape depicted in an elevation drawing is measurable, while the same shape depicted in a perspective drawing is not measurable due to its foreshortening effect (Fig. 7.1).

Elevation drawings are created for construction purposes. They are drawn to scale and complete with dimensions, notations, and drawing titles. whereas perspective drawings are not measurable even if they are created on a certain scale. They can

DOI: 10.4324/9781003266242-7

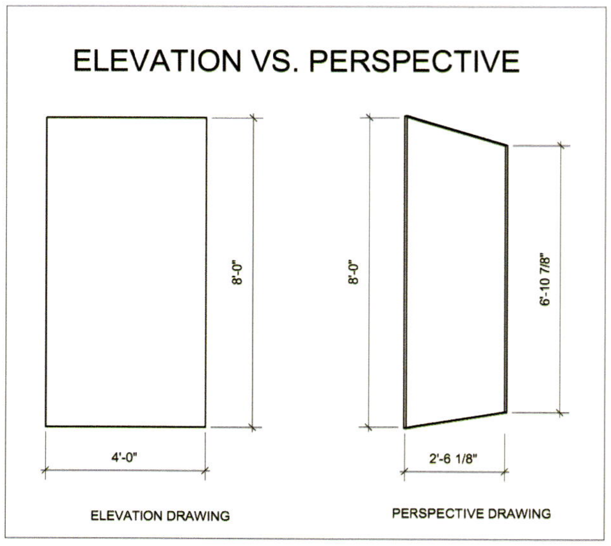

Figure 7.1 *Elevation vs. Perspective*. An illustration comparing an elevation drawing of a ***Flat*** to a perspective drawing of the flat. A flat of 8′ tall and 4′ wide is measurable in the Elevation of the flat but not in the perspective drawing of that flat.

only serve as a reference image during construction processes. In scenic drafting, a set unit with a known thickness, such as a Flat (1″ thick), is often drawn as a single Elevation.

In a set design that employs series walls, the designer/drafter should properly label and number the walls on a floor plan, starting from the wall located furthest downstage right to the wall located upstage center and ending at the wall located furthest downstage left. These labels/numbers are keyed to the Elevation of the walls shown in the construction plan. Fig. 7.2 illustrates the proper application of drafting conventions in the positioning and labeling of the walls on both the Floor Plan and the Elevation drawing of the flats.

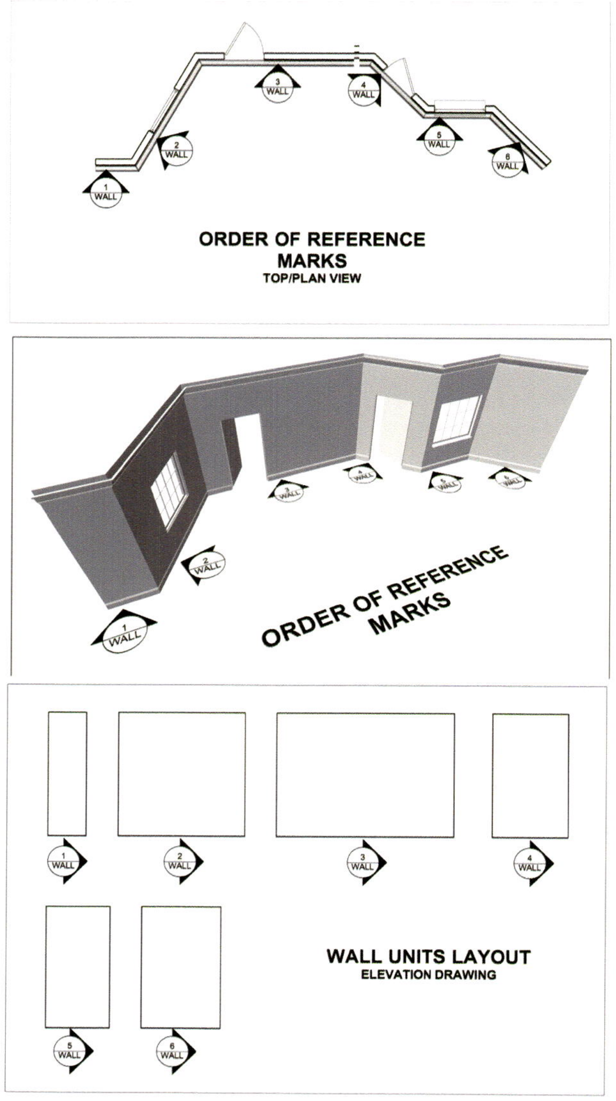

Figure 7.2 *Labeling Convention of Flats*. This illustration consists of three images. The image on the top displays the proper order of *Reference Markers* for the walls on a floor plan. The image in the middle shows the set in a perspective view. The image at the bottom demonstrates the close relationship between the labels for the walls on a floor plan and the labels, as well as the wall layout, in the elevation drawing of the walls.

Orthographic Projection

Definition

The term ***Orthographic Projection*** refers to a method of drafting that uses a series of Elevations to depict a 3D object in 2D shapes. Fig. 7.3 visualizes the concept of Orthographic Projection.

The six standard views of Orthographic Project are top view, front view, left-side view, right-side view, back view, and bottom view.

In Orthographic Projection drawings, the views are drawn to scale and complete with dimensions, notations, and drawing titles for construction purposes.

Projection Views

Orthographic Projection in scenic drafting will often include top view, front view, and side views. In special circumstances, it might also include a back

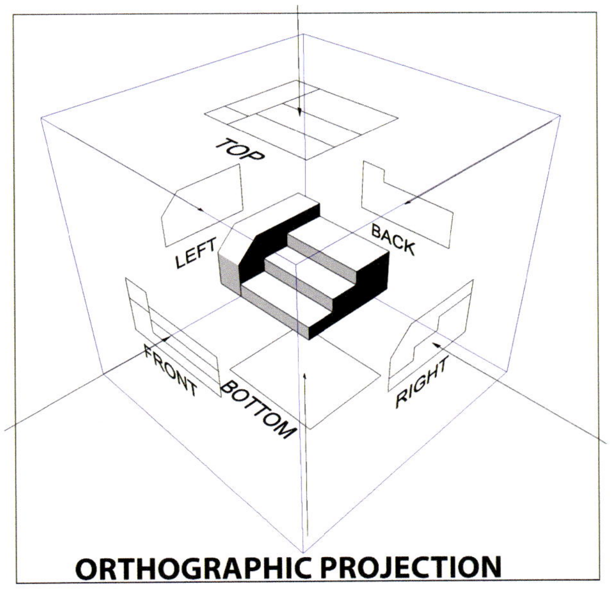

Figure 7.3 *Orthographic Projection*. This image shows how a 3D object can be described through a series of elevations taken from six directions perpendicular (straight on) to the object. Each of the six views projected on the planes of an imaginary glass box is parallel to the object being viewed from that direction.

view and even a bottom view. That said, not all objects are necessarily drawn in a full set of views.

- For a flat with a known thickness (e.g., 1″), only a front view is needed.
- For a cylinder, a top view and a front view are sufficient, because the side views are the same as the front view.
- For a symmetrical 3D object, you can convey your idea clearly with a top view, a front view, and a side view because the views on both sides are identical.
- For an asymmetrical 3D object, you want to provide a top view, a front view, a right-side view, and a left-side view.
- For an asymmetrical 3D object that will be turned around for the audience to see its back, you will need to provide a back view in addition to a top view, a front view, a right-side view, and a left-side view.
- For an 3D object that will be hanging in the air and being seen from below, a bottom view may be necessary, in addition to the regular views.

Placement and Alignment of the Views

In an Orthographic Projection drawing, the placement of each view of a 3D object is predetermined. The top view is always placed above the front view; the bottom view (or plan view) is always placed below the front view; the left view is always placed on the left side of the front view; the right view is always placed on the right side of the front view; and the back (rear) view can be placed either on the left side of the left view (convention) or on the right side of the right view (VW default). The conventional placement of views can not only facilitate the viewer's understanding of the object but also streamline the dimensions in the drawing. See Fig. 7.4 for further clarification.

During the drafting process, the projection views should be placed properly and aligned accurately. The top view, front view, and bottom (or plan) view of an object should be aligned vertically to share the horizontal dimensions, while the left view, front view, right view, and back (rear) view of the object should be aligned horizontally to share the vertical dimensions. The depth dimensions are shared among the top, bottom, left, and right views.

Since many dimensions are shared among projection views and drafters are expected to avoid redundancy of dimensions in their drafting, you might wonder what an orthographic projection drawing done properly would look like. Fig. 7.5 demonstrates just that.

Generating Orthographic Projection in VW Program

As stipulated previously in Chapter 1, the VW program makes the process of drafting pleasurable. As soon as the 3D model of a set unit is created, it only takes a few mouse-clicks to generate an orthographic projection drawing of the set unit. The steps involved in making such drawings, will be described in Technique 7 of this chapter. One important thing to remember for this process is that, in Top/Plan view, you need to ensure that the line representing the front side of the set unit is parallel to the bottom edge of the sheet before generating the orthographic projection views.

Auxiliary View

An ***Auxiliary View*** displays the true shape and size of the surface of an object that is neither parallel nor perpendicular to the standard orthographic projection planes. The slanted plane of the short wall in the Stair Unit shown in Figs. 7.3 and 7.4 is such an example. The true shape and size of this plane may not be as important in the drafting of this unit, as it

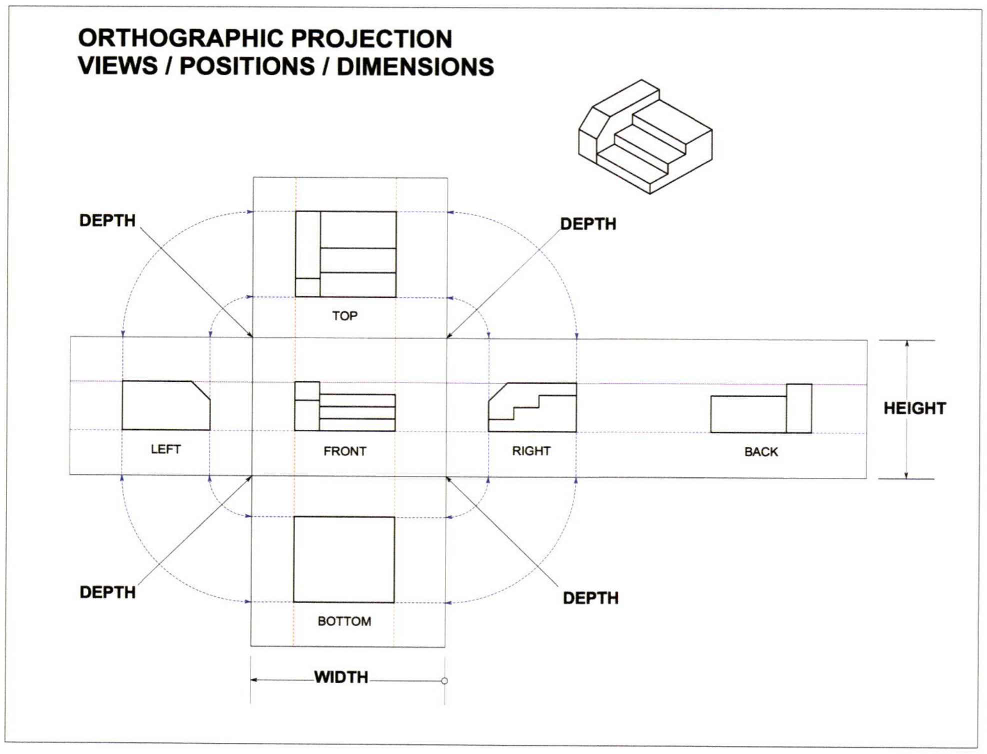

Figure 7.4 Orthographic Projection Views, Positions, and Dimensions. This image displays the positional relationships among the views of an Orthographic Projection drawing and explains the ways these views share dimensions. It uses color-coded lines (blue, purple, and orange) to indicate the sharing of vertical, horizontal, and depth dimensions among the various views.

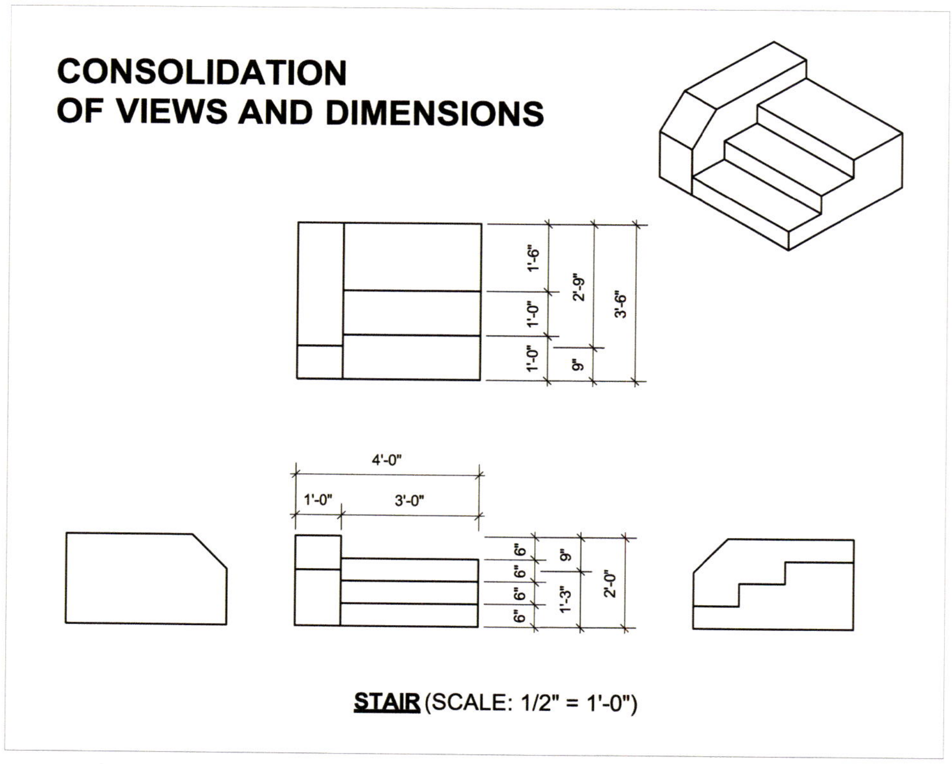

Figure 7.5 *Consolidation of Views and Dimensions*. An example of orthographic projection drawing, showing the views and dimensions necessary to get the design ideas across in a clear and concise manner.

can be easily figured out during the construction process, yet if you are dealing with a slanted surface on a grand scale, the case will be rather different.

Imagine that you want to estimate the cost of the material for the gable roof on a building. The true shape and dimensions of the gable surface would be crucial in the design and construction processes.

Fig. 7.6 shows an example of an orthographic projection drawing where an Auxiliary View of the object and its dimensions are important and should be included in the drafting of this set unit.

In an orthographic projection drawing with an Auxiliary View or views, the top view, side views, and auxiliary view share depth dimensions. The Auxiliary View can be drawn at a convenient location but must be drawn in alignment with the slanted object line that the Auxiliary View is referring to at a right angle (90 degrees).

Technically speaking, Auxiliary View is an extension of Orthographic Projection views. In this chapter, Auxiliary View is discussed separately from standard views because this type of view is abnormal and cannot be generated through View command in Vectorworks. It is recommended that Auxiliary Views be created on the Sheet Layer after the normal orthographic projection views are generated. You will go through the process of producing an Auxiliary View in Technique 7 of this chapter.

Section

A ***Section*** is a dissect view of a set unit. It is produced by cutting the unit with an imaginary knife. A Section can be either a vertical cut-through or a horizontal cut-through or a combination of both. Designer/Drafter need to provide a Section drawing when the information regarding the interior of an object is important. For instance, when Kennesaw State University produced *Big River*, it did not have a budget big enough to build the automated raft that the script calls for. Therefore, manpower must be involved. The design for this raft includes two big crates, inside of which a run crew (not being seen by the audience) can stand and push the raft around when the raft needs to move and sit down when the raft stays in place during the performances.

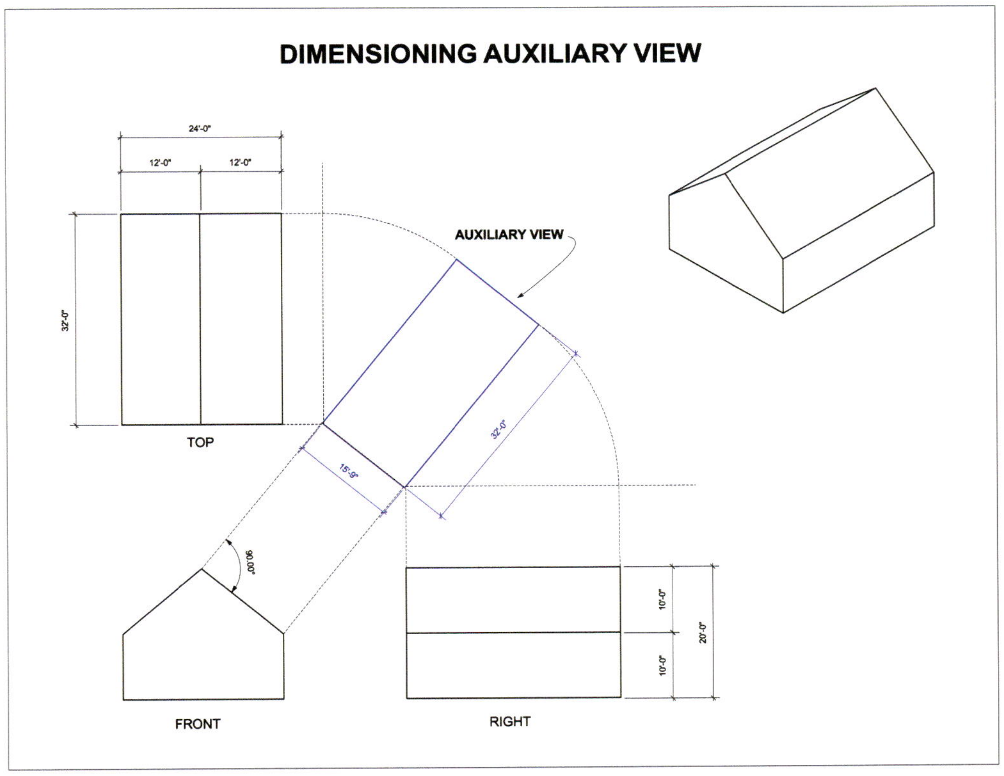

Figure 7.6 *Auxiliary View*. An example of an Orthographic Projection drawing with an Auxiliary View.

This specific need for the raft requires a Section drawing of this set unit to show the interior space arrangement and placement of the pushing handle.

Fig. 7.7 showcases a scenario when a section drawing or drawings are necessary, because the standard orthographic projection views do not provide depth information on the shapes and dimensions of the interior cuts, which are necessary to the construction of this unit.

- A Section drawing should include a view that is the most telling of the cuts (a front view in Fig. 7.8), and a section view or views (a vertical Section on the left and a horizontal Section at the bottom in Fig. 7.8).
- The drafter should select the location of the cutting plane that provides most information possible.
- The cut-through plane of a solid mass needs to be outlined with heavy-weight lines and filled with hatches drawn with light-weight diagonal lines (Fig. 7.8).
- Object lines behind the cutting plane will be visible using a medium-weight line (Fig. 7.8).

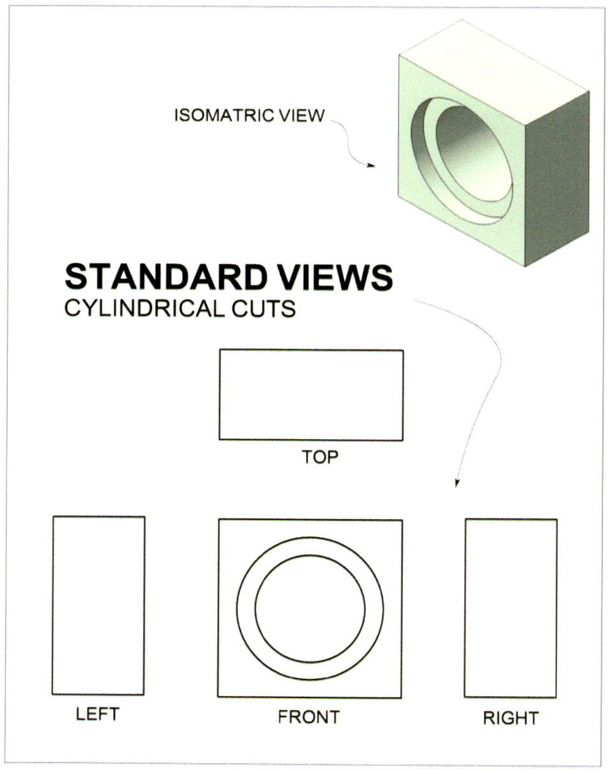

Figure 7.7 *Standard Views – Cylinder Cuts.* The cuboid shown in this image is subtracted inside by two cylindrical forms, but the interior cuts are not reflected in the standard views of an Orthographic Projection drawing.

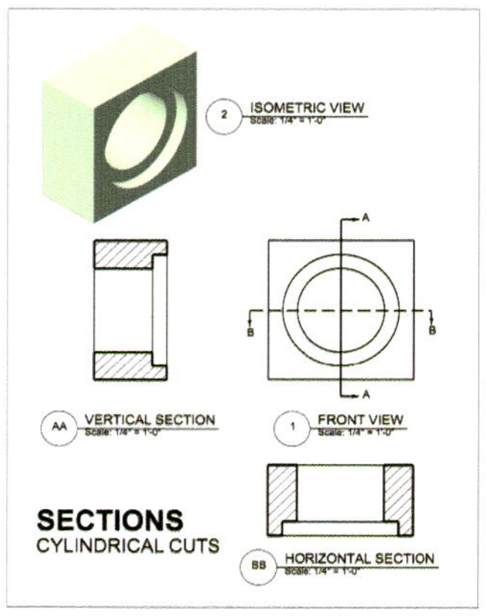

Figure 7.8 *Sections – Cylinder Cuts.* An example of section drawings of a cuboid form with cylindrical cuts inside. Conformed with drafting conventions, these sectional drawings provide information concerning the depth of the cylindrical cuts.

- On the front view, the cutting line is expressed through a thick, dashed line (one long dash and two short dashes). The line is stopped slightly beyond object lines on both ends, then made a 90-degree turn towards the direction the section is taken. This line is ended with an arrowhead, indicating the viewing direction of the Section, and an alphabetic label on both ends identifies the cut. (In the case of Fig. 7.8, the horizontal Section is a top/plan view of the object, with the upper half of the object removed to reveal the inner structure of the object. The vertical Section is a left view of the object, with the left half of the object removed to reveal the inner structure of the object.)
- The specific label used on the cutting line is used again as the drawing title for the relevant Section view. (In Fig. 7.8, the horizonal section view is labeled "BB" and the vertical section view is labeled "AA.")

Fig. 7.8 is an example of a section drawing that provides depth information and conforms with the drafting conventions for section drawings as stipulated below.

In the case of Fig. 7.9, the standard orthographic projection drawing, again, fails to communicate the depth information regarding the concave with a hemispheric cut.

The section drawings shown in Fig. 7.10 shows the depth at which the hemisphere forms, cutting into the cuboid form. It provides a vertical Section viewing from the right and a horizontal Section viewing from above.

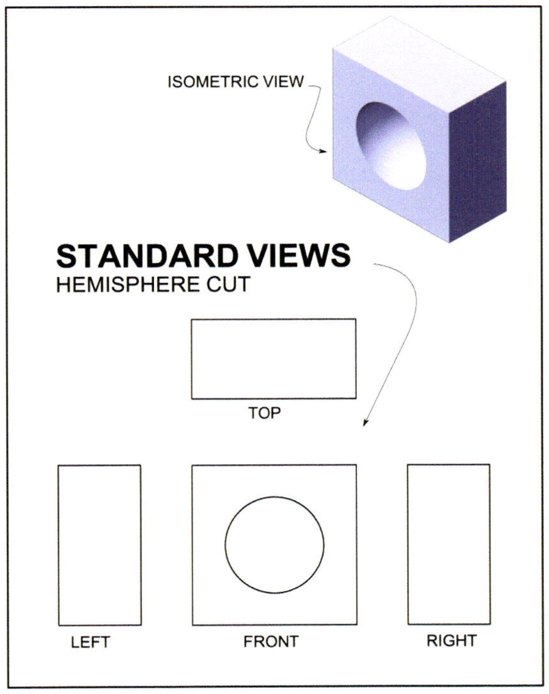

Figure 7.9 *Standard Views – Hemisphere Cut*. The cuboid shown in this image is subtracted inside by a hemisphere. Neither the top view nor the side views of the orthographic projection drawing reflect the depth information of the cuts.

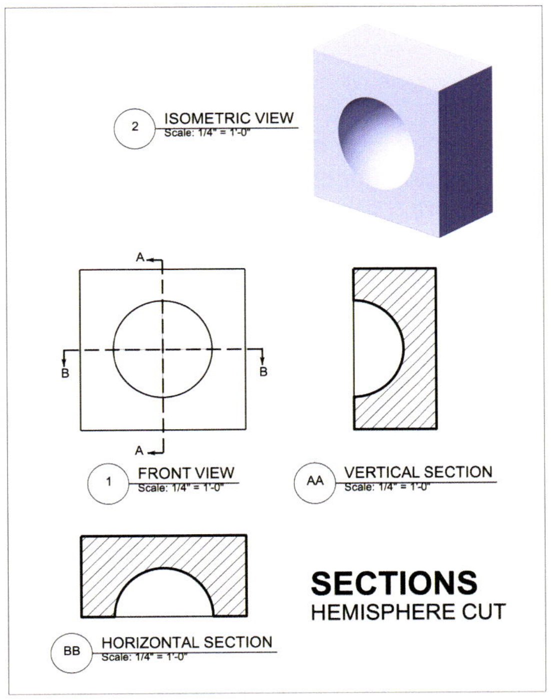

Figure 7.10 *Sections – Hemisphere Cut*. Another example of Section drawing with a different cutting shape and viewing direction to show how the convention of section drawing works.

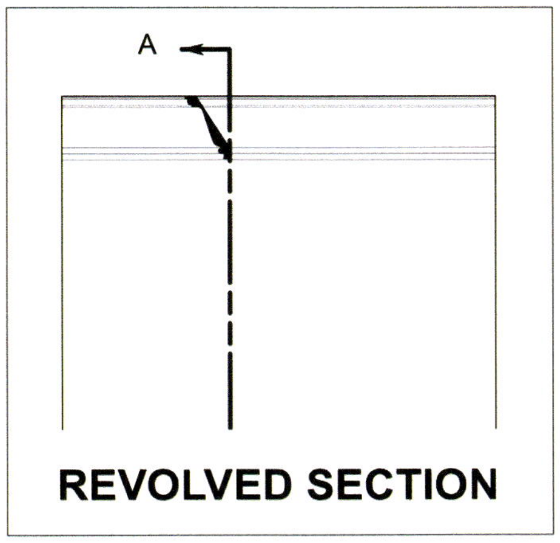

Figure 7.11 *Revolved Section*. This cropped drawing demonstrating how the section view of a crown molding is imposed on the front view of a wall in a Revolved Section. The cutting line indicates the direction in which the crown modeling section was taken.

As a special form of Section, ***Revolved Section*** imposes a Section view drawing onto the Front view drawing. This type of drawing best serves the scenario when the depth of the object is relatively shallow but detailed. Fig. 7.11 illustrates what a revolved section drawing looks like.

Detail

In drafting, ***Detail*** refers to a blow-up view of a set unit or part of a set unit. A detailed drawing is needed when the standard orthographic projection views are not large enough to sufficiently convey all the information in the drawing (Fig. 7.12).

In hand drafting, the drafter would use a larger scale to draw the Detail in addition to the standard projection views. In VW, after the drafter makes a choice of scale, the detailed drawing with a zoom-in effect of the part to be detailed as well as the reference labels will both come out automatically. The best placement for a detailed drawing is next to where the detail is taken. The steps to complete a Detail drawing can be found in Technique 7 of this chapter.

Floor Plan

Terminology and Purpose of the Floor Plan

In theatre, "***Floor Plan***," "***Ground Plan***," and "***Plan***" are alternative names for the same concept. In film and television, it is called "***Staging Plan***."

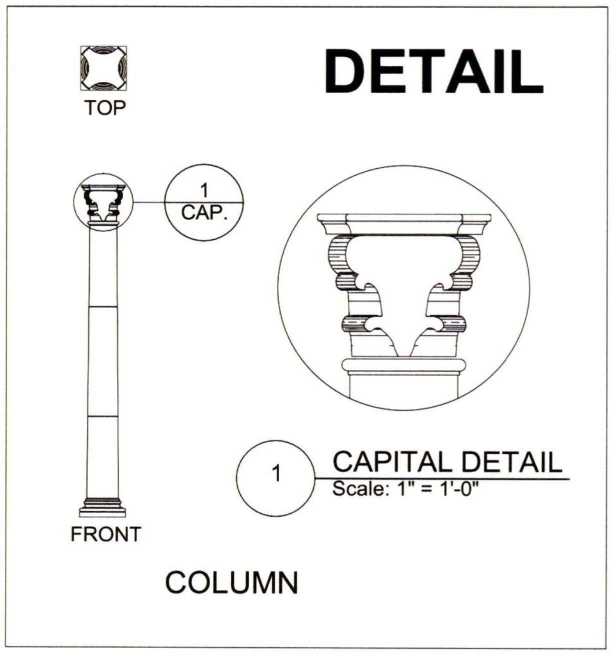

Figure 7.12 *Detail*. This illustration presents a scenario when a detailed view is needed. It also showcases how the labeling system works for the Detail.

Rich Rose, the author of *Drafting Scenery for Theatre, Film, and Television*, alludes to a floor plan as "a roadmap of the performance space," because "It aids the designer in developing the architecture of the setting. It is also a tool for the director to use in establishing the flow of the action. To the lighting designer, it is a mandatory instrument for planning the lighting design, and for the stage technician, it is invaluable regarding the placement of the scenery." (Rose, 54) Likewise, Harvey Sweet, the author of *Complete Book of Drawing*, believes that "The ground Plan is the single most important drawing made by the designer" (Sweet, 84).

Although they are similar in appearance, the Floor Plan of a theatre is different from the top view (a bird's eye view) of it. Looking down from above, you will see the roof of a theatre building in a Top view of it, but not in a Floor Plan of it, because a Floor Plan is made for the planning of the stage traffic, with a need to show where the actors can or cannot pass through. The walls, doors, and furniture pieces under the roof will all affect the planning of the stage traffic. Technically speaking, a Floor Plan, as mentioned in Chapter 1, is a horizontal cut-through of a theatre. The imaginary cutting line is conventionally set at 4′ above the stage floor to show the viewer where the actors can enter/exit the stage and where the actors are blocked by the walls of the theatre. This is the same in the case of the floor plan for the scenery.

Components of a Floor Plan

In the floor plan of scenic design, you may see lines, shapes, and symbols representing architectural elements, set units, and furniture pieces; you may see labels of scenic units and set props; you may see height dimensions of platforms and staircases; you may see dimensions indicating how a crucial point on a set unit is related to the centerline and plaster line of the theatre for the purpose of a proper placement of the set unit on stage; you may also see a Title Block that summarizes what this drawing is for, about, and who it was created by (Fig. 7.13).

What you will not see on a floor plan, however, are the length and width of a set unit shown on this plan, because a floor plan is not made for set construction; rather, it is made for the placement of the set units after these units are built.

Types of Floor Plan/Staging Plan

For a small-scale set design, the designer might want to create a ***Composite Floor Plan*** (see Fig. 7.13) for everyone in a production team, which will include all components required of a Floor Plan. In contrast, when a scenic design is complex, a Composite Floor Plan may be crowded with a huge amount of information that is difficult to read. Working with a CAD program makes it easier to duplicate a floor plan and spread the information among its versions, each customized for a different group of people. For instance, directors and choreographers are more interested in information concerning actors' position and movement (stage traffic) in the space. A Floor Plan for them may include height dimensions for walking surfaces, furniture pieces, etc. Unlike directors and choreographers, technicians, such as the technical director and stage manager, are more interested in the placement of the scenery in space. For them, a floor plan must include dimensions relating to the placement of the set units. In comparison, stage managers and shifting crews would like to see a set of ***Shift Plans***, especially if a design involves numerous scene changes. Fig. 7.14 samples shift plans that reflect the positions of the set units on and off stage for each scene.

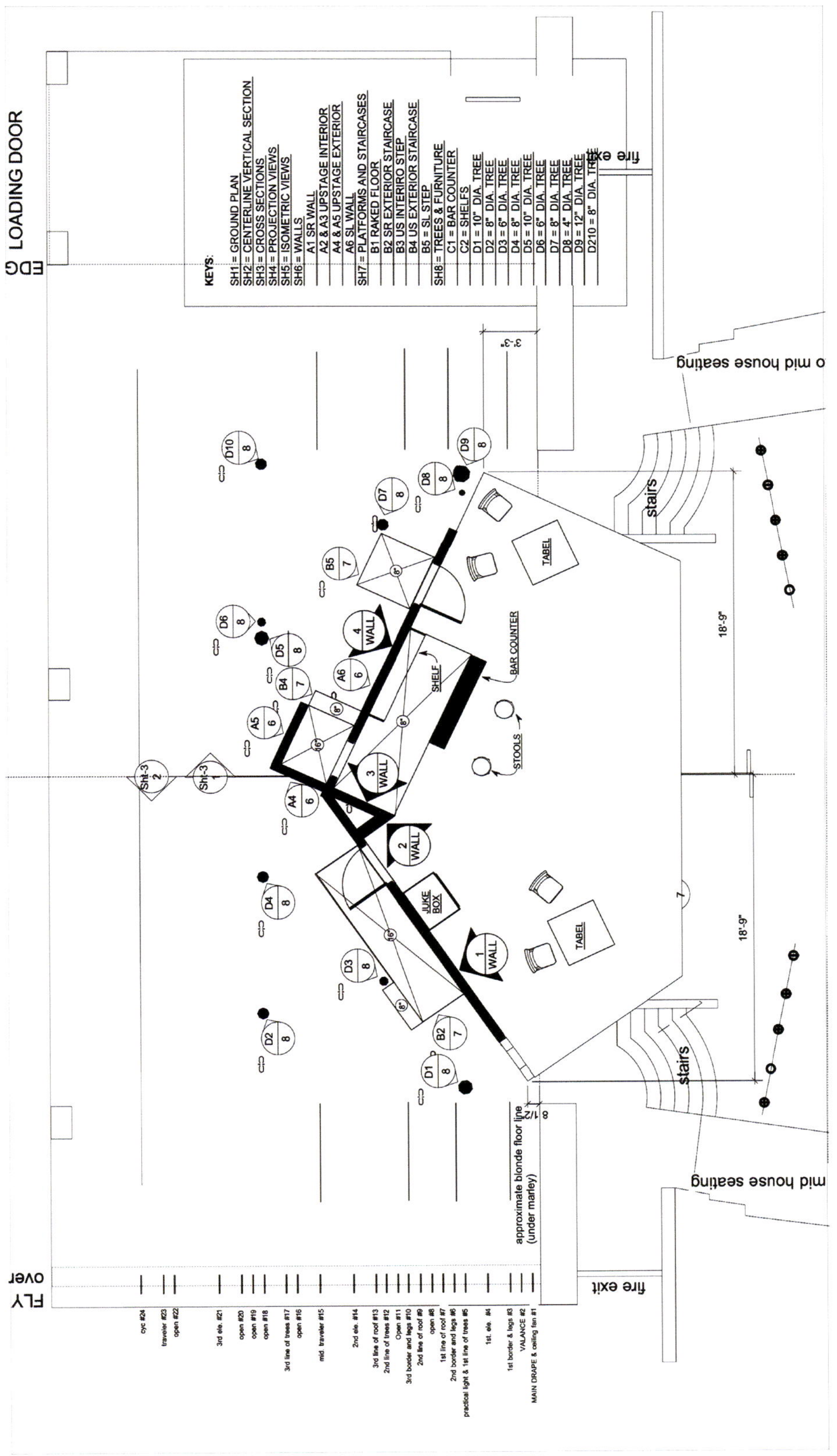

Figure 7.13 *Ground Plan Sample.* A floor plan for *East Texas Hot Links* by Eugen Lee, a theatre production of Kenny Leon's True Color's Theatre Company in Atlanta.

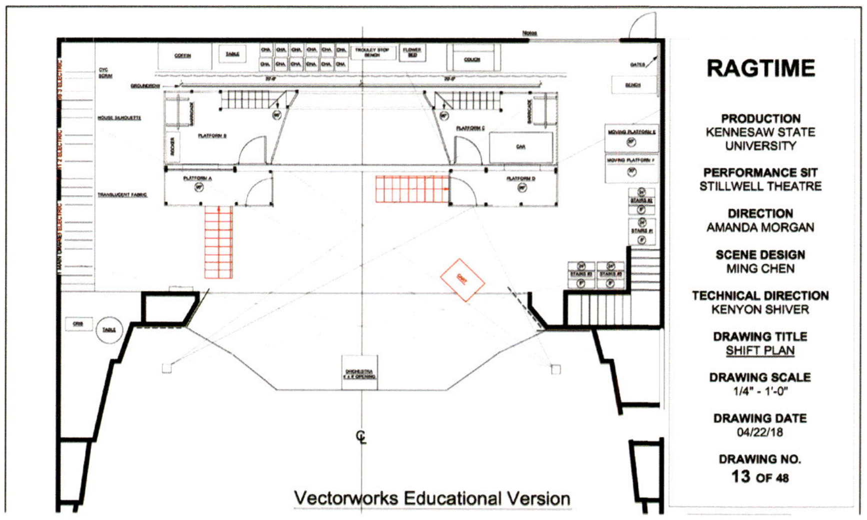

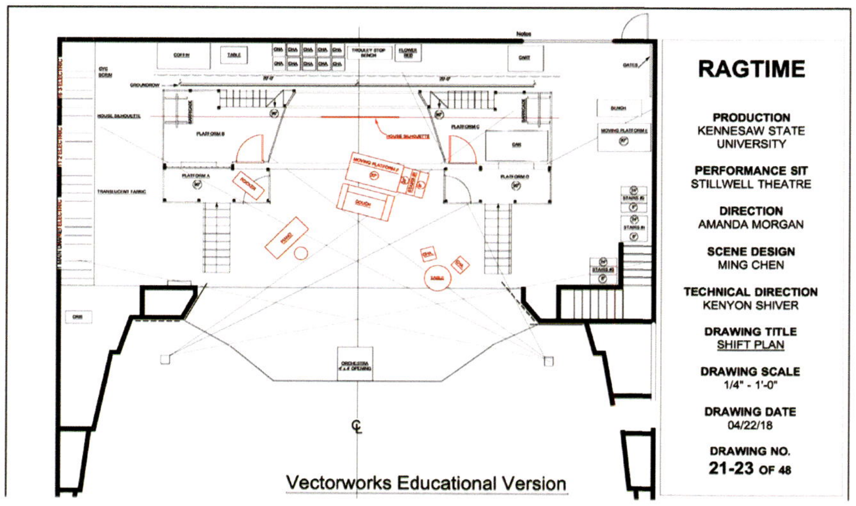

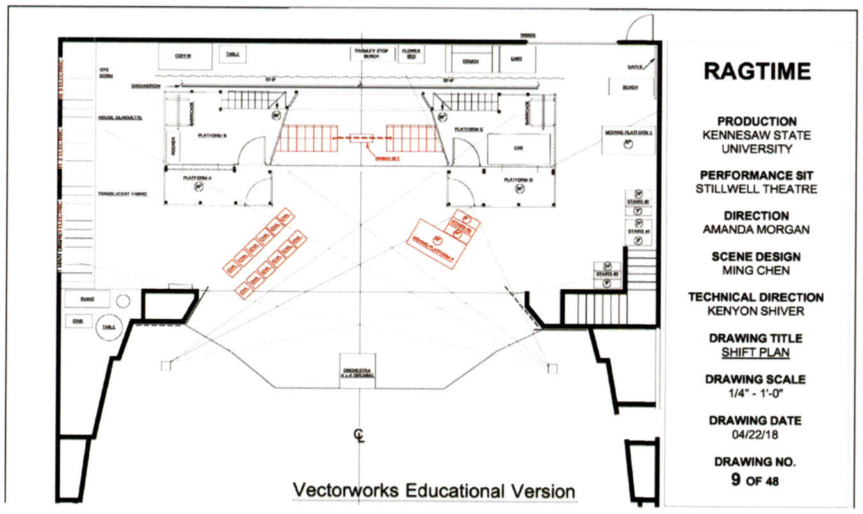

Figure 7.14 *Shift Plan Samples*. An illustration of Shift Plan samples created for *Ragtime* performance at Kennesaw State University. Objects in red are set units moved on stage (from off-stage areas) for that particular scene. The scene design for this production contains more than 36 scene shifts. The shift plans featured in this illustration include (from top to bottom) No. 13_Success_Street of New York, No. 21–23_Courtship_Kitchen Parlor, and No. 9_Journey On_Crime of the Century.

Creating a Floor Plan in the VW Program

To create a floor plan in a VW working environment, you may apply the following procedure:

1. In the Top/Plan view, open the theatre floor plan.
2. Locate horizontal critical seats in the auditorium and check sightlines to get a sense of the space, including the area on stage that can be seen by all audience members in the house and the sightline limits. Keep this information in mind as you plan the space.
3. Establish a set structure by creating the major set elements, such as walls, platforms, and curtains, starting with drawing 2D shapes of the elements, and then extruding them in 3D forms if you are not using 3D modular and/or symbol objects.
4. Set entrances and exits, such as doors and windows.
5. Place the set props in space.
6. Recheck the sightline for masking purposes.
   a. Install conventional masking devises, such as a cyc and the legs, and assign them to battens available in the Flying Gallery. Even if you have walls enclosing the performance space, remember that the audience can usually see the off-stage space above the walls and through the doors when they are open. So, you will still need to install the standard masking devices, such as legs, if you want to conceal the objects in the wing space, and back wall of the theatre, if you want to create Realism on stage.
   b. Install additional masking devices for the openings, such as doors and windows.
7. Create a horizontal section view (floor plan) on a new sheet layer and viewport. (See Technique 7 of this chapter for details.)
8. Label the set units and set props.
9. Designate hanging positions beside the counterweight system.
10. Provide dimensions for the positioning of the set units. Select points on the set units that are crucial to the positioning of the set units. Measure and place the horizontal dimensions between each crucial point and the centerline of the stage. Measure and place the vertical dimensions between each crucial point and the plaster line of the stage. Measure and place the angle dimensions if needed.
11. Create a Title Block for the floor plan (see Technique 6 of previous chapter for details).

Theoretically, the horizontal section view of a set model should be able to serve as the Floor Plan of the set. In practice, however, some symbols available in VW symbol libraries were created using modeling methods that do not allow dissection. So, what happens is that, when a horizontal section view is created through Viewport on a sheet layer, these symbols will simply disappear. Plant symbols are notoriously troublesome in this regard. One way to deal with this issue is to add the missing symbols to the sheet layer by double-clicking an object on the floor plan, selecting Annotation, which will bring you to the Design Layer, and then inserting the missing symbols into the design layer and exiting the annotation window. Another way to deal with this issue is to use the Top/Plan view of the set as the Floor Plan while acknowledging the differences and using the horizontal section view of the set as a reference. Either of the two ways is not ideal, but a temporary fix until a better solution is discovered by VW software developers.

Centerline Vertical Section/Cross Section/Section Plan

The terms ***Centerline Vertical Section***, ***Cross Section***, and ***Section Plan*** share the same definition. Each refers to a vertical cut-through of an entire set or theatre. The cutting line of the Cross Section is the centerline of the stage, looking towards either side of the scenery or theatre.

A Cross Section serves multiple purposes. First, it allows the scenic designer to check the audience's vertical sightlines and determine the height dimensions of the set units. Secondly, it facilitates the scenic designer in setting the trim positions of any hanging or flying pieces of scenery. Finally, it shows the heights of the scenic units in relation to the lighting pipes and instruments that benefit the lighting designer in plotting the lighting instrument positions.

Fig. 7.15 illustrates the employment of cross sections in the process of checking the audience's vertical sightlines, setting the trim positions for the boarders, and placing lighting instruments.

Before CAD programs made their way to the entertainment world, scenic and production designers were asked to provide lighting designers and others in the production team with a centerline vertical section (or cross section) on the most telling

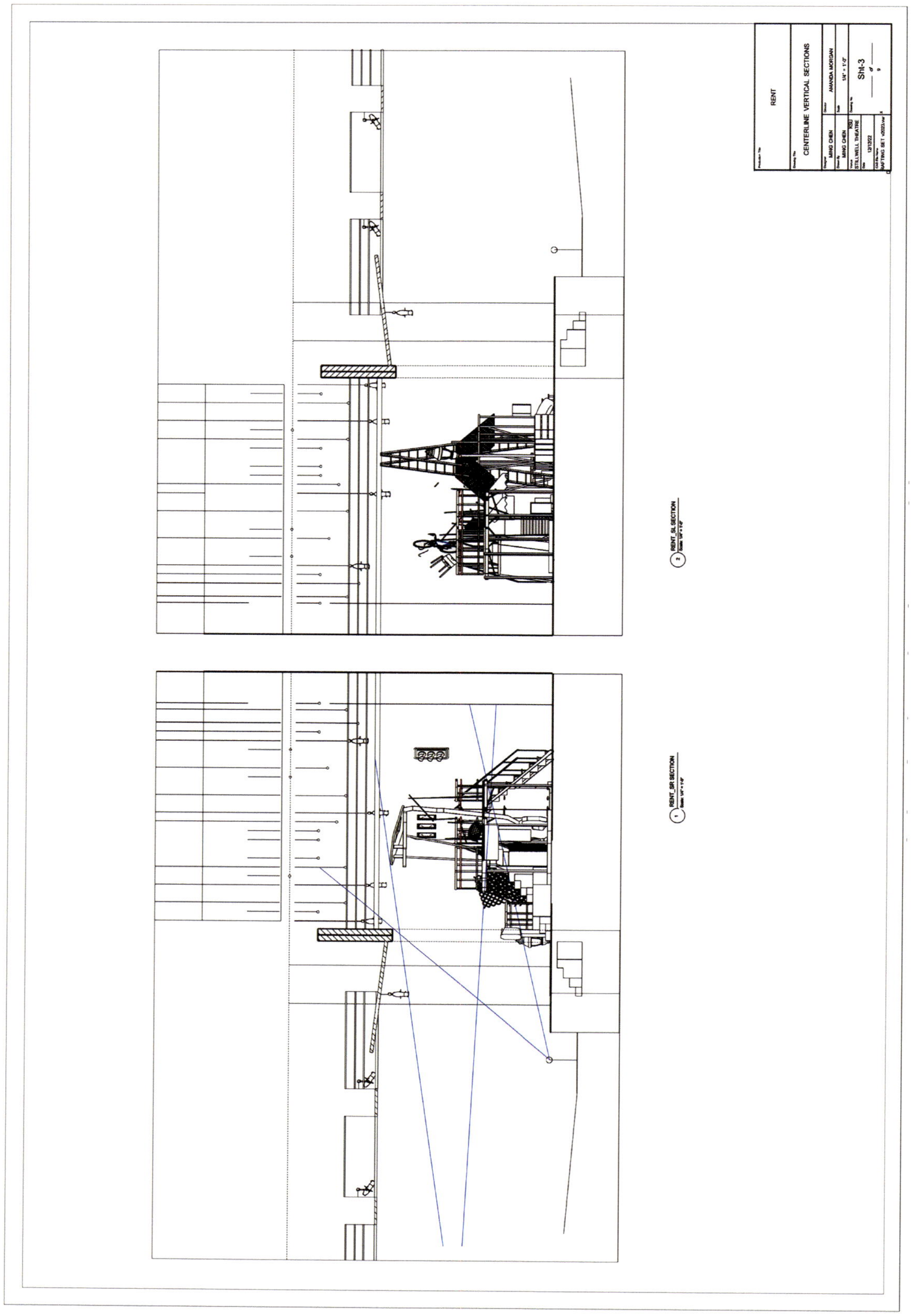

Figure 7.15 *Cross Section Sample.* Cross Sections for the musical production of *Rent* at Kennesaw State University. The SR SECTION is on the left, and the SL SECTION is on the right. Sightlines on the SR SECTION are drawn in BLUE.

side of the set, meaning either SL Section or SR Section. The emergence and rapid advancement of CAD programs have significantly changed the professional practice of the industry. Since it is now so easy to produce Centerline Vertical Sections using CAD programs, it is highly recommended for the scenic and production designers to provide both SL Sections and SR Sections when the sets are asymmetrical, as they usually are. Lighting designers and others in the production team seek as much information as they can get about the space, and the plans by scenic and production designers are the primary source of information on which lighting designers base their creations.

Fig. 7.16 showcases what a ***Hanging Section*** plan looks like.

In this plan, you can see the available battens being designated for specific items that may be flying on/off stage during the performance. Although not seen as often nowadays as other types of plans,

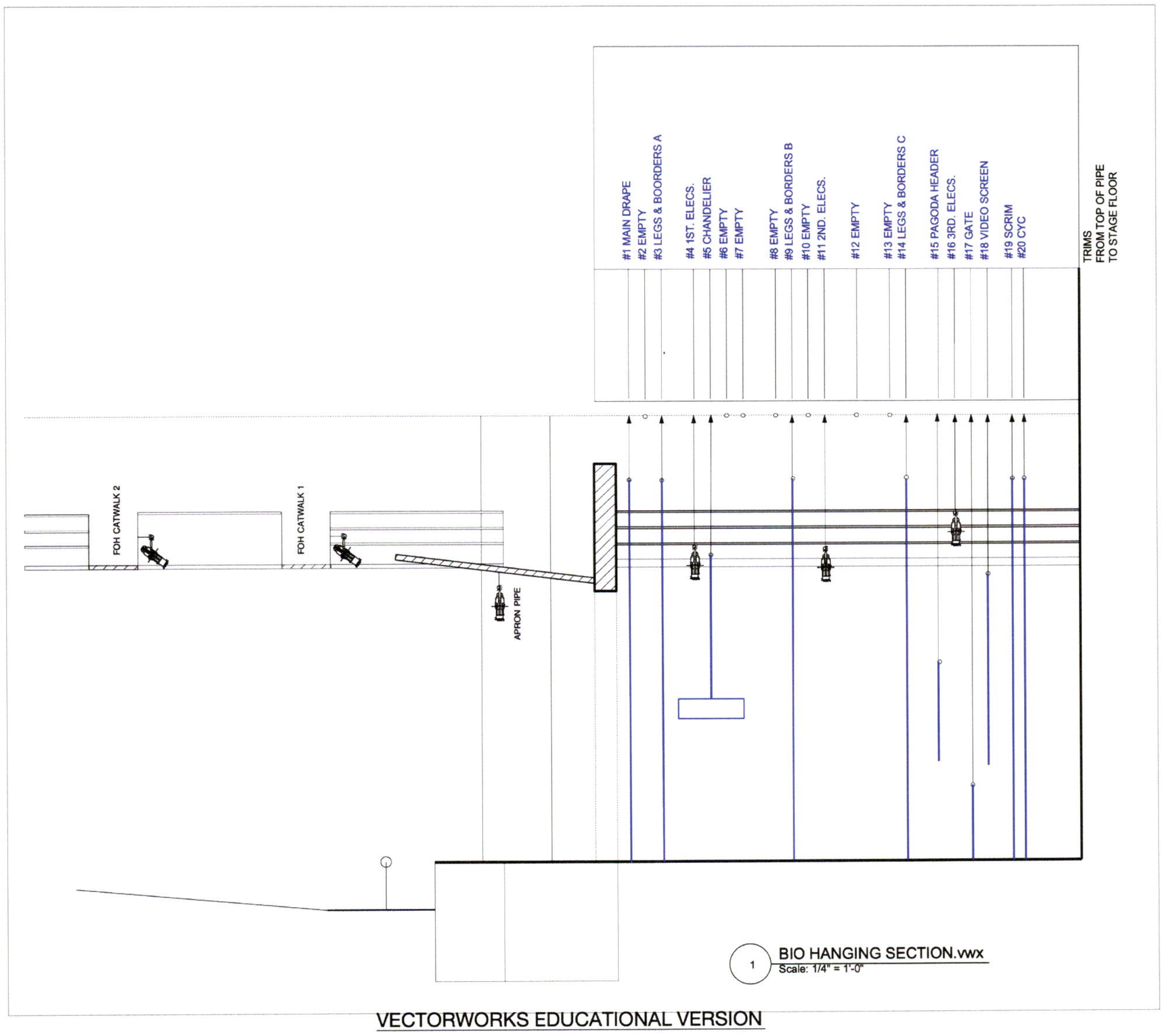

Figure 7.16 *Hanging Section Sample*. A Hanging Section plan created for Kennesaw State University's musical production of *Bring it On*. The hanging scenic pieces are on the lower right side of the drawing, while the item descriptions are on the upper right side of the drawing. Both are highlighted in BLUE.

since two-dimensional sceneries have given way to three-dimensional sceneries (a shift in fashion starting in the early 20th century), this type of plan is helpful for the scenic and production designers to organize the hanging items and spot problems, such as set dimensions, in a more systematic way. In this plan, you can see the depth and height of the hanging pieces to make sure that the space is clear for the hanging pieces to fly in/out, and the gridiron is placed high enough to allow sceneries to be flied all the way out of the audience's sight.

Isometric Views

Although drawings of *isometric* views of a scenic design are not required in a standard set of scenic drafting, they are now often included in the designer's drafting set as these drawings can help the shop technicians to see an image of the end product of their work. In addition, it takes no time for the designers/drafters to produce drawings of *isometric* views in the VW Program. Technique 7 will also include instructions to produce such drawings.

Technique 7 – Drafting

In Vectorworks, the primary functions of Sheet Layers and Viewports are for the designer to generate various technical drawings from 3D models and get the drawings ready for printing. In Technique 7, you will learn to produce Orthographic Projection, Section, Detail, Ground Plan, Centerline Vertical Section, and Isometric View drawings on Sheet Layers and Viewports.

Create Orthographic Projection Drawings

Generate Standard Projection Views

To generate standard Orthographic Projection views of a set unit, do the following:

1. Open the drawing of the stair that you created previously in Chapter 3.
2. Create a new Design Layer and name it "YOUR LAST NAME_ORTHOGRAPHIC PROJECTION."
3. Check to confirm that you are in the Architect workspace, your drawing scale is ½", and your page size is set to US Arch D (36" × 24").
4. Copy and paste the set unit named Stair onto your new design layer.
5. View your set unit in Top/Plan view.
6. Verify that the line representing the front surface of the set unit is parallel with the bottom edge of the drawing area. If not, rotate the object to meet this requirement. (Note: This is an important step to take before generating views because it will tell the computer which side is the front view, and ensure the front view is a straight on, non-perspective projection drawing.)
7. With the object selected, go to View (located on the Top Menu bar) – Create Multiple Viewports… A dialogue box appears.
8. Check "Front," "Top," "Right," and "Right Isometric" views for an object that is symmetrical. Check an additional "left" view for an object that is asymmetrical.
9. Click "OK." Your drawing of the orthographic projection appears on a Sheet Layer.
10. Click on the "Update" button located on the Object Info palette, if it is lit in RED, to update the drawing.
11. Deselect the views by clicking anywhere outside of the views.
12. If needed, drag each view to an appropriate location in relation to other views, while taking into consideration the space needed for dimensioning in between the aligned views.

    Note: Click on a view that you intend to move. Hover your mouse over the view. When a cross mouse-icon appears, click on the view, then press the shift key while dragging the view to ensure that the view moves in alignment with the other view that shares the dimension. As a default, the top view is located on the top of the front view; the right-side view is located on the right side of the front view; the left-side view is located on the left side of the front view; and the right isometric view is located on the upper right corner of all the views combined.

Dimension a Set Unit

To dimension the set unit, do the following:

1. On the Sheet Layer, double-click on a view, and the Edit Viewport dialogue box appears.
2. Check the Annotation and click "OK." You are now in the edit mode of Viewport Annotation.

Note: The beginning users of the VW program often find themselves in a situation where the dimensions of the objects are very small and do not match the dimensions they intended. This is because they have missed this step of dimensioning in the Viewport Annotation window. The scale in the Annotation window is the same as in a Design Layer, while in the Sheet Layer, the scale is always 1:1.

3. In the Viewport Annotation window, zoom in the view of your set unit to a comfortable size for dimensioning.
4. Click on the dimension tool in Tool Sets – Dims/Notes to provide dimensions for this view.

   Note: Remember to put the dimensions of smaller increments closer to the view from which you draw the dimensions and put overall dimension furthest away from the view. Use the second dimensioning mode for Continuous Dimensions and the first dimensioning mode for Single Dimensions. The views should be lined up accurately. Since some dimensions are shared by different views, you should avoid duplicate dimensions that are not necessary.

5. After you have finished dimensioning this view, zoom out to find another view to dimension.

   Note: For the Stair, you can provide width and height dimensions on the front view and depth dimensions on the top view of the stair to streamline and consolidate the dimensions.

Draw an Auxiliary View

1. To draw an Auxiliary View of the slanted plane on the Stair unit, go to the Annotation Edit window and click on Rectangle Tool in the Basic palette to select it.
2. Click on "Three Point Rotated Mode" located on the Mode bar and draw a reference rectangle, which will give you the reference to the length, the right angle, and the location needed for your Auxiliary View.
3. Alongside the reference rectangle, draw another rectangle that shares the length dimension with the slanted line and the depth dimension with the width of the short wall in front view. Adjust the dimensions in the Object Info palette if needed.
4. After the shape of the slanted wall surface is established, delete the reference rectangle and add dimensions to that view using the Unconstrained Linear Dimension Tool located in Tool Set – Dims/Notes.

Create Notes and Labels

1. While the drawing is still in the Annotation edit window, make notes where needed.

   Note: Use 12 pt. font size and capital letters to make notes. For local notes, use a leader line and an arrowhead to point out the parts that the notes are referring to. General Notes can stand alone. They are usually located on the top right corner of the drawing sheet.

2. While the drawing is still in the Annotation edit window, label the drawing with a drawing title placed below all the views of the object combined (using 18 pt. font size; capital letters; bold, underline for the drawing title).
3. After you have finished dimensions, notes, and labels, click the "Exit Viewport Annotation" button to exit the editing mode.

Install a Title Block

To install a title block for the drawing, refer to the section named Create a Title Block for the Drawing in Technique 6, Chapter 6.

Export and Save the Drawing

1. When you are ready to export or print your drawing, zoom in your drawing to its fullest size on your VW window.
2. Go to File – Export – Export to PDF file. A dialog window pops up.
3. Under Export Range, select "Current View."
4. Under Resolution, type in "200" DPI. Click "Export."
5. Save the file to your computer desktop for easy access.

Create a Detailed View

To create a detailed view, do the following:

1. Go to File – New… – Create blank document.
2. Right click (PC) or Ctrl+Click (Mac) to set the Active Layer Scale to ¼″ scale.
3. Click on the Symbol Tool in the Basic palette.

4. In Resource Manager, search for "ArchElement Haddonstone Corinthian Column M5" and double-click on the column icon to select it.
5. In the Top/Plan view, place the column in the drawing area.
6. Go to the Top Menu – View – Create Multiple Viewport…
7. When a dialog box opens, select Top and Front views and click "OK." The Orthographic Projection views now appear on a Sheet Layer.
8. Invoke a shape tool in the Basic palette to draw a shape on the part of the column that you want to zoom in.
9. Go to the Attributes palette and select "none" in the Fill slot to reveal the part you selected.
10. While the shape is still selected, go to Top Menu – View – Create Detail Viewport. A dialog window appears.
11. In this window, insert "DETAIL" in the "Drawing Title" slot, change the Scale to 1″ = 1′-0″, and click "OK" to exit the window. The detailed drawing shows up on the same Sheet Layer as the Orthographic Projection drawing.
12. Move to place the detailed drawing next to the drawing from which the detailed is taken.
13. Use the same shape tool that you used previously and draw the shape around the Detail to enclose it.
14. Select "None" in the Fill slot (Attribute Palette) to reveal the Detail.
15. You can now add dimensions, notations, and a sheet title to complete the Detail.

Create Section Drawings

Create a Model for Set Unit 1

1. Create a New Blank document and set the scale to ½″ and the document size to US Arch D.
2. Draw a rectangle: 7′ (w) × 6′ (h)
3. Align with the upper-left corner of the previous rectangle, draw a square: 5′ × 5′.
4. Double-click on the Offset Tool in the Basic palette. A dialog box appears.
5. Check Offset by Distance, insert 6″ to the Distance slot, and click "OK."
6. Click on the 5′ × 5′ square to create a smaller square.
7. While the square is still selected, extrude it to 7′, and set the Bot Z to 1′ 6″.
8. Select the larger square, extrude it to 8′, and set the Bot Z to 1′.
9. Select the rectangle, and extrude it to 1′.
10. Select both squares. Go to Top Menu – Model – Subtract Solids… When the large square is lit in RED, click "OK."
11. Select all the shapes. Go to Top Menu – Model – Add Solids.
12. Observe Set Unit 1 in an isometric view.

Generate Orthographic Projection Drawings

1. Go to the Top Menu – View – Create Multiple Viewports… A dialog box opens.
2. Click on Third Angle Projection and check Front, Top, Right, and Left views, and click "OK." The views you selected appear on a Sheet Layer.
3. While the views are still selected, go to the Object Info palette and click on "Update" (if it is in RED) to update the views.
4. Move the views to comfortable positions with space for dimensions and notations in mind.

Create Horizontal and Vertical Section Drawings

Generate a Horizontal Section View

1. Make the Design Layer the active layer.
2. Switch to Top/Plan view to verify that the line representing the front façade of the set unit is parallel with the bottom edge of the sheet. If not, rotate the set unit to meet this requirement.
3. Go to Top Menu – View – Create Horizontal Section Viewport… A dialog window opens.
4. Make the following selections:
   a. Create on Layer: Sheet Layer-1
   b. Confirm that the "Create drawing label" box is checked.
   c. Drawing Number: AA
   d. Drawing Title: HORIZONTAL SECTION
   e. Uncheck both "Display planar objects" and "Display 2D components."
   f. Cut Plane: 4′0″
5. Click on the "Advanced Section Properties" button. Another dialog window appears.
6. Under the Attributes tab, in Attribute Class dropdown menu, select "New Class…"
7. In the popup window, name the class "SECTIONS" and click "OK." An "Edit Class(es)…" window pops up. Make the following selections:
   a. Check the "Use at Creation" box.
   b. Fill – Style: Hatch
   c. Click on the arrows by the hatch icon and select "Cast Iron HF".

   d. Pen Thickness: 1.00
   e. Click "OK" to close the window. The Name "SECTIONS" appears in the Attribute Class slot.
8. Under Fill, check the "Use Class" box, and select "SECTIONS."
9. Under Line Style, check the "Use Class" box, select "SECTIONS," and click "OK" to close the window.
10. Click "OK" again to exit the "Create Horizontal Section Viewport" window. The Horizontal Section view appears on the same Sheet Layer where the Orthographic Projection is located.
11. Update the drawings and move the Horizontal Section view below and in alignment with the front view.

Generate a Vertical Section View

1. Make your Design Layer the active Layer.
2. In the Top/Plan view, verify that the line representing the front façade of the set unit is parallel with the bottom edge of the sheet. If not, rotate the set unit to meet this requirement.
3. Go to Top Menu – View – Create Section Viewport…
4. On your drawing area, make the cut for the Section view by drawing a straight line that starts with a click above the object but meets its centerline, going downwards through the object and making the second click on a point below the object.
5. Make a turn towards the left side of the object (the big arrow in the middle of the drawing is pointing towards the direction the section is taken), and then make the third click (a double click). A dialog window appears.
6. In this window, make the following selections:
   a. Create on Layer: Sheet Layer-1
   b. Confirm that the "Create drawing label" box is checked.
   c. Drawing Number: BB
   d. Drawing Title: VERTICAL SECTION
   e. Uncheck both "Display planar objects" and "Display 2D components."
7. Click on the "Advanced Section Properties" button. Another dialog window appears.
8. Under the Attributes tab, check to confirm that the Attribute Class is set on "SECTIONS," Fill – Use Class is set on "SECTIONS," and Line Style is also set on "SECTIONS," and then click "OK" to close the window.
9. Click "OK" again to exit the "Create Section Viewport" window. The Vertical Section view appears on the same Sheet Layer where the Orthographic Projection is located.
10. Update the drawings and move the Vertical Section view on the right side of and in alignment with the right view.

Note: As an alternative to the method used to generate horizontal and vertical Section Views explained above, you can generate these views using the Clip Tube command. The following steps explain the process of generating a Vertical Section view with the Clip Cube command.

1. Switch back to Design Layer.
2. In Top/Plan view, draw a vertical reference cutting line in the center of the object. In fact, you can draw the cutting line in any position as needed, as long as the position of this cutting line is reflected accurately on the front view of the drawing in Sheet Layer.
3. Switch to the Right Isometric view and select the object.
4. Go to Top Menu – View – Clip Cube, a transparent box will appear around the selected object.

   Note: To install an icon of Clip Cube for easy access to the tool, click on the downward arrow located at the furthest right of the Mode bar and select Clip Cube from the dropdown list. With the Tool on the Mode bar, you can turn on and off the tool anytime you want.

5. Click on one of the edges of the box; the edges of the box are lit in RED.
6. You can now click and push/pull the right side of the box to let the right side of your object meet the centerline that you created in Top/Plan view.
7. Use the Selection Tool to select the right surface of the box.
8. When the surface is lit in RED, Right-Click on Mac or Ctl+Click on PC to select "Created Section Viewport…" at the bottom of the dropdown list.
9. You are now in the same "Create Section Viewport" window as before.
10. Follow Steps 6–10 in the previous section named "Generate a Vertical Section View" to complete the drawing of a Vertical Section View on a Sheet Layer.

Draw and Label the Cutting-Plane Lines

1. Go to the Attributes palette, in the Pen dropdown menu, select Line Type.
2. Click on the slot below to select "ISO 09 Long Dashed Double-Short Dashed."
3. Click on "2D Polygon Tool" in the Basic palette to invoke the tool.
4. Draw a horizontal cutting-plane line alongside the vertical centerline of Set Unit 1 (with small right-angle returns at both ends pointing downward) and install arrows on both end of the line.
5. Label the line "A" at the beginning and ending of the line (font size: 18 pt.).
6. Draw a vertical cutting-plane line alongside the horizontal centerline of Set Unit 1 (with small right-angle returns at both ends pointing left) and install arrows on both ends of the line.
7. Label the line "B" at the beginning and ending of the line (font size: 18 pt.).
8. Select both cutting plane lines and change the lines to a heavy-weight line in the Attributes palette.
9. Put the drawing title "SET UNIT 1" below all the views combined (font size: 36 pt.). Your Section drawings are now complete.

Create Floor Plans

Note: If you want to create a Composite Floor Plan for everyone to see, you can create labels and dimensions, as well as assign hanging positions either on a Design Layer before generating a Horizontal Section view on a Sheet Layer or create them directly on a Sheet Layer in the Viewport Annotation (Edit) window after the view is generated. To access the Viewport Annotation (Edit) window, you just need to double-click on one of the components in the drawing, select "Annotations," and click "OK." The process of creating labels and dimensions and assigning hanging positions are the same as detailed in Technique 6 of the previous chapter.

That said, if you want to customize floor plans for individuals or subgroups, it is recommended that you create these components in a Design Layer and put them in different Classes and Sub-Classes before generating Horizonal Sections on Sheet Layers. In this way, you will avoid repetitive processes and have better control over what to show in a specific type of Ground Plan.

Produce a Composite Floor Plan

Preparation

1. Open an existing set model created in a theatre space, with labels, dimensions, hanging positions, and standard masking devices installed. (Note: See Technique 4 for instructions on installing masking devices. See Technique 6 for instructions on creating labels and dimensions and assigning hanging positions.) You may use the Mock Box Set that you created in Technique 6 for this exercise.
2. Set the model in the Top/Plan view.
3. In the Navigation palette, put the set model in an independent layer, name the layer "SET" if the model is not already on a Layer named "SET," and make it the active layer.
4. Make all Layers and Classes that you want to see on the Composite Floor Plan Visible (others invisible).
5. Select "Show/Snap/Modify Others in Navigation – Layer Options" dropdown menu.
6. In the Attributes palette, check to see if the Fill slot of any walking surface is solid. If so, change it to "None," as this will allow the 2D dimensions and labels to show up in the Horizontal Section.
7. If you have labels created on the top of a furniture piece, double-click on the piece to get into the Annotation Edit window. Then change the fill of the furniture pieces to "None."
8. Make sure that none of the 2D elements that you want to show on your Floor Plan are accidentally set on "Screen" Plane," because if they are on "Screen "Plane, they will not appear on your Floor Plan after the drawing is generated on a Sheet Layer. If they are assigned to the "Screen" Layer (shown in the Object Info palette), reassign them to the Design Layer before generating a Horizontal Section drawing.

   Note: In Technique 6, we have introduced the process of using the "View – Create Viewport…" command to generate a Top/Plan view of a set model on a Sheet Layer. The steps below demonstrate the process of using the "View – Create Horizontal Section Viewport…" command to generate a Floor Plan (Horizontal Section) on a Sheet Layer.

Generate a Horizontal Section View

To generate a Horizontal Section View from a 3D model, proceed as follows:

1. In Architect Workspace, go to View – Create Horizontal Section Viewport…
2. When a "Create Horizontal Section Viewport" window appears, make the following selections:
   a. In the "Create on Layer" dropdown menu, select "New Sheet Layer…"
   b. When a New Sheet Layer dialog box appears, in the Sheet Title slot, give a title to the drawing (E.G., MOCK BOX SET_FLOOR PLAN).
   c. Check the "Edit Properties after Creation" box and click "OK." The Edit Sheet Layer dialog window appears.
   d. In this window, change Raster Rendering DPI to 150.
   e. Click on the Page Setup button.
   f. When the Page Setup dialog window opens, confirm that the drawing size is set to US Arch D and click "OK" to exit the Page Setup window.
   g. Click "OK" again to exit the Edit Sheet Layer dialog window.
   h. In Create the Horizontal Section Viewport dialog window, insert "MOCK BOX SET_COMPOSIT FLOOR PLAN" in the Drawing Title slot.
   i. Make sure that the Scale is set to a ¼" scale and the cut plane is set to 4′0″. You may change the cut plane to a different height if needed by clicking on Cut Plane and Extents… and making a choice.
   j. Click "OK" to exit the dialogue window. Your Floor Plan (Horizontal Section) now appears in a new sheet layer ready for exporting, saving, and printing. (Note: In this Horizontal Section, everything else, but the chandelier, remain in place, because the chandelier is above the 4′ cutting plane)

(Note: If you want the Section to conform with the conventional scenic drafting standard, click on the button named Advanced Horizontal Section Properties… and follow the instructions in the section named Create Horizontal and Vertical Section Drawings, *Generate a Horizonal Section View*, steps 7–11.)

Produce a Director's Floor Plan

Note: As stipulated previously in this chapter, different individuals and subgroups in a production team will be interested in a different set of information on a scenic designer's Floor Plan. If a Composite Floor Plan contains too much information and appears to be too crowded, spreading information on different versions of customized Floor Plans might be a wise solution. The instructions below provide a sample of such a customized Floor Plan.

1. Make the SET Layer as the active Layer.
2. Double-click on the Class Icon located in the Navigation palette.
3. Create the following new Classes and Sub-Classes:
   a. DIMENSION – SET POSITIONS
   b. DIMENSION – WALKING SURFACES
   c. LABEL – WALLS
   d. LABEL – FLATS
   e. LABEL – FURNITURE
4. Reassign the components to the new Classes and Sub-Classes:
   a. Select all the dimensions that you drew for set positions and reassign them to "DIMENSION – SET POSITIONS."
   b. Select all the dimensions that you drew for walking surfaces and reassign them to "DIMENSION – WALKING SURFACES."
   c. Select all the labels that you drew for the walls and reassign them to "LABEL – WALLS."
   d. Select all the labels that you drew for the flats and reassign them to "LABEL – FLATS."
   e. Select all the labels that you drew for the furniture pieces and reassign them to "LABEL – FURNITURE."
5. In the Navigation palette, click on the Class icon if it is not already selected, and make the following sub-classes invisible:
   a. DIMENSION – SET POSITIONS
   b. LABEL – WALLS
   c. LABEL – FLATS
6. Go to Top Menu – View – Create Horizontal Section Viewport… A dialog window shows up.
7. In the "Create on Layer" dropdown menu, select "New Sheet Layer…"
8. When a New Sheet Layer window pops up, insert "MOCK BOX SET – DIRECTOR'S FLOOR PLAN" as the Sheet Title and click "OK."

9. When the "Edit Sheet Layer" window appears, insert 150 in the "Raster Rendering DPL" slot and click "OK" and "OK" again to exit the windows. The Director's Floor Plan, a less crowded and more focused version of the plan, is now on a Sheet Layer and ready for exporting, saving, and printing.

Create Centerline Vertical Sections

To produce Cross Sections from a 3D model, perform the following steps:

Create SR Section

1. In the Navigation palette, make the SECTION (theatre section) Layer the active Layer and select "Active Only" in the Layer Option dropdown menu.
2. Check to see if the Section drawing is right side up. If not, rotate it so it is right side up.
3. Click on View located on the Top Menu bar. In the dropdown menu, select "Create Viewport…" A dialog box appears.
4. In the Create Layer dropdown menu, select "New Sheet Layer…" Another dialog box appears.
5. Give a title to the Drawing (e.g., MOCK BOX SET_SECTIONS), check the "Edit Properties After Creation" box, and click "OK." An Edit Sheet Layer window appears.
6. Change the Raster Rendering DPI to 150 and click "OK" to exit the window.
7. In the Create Viewport window, check the "Create drawing label" box, insert "MOCK BOX SET_SR SECTION" in the Drawing Title slot, and click "OK."
8. A new Sheet Layer appears with the Theatre SR Section drawing placed on it.
9. Make the SET Layer as the active Layer, the THEATRE Layer gray, the HORIZONTAL MASKING Layer, and the SECTION Layer invisible.
10. Go to Navigation palette, in Layer Options dropdown menu, select "Show/Snap/Modify Others."
11. On the Set Layer, draw a line aligned with the last batten position of the Flying Gallery in the width of a backdrop (52′-0″) if it does not already exist.
12. Extrude this line into a 3D Cyc (24′-0″).
13. Again, on the Set Layer, draw a line that coincides with the centerline of the Theatre Plan.
14. Make the THEATRE Layer invisible.
15. Go to Top Menu – View – Create Section Viewport…
16. Click on the top of the Centerline (above the Cyc line). Drag your mouse down along the Centerline to anywhere below the set and make the second click. Lead your mouse horizontally in the direction of Stage Right (press the SHIFT key while dragging the mouse) and make a third click (double click). A dialogue window appears.
17. In this window, make the following selections:
    a. Confirm that the "Create on Layer" slot is set on the MOCK BOX SET_SECTIONS sheet layer.
    b. Uncheck the "Create Drawing Label" box if it is checked.
    c. Make sure that the Scale is set on a ¼″ scale.
    d. To use VW default Section Style for your SR Section, click "OK" to exit the "Create Section Viewports" dialog window. Your SR Section drawing of the set now appears on the MOCK BOX SET_ SECTIONS Sheet Layer.
18. Move the Section drawing of your set so that the bottom of the set is aligned with the stage level and the Cyc line is aligned with the last batten position of the Flying Gallery, and group the two drawings together as one.
19. Draw a rectangle around it, group the drawing and the rectangle together, and move the drawing to the upper right part of the drafting sheet. Your SR Section is now complete.

Create SL Section

1. In the Navigation palette, make the SECTION layer the active Layer again and select "Active Only" in the Layer Options dropdown menu.
2. Check to ensure that the Section drawing is right side up.
3. Select the Section drawing.
4. Go to the Mirror Tool in the Basic palette and draw a mirror image of the Section drawing.
5. Select the new Section drawing and cut it.
6. Go to the Navigation palette and double-click on the Layer icon to create a new Layer named "SL SECTION."
7. On the new Design Layer, paste your Section drawing of the theatre.
8. While the drawing is still selected. Go to Top Menu – View – Create Viewport… A dialog box appears.
9. In this window, confirm that the "Create on Layer" slot is set on the MOCK BOX SET_SECTIONS sheet layer.
10. Check the "Create Drawing Label" box.

11. Give a title to the Drawing (e.g., MOCK BOX SET_SL SECTION) and click "OK" to exit the dialog box.
12. The Theatre SL Section drawing appears on the same Sheet Layer as MOCK BOS SET_SR SECTION. Move the SL SECTION to the upper left part of the drafting sheet.
13. Make your Set Layer an active layer and other Layers invisible.

    Note: Generally speaking, in theatre, the proportion of scenery is seen in relation to the actors. Before we generate the SL Section, let us bring a human figure into the scene. In Resource Manager, search for "3D People." When the figures appear in the Resource Manage window, drag-and-drop one of the figures onto your drawing area (on the SL side of the stage). If an Import Resource dialog box appears, click "OK" to accept the default.

14. Click on View located on the Top Menu bar. In the dropdown menu, select "Create Section Viewport…"
15. Click on the top of the Centerline (above the Cyc line). Drag your mouse down along the Centerline to anywhere below the set and make the second click. Lead your mouse horizontally in the direction of Stage Left and make a third click (double click). A dialogue window appears.
16. In this window, make the following selections:
    a. Confirm that the "Create on Layer" slot is set on the MOCK BOX SET_SECTIONS sheet layer.
    b. Uncheck the "Create Drawing Label" box and click "OK" to exit the "Create Section Viewports" dialog window. Your SL Section drawing of the set now appears on the MOCK BOX SET_ SECTIONS Sheet Layer.
17. Move your set Section drawing so that the bottom of the set is aligned with the stage level and the Cyc line is aligned with the last batten position of the Flying Gallery.
18. Draw a box around the drawings and group the three together as one.
19. Your SL SECTION is now complete. You can add a Title Block to the Sections.

Create Isometric View Drawings

1. Make the Set Layer the active layer and select "Active Only" in the Layer Options dropdown menu.
2. Go to the Navigation palette and click on the "Class" icon. Make all the 2D Classes, such as DIMENSIONS and LABELS invisible.
3. Create a new class and name it "LABELS-CROSS SECTIONS."
4. Select the two Cross Section labels and reassign them to "LABELS-CROSS SECTIONS" class and make this class invisible.
5. Go to the View bar and make the following selections:
    a. Current View: Right Isometric
    b. Current Projection: Perspective (If a camera frame shows up, go to File – Document Settings – Document Preferences and turn off the "Crop perspective view" box and click "OK" to make the frame go away.)
    c. Current Render Mode: Hidden Line
6. Use the Flyover Tool located in the Basic palette to slightly adjust the model if needed for an optimal viewing angle.
7. Go to Top Menu – View – Create Viewport… A dialog window opens.
8. In this window, make the following selections:
    a. Create on Layer: New Sheet Layer… and name the Sheet Layer "MOCK BOX SET_ISOMETRIC VIEWS."
    b. Check the "Create drawing label" box.
    c. Drawing Number: 1
    d. Drawing Title: RIGHT ISOMETRIC VIEW
    e. Click "OK" to close the window. The Right Isometric view of your set model is now displayed on a Sheet Layer named "MOCK BOX SET_ISOMETRIC VIEWS."
9. Make a frame around the drawing, group the frame and the drawing, and place the view on the right side of the sheet.
10. Make the Set layer the active layer again.
11. View the model in Left-Isometric view. Slightly adjust the model if needed.
12. Go to Top Menu – View – Create Viewport… A dialog window opens.
13. In this window, make the following selections:
    a. Create on Layer: MOCK BOX SET_ISOMETRIC VIEWS
    b. Check the "Create drawing label" box.
    c. Drawing Number: 2
    d. Drawing Title: LEFT ISOMETRIC VIEW
    e. Click "OK" to close the window. The Left Isometric view of your set model is now displayed on the same Sheet Layer as the Right Isometric view of your set model.

14. Make a frame around this drawing, group the drawing and the frame, and place the view on the left side of the sheet.
    a. Create a title "MOCK BOX SET_ISOMETRIC VIEWS" in 36 pt. font for the two drawings and put the title below the two views combined. The Isometric View drawings are now complete. You can add a Title Block to this sheet.

Project #4: Producing Technical Drawings

Objectives

The purpose of this project is for you to

- demonstrate your understanding of the method, process, and technique of using Sheet Layer and Viewport to transfer a 3D model into various types of technical drawings, including Orthographic Projection, Section, Detail, Ground Plan, Centerline Vertical Section (with a human figure), and Isometric View.
- Produce dimensions, labels, notations, and title blocks for technical drawings that comply with drafting conventions recommended by USITT.
- practice the skills of checking audience sightlines, assigning battens, and creating masking devices in technical drawings.
- develop patience, concentration, attention to details, and professionalism.

Tasks

Your task for this project is to produce a set of technical drawings, namely drafting, based on the set model that you created in Project #3. This includes:

- use Sheet Layer and Viewport to generate a Composite Ground Plan (Wireframe), two Centerline Vertical Sections (Wireframe with a human figure), and two Isometric Views (Hidden Line) of your set model (Mock Box Set).
- produce Orthographic Projection views for a single set unit of your choice (also from your set model) and a Detail view for a part of that set unit.
- Conform with drafting conventions discussed in Chapters 6 and 7 in creating dimensions, labels, notations, and title blocks for your technical drawings.
- check audience sightlines, put masking device(s) in positions where needed, and assign battens for the hanging pieces of your design.
- save your vwx file(s) on your computer.
- export your drafting set to PDF files and save them on your computer. This set of drawing includes 1) a Composite Ground Plan of your set model, 2) two Centerline Vertical Sections (SR Section and SL Section) of your set model, 3) two Isometric Views SR and SL) of your set model, 4) Orthographic Projection drawings of a single set unit selected from your set model, and 5) a Detail view blowing up a part of this set unit.

Required Equipment and Materials

To complete this project, you will need a computer with internet access and Vectorworks Version 2023 installed.

Drawing Scales

¼″ = 1′-0″ for the Ground Plan and Centerline Vertical Sections
½″ = 1′-0″ for Orthographic Projection views
1″ = 1′-0″ for the Detail view

Evaluation Criteria

Problem-Solving

1. The work shows a successful transformation from a 3D model to a Composite Ground Plan, two Centerline Vertical Sections (SR and SL), two Isometric Views (SR and SL) drawings, Orthographic Projections of a set unit, and a Detail view of that unit, all being drafted on Sheet Layers.

Mechanics

1. The work complies with drafting conventions for dimension, label, notation, and title block.
2. It solves the problem of audience sightlines.
3. It provides sufficient masking device(s).

Requirements and Presentation

1. The work is complete and meets the required components and format.
2. It is executed with accuracy and professionalism.

Student Work Samples

Figs. 7.17–7.24 showcase the student work samples for Project #4 – Producing Technical Drawings.

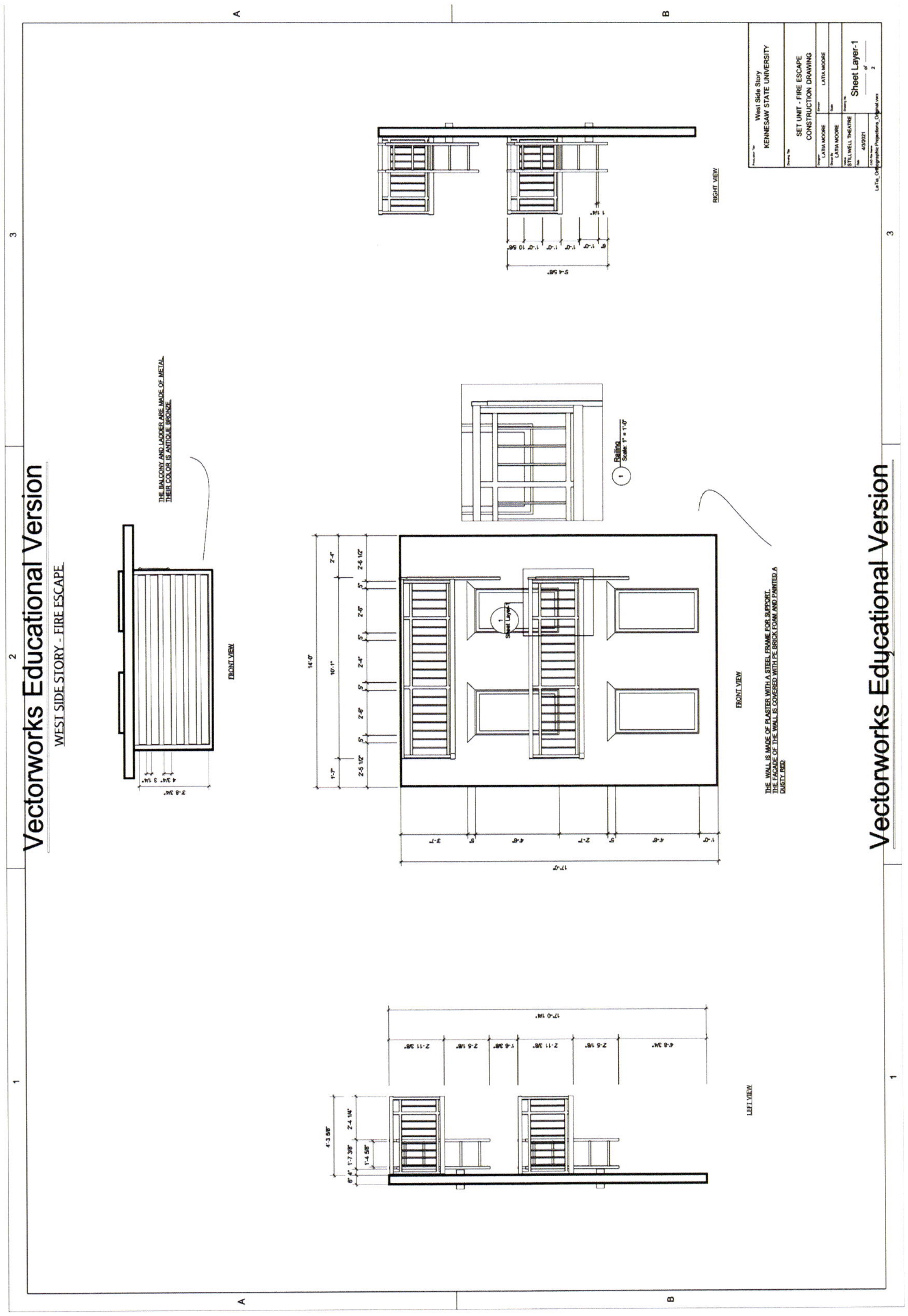

Figure 7.17 *West Side Story_Orthographic Projection*. An Orthographic Projection drawing of a set unit designed and drafted by LaTia Cunningham-Moore for *West Side Story*. This drawing is for the class project titled Producing Technical Drawings.

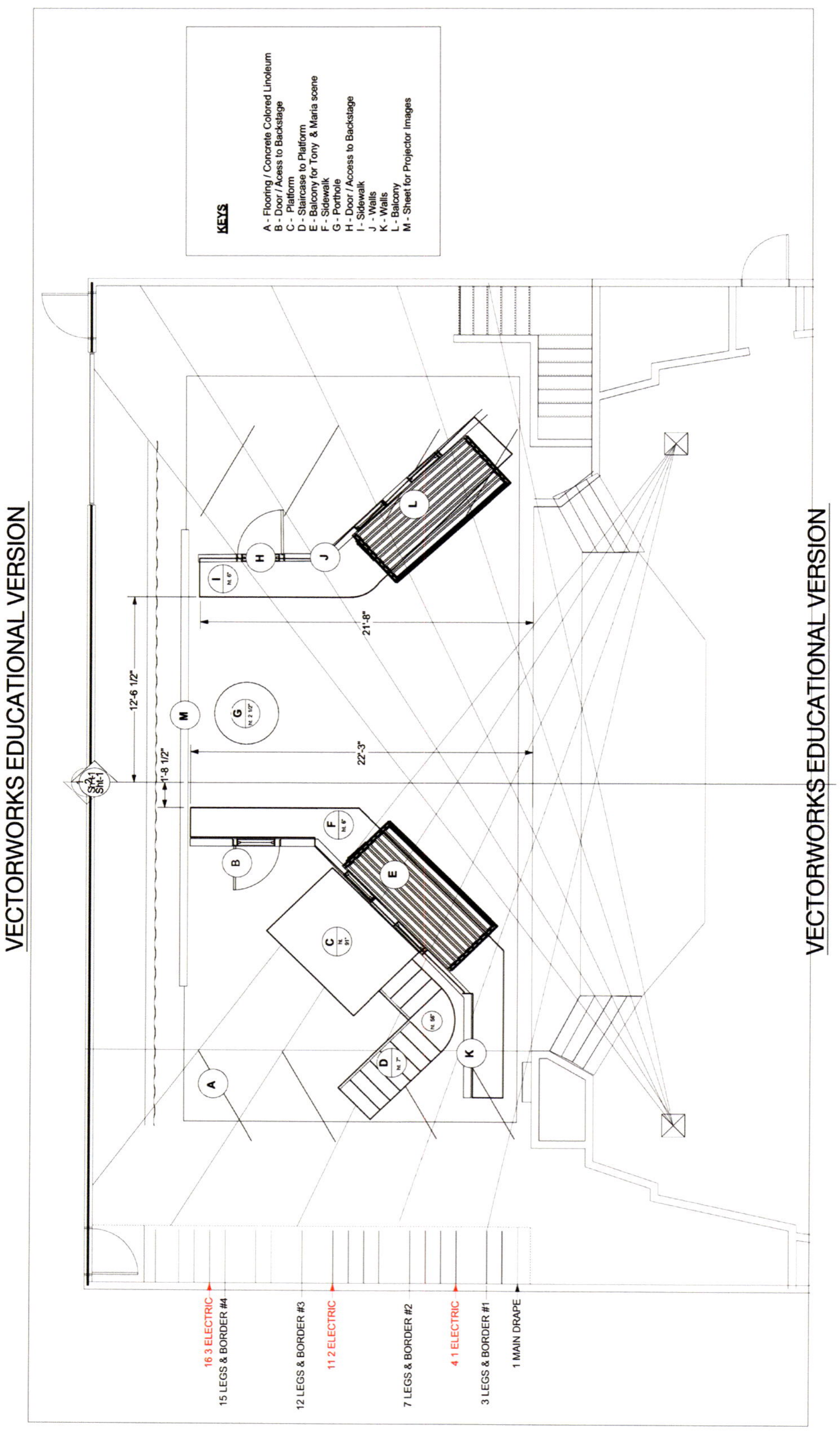

Figure 7.18 *West Side Story_Top/Plan View*. The Top/Plan view drawing of a set design created and drafted by LaTia Cunningham-Moore for *West Side Story*. This drawing is for the class project titled Producing Technical Drawings.

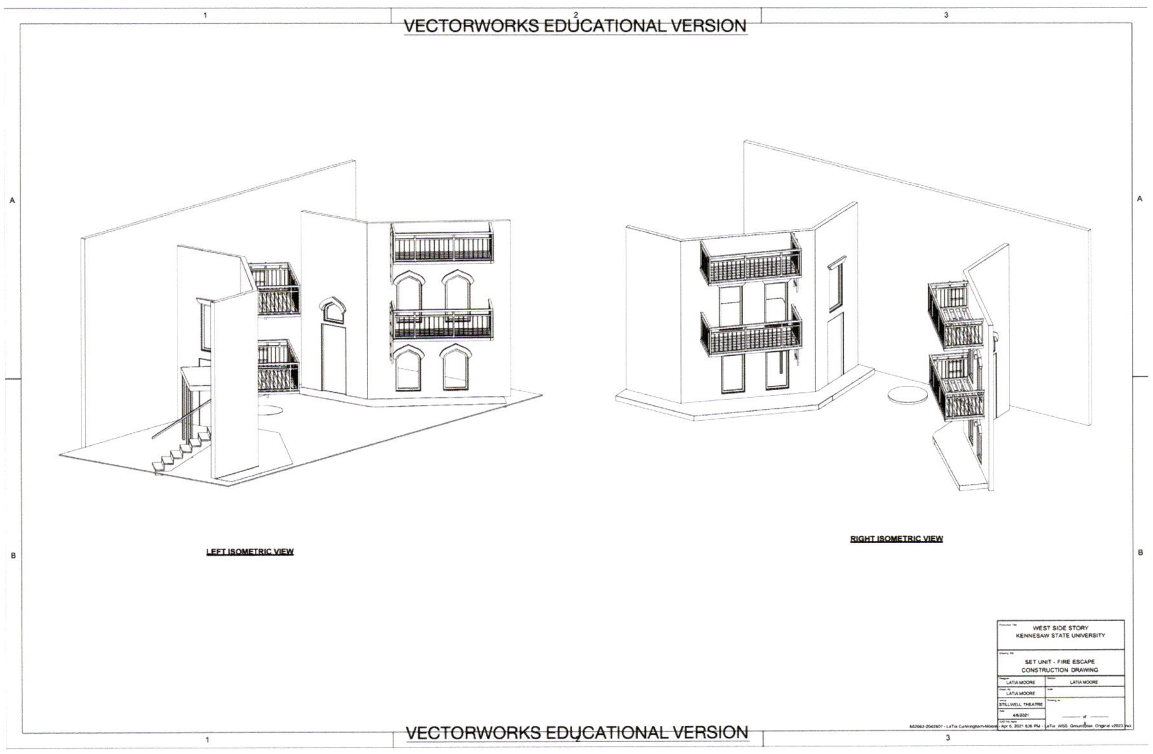

Figure 7.19 *West Side Story_Isometric Views*. Two isometric views of a set design created and drafted by LaTia Cunningham-Moore for *West Side Story*. This drawing is for the class project titled Producing Technical Drawings.

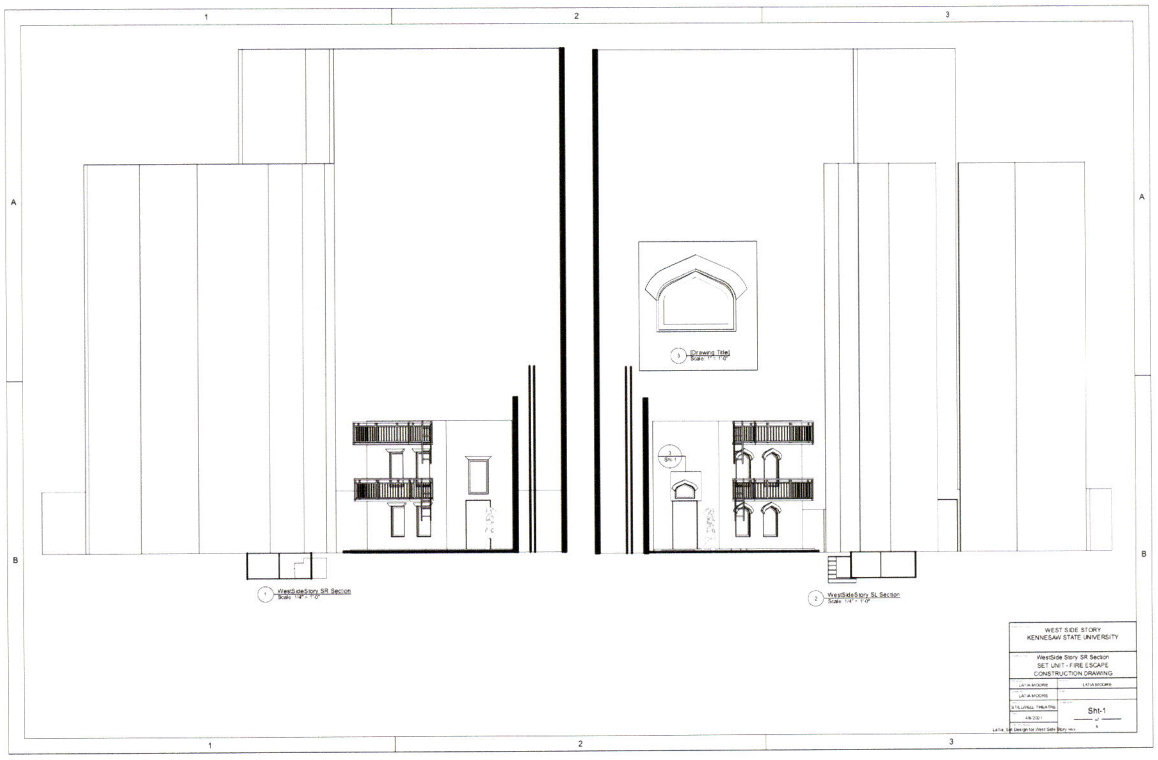

Figure 7.20 *West Side Story_Sections*. The SR and SL sections of a set design created and drafted by LaTia Cunningham-Moore for *West Side Story*. This drawing is for the class project titled Producing Technical Drawings.

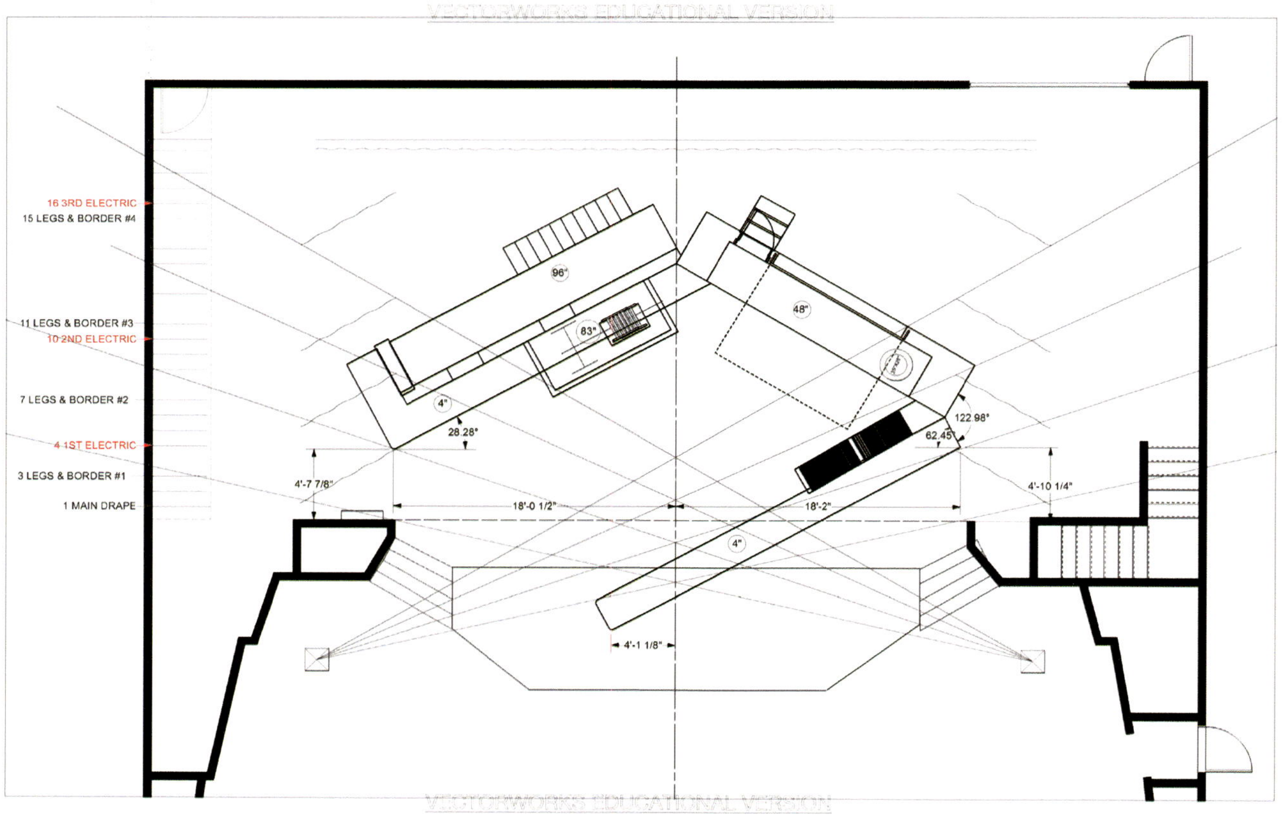

Figure 7.21 *West Side Story_Floor Plan*. The floor plan of a set design created and drafted by Mace Gallagher for *West Side Story*. This drawing is for the class project titled Producing Technical Drawings.

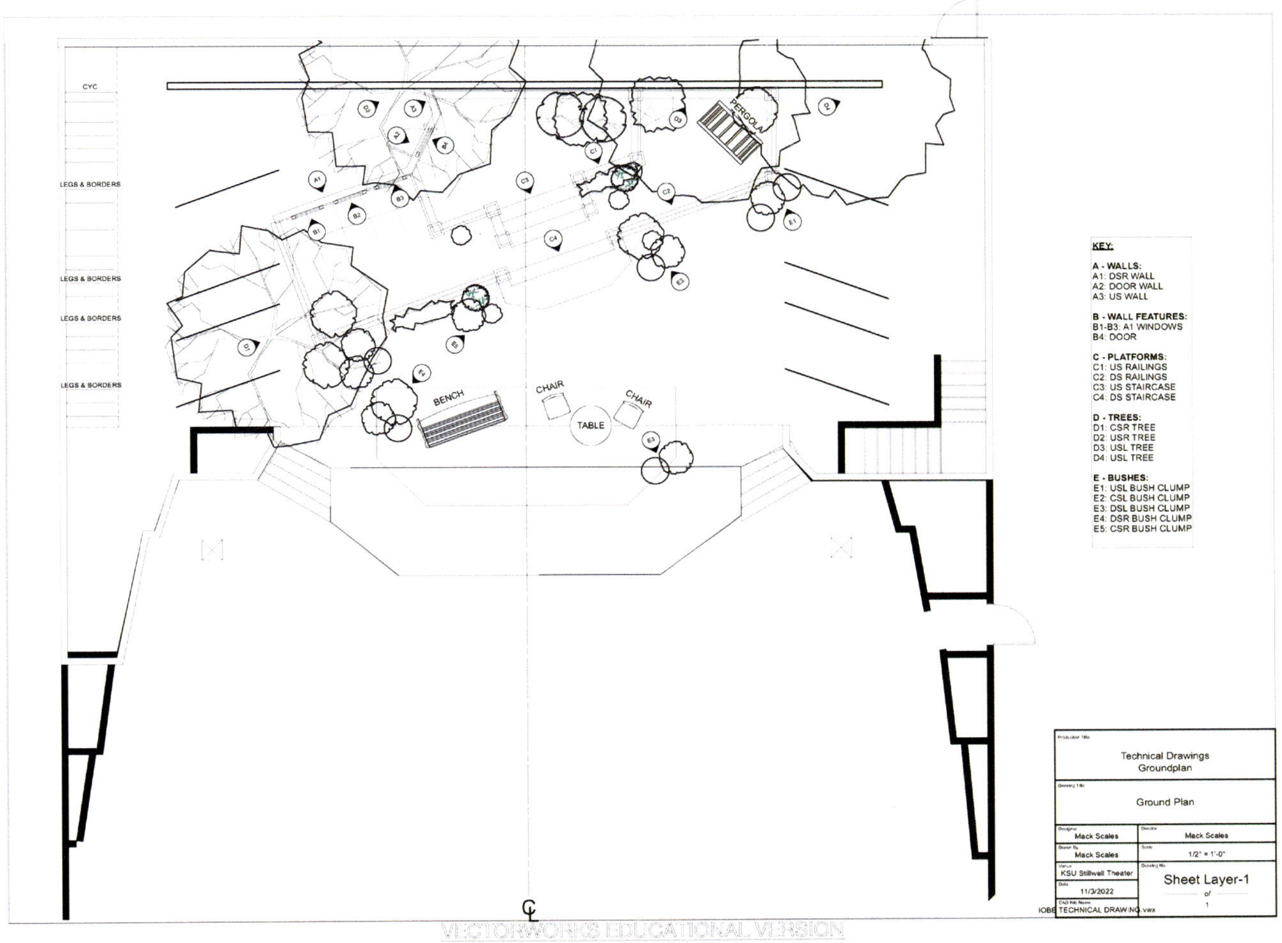

Figure 7.22 *The Importance of Being Earnest_Ground Plan*. The ground plan of a set design created and drafted by Mackenzie Scales for *The Importance of Being Earnest*. This drawing is for the class project titled Producing Technical Drawings.

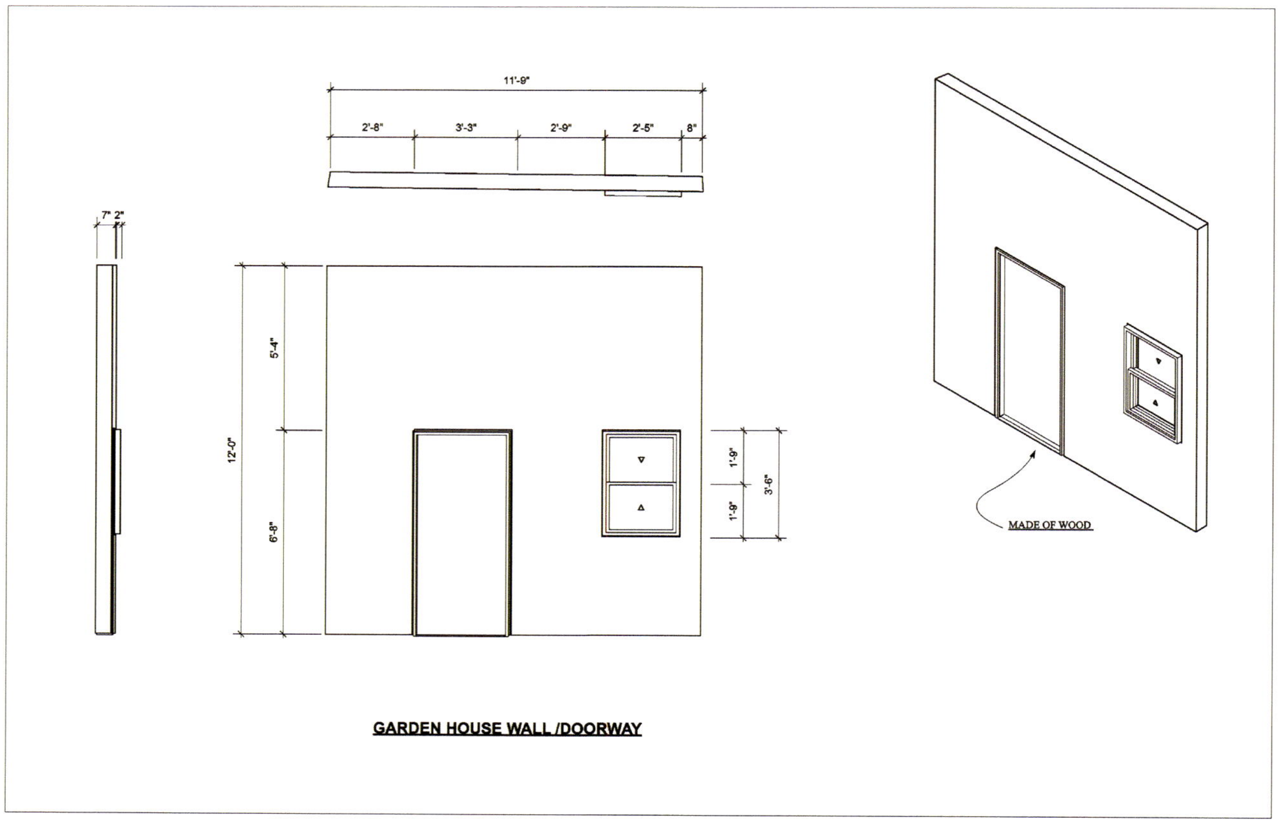

Figure 7.23 The *Importance of Being Earnest_Orthographic Projection*. An Orthographic Projection drawing of a set design created and drafted by Raechel Sigur for *The Importance of Being Earnest*. This drawing is for the class project titled Producing Technical Drawings.

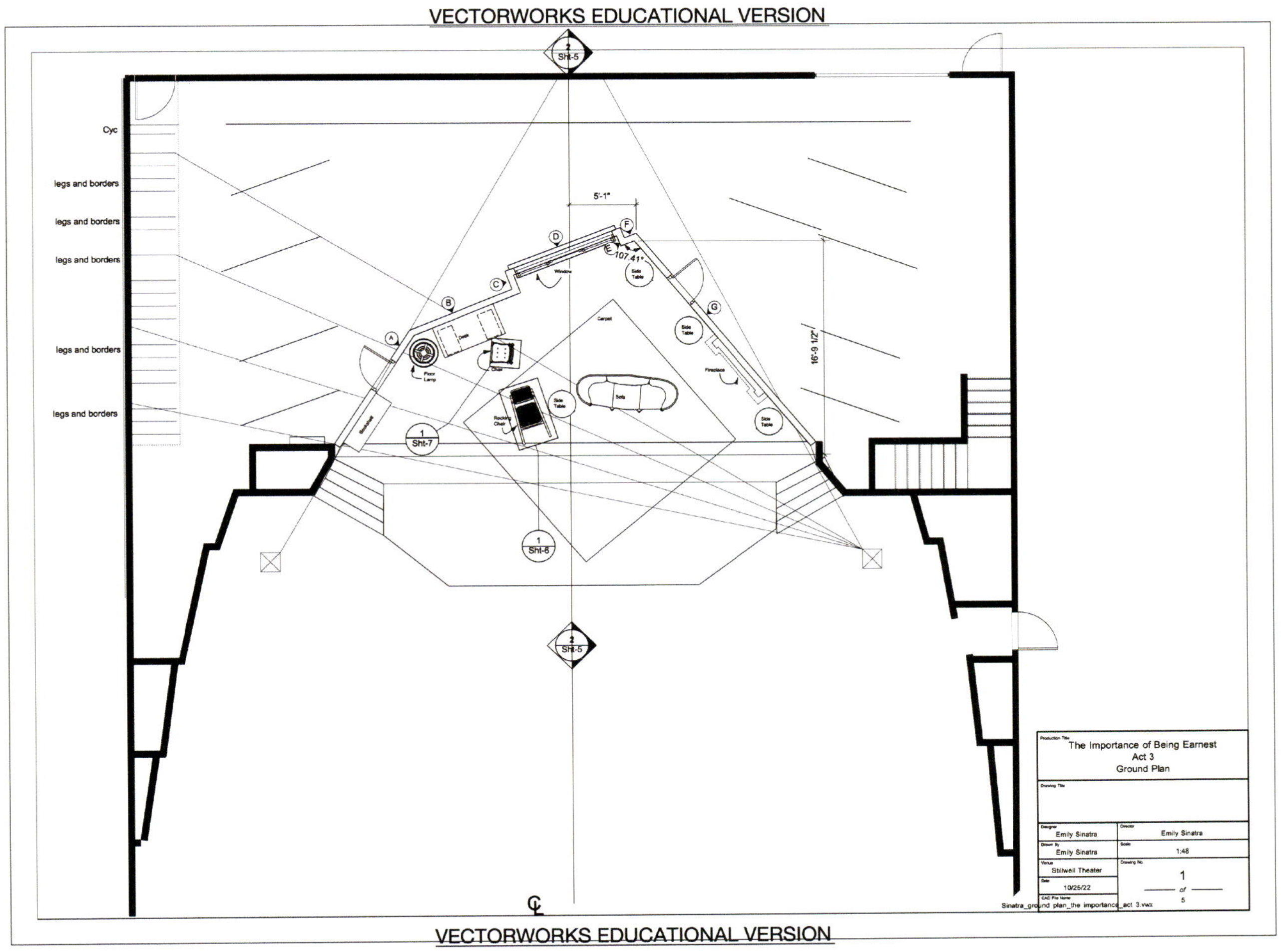

Figure 7.24 *The Importance of Being Earnest_Floor Plan*. The Floor Plan of a set design created and drafted by Emily Sinatra for *The Importance of Being Earnest*. This drawing is for the class project titled Producing Technical Drawings.

Bibliography

Cunningham-Moore, LaTia. Fig. 7.17 *West Side Story_Orthographic Projection*. Design Skills class project. 2021.

Cunningham-Moore, LaTia. Fig. 7.18 *West Side Story_Top/Plan View*. Design Skills class project. 2021.

Cunningham-Moore, LaTia. Fig. 7.19 *West Side Story_Isometric Views*. Design Skills class project. 2021.

Cunningham-Moore, LaTia. Fig. 7.20 *West Side Story_Sections*. Design Skills class project. 2021.

Gallagher, Mace. Fig. 7.21 *West Side Story_Floor Plan*. Design Skills class project. 2021.

Gillette, J. Michael. *Theatrical Design and Production: An Introduction to Scene Design and Construction, Lighting, Sound, Costume, and Makeup*. McGraw Hill, 2012.

Nemetschek Group. Fig. 7.12 *Details* (a Corinthian column obtained from VW Libraries), Vectorworks, 2023.

Rose, Rich. *Drafting Scenery for Theatre, Film, and Television*. Betterway Publications, Inc., White Hall, Virginia, 1990.

Scales, Mackenzie. Fig. 7.22 *The Importance of Being Earnest_Ground Plan*. Design Skills class project. 2022.

Sigur, Raechel. Fig. 7.23 *The Importance of Being Earnest_Orthographic Projection*. Design Skills class project. 2022.

Sinatra, Emily. 7.24 *The Importance of Being Earnest_Floor Plan*. Design Skills class project. 2022.

Sweet, Harvey. *The Complete Book of Drawing for the Theatre*. Allyn and Bacon, 1995.

CHAPTER 8

Modeling Nuances and Texture Manipulation

Vocabulary

- 2D Fillet
- 3D Fillet
- Extract
- Subdivision
- Reshape
- Shell Solids
- Texture Shaders
- Displacement Mapping
- Hardscape
- Softscape
- Image Props
- Proxy Objects
- VBvisual Plants

Learning Objectives

- Apply commands such as Extract (lines and surfaces), Fillet (2D and 3D), and Shell Solids in the modeling process.
- Demonstrate the ability to manipulate Texture Shaders, Displacement Mapping, and Scale perimeters in the enhancement of visual texture.
- Practice ways of combining various tools, commands, and techniques to create complex objects and structures.

Set Model and Rendering: Nuances and Complexity

In this chapter, you will learn new tools, commands, methods, and techniques in interior decoration, architecture design, and landscape planning. Although in stage and production design, a faucet may not need to run water and a building may be more expressive than functional, fundamentally, set design involves design aspects ranging from architecture and landscape designs as well as interior decoration. The interior decoration technique covered in this chapter includes topics such as how to use the Extract-Curves command to install mouldings and trims on interior walls, how to create a bathtub using 2D and 3D fillet tools, how to apply the Subdivision tool and its various modes to create curtains from scratch, and how to customize modular windows to supply details to the interior room. The landscape planning technique introduced in this chapter encompasses topics such as how to use Hardscapes tools to plan landings and paths and how to apply Softscapes tools to install bushes, trees, and flowers. You will be exposed to ways of manipulating Texture Shaders, Displacement Mapping, and Scale perimeters to control the texture properties of an object and to arose audience's tactile sensation of a given material. In addition, you will practice building complex architecture structures by applying tools and commands such as Shell Solids, Extract-Surface, and Sweep.

DOI: 10.4324/9781003266242-8

Interior Decoration

Install Mouldings and Trims

In the VW program, after walls are established and doors, door openings, and windows are inserted, baseboard moulding, crown moulding, trims around doors and windows, as well as picture frames, can all be created by using the "Extrude Along Path…" command. To make this command work, you must have a line and a moulding profile. To create a line for baseboard moulding, for example, you may use the Polyline Tool (Basic palette) and draw a line along the front edges of the wall in Top/Plan view, use the Rectangle Tool (Basic palette) to draw a rectangle along the outer edges of a picture in a front view or Isometric view, or even use the ***Extract Tool*** (Tool Set – 3D Modeling) and Extract Curve Mode in an Isometric view. Then select the edges of the wall and click "Check Mark" on the Mode bar to execute the command. The Extract Curve comment takes the edge of an object and converts it into a line. As for the moulding profile, you can either create it from scratch or adopt it from VW Libraries in Resource Manager. VW Libraries store numerous beautiful mouldings for you to use. After a line and a moulding profile are ready, you can then select both and go to Model – Extrude Along Path to execute the command. That said, since there are default settings for the moulding profiles that you adopt from the VW Library, often you will need to access the profile edit window after the moulding is created to adjust the position and orientation of its profile so that the base moulding is attached to the wall(s) properly. Please note that it may take a few trials to get to the correct orientation and position of the moulding profile in the Edit Profile window. Patience is needed to get used to this method of working. Fig. 8.1 features a sample of a wall unit with mouldings, casings, and frames installed (see Technique 8 of this chapter for step-by-step instructions to install mouldings and Trims).

Figure 8.1 *mouldings and Trims.* An image showing the result of moulding/trim installation using a combination of Line Tool, Polyline Tool, Rectangle Tool, or Extract Tool and Extrude Along Path command. Wedding photo by Beautiful Life Studio. Curtesy of Grace Lu and Bing Luo.

For a smoother modeling process, it is highly recommended that you install the mouldings, casings, and frames in the following order.

1. Install casings for the doors and door openings.
2. Install base mouldings.
3. Install crown mouldings.
4. Install casings and frames for the windows and pictures.

Construct a Bathtub

2D Fillet Tool in Basic palette and ***3D Fillet*** Tool in Tool Sets – 3D Modeling round the sharp corners and edges of an object by a given radius. You set the perimeters in the tool preference window and select the relevant lines or surfaces; the software will do the job for you. While the 2D Fillet Tool, round the corners formed by two joining lines, the 3D Fillet Tool can round edges formed by two surfaces. They can be either concave or convex surfaces. The image presented in Fig. 8.2 offers such an example (see Technique 8 of this chapter for step-by-step instructions to create a bathtub).

Figure 8.2 *Bathtub.* An example of applying 2D and 3D Fillet Tool in the creation of a bathtub.

Create a Curtain

VW program allows you to create tailor-made curtains for the windows on your set. By accessing the ***Subdivision*** Tool and its various modes, you can make the fabric folds look natural and decent. Fig. 8.3 shows curtains created from scratch by employing the Subdivision Tool with Split and Transform Tool Modes (see Technique 8 of this chapter for step-by-step instructions to create a custom-made curtain).

It may take a few practices for you to get used to the tools and tool modes, as it requires you to operate under a 3D coordinate system

Figure 8.3 *Custom-Made Curtains.* An illustration of natural looking curtains made by using Subdivision Tool with Split and Transform Tool Modes.

(the YELLOW arrow pointing toward the direction your cursor will be moving), but you will find it worthy of the effort. (See Technique 8 for step-by-step instructions on how to create a custom-made curtain.)

Customize a Window

In Tool Sets, there are dozens of modular tools that provide frameworks for you to customize the most used objects, such as walls, doors, windows, stairs, plants… You name it. You select a tool and insert the object in your drawing area. From there, you can change the perimeters for that object either in OIP or in OIP – Settings window. The Modular Window Tool is such an example. The window that comes with the Window Tool has default settings. It is called Unstyled. However, the basic components of the window can all be altered and adjusted to satisfy your set design style needs. This will happen after you drop the Unstyled window in the Drawing Area. Furthermore, you can customize the window by selecting "New Plug-in Style" from Unstyled Plag-in… in OIP – Style dropdown menu and saving it under a name of your choice in your home folder for future use.

Fig. 8.4 offers an example of a custom window created by changing the perimeters of an Unstyled window that comes with the modular Window Tool found in Tool Sets (see Experiment and Practice in this chapter for step-by-step instructions on how to customize a window).

Figure 8.4 *Customized Window Style.* An illustration of a window style created through changing the default perimeters of an Unstyled modular window.

With the experience of customizing a window style using a modular window under your belt, you can customize other commonly used objects found in Tool Sets. The perimeters of each object might vary, but the process is similar.

Exterior Landscape Planning

Landscape design involves the planning of hardscapes and softscapes to shape a purposeful environment. ***Hardscape*** refers to manmade components, such as patios, pavements, retaining walls, and water features, whereas ***Softscape*** denotes living elements, such as plants, soils, shrubs, and flowers. As their names imply, hardscapes are made with hard and durable materials like stones, concrete, and bricks, while softscapes are formed with natural growing materials like flowers, grass, and trees.

Hardscape

In VW Landmark Workspace, modular tools such as the Hardscape Tool, Parking Area Tool, and Roadway (Poly) Tool, as well as their various tool modes, provide convenience to designers in creating sensible and visually appearing hardscape features in a speedy manner.

Hardscape Tool resides in Tool Sets – Site Planning. Once the tool is activated, you will be able to access the various tool modes on the Mode bar. First, you can select an existing hardscape style in the Style dropdown menu. Next, you can select one of the three configuration modes to create hardscape in the style you pre-selected. Boundary Configuration Mode lets you use a polyline tool to shape the boundary of hardscape. Aligned Configuration Mode takes the edge of an existing object as a line and lets you add more polylines to provide a boundary. Pathway Configuration Mode let you draw a polyline to define a path for the hardscape. As soon as you have defined the boundary or path of the hardscape, the area or path appears on the drawing board in the style you selected. There are also sub-modes to assist you in drawing polylines and polygons with curves and to give you insertion options to accurately position the hardscape objects. Lastly, there is a tool preference icon also on the Mode bar, which permits you to configure the tool before using it. After you have created a hardscape object, you can still edit its settings and perimeters in OIP.

Aside from using modular tools to create hardscape, you can convert existing geometry to a hardscape object. For instance, you can use the Polygon Tool with Inner Boundary Tool Modes selected and click on an area that is bounded by other objects. With the shape selected, right-click on PC or Ctrl-Click on Mac to select "Create Objects from Shapes…" In the popup window, click on the dropdown menu to select "Hardscape," check "Show Properties Dialog," and click "OK." This will open the Hardscape Preferences window for you. As soon as you set the preferences and click "OK" to close the window, the hardscape with your preferred style and perimeters appears in your drawing area.

Additionally, it is possible to create hardscapes from scratch. Fig. 8.5 shows a landscape image created by a combined use of tools and modes to shape its hardscape objects. The manmade lake (the water container) is created from scratch by using the ***Reshape*** Tool and the ***Shell Solids*** Tool, among others. The paved circular landing and paved winding path are both generated by using the Hardscape Tool. The short walls are erected by using the Wall Tool.

Figure 8.5 *Hardscape.* An illustration of hardscape objects, such as a manmade lake, a paved a paved walkway and a winding path, as well as a short wall, created by a combined use of tools and commands.

Softscape

What is a Plant in VW?

A plant in VW has two aspects, its 2D representation and its 3D representation. A 2D representation is composed of several elements. For example, a tree can have its linear silhouette, its branches, and its leafy canopy. Each element is set in a separate class and laid one on the top of another. You can change their sizes and transparency, as well as the stack order and visibility of each in the Edit window, even create a 2D representation of a plant from scratch by yourself.

The 3D representations of plant objects in VW can be divided into three types. One type is called "***Image Props***." An Image Prop is photo based. It shows you a realistic image of a plant without modeling it in 3D. This type of plant renders quickly. However, if you do not render it in a rendering mode that supports texture, you may only see a linear cross image in Top/Plan view or an image of two intersecting planes in Isometric view. Different from the "Image Props" type, a "***Proxy Objects***" type is a 3D model that captures only the basic form of the plant with no texture details. This type of plant is usually used for initial schematic plans rather than the final presentation. Compared to "Image Props," this type of plant object may take a bit longer to download and render. ***VBvisual Plants*** is a type of plant that is a 3D model of a plant with realistic details. You have the choice of setting it to render either in low detail, medium detail, or high detail in the Preference window (Global Setting). Comparing to an "Image Prop" or "a "Proxy Object," a VBvisual Plant with a "high detail" setting will take a significantly longer time to render. Like its 2D representation, the size and orientation of the 3D representation of the plant can be edited in OIP. You can even create a 3D plant yourself.

Where are the Plants Stored and How to Access Them?

The Plant Tool can be found either in the Landmark workspace or in the Design Suite workspace. You can access the plant resources through the following routes.

- Find a plant by searching for it in Resource Manager – VW Libraries.
- Find a plant by going to Tool Sets – Site Planning – Plant Tool and click on the Plant Style dropdown menu or the Tool Preference icon – Use Style dropdown menu, both located on the Mode bar.

- Find a plant by going to Tool Sets – Visualization – Laubwerk Plant Tool and click on the Laubwerk Plant dropdown menu located on the Mode bar.
- Find a plant by going to Tool Sets – Visualization – Render Mall Plant Tool and click on the Render Mall Plant dropdown menu located on the Mode bar.

Through the first two routes, you can access the plant resources available in VW Libraries. Through the third route, you can find plants available in Laubwerk Plant Catalog. Through the fourth route, you can find plants available in Render Mall Catalog.

Among the available resources, Render Mall provides you with high-quality 3D realistic plant images that take only a few seconds to download. Laubwerk offers you several choices in a Global setting to render the plants. It shows you a frontal view of each plant image with a human figure on the side to compare its proportion with the plant. In addition, it lets you select the age and season of the plant. That said, the Plant Tool in the Site Planning tool set is the best route for softscape planning, for it not only allows you to select plants available in VW Libraries but also offers several tool modes and sub-modes to assist you in the planning process.

How Can I Use the Tools to Create Softscapes?

If you click on the Plant Tool in Site Planning tool set, three tool modes will be available for you to select. The first mode lets you download a plant. The second mode lets you pick up a plant that exists on your drawing board. The third mode is for mass planting. After selecting the mode, you can then click on the Plant Style dropdown menu to select a plant in Resource Manager. Before inserting the plant on your drawing board, you will need to select a sub-mode for plant placement.

- Single Plant Placement Mode lets you place one plant per click.
- Poly Vertex Placement Mode lets you place multiple plants along a polyline path you set with multiple clicks, but still one plant per click.
- Poly-Edge Spaced Mode lets you place a row of plants with a click at the beginning of the row and a double-click at the end of the row.
- Both Rectangle Array Mode and Triangular Array Mode let you place rows of plants by defining the boundary of an area where you want to place the plants.

If you click the Preference Tool (also located on the Mode bar) before you place the plant, you can set the default perimeters, including plant size, spacing, insertion option, etc. for the tool. After you place the plants, you can still change the settings and perimeters in OIP.

The plants in Fig. 8.6 came from various routes. A few of them are from VW Libraries; others are either from Render Mall or from Laubwerk. In this image, you may also observe that different placement modes were employed.

Figure 8.6 *Softscape.* The image illustrates the use of plants from VW Libraries, Render Mall, and Laubwerk routes. You may also observe the application of plant modes and sub-modes in this image.

Texture Manipulation

Texture, Tactile Sensation, and Visual/Digital Texture

When you dig your hands in the sand to make a sandcastle, or flip a page of your textbook, you will feel the texture of the material. The term "texture" most often refers to the surface characteristics of an object (e.g., Sand is gritty; paper is smooth). It is also closely related to what the material is made of and how it is structured and finished. In other words, materials made of different substances, constructed in different ways, or given different surface treatments will result in different textures. Take fabrics, for example: fiber, yarn, weave, and finish are four basic structural elements of fabrics. Varying any of the four elements will result in fabrics with different tactile traits and draping and moving qualities. If you want your skirt to flow, you will get silk or chiffon; if you wish your suit to have weight and structure, you will get wool. While texture is a physical quality of a material, the feel aroused through touch, however, is called "Tactile Sensation." It is a human being's response to a given texture. By the time we are adults, we have such a vast experience with texture that we no longer need to touch to understand; just by seeing, we can relate a certain sensation to a given texture. It is based on this premise, visual texture claims its existence. It is also on this premise, the digital texture is founded.

In the VW program, you can create a texture style to be applied to an object or alter the texture properties of an existing object by manipulating four ***Texture Shaders*** of the object or its *Displacement Mapping*.

Texture Shaders

A texture is composed of one or several shaders. Color, Reflectivity, Transparency, and Bump are four Texture Shaders available in the VW program. Each Shader comes with several sub-shaders and perimeters. Just like manipulating the four structural elements of fabrics, the choices of sub-shaders and the manipulation of their perimeters will result in textures with different tactile traits.

In Resource Manager, if you find a texture in VW Libraries, you can right-click your mouse (PC) or Ctrl + Click (Mac) to access the "Edit" window, in which you can change the perimeters of the texture. If you want to create a texture from scratch, you can click on the button named "New Renderworks Texture" in Resource Manager, then select Renderworks Texture to access the Edit Texture window, in which you can set the perimeters for the new texture.

After you have made the selections, you can then Click "OK" to apply the new texture to the object and adjust the scale, rotation, and mapping type in OIP (under the Render tab) to your satisfaction.

Experimenting Texture Shader Options and Perimeters

It will take you a period of trial-and-error to learn what these texture Shader options and perimeters can do in the creation of various textures. Fig. 8.7 through Fig. 8.9 show you an example of experimenting with Shader options and perimeters. In this experimentation, except for a few changes made in the Edit Texture window, which are indicated in Fig. 8.7 (the Chart), all other perimeters of the shaders are default settings. Please note that the first column shows the preset for all the rows in this chart.

Fig. 8.8 reflects the changes made in the Shaders as indicated in the chart, except for the cubes in the fourth row. The changes made in the Bump Shader sometime can only show up in Final Quality Renderworks rendering mode. The cubes in the fourth row still look the same despite the changes, because 8.8 is rendered in Shaded rendering mode.

Fig. 8.9 is rendered in Final Quality Renderworks mode. The changes made in Bump Shade settings for the cubes on the fourth row appear. You can see a variety of bumps displayed on the surfaces of the cubes.

Below are observations made from this experiment on Texture Shaders (see Fig. 8.8):

1. On the first row, the differences among the four tubes demonstrate that you can change the color of a glass texture by selecting "Color" in Color Shader and assigning a color to the object. (Note: The color of a Glass material will not be visible if the Transmission setting is at 100%. The transmission settings for the cubes on the first row are at 80%.)
2. On the second row, the differences among the four tubes show us that you can make changes to materials of different reflectivity and their perimeters under the Reflectivity Shader to alter the color, transparency, and even light emission of a glass texture.

Experimenting Texture Shaders

Shader Settings

Preset: 1st Column (Start Settings for All Rows)	Changes on the 1st Row	Changes on the 2nd Row	Changes on the 3rd Row	Changes on the 4th Row
Color a. Color Edit a. Color: Cyan-Azure a. Brightness: 90%	***Color Change*** a. Cube #2: Azure 7 b. Cube #3: Azure Blue 2 c. Cube #4: Blue 3			
Reflectivity a. None		***Reflectivity Change*** a. Cube #2: Mirror Reflection: 1000% b. Cube #3: Metallic Reflection; 100% Roughness: 40% c. Cube #4: Glow Brightness: 200% Check Emit Light		
Transparency a. Glass Edit a. Transmission: 90% b. Index of Refraction: 1.5			***Transmission Change*** a. Cube #2: 70% b. Cube #3: 40% c. Cube #4: 10%	
Bump a. None				***Bump Change*** a. Cube #2: Noise Pattern: Turbulence Strength: 300% Scale: 10 (in OIP) b. Cube #3: Noise Pattern: Zata Strength: 300% Scale: 10 (in OIP) c. Cube #4: Noise Pattern: Random Strength: 300% Scale: 10 (in OIP)

Figure 8.7 *Texture Shader Variations – the Chart.* A chat illustrating the preset perimeters (first column) for all four rows and the changes made on the Shader options and perimeters (second, third, and fourth columns).

Figure 8.8 *Texture Shader Variations – Visual Result*. An image reflecting the changes made in Texture Shaders, except for those made on the Bump Shader because 8.07 is rendered in Shaded rendering mode as opposed to Final Quality Renderworks rendering mode.

3. On the third row, the differences among the four tubes tell us that, if you change the transmission level under Transparency Shader, you can not only add opacity to a glass texture, but also change the color intensity of the glass texture. The more transparent the glass is, the less intense the color of the glass is, and vice versa.
4. On the fourth row, the sameness of the four tubes reveals that the settings in Bump Shader will not show in Shaded rendering mode. The differences among the four tubes are shown in Fig. 8.9, because Fig. 8.9 is rendered in Final Quality Renderworks. The differences among the four tubes are due to the three choices made for #2, #3, and #4 under Bump Shader – Noise. These choices provide various rough texture surfaces for the three tubes.

Powerful Shader Options

"Grow" under Reflectivity Shader and Displacement Mapping in "Noise" under Bump Shader are two powerful shader options due to their unique functionalities. Grow can be an alternative to a light fixture because this sub-shader option can emit lights, especially in dark environment. An object coated in Grow sub-shader renders faster than a normal light object. In Fig. 8.10, you can see how the Glow texture option can be applied to a television screen to make the screen appear to emit light.

Another powerful shader option is Displacement Mapping. This option is in Bump Shader – Noise. Unlike any other shader option, Displacement Mapping can add a depth dimension to the 2D surface.

Figure 8.9 *Texture Shaders Variations – The Bump Shader.* As a supplement to Fig. 8.8, Fig. 8.9 shows the visual result of the changes made on the fourth row, the Bump Shader. Fig. 8.9 is rendered in Final Quality Renderworks mode.

Figure 8.10 *Reflectivity Shader – Glow_TV Screen*. Another example of Glow texture option used in the creation of a television screen.

No matter how 3D a normal texture can appear, if you carefully look at the edge of the texture surface, you will find that the perception of depth in those textures is illusory. Displacement Mapping option, nevertheless, lets you set a depth perimeter that will bump up the 2D texture surface into a 3D form that is observable on the edges of the texture surface and can even receive and cast shadows. The image of pebbles shown in Fig. 8.11 is enhanced by adding a depth dimension in the Texture Edit window – Bump Shader – Noise – Displacement Mapping.

Texture Application

VW 2023 makes the application of texture easier by providing a drag-and-drop option. To apply a texture to an object, click on the object, select "Texture" in the Texture dropdown menu in OIP (under the Render tab), find the texture you want in Resource Manage, drag it from the Resource Manager, and drop it on the object. In addition, you have the option of applying the texture either to a single surface or to the entire object. For a single surface application, drag-and-drop the texture while pressing the Command key (mac) or Control key (PC) on the keyboard. For an application to

Figure 8.11 *Pebbles – Displacement Mapping*. An example showing how the Bump Shader Option – Noise – Displacement Mapping can enhance the feeling of depth in texture.

the entire object, drag-and-drop the texture while pressing Command+Shift (mac) keys or Control+Shift (PC) keys on the keyboard. As an alternative, you can also select "Apply to Object Mode" or "Apply to Face Mode" on the Mode bar after you select the desired texture in Resource Manage. In this way, you can then click on the object or face you want to apply the texture to.

Editing Texture Shaders and Perimeters

Texture shaders and perimeters can be edited either in OIP, under the Render tab, or in Resource Manager with the "Edit" command (right-click on PC and Ctrl+Click on Mac). The advantage of editing texture in OIP is that it allows you to observe the changes made while you are editing.

Technique 8 – Modeling Nuances and Texture Manipulation (Episode One)

Technique 8 contains three episodes. In this episode, you will learn to apply new tools, commands, and techniques to mount a framed picture and install mouldings and trims on walls, to produce a bathtub, a curtain, a sunroom, and a winding path, and to manipulate texture shaders to create a glowing effect.

Install Mouldings and Trims

Fig. 8.12 illustrates the outcome of the following procedure intended to install mouldings and trims.

Preparation

1. Find an image that is about 4′ (w) × 3′ (h) and save the image on your desktop.
2. Create a blank document and set the scale to ¼″ scale and document size to US Arch D (in Architect Workspace).

Build Walls

1. Go to Tool Sets – Building Shell – Wall Tool.
2. Click on the Wrench/Pencil (Preference) icon. A dialog window appears.
3. Under "Definition" tab, set the wall thickness to 6″.
4. Under "Insertion Option" tab, set the wall height to 10′ and click "OK."

Figure 8.12 *Mouldings and Trims Installation.* This image shows the result of the following practice. Wedding photo by Beautiful Life Studio. Curtesy of Grace Lu and Bing Luo.

5. In Top/Plan view, draw three walls.
   a. Wall A: From the top of the document, draw a wall starting from Upstage to Downstage (L: 8′).
   b. Wall B: Continue to draw a wall in a right-angle toward Stage left (L: 6′).
   c. Wall C: Continue to draw a wall in a right-angle toward Downstage (L: 5′6″) and make a double-click to end the wall.

Insert a Door and a Window

1. Go to Tool Sets – Building Shell – Door Tool.
2. Insert a door into Wall A and swing the door to the right-side.
3. Go to Tool Sets – Building Shell – Window Tool.
4. Insert a window into Wall C.

Create a Picture

1. In Front view, go to Tool Sets – 3D Modeling – Set Working Plane Tool.
2. Set the working plan on Wall B.
3. (At the eye level) Draw a rectangle (width: 4′; Height: 3′) and extrude it by 1″. You have now created a canvas!
4. Go to Resource Manage and double-click on the "New Resource" button located at the lower left corner of the window. A dialog box opens.

5. Check "Renderworks Texture" and click on "Create." An edit texture window appears.
6. Give the texture a name. In Color shader dropdown menu, select "Image."
7. When the "Choose Image" dialog box appears, click "OK" to import an image file.
8. Locate the image that you have previously saved on your desktop, choose the image to open it, and click "OK" in Edit Image Color window to accept the default. The image now shows up in the "Edit Texture" window.
9. Under "Size," insert 4′. Under "Object Size," insert 4′. Click "OK."
10. Select the "Canvas." In OIP, select "Texture" in Texture dropdown menu and find the Renderworks texture you have created previously and double-click on it to select it.
11. In OIP, adjust the scale of the image if needed. You are now ready to install mouldings, casings, and a picture frame for the interior of the room.

Install Door Casing

1. Switch to the Left view and select Wall A.
2. Go to Tool Sets – 3D Modeling – Set Working Plane Tool.
3. Set the working plane on Wall A and use the Polyline Tool to draw lines around the outer edge of the door (on three sides).
4. Go to Resource Manager and search for "Moulding" and select the moulding named "Profile Copper Beech Millwork CB1105."
5. In Top/Plan view, drop the moulding somewhere near the door.
6. Zoom in the moulding to adjust its size (Length: about 4″; Hight: about 1.5″).
7. In Left Isometric view, select both the line that you created previously and the moulding profile, and go to Top Menu – Model – Extrude Along Path. A dialog box opens.
8. When the line is lit in RED, click "OK."
9. Double-click on the moulding. A dialog box opens.
10. Select "Profile" and click "OK." You are now in the Edit Profile window.
11. Zoom in on the moulding profile. Go to Top Menu – Modify – Rotate… To adjust the orientation of the moulding. (See Fig. 8.13 for reference.)

Note: Please pay attention to how the moulding is related to the green line and red line, which represent vertical and horizontal coordinate planes.

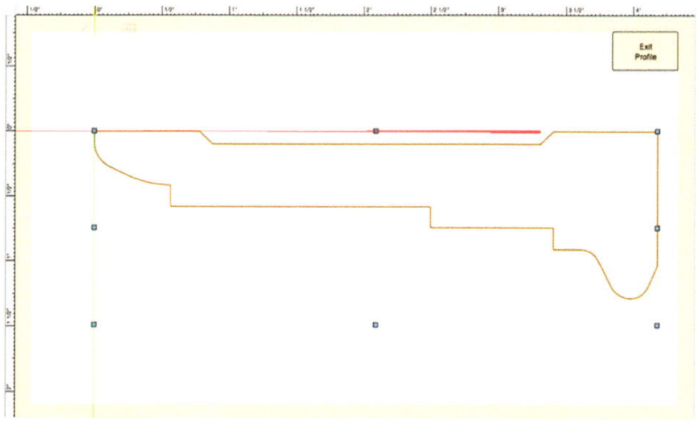

Figure 8.13 *Door Casing Profile.* An illustration demonstrating the moulding orientation and position in the Edit Profile window for the door casing. The upper left corner of the profile must hit the origin.

12. Use the Arrow key while pressing the Shift key to nudge the moulding to the exact position shown in Fig. 8.13.
13. Click the "Exit Profile" button to exit the window.
14. See the result of the door casing in Left Isometric view.

Install Baseboard Moulding

1. Go to Top/Plan view. Use the Line Tool to draw a line starting from the top-left corner of Wall A and ending at the point where the door casing starts.
2. Go to Resource Manager to search for moulding and select the moulding named "Profile Copper Beech Millwork CB2135."
3. In Top/Plan view, drop the moulding profile somewhere near Wall A.
4. Zoom in on the moulding profile to adjust its size (Length: about 9″; Height: about 1.5″).
5. Select both the line that you created previously and the moulding profile, and go to Top Menu – Model – Extrude Along Path. A dialog box opens.
6. When the line is lit in RED, click "OK."
7. Double-click on the moulding. A dialog box opens.
8. Select "Profile" and click "OK." You are now in the Edit Profile window.
9. Zoom in on the moulding profile. Go to Top Menu – Modify – Rotate… To adjust the orientation of the moulding (see Fig. 8.14 for reference).
10. Use the Arrow key while pressing the Shift key to nudge the moulding to the exact position shown in Fig. 8.14. Copy the profile for later use.
11. Click the "Exit Profile" button to exit the window.
12. See the result of the baseboard moulding in Left Isometric view.

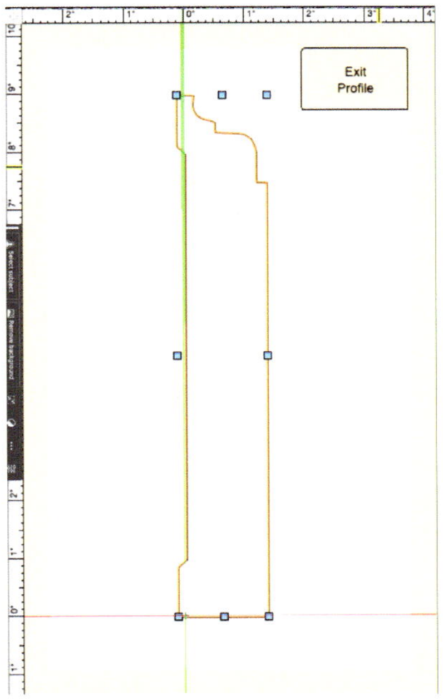

Figure 8.14 *Baseboard Profile*. An illustration demonstrating the moulding orientation and position in the Edit Profile window for the baseboard. The lower right corner of the profile must hit the origin.

13. In Top/Plan view, drop the moulding profile near Wall A.
14. Use the Polyline Tool to draw a polyline, starting from the door casing on Wall A and ending at the end of Wall C.
15. Select both the polyline and the moulding profile. Go to Top Menu – Model – Extrude Along Path.
16. When the line is lit in RED, click "OK" to execute the command.
17. Double-click on the moulding. A dialog box opens.
18. Select "Profile" and click "OK." You are now in the Edit Profile window.
19. Zoom in on the moulding profile. Use the Arrow key while pressing the Shift key to nudge the moulding to the exact position shown in Fig. 8.14.
20. Click "Exit Profile" button to exit the window.
21. View the result of the baseboard installation in Left Isometric view.

Install Crown Moulding

1. Go to the Navigation palette. Double-click on the Class icon.
2. Create a new class and name it "Baseboard."
3. Select all the baseboard mouldings and reassign them to a class named "Baseboard" in OIP.
4. In the Navigation palette, make the Baseboard class invisible.
5. In Top/Plan view, use the Polyline Tool to draw a polyline along the front edge of the walls.
6. In Resource Manager, search for a moulding profile named "Profile Copper Beech Millwork CB3153" and double-click on the moulding to select it.
7. Drop the moulding profile near the walls.
8. Zoom in the moulding profile to adjust its size (width: around 7.2"; height: around 9.3").
9. Select both the line that you created previously and the moulding profile, and go to Top Menu – Model – Extrude Along Path. A dialog box opens.
10. When the line is lit in RED, click "OK."
11. Double-click on the moulding. A dialog box opens.
12. Select "Profile" and click "OK." You are now in the Edit Profile window.
13. Zoom in on the moulding profile. Go to Top Menu – Modify – Rotate… To adjust the orientation of the moulding (see Fig. 8.15 for reference).
14. Use the Arrow key while pressing the Shift key to nudge the moulding to the exact position shown in Fig. 8.15.

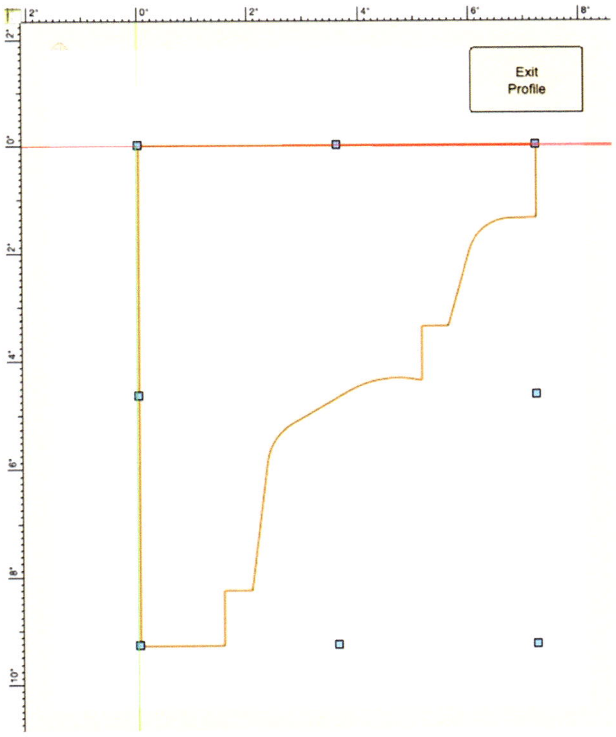

Figure 8.15 *Crown moulding Profile*. An illustration demonstrating the moulding orientation and position in the Edit Profile window for the crown moulding. The upper left corner of the profile must hit the origin.

15. Click the "Exit Profile" button to exit the window.
16. Switch to Front View. While pressing the Shift key, lift the moulding up to flash the top of the moulding with the top of the wall.
17. See the result of the crown moulding in Left Isometric view.
18. Go to the Navigation palette to make the Baseboard moulding visible.

Install a Picture Frame

1. In Front view, click on Wall B.
2. Go to Tool Sets – 3D Modeling – Set Working Plane Tool.
3. Set the work plane on the surface of the picture.
4. Use the Rectangle Tool to draw a rectangle along the edge of the picture.
5. Search moulding in Resource Manager and select a moulding named "Profile Copper Beech Millwork CB1110."
6. In Top/Plan view, drop the moulding profile near the picture.
7. Zoom in on the moulding profile and adjust the moulding size (width: 6″; height: 2″).
8. Select both the rectangle that you created previously and the moulding profile and go to Top Menu – Model – Extrude Along Path. A dialog box opens.
9. When the line is lit in RED, click "OK."
10. Double-click on the moulding. A dialog box opens.
11. Select "Profile" and click "OK." You are now in the Edit Profile window.
12. Zoom in on the moulding profile. Go to Top Menu – Modify – Rotate… To adjust the orientation of the moulding (see Fig. 8.16 for reference).

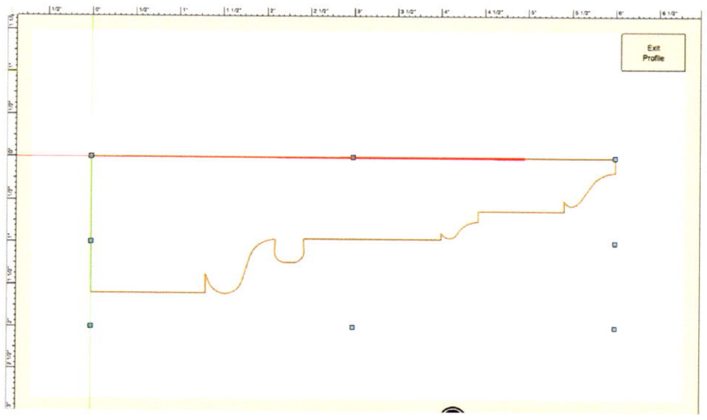

Figure 8.16 *Picture Frame Profile*. An illustration demonstrating the moulding orientation and position in the Edit Profile window for the picture frame. The upper left corner of the profile must hit the origin.

13. Use the Arrow key while pressing the Shift key to nudge the moulding profile to the exact position shown in Fig. 8.16.
14. Click the "Exit Profile" button to exit the window.
15. See the result of a picture frame in Front view.

Install a Window Casing

Except for the moulding profile, which is the same moulding profile as the door casing (Profile Copper Beech Millwork CB1105), the process of installing a window casing is the same as that of installing a picture frame. You can double-click on the door casing to copy the profile in the edit window and paste it near the window during the installation process.

Build a Bathtub

Fig. 8.17 illustrates the outcome of the following procedure intended to build a bathtub.

Construct the Body of a Bathtub

1. Create a new document and set the scale of the document to 1″ scale by right-clicking the mouse (PC) or Ctrl-Clicking (Mac) and selecting Active Layer Scale.
2. In Top/Plan view, draw a rectangle (width: 5′; height: 2′6″) and extrude it by 1′2″.
3. In the middle of the rectangle, draw another rectangle (width: 4′6″; height: 1′10″).
4. In the Basic palette, click on the "Fillet Tool" to select it.
5. In the Mode bar, select Trim Mode and insert a 6″ in the Radius slot.
6. On the smaller rectangle, click on the two lines that make a corner one by one. The lines turn RED, and then the corner becomes rounded.
7. Perform this action on the rest of the three corners of the smaller rectangle.
8. Extrude this shape by 1′3″.
9. In OIP, change the Bot Z to 2″.
10. Select both forms and go to Top Menu – Model – Subtract Solid.
11. When the large form is turned into RED, click "OK" to execute the command.
12. View the result in the Right Isometric view.
13. Go to Tool Sets – 3D Modeling – Fillet Edge.
14. Click on the "Fillet Edge Preferences" icon in the Mode bar. A dialog window opens.

Figure 8.17 *Bathtub*. This image shows the result of the following practice.

15. Check "Select Tangent Entities." Under Constant Radius, insert 1.25″ in the Radius slot, check "Select Faces," and click "OK" to exit the window.
16. While pressing the Shift key on the keyboard, select the top face and all the faces inside the tub one by one. When these faces turn into RED, click on the Check Mark on the Mode bar to execute the Fillet command. The corners and edges on the inside of the bathtub is now rounded.
17. Deselect the tub. Go to Tool Sets – 3D Modeling – Fillet Edge.
18. Click on the "Fillet Edge Preferences" icon in the Mode bar. A dialog window opens.
19. Uncheck "Select Tangent Entities." Under Constant Radius, insert 0.5″ in the Radius slot, check "Select Faces," and click "OK" to exit the window.
20. While pressing the Shift key, select all the faces outside of the bathtub, using the Current View dropdown menu to switch the views (from the Right Isometric view to the Left Rear Isometric view).
21. When these faces become RED, click on the Check Mark in the Mode bar to execute the Fillet command. The corners and edges on the outside of the bathtub are now rounded.

Install Hardware Inside of the Tub

Install a Symbolic Tub-Overflow-Plate

1. In Right-Isometric view, go to Tool Sets – 3D Modeling – Set Working Plane and set your working plane on the left-end vertical face of the tub.
2. Use the Circle Tool to draw a circle (radius: 1.5″) near the top of the face.
3. Extrude the circle by 0.5″.
4. Switch to the Top/Plan view and use the snap function to center the plate on the vertical plane.
5. While the shape is still selected, in OIP, click on the Render tab and select "Texture" in the Texture dropdown menu.
6. In Resource Manager, search for a texture named "Metal Chrome RT" and double-click on the item to select and download it. A dialog window appears. Click "OK" to accept the default.

Install a Symbolic Tub-Waste-Plug

1. In Top/Plan view, draw a circle (radius: 1.1″) and extrude it by 3″.
2. Select both the tub and the cylinder and go to Top Menu – Model – Subtract Solid. A dialog window opens.
3. If the tub turns RED, click "OK" in the dialog window to execute the command.

4. On the top of the hole, draw a circle (radius: 1.5″) sharing the center point with the hole.
5. In the middle of the circle, draw a smaller circle (radius: 1.1″).
6. Select both circles, go to Top Menu – Modify – Clip Surface, and delete the small circle.
7. Extrude the new shape by 0.25″.
8. While the shape is still selected, in OIP, change the Bot Z to 2″.
9. Click on the Render tab and select "Texture" in the Texture dropdown menu.
10. In Resource Manager, click on the "Home" icon and double-click on the texture named "Metal Chrome RT," if needed.

Render the Tub in Light

1. Go to Tool Sets – Visualization – Light.
2. Click on "Directional Light Mode" in the Mode bar.
3. In Top Plan view, place the light near the lower right corner of the tub, pointing toward the center of the tub.
4. In OIP, change "Z" to 3′ and "Elevation" to 45″.
5. Go to View – Set Renderworks Background, select SimpleSky Morning in the Renderworks Background dropdown menu, and click "OK."
6. Render the bathtub in Shaded rendering mode.
7. Go to the Teapot icon in the View bar, select Shaded Options… A dialog window opens.
8. Under Option, check "Textures," "Colors," "Anti-aliasing," and "Shadows," uncheck "Draw edges," and check "Environment lighting," "Environment reflections," and "Object Reflections."
9. Under "Quality," select "Very High" in Details and "High" in shadows and click "OK."
10. View the result in the Rear Right Isometric view and the Normal Perspective view.
11. Zoom in and use the Flyover Tool to see the details.
12. Save your document on your computer as "Bathtub."

Create a Curtain

Fig. 8.18 illustrates the outcome of the following procedure intended to create a Curtain.

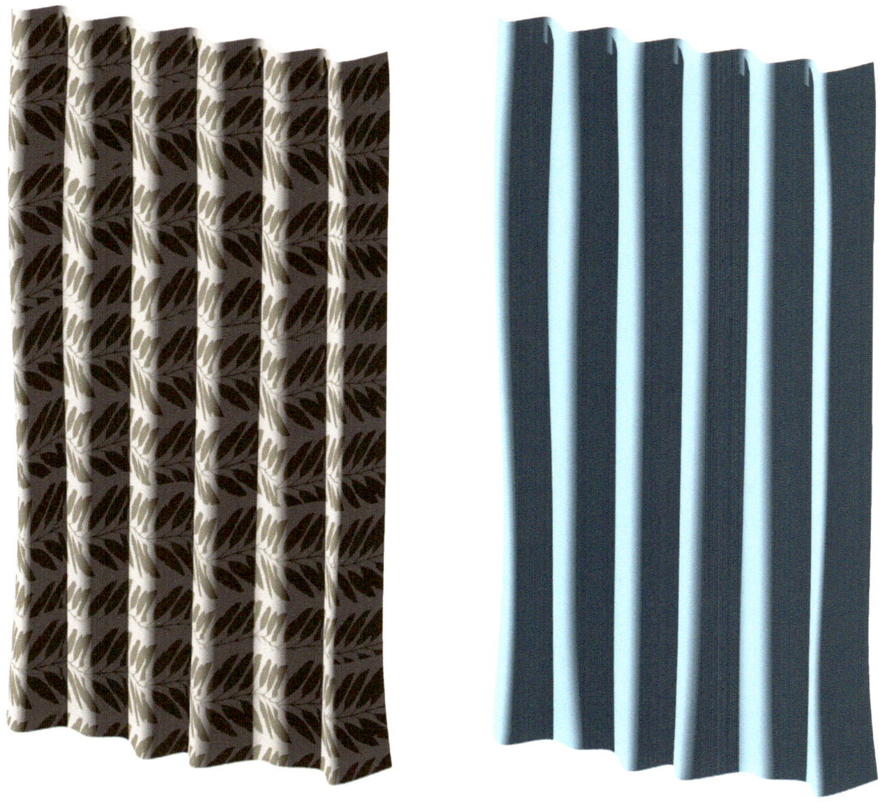

Figure 8.18 *Curtain*. This image shows the result of the following practice.

Weave a Sheet of Fabric

1. Create a new document and set the scale of the document to 1″ scale by right-clicking the mouse (PC) or Ctrl + Click (Mac) and selecting Active Layer Scale.
2. In Top/Plan view, draw a horizontal line (4′).
3. Extrude the line by 8′.
4. Turn off all the snap options located on the Snap palette.

Make Fabric Folds

1. While the line is selected, go to Top Menu – Modify – Convert – Convert to Subdivision. A dialog box opens.
2. In the subdivision Iteration dropdown menu, select "0" and click "OK" to exit the dialog box.
3. Use the Selection tool to double-click on the line; a range of subdivision tools is now available to you.
4. Zoom in the line to its fullest size.
5. Click on the Split Mode on the Mode bar and make a dozen division dots on the line with two clicks for each. First click locates a placement on the line. You can slide along the line before making the second click to drop the dot.
6. See the result in an isometric view.
7. Go back to Top/Plan view. Double-click on the line. The dots are now showing up on the line.
8. Click on Transform Mode and make sure the Translate and Rotate Mode is also on.

   Select even-numbered dots one by one while pressing the shift key on the keyboard. (Note: you need to use the selection tool to click and drag the cursor to ensure that the overlapping dots on the top and bottom of the curtain are both selected.) All the even-numbered dots have now turned RED.

9. After you have selected the last even-numbered dot, drag the Translate and Rotate 3D Drager down to create fabric folds for the curtain.
10. Go to OIP to change the Iteration number to 3 to curve the folds.
11. See the result in the Right Isometric view.

Create Organic Feel to the Curtain

1. After creating fabric folds, you need to make a few vertical divisions in the Right Isometrical view.
2. Double-click on the curtain (if needed to reveal the original dots).
3. While the Split Mode is still active, click on the vertical line furthest left to locate the placement of a horizontal line. Move the cursor to the right and make the second click to drop the horizontal line.
4. Repeat Step 2 four more times. Now, you are in a position to make some adjustments to fine-tune the fabric folds you previously made, with an eye toward creating an organic feel for the curtain.
5. Select Transform Mode, click a dot, and drag it slightly up, down, right, or left based on your intuition.
6. Repeat the previous step (Step 4) as many times as needed to complete the adjustments.
7. To scale the width of the curtain, go to Top/Plan view and double-click on the curtain.
8. Click on "Scale Mode" on the Mode bar and use the selection tool to select everything on the curtain. A "Scale 3D Dragger" appears in the middle of the curtain.
9. Hover your cursor over the horizontal arrow. When the arrow turns to YELLOW, click on it. Now you can either slide along the direction of the arrow or input a number in the scale slot to scale the width of the curtain. You can do the same to scale the depth of the curtain.
10. See the result in the Right Isometric view.

Render the Curtain with Light and Pattern

1. In Top/Plan view, go to Tool Sets – Visualization – Light. Select Directional Light mode.
2. Place a light source on the left side of the curtain, with the light pointing toward the curtain at a steep angle.
3. In OIP, click on the "Render" tab and select "Texture" in the Texture dropdown menu.
4. Go to Resource Manager to search for Fabric. When the fabric swatches show up in the middle column of the window, scroll down to the end of the list and select a fabric with a bold pattern (e.g., "Leaf Green RT").
5. Double-click on the swatch to select it. The pattern shows up on the curtain you made.

Manipulate Texture Shaders: Glow

Fig. 8.19 illustrates the outcome of the following procedure intended to manipulate texture shaders for a "glow" effect.

1. Create a new document and set the active layer scale to ½″ scale.
2. Save the document and name it "Glow Texture_ Florescent Light."

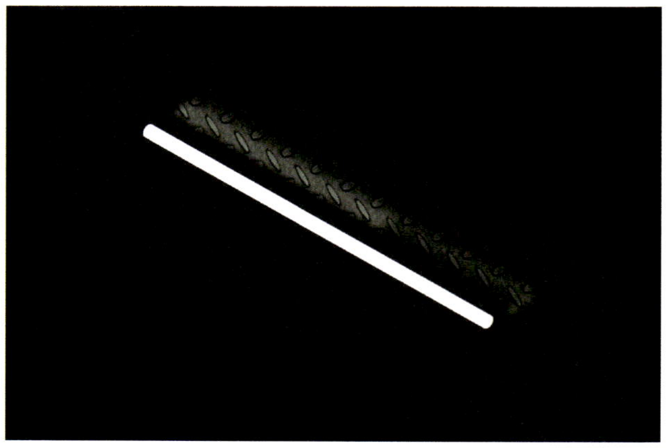

Figure 8.19 *Reflectivity Shader – Glow_Tube*. An example showing how the texture shader option "Glow" works in a low lighting environment. The image shows the result of the following practice.

3. In Top/Plan View, draw a line (length: 8′).
4. Draw a circle (diameter: 3″).
5. Select both objects and go to Top Menu – Extrude Along Path. A dialog window appears.
6. If the line is lit in RED, click "OK" to execute the command. A tube is now created.
7. On the top of the tube, draw a line (length: 14′) next to it and extrude the line by 5′.
8. In OIP, under the Render tab, select "Texture" in the Texture dropdown menu.
9. In Resource Manage, search for "Metal Treadplate 01 RT" and double-click on it.
10. Go to OIP to change the scale of the texture to 2.
11. Select the tube. In OIP, set the Bot Z to 3′.
12. Click on the Render tab and select "Texture" in the Texture dropdown menu.
13. Go to Resource Manager, click on "New Resources." A "Create Resource" box opens.
14. Check "Renderworks Texture" and click on "Create."
15. In the "Edit Texture" dialog window, name the texture "Glow 1."
16. Under "Shaders," make the following selections.
    a. Color: Fresnel. Click on "Edit…" and change the Center Color to "Lime-Green 6."
    b. Reflectivity: Glow. Click on "Edit…" and change the Brightness to 300, and check the "Emit Light" box.
17. Under Shadows, check "Cast," uncheck "Receive," and click "OK" to exit the window.
18. In Resource Manage, double-click on the texture named "Glow 1" to select the texture for the tube.
19. Go to Top Menu – View – Set Lighting Options… to turn off the ambient light.
20. Go to Top Menu – View – Set Renderworks Background… to select "Curvy Dome."
21. Go to Tool Sets – Visualization – Light and select the "Directional Light Mode."
22. Install a light on the lower left side of the tube.
23. In OIP, deselect "Cast shadows" and change the brightness to 50.
24. View the result in Right Isometric view.
25. Go to the Teapot icon in the View bar and select Shaded Options… A dialog window opens.
26. Under Option, check "Textures," "Colors," "Anti-aliasing," and "Shadows." Uncheck "Draw edges" and check "Environment lighting," "Environment reflections," and "Object Reflections."
27. Under "Quality," select "High" in Details and "High" in shadows and click "OK."
28. Select the light object. In OIP, make the final light angle/direction adjustments by sliding the bars in Azimuth and Elevation slots so that the panel behind the glowing tube is barely lit, as this will emphasize the glowing effect of the tube.

Construct a Sunroom

Fig. 8.20 illustrates the outcome of the following procedure aiming to construct a sunroom.

Create a Base Structure for the Sunroom

1. In Architect Workspace, create a blank document (Scale: ¼ inch; Size: US Arch D).
2. In Top/Plan view, draw a rectangle (16′ w × 24′ h).
3. Extrude the rectangle by 8′.
4. Draw a smaller rectangle (8′ w × 24′ h) overlapping the left side of the big rectangle.
5. Extrude the smaller rectangles to 4′.
6. In OIP, set the Bot Z of the smaller rectangle to 8′.
7. Use the Mirror Tool in the Basic palette to draw a vertical line aligning with the centerline of the big rectangle to create a mirror image of the smaller rectangle, overlapping the right side of the big rectangle.
8. Switch to Front view to see the base structure.
9. Go to Tool Sets – 3D Modeling and use the Set Working Plane Tool to set the Working Plane on the front face of the rectangle located at the upper right corner of the structure.
10. In the Basic palette, select Split Tool and Line Split Mode (on the Mode bar) to make a diagonal cut, starting from the upper left corner of the rectangle and ending at the lower right corner of the rectangle.

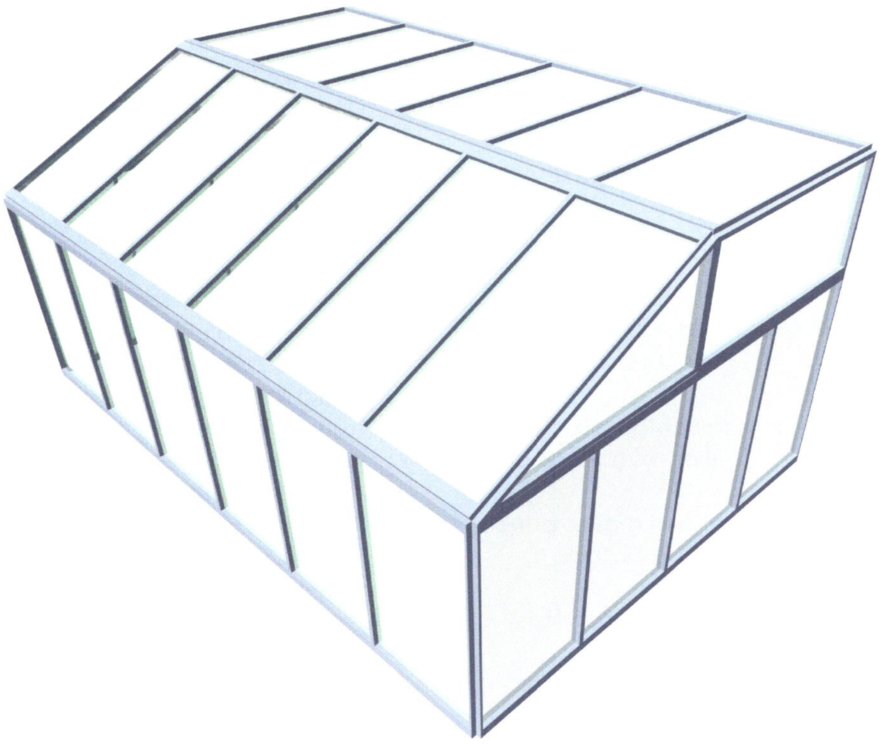

Figure 8.20 *Sunroom*. An example of using Extract Tool in the creation of a sunroom.

11. Deselect everything, and then select the triangle located at the upper right corner of the structure and delete it. Now the base structure of the sunroom is complete.

Create a Shell of the Base Structure

1. Still in Front view, go to Tool Sets – 3D Modeling – Extract Tool.
2. Use the tool to select the front, right, and back surfaces of the big cuboid. (Hover your mouse over a surface. When it is lit in RED, click on it to select it.)

   Note: You need to select multiple surfaces of the cuboid. You can do so by pressing the Shift key on the keyboard while switching views using either the Current View dropdown menu or the number keys on the keyboard to select the surfaces. (No. 2 for Front View; No. 8 for Back view; No. 4 for Left view; No. 6 for Right view.)

3. After selecting the front, right, and back surfaces of the cuboid, click on the Check Mark icon located on the Mode bar.
4. Switch to the Left view, select the cuboid base, and delete it.
5. Use the Flyover Tool to see that a shell of the cuboid is being created.
6. Use the same method to create a shell (front, back, and top surfaces) for the small cuboid.
7. Use the same method to create a shell (front, back, and right surfaces) for the triangular solid.

Create a Framed Glass Panel

1. In Top/Plan view, draw a rectangle (4′ w × 8′ h).
2. Use Offset Tool in Basic palette (Offset Distance: 2″) to create a smaller rectangle inside of the previous rectangle.
3. Select both rectangles and go to Top Menu – Modify – Clip Surface.
4. While the smaller rectangle is still selected, extrude it by 0.2″.
5. Go to OIP and click on the "Render" tab.
6. Select "Texture" in Texture dropdown menu.
7. In Resource Manager, search for a texture named "Glass Mirror Finish Green RT."
8. Drag and drop the texture icon onto the rectangle to give the rectangle a glass texture.
9. Select the large rectangle (It is now a frame.) and extrude it by 2″.

10. While the frame is still selected, go to the Attributes palette to select HSV (220, 51, 204) in the list of Classic Vectorworks Colors.
11. Render the panel in Shaded rendering mode to see the result.
12. Select both the glass and the frame and group them together.

Install the Glass Panels

1. Still in Top/Plan view, select the glass panel and go to Top Menu – Edit – Duplicate Array… to create six more panels.
2. In the Right Isometric view, select the big cuboid-base shell and ungroup the shell to make each side of the shell independent.
3. Select the left side of the shell and a glass panel.
4. Go to Top Menu – Model – Create Surface Array… A dialog window appears.
5. In the "Repetition Mode X – No. of Repetitions" slot, type "1."
6. In the "Repetition Mode Y – No. of Repetitions" slot, type "4."
7. Uncheck "Display Base Surface" and click "OK" to exit the window.
8. Select the right side of the shell and a glass panel.
9. Repeat Steps 4–8 to install six glass panels on the right side of the structure. The only difference this time is to change "4" to "6" in No. of Repetitions (Repetition Mode Y).
10. Switch to Back view and use the same method (Step 4–8) to install four glass panels on the back side of the structure.
11. Select the smaller cuboid, ungroup the surfaces, and use the same method to install six panels on the top side of the cuboid (Repetition Mode X – No. of Repetitions: 1; Repetition Mode Y – No. of Repetitions: 6).
12. Install one panel on the front side and one panel on the back side of the cuboid (Repetition Mode X – No. of Repetitions: 1; Repetition Mode Y – No. of Repetitions: 1).
13. Select the triangular shell and ungroup the surfaces.
14. Select the slanted roof top and use the same method to install six panels on it. (Repetition Mode X – No. of Repetitions: 1; Repetition Mode Y – No. of Repetitions: 6).
15. For the two triangular shells, go to Tool Sets – 3D Modeling – Set Working Plane Tool.
16. Use the tool to set the Working Plane on the triangular shell.
17. Use the 2D Polyline Tool in the Basic palette to draw a triangle (4′ h × 8′ w).
18. Use the Offset Tool in the Basic palette (Offset Distance: 2″) to create a smaller triangle inside the large triangle.
19. Select both triangles and go to Top Menu – Modify – Clip Surface.
20. While the smaller triangle is still selected, extrude it by 0.2″.
21. Go to OIP and click on the "Render" tab.
22. Select "Texture" in the Texture Dropdown menu and use "Glass Mirror Finish Green RT."
23. Select the large triangle (it is now a frame) and extrude it by 2″.
24. While the frame is still selected, go to the Attributes palette to select HSV (220, 51, 204) in the list of Classic Vectorworks Colors.
25. Repeat Steps 15–24 to install a triangular glass panel on the back side of the structure.
26. Your sunroom is now complete. View the result in an Isometric view, Normal Perspective projection, and Final Quality Renderworks rendering mode.

Create a Winding Path

1. In Architect Workspace, create a blank document (Scale: ¼ inch; Size: US Arch D).
2. Go to Top/Plan view. Use the Circle Tool and Radius mode to draw a circle (Radius: 12′).
3. Again, use the Circle Tool and Radius mode to draw a smaller circle (Radius: 4′) on top of the large circle, starting from the center of the large circle.
4. Select both circles and go to Top Menu – Modify – Clip Surface.
5. Delete the smaller circle. The large circle now takes on the shape of a ring.
6. Select the ring and extrude it by -2″
7. In Top/Plan view, use Split Tool and Line Spilt mode to cut the Rings horizontally, vertically, and diagonally, so that it becomes six slices (4 small slices; 2 large slices).
8. Move the pieces apart. and then move them next to each other one by one to form a winding path.
9. Make sure that the first 5 snapping modes on the Snapping palette are selected.
10. Apply the Rotate Tool in the Basic palette to connect them seamlessly, using the Z key to zoom in and the Shift+Arrow key to nudge if needed. (Refer to Fig. 8.21 *Winding Path* for the orientation and order of the components.)

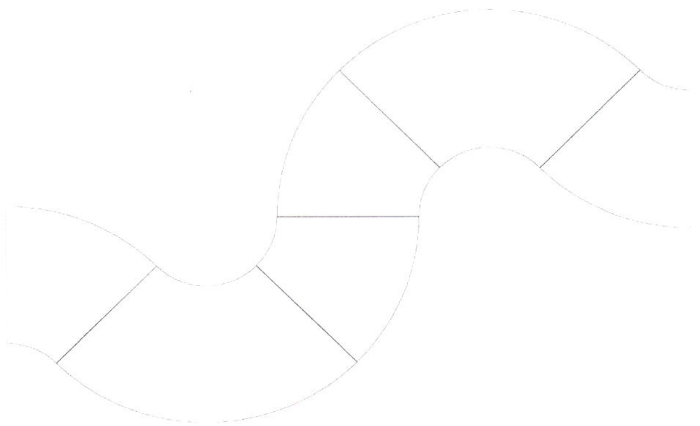

Figure 8.21 *Winding Path*. This image shows the practice of creating a winding path from a geometric shape.

Technique 8 – Modeling Nuances and Texture Manipulation (Episode Two)

In this episode, you will practice tools, commands, procedures, and techniques for modeling complex 3D structures.

Construct a Blue Dragon – A Roofed Walkway

Fig. 8.22 illustrates the outcome of the following procedure aiming to construct a roofed walkway named "Blue Dragon."

Preparation

1. Create a new blank document, set the scale to ¼″ and size to US Arch D.
2. In Architect Workspace, go to Top Menu – Tools – Options… – Vectorworks Preferences… A dialog box opens.
3. Click on 3D located on the left column. In the right column, make the following selections.
   a. 3D Conversion Resolution: High
   b. Default 3D view Render Mode: Shaded
4. Click "OK" to exit the window.
5. Create 13 Classes and name them:
   a. FLOOR
   b. GALLERY-ROOF BASE
   c. GALLERY-ROOF GLASS
   d. GALLERY-ROOF FRAME
   e. GALLERY-ROOF
   f. GALLERY-WALL BASE
   g. GALLERY-WALL GLASS
   h. GALLERY-WALL FRAME
   i. GALLERY-WALL
   j. ATRIUM-ROOF BASE
   k. ATRIUM-ROOF
   l. ATRIUM-FLOOR
   m. ATRIUM-POSTS
6. Save the file and name it "Blue Dragon."
7. Before you start drawing, make the default class "None" the active class.

Building a Gallery

Create a Roof Base for the Gallery

1. In Front view, use the 2D Locus Tool in the Basic palette to place a locus mark on the center of the page (the origin).
2. Use the Circle Tool and Radius Mode to draw two circles (Radius: 8′), one on top of the other, both starting from the center of the page.
3. Move one circle to the right side of the other circle, align them horizontally (press the "shift" key on the keyboard while moving the circle), and leave a small gap in between them.
4. Delete the circle located in the middle of the page.
5. Select both the locus mark and the circle and go to Top Menu – Model – Sweep…
6. When a dialog box opens, click "OK." A large ring mass has now taken shape.
7. Still in Front view, double-click on the ring to get to the "Sweep Profile" edit window.
8. While the circle is still selected, use the Clip tool in the Basic palette to draw a rectangle that covers the bottom half of the circle.
9. Click the "Exit Sweep Profile" button. The bottom half of the ring has now disappeared. This is the base for the roof of the gallery.

Create a Floor for the Gallery

Note: Here, we will apply the same method and technique that we used in Episode One, "Create a Winding Path," to create a winding path for the gallery.

1. Go to Top/Plan view. Use the Circle Tool and Radius mode to draw a circle (Radius: 24′) on the side of the ring.
2. Again, use the Circle Tool and Radius mode to draw a smaller circle (Radius: 8′) on top of the large circle, starting from the center of the large circle.
3. Select both circles and go to Top Menu – Modify – Clip Surface.
4. Delete the smaller circle. The large circle now takes on the shape of a ring.
5. Extrude the ring to -3″.

Figure 8.22 *Blue Dragon – A Roofed Walkway*. This image represents a Blue Dragon in a form of a roofed walkway as the material used for the walls and the roof are blue glass and aluminum. The roofed walkway in this image shows the result of the following practice.

6. Go to OIP, under the Render tab, select "Texture" in the Texture dropdown menu.
7. Go to Resource Manager, search for "Pavers (Arroway Pavement 006)"
8. When the texture swatch appears, click on it. Then drag and drop the texture onto the floor surface. When a dialog box appears. Click "OK" to close the window.
9. View the floor in Shaded rendering mode to verify the texture application.
10. Go to OIP, to increase the scale setting of the texture to "3."
11. Move the white ring (roof base) onto the top of the textured ring (floor).

Dissect the Rings and Form a Winding Path

1. In Top/Plan view, use Split Tool and Line Spilt mode to cut the Rings horizontally, vertically, and diagonally, so that it becomes six slices (4 small slices; 2 large slices).
2. Group each floor piece with its roof base.
3. Move the pieces apart. and then move them next to each other one by one to form a winding path.
4. Make sure that the first 5 snapping modes on the Snapping palette are selected.
5. Apply the Rotate Tool in the Basic palette to connect them seamlessly, using the Z key to zoom in and Shift + Arrow to nudge if needed.

Create a Shell for the Roof

1. Select all pieces and go to Top Menu – Modify – Ungroup so that the floor pieces are separate from the roof base pieces.
2. Select all the roof base pieces and group them.
3. Go to the Front view. Press the shift key on the keyboard while lifting the roof base significantly above the ground.

   Note: Here, we will apply the same method and technique that we used in Episode One, "Construct a Sunroom," to create a shell for the roof base and install the glass panels on the roof.

4. Ungroup the roof base pieces.
5. Go to the Right Isometric view. Click on the first roof base.
6. Go to Tool Sets – 3D modeling and click on "Extract." Select "Extract Surface Mode" on the Mode bar.
7. Hover your mouse over the first roof base. When it is lit in RED, click on it.
8. Click on the check mark on the Mode bar to execute the Extract Surface command.
9. View your model in the Lower Right Isometric view.
10. Use the Selection Tool to select the bottom surface of the first roof base.
11. Reassign this roof base to the "Gallery-Roof Base" class.
12. Go to the Navigation palette to make the Gallery Roof Base class invisible. A shell of the first Gallery roof base is now shown in your drawing area.
13. Repeat Steps 5–12 until the shells are created for all the roof pieces.

Create a Framed Glass Window for the Roof

1. Go to Top/Plan view, click on Regular Polygon Tool in the Basic palette and input 6 in Number of Sides on the Mode bar.
2. On the side of the roof shell, draw a six-sided polygon starting from the center to the right side (2′ diameter; 4′ total).
3. Click on the Off-Set Tool in the Basic palette, click on the Preference button on the mode bar, and Set the Offset by Distance preference to 3″.
4. Make a click inside the polygon to create a smaller polygon of that shape.
5. Select both polygons and go to Top Menu – Modify – Clip Surface.
6. While the smaller polygon is still selected, extrude it by 0.2″.
7. Go to OIP, under the Render tab, select "Texture" in the Texture dropdown menu.
8. Select the glass texture named "Glass Blue 03 RT" for the smaller polygon.
9. While the smaller polygon is still selected, go to OIP (under the Shape tab) to reassign it to a class named "Gallery-Roof Glass."
10. In your drawing area, select the large polygon, which is now a frame, and extrude it by 2″, and assign this polygon a medium gray color (Gray 40%) in the Attributes palette.
11. While the frame is still selected, go to OIP to reassign it to a class named "Gallery-Roof Frame."
12. Group both the glass and the frame.

Create an Arched Glass Roof for the Gallery

1. Select both the framed glass and the roof shell. Go to Top Menu – Model – Create Surface Array… A dialog window appears.

2. In this window, after making the following selections, click "OK" to close the window.
   a. Repetition Mode X, Number of Repetitions: 6
   b. Repetition Mode Y, Number of Repetitions: 4
   c. Uncheck "Display Base Surface."
3. See the first piece of Gallery Roof in Shaded rendering mode and Right Isometric view.
4. Go back to Top/Plan view and double-click on the newly created roof piece.
5. When a dialog box opens, check Array Items, and click "OK."
6. Select and copy the framed window and exit the dialog window.
7. Paste the framed window on the drawing area.
8. Select both the framed window and the second roof shell (a bigger one). Go to Top Menu – Model – Create Surface Array… A dialog window appears.
9. In this window, after making the following selections, click "OK" to close the window.
   a. Repetition Mode X, Number of Repetitions: 6
   b. Repetition Mode Y, Number of Repetitions: 8
   c. Uncheck "Display Base Surface."
10. See the second piece of Gallery Roof in Shaded rendering mode and Right Isometric view.

    Note: The only difference between the process of creating the first roof piece and the second roof piece is the Number of Repetitions in the Y slot (4 for the smaller first roof piece and 6 for the larger second roof piece.

11. Keep in mind two different sizes of the roof pieces while repeating Steps 7–9 to complete the rest of the Gallery roof pieces.
12. After the Rood is completed, select and group all the roof pieces and reassign them to a class named "Gallery-Roof."

Create a Wall-Base for the Gallery

1. Go to the Navigation palette to make the "Gallery-Roof" Class invisible.
2. Turn on the first five snapping tools in the Snapping palette.
3. Go to Tool Sets – Building Shell and click on the Wall Tool.
4. Select "Arc Path Mode," "Left Control Line Mode," and "Three Points Mode" on the Mode bar.
5. Click on the preference Tool on the Mode bar. In the dialog window, click on the Insertion Options tab, set the wall height to 8′, and click "OK" to close the window.
6. Alongside the curved floor, draw curved walls on the upper side of the winding path by making the first click at the beginning of the curve, the second click in the middle of the curve, and the third click at the end of the curve for each of the connected curves.

   Note: Before you make the first click for the next curve, make sure that the previous curve is lit in RED. This will ensure all the curved walls are connected.

7. After you have finished drawing the walls on the upper side of the winding path, switch from Left Control Line Mode on the Mode bar to Right Control Line Mode.
8. Draw the walls on the lower side of the winding path.

Insert Glass Doors for the Entrances/Exits of the Gallery

1. Go to Resource Manager to search for "Door Hinged French Patio."
2. Double-click on the Door Icon (a double paneled door) to select and download the door.
3. Insert the doors into the four shortest curved walls when they are lit in RED.
4. Go to OIP to adjust the door size to 6′ (w) × 8′ (h) for each of the four doors.

Create Glass Panels for the Gallery Walls

1. In Top/Plan view, draw a rectangle (6′ w. × 8′ h.).
2. Click on Offset Tool in the basic palette.
3. Click on the Preference button on the Mode bar to set the Offset Distance to 3″ and click "OK" to exit the preference window.
4. Click once inside the rectangle to create a smaller rectangle.
5. Select both rectangles and go to Top Menu – Modify – Clip Surface.
6. While the smaller rectangle is still selected, extrude it to 0.2 inches.
7. Go to OIP, click on the Render tab, and select "Texture" in the Texture dropdown menu.
8. Go to Resource Manager to search for a glass texture named "Glass Figured Light Blue RT."
9. Drag and drop the glass texture on the smaller rectangle when it is lit in RED. When a dialog box opens, click "OK" to accept the default.
10. Go to OIP to click on the Shape tab, reassign the glass to a Class named "Gallery-Wall Glass."

11. Select the larger rectangle, which is now a frame, and extrude it by 2″.
12. Go to the Attributes palette to select a medium gray (Gray 40%) for the frame.
13. Go to OIP to reassign the frame to a class named "Gallery-Wall Frame."
14. Select both the glass and the frame and group them.

Replace Walls with Glass Panels

Note: There are three widths of curved walls installed alongside the path. We will call them short walls, medium walls, and long walls. For the short walls, we will install 3 glass panels. For the medium walls, we will install 4 glass panels. For the long walls, we will install 8 glass panels. There is no repetition vertically.

1. Select the framed glass panel and copy it. You will paste it multiple times during this process.
2. In Right Isometric View, select the first wall on the left side.
3. Go to Tool Sets – 3D Modeling – Extract.
4. Make sure that the Extract Surface Mode on the Mode bar is selected.
5. Hover your mouse over the left side of the first wall and make a click when this side of the wall is lit in RED.
6. Click on the Check Mark located on the Mode bar.
7. Zoom in on the wall and use the Selection Tool to select the top side of the wall (wall base)
8. Go to OIP to reassign the wall base to a Class named "Gallery-Wall Base."
9. Go to the Navigation palette to make the "Gallery-Wall Base" class invisible. You will now see that a shell of the wall appears in your drawing area.
10. Select both the shell of the wall and the glass panel and go to Top Menu – Model – Create Surface Array.
11. When a dialog window appears, make the following selections.
    a. Repetition Mode X, No. of Repetitions: 8
    b. Repetition Mode Y, No. of Repetitions: 0
    c. Uncheck the "Display Base Surface" box.
12. Click "OK" to exit the window. (The solid wall is now replaced by eight glass panels.)
13. Repeat this process for all the solid walls in the gallery, starting your process by pasting the framed glass panel on the side of a solid wall. Refer to the number of glass panels needed for short walls, medium walls, and long walls stipulated in the note at the beginning of this process. (Replace Walls with Glass Panels.)
14. After the solid walls on one side of the Gallery are replaced by glass panels, switch to the Left Rear Isometric view to install the glass panels for the walls on the other side.

Bring the Components of the Gallery Together

1. Go to the Navigation palette to make the "Gallery-Roof" Class visible.
2. Go to Front view, select the roof, and drag the roof downward to meet the top of the glass panels while pressing the shift key to make sure that the horizontal position of the roof does not shift.
3. See the result of the complete gallery in an isometric view.

Building the Atrium

Fig. 8.23 illustrates the outcome of the following procedure aiming to build an atrium for the "Blue Dragon."

Create a Floor for the Atrium

1. In Top/Plan view, use the Circle Tool in the Basic palette to draw a circle (Radius: 15′) adjacent to the gallery.
2. Extrude the circle by -3″.
3. Go to OIP, under the Render tab, select "Texture" in the Texture dropdown menu.

Figure 8.23 Blue Dragon – Atrium Roof. This image shows how the atrium glass ceiling looks from a lower angle.

4. Go to Resource Manager, search for "Pavers (Arroway Pavement 006)"
5. When the texture swatch appears, click on it. Then drag and drop the texture onto the floor surface. When a dialog box appears. Click "OK" to close the window.
6. View the floor in Shaded rendering mode to verify the texture application.
7. Go to OIP, to increase the scale setting of the texture to "3."

Create a Roof for the Atrium

1. In Top/Plan view, use the Hemisphere Tool available in Tool Sets – 3D Modeling to draw a hemisphere (diameter: 15′) on the top of the Atrium Floor.
2. In Front view, drag the hemisphere upward above the gallery roof while pressing the Shift key to ensure that the horizontal position of the hemisphere does not move.
3. In Lower Right Isometric view, go to Tool Sets – 3D Modeling – Extract.
4. Hover your cursor over the curved surface and make a click when the surface is lit in RED.
5. Click on the Check Mark on the Mode bar to execute the "Extract Surface" command.
6. Use the Selection Tool to select the bottom surface of the hemisphere.
7. Go to OIP and reassign the hemisphere to a class named "Atrium-Roof Base."
8. Go to the Navigation palette to make the "Atrium-Roof Base" class invisible.
9. A shell of the Atrium Roof appears in your drawing area.
10. Ungroup the Gallery Roof and double-click on one piece of the glass roof. A dialog box opens.
11. Check "Array Items" and click "OK."
12. Select the framed polygon panel and copy it.
13. Press the "Exit Array Items" button.
14. In Top/Plan view, paste the polygon panel on the side of the atrium roof shell.
15. Select both the roof shell and the polygon panel.
16. Go to the Top Menu – Model – Create Surface Array... A dialog window opens.
17. In this window, make the following selections.
    a. Repetition Mode X, No. of Repetitions: 6
    b. Repetition Mode Y, No. of Repetitions: 24
    c. Uncheck the "Display Base Surface" box.
18. Click "OK" to exit the window. Now, you can see a glass dome shows up in the drawing area.
19. Go to Front view, move the dome downward to level it with the top of the rectangle frame, and press the Shift key to make sure that the dome does not move horizontally.

Create Supporting Posts for the Atrium Roof

1. In Top/Plan view, select the glass dome and go to OIP to reassign the dome to the class named "Atrium Roof."
2. Go to the Navigation palette to make the Atrium Roof class invisible.
3. Use the Rectangle Tool and Center to Corner mode to draw a square (32′ × 32′ total) on the top of the Atrium circle.
4. Use the square as a reference to draw a horizontal line, a vertical line, two cross diagonals starting from the corners of the square, each longer than the circle and passing through the center of the square…
5. Delete the square.
6. Select all four lines and go to Top Menu – Modify – Rotate.
7. When a dialog window opens, type -7.5 in the angle slot and click "OK." The positions of these lines indicate the positions of the posts.
8. Draw a circle (6″ radius; 1′ diameter) on the side of the Atrium.
9. Extrude the circle to 8′3″ to create a post.
10. Duplicate the post 6 times so that you have 7 posts.
11. Place each post on a line, except for the line that goes into the gallery, and inside the largest circle of the Atrium.
12. Select all the posts, go to the Attributes palette, and assign a medium gray color (Gray 40%) to the posts.
13. Delete the lines.
14. Go to the Navigation palette to make the Atrium Roof class visible.
15. See the result in the Right Isometric view.

Presentation

1. Go to Tool Set – Visualization – Light
2. Select Directional Light Mode on the Mode bar.
3. Place the light somewhere on the lower left side of the Blue Dragon.
4. Go to Top Menu – View – Set Renderworks Background…
5. When a dialog window opens, select HDRI Sky Day Partially Cloudy in the Renderworks Background dropdown menu.
6. Your Blue Dragon is now complete.

Technique 8 – Modeling Nuances and Texture Manipulation (Episode Three)

In this episode, you will learn to use new tools, commands, procedures, and techniques in the creation of exterior hardscapes and softscapes.

Create a Manmade Lake and the Environment for the Blue Dragon

Fig. 8.24 illustrates the outcome of the following procedure designed to create a manmade lake and an environment for the "Blue Dragon."

Preparation

1. Create a new blank document.
2. Set the scale to ¼" by right clicking your mouse (PC) or Ctrl + Click (Mac) and selecting Active Layer Scale.
3. Turn on the first five snapping icons on the Snapping palette.
4. In Top/Plan view, draw an oval shape (width: 220′; height: 160′) to create the surface of a grassland.
5. In the middle of the oval, draw a reference square (120′ × 120′) for the lake.
6. Go to Tool Sets – Visualization – Light. Select "Directional Light Mode" on the Mode bar.
7. Install a Directional Light on the left side of the square, pointing toward the top middle of the square.
8. In OIP, make the following selections.
   a. Check both "Cast Shadows" and "Soft Shadows."
   b. Brightness: 100
   c. Color: White
   d. Z: 25′
9. Save the file and name it "Manmade Lake – Blue Dragon Resort."

Create a Water Container

1. On the top of the square, use the Polygon Tool to draw an irregular polygon about the same size as the square and in the shape of a lake. Before you make the last click, press the "Z" key to make sure that the polygon is closed. If not, go to OIP to close it.
2. Double-click on the polygon to select the Reshape Tool.

Figure 8.24 *Blue Dragon Playing with Water*. This image situates the Blue Dragon in a resort-like environment. It places the dragon in a manmade lake surround by a grassland with some plants. It shows the result of the following practice.

3. Click the "Change Vertex Mode" icon located on the Mode Bar.
4. Click on the "Reshape Tool Preferences" icon, a "Fillet Setting" dialog box appears.
5. Insert 10′ in the Fillet Radius slot and click "OK" to close the window.
6. While the Change Vertex Mode is still selected, click on Bezier Control Point Mode to select it.
7. Click on the corners of the polygon one by one to make the polygon appear rounded and organic.
8. Copy and paste the organic shape, and drag one copy of the organic shape (the water surface) to the side.
9. Delete the reference square.
10. Select both the oval and the other copy of the organic shape and go to Top Menu – Modify – Clip Surface. A grassland shape is created. Drag the grassland shape to the side.
11. Select the organic shape in the model and extrude it by –40′.
12. Switch to Front view and go to Tool Sets – 3D Modeling – Set Working Plane.
13. Use the "Set Working Plane Tool" to set the working plane that is parallel to the picture plane.
14. Use the Polygon Tool to draw an irregular polygon that covers the lower part of the organic form that you have just created.
15. Extrude this polygon by –140′.
16. Switch to the Top/Plan view and move the new form to cover the entire body of the organic form.
17. Select both forms and go to Top Menu – Subtract Solid.
18. When the organic form is lit in RED, click "OK."
19. See the result in the Right Isometric view.
20. Select the organic form.
21. Go to Tool Sets – 3D Modeling – Shell Solid.
22. Click on the "Shell Solid Tool Preferences" icon. A dialog window appears.
23. Under "Shell," select Outside. Under "Thickness," insert 3′. Check "Select Tangent Surfaces," and click "OK."
24. Click once on the top of the organic shape to select it. The form turns RED.
25. Click on the Check Mark on the Mode bar to execute the "Shell Solid" command. The organic shape is now hollowed out and becomes a water container.
26. In OIP, set the Z Scale to 1.05.

Create a Body of Water

1. In Top/Plan view, select the organic shape (the water surface) and drag it to place it inside the water container.
2. Extrude the water surface by -6″ to create a body of water.
3. In OIP, change the Bot Z to -6″. See the result in the Right Isometric view.

Apply Water Texture

1. Select the body of water.
2. In OIP, click on the "Render" tab and select "Texture" in the Texture dropdown menu.
3. In Resource Manager, search for a texture named "Landscape Water Clear RT" and double-click the icon to select it.
4. When the "Import Resources window" shows up, check "Select destination folder:" and click "OK."
5. The water texture icon shows up in OIP and is applied to the body of water in the drawing area.

Manipulate Texture Shaders

1. Still in Resource Manager, click on the "Home" icon and select the texture swatch that you imported (E.G., "Landscape Water Clear RT") and right click your mouse (PC) or Ctrl + Click (Mac) to select "Edit." An Edit Texture window appears.
2. In the window named "Landscape Water Clear RT," make the following choices.

   Shaders

   a. Color: Image
      Click on "Edit..." and make the following choices in Image Color Shader.
        Tile Image
          Check Horizontal.
          Check Vertical.
        Filter Color
          Check No Filter and click "OK."
   b. Reflectivity: Mirror
      Click on "Edit..." and make the following choices in Mirror Shader.
        Color: White
        Reflection: 100
        Blurriness: 0
   c. Transparency: Color
      Click on "Edit..." and make the following choices in Color Shader.
        Color: Azure-Blue 12
        Brightness: 100

d. Bump: Noise
   Click on "Edit…" and make the following choices in Noise Shader.
   Pattern: Box
   Bumps
   Strength: 50
   Parallax Offset: 50
   Heights: 0; 100
   Scale
   Global: 100
   Relative U: 100; V: 100; W: 100
   Options
   Dimensionality: 2D Wrapped
   Detail: 3
   Cycles: 0
   Low Clip: 0
   High Clip: 100
   Displacement Mapping
   Height: 3″
   Detail: Medium
   Uncheck Self-Shadowing

Note: Displacement Mapping setting will overwrite the strength setting in Bump Shader.

Size: 3′0″
Shadows: Check both "Cast" and "Receive" boxes.
Preview Options
e. Obj Type: Plane
f. Obj Size: 6′0″
g. Check "Color," "Reflectivity," "Transparency," and "Bump."
3. Click "OK" to exit the Edit Texture window.
4. In OIP, change the scale to 5.

Complete the Grassland

1. Select the grassland shape and extrude it by -6″.
2. In OIP, change the Bot Z to 0.
3. Place the grassland outside of the lake.
4. In OIP, click on the Render tab. Select "Texture" In the Texture dropdown menu.
5. In Resource Manager, search for "Grass" and double-click on a swatch named "Grass Sports Lawn 02 <Displace Map> RT" to select it.

Plant Trees and Bushes

Plant Trees and Bushes through Softlandscape

1. Go to Top Menu – Tools – Workspaces – Landmark
2. In Top/Plan view, go to Tool Sets – Softlandscape – Plant.
3. In the Mode bar, select "Insertion Mode" and "Poly-Edge Spaced Mode."
4. Click on the "Plant Tool Preferences" icon. A preferences window opens.
5. Click on the "Use Style" dropdown menu. A Resource Manager selection window appears.
6. On the left column, go to Vectorworks Libraries – Plant -Plant Styles. Scroll down to look for a folder named "Shrub Evergreen."
7. Click on "Buxus.vwx." Several choices appear in the middle column.
8. Click on a shrub named "Buxus microphylla var. koreana" and select the plant.
9. In the preference window, click on "Size and Spacing," located on the left column.
10. Insert 5′ in Spacing – Fixed Spacing slot and click "OK" to exit the window.
11. In your drawing area, along the left side of the lake, plant a row of shrubs.
12. Use the same method (Steps 1–10) to select a palm tree named "Phoenix canariensis."
13. Select "Single Plant Placement Mode" on the Mode bar.
14. In the drawing area, plant a few palm trees on the grassland.

Plant Trees and Bushes through Visualization

Laubwerk plant route

1. Go to Tool Sets – Visualization and click on "Laubwerk Plant."
2. In the Mode bar, click on the "Laubwerk Plant Tool Preferences" icon. A dialog box appears.
3. Click "Global Settings" tab. In the 3D Representation dropdown menu, select "Low Detail."
4. Click the "Object Properties" tab.
5. Click on the "Select plant…" button. A Laubwerk Plant Catalog opens.
6. Double-click on the tree named "juneberry – Amelanchier lamarckii" to select and download the tree.
7. Click "OK" to exit the Preferences window.
8. In the drawing area, plant a few trees in the grassland.

RenderMall Plant Route

1. Go to Tool Sets – Visualization and click on "RenderMall Plant."
2. In the Mode bar, click on the "RenderMall Plant" dropdown menu and select a plant named "Lonicera 1."
3. Place a few clusters of this plant along the top edge of the grassland.

Set the Background for the Scene

1. View the lake in the Right Isometric view and the Normal Perspective view.
2. Go to the Top Menu – View – Set the Renderworks Background. A dialog window opens.
3. In the Renderworks Background dropdown menu, select "HDRI Sky Day Mostly Sunny" and click "OK."

Place the Blue Dragon Inside the Lake

1. Open the file named "Blue Dragon" and select and copy the model.
2. In the file named "Manmade Lake – Blue Dragon Resort," paste the model in the middle of the lake.

Render the Scene

1. Go to the View bar, and under the Current Render Mode (Teapot icon) dropdown menu, select "Shaded."
2. Still under the current Render Mode dropdown menu, select Shaded Options.
3. When a dialog box appears, make the following choices:
   a. Options
      Check "Textures," "Colors," "Anti-aliasing," and "Shadows."
      Uncheck "On ground only" and "Draw edges."
      Check "Environment lighting," "Environment reflections," and "Object reflections."
   b. Quality
      Details: High
      Shadows: High
4. Click "OK."

   Note: For details, you might want to put another directional light source from the right side of the scene to soften the shadows. Deselect "Cast Shadows." in OIP and set the brightness to 60. You might want to assign a texture to the edge of the lake container (Concrete Lightest IF). You might also want to assign the doors and walls the same gray as the frames of the glasses (Gray 40%).

5. Use the Space Bar on your Keyboard and the Flyover Tool to customize your view and go to the View bar to click on the Save View dropdown menu to select Save View…
6. When a dialog window opens, give the view a name and click "OK" to save the view for later access.

Experiment and Practice

Customize a Window

Fig. 8.25 illustrates the outcome of the following procedure aiming to customize a window.

1. Create a new document. Set the scale to ½″ and the size to US Arch D.
2. Go to Tool Sets – Building Shell – Wall tool.
3. Click on the tool preference icon in the Mode bar.
4. When the preference window opens, under Definition, insert 6″ in the Overall Thickness slot. Under Insertion Options, insert 10′ in the Height slot. Click "OK."
5. In Top/Plan view, draw a wall (length: 10′) that is parallel with the picture plane.
6. Go to Tool Sets – Building Shell – Window Tool.
7. Insert a window in the middle of the wall.

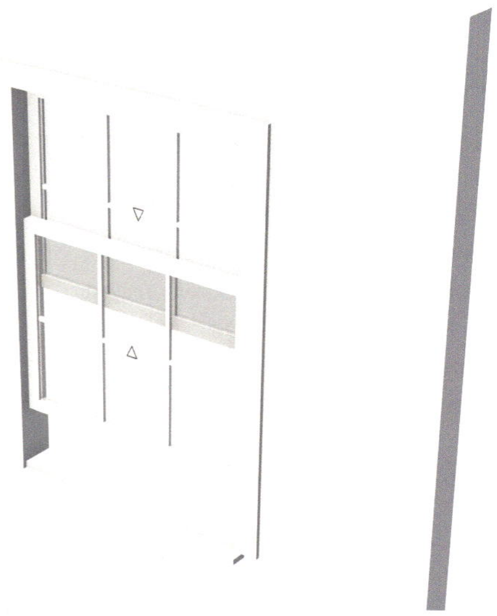

Figure 8.25 *Custom Window*. This image shows the result of the following practice.

8. Go to OIP and double-click on Settings… A Window Settings dialog window opens. (Note: all the changes you make in this window will be reflected on the 3D Preview box located on the right column.)
   - In the left column, click on "General" and make the following changes.
     i. Width: 4′
     ii. Height: 6′
     iii. Elevation in Wall: 8′
     iv. Configuration: Hang
     v. Operation: Double Hung
   - In the left column, click on "3D Visualization."
     i. Uncheck "Show interior marker."
     ii. Check "Show 3D open."
     iii. Open Angle: 30.
   - In the left column, click on "Sill."
     i. Check "include sill."
   - In the left column, click on "Trim."
     i. Check "include interior trim.
   - In the left column, click on Muntins
     i. Check both "Top sash" and "Bottom sash."
     ii. Pattern: Colonial
     iii. Vertical Bars: 2
     iv. Horizontal Bars: 1
     v. Bar Width: ¾″
     vi. Bar Depth: ½″
9. Click "OK" to close the window.
10. See the result in an isometric view and render it in Final Quality Renderworks.

Give the Room a Finishing Touch

Open the file named "Mock Box Set" that you created previously (refer to Chapter 6 – Technique 6) and give the room a finishing touch by complete the following tasks.

- Use the technique you acquired in Customize a Window (See the exercise above) to customize the window in the room.
- Use the technique you acquired in Create a Curtain (Technique 8, Episode 1) to install two folded curtains on both sides of the window.
- Use the technique you acquired in Install mouldings and Trims (Technique 8 Episode 1) to install casings for the door(s), the door opening, and the window.
- Use the technique you acquired in Install mouldings and Trims (Technique 8 Episode 1) to install baseboard and crown moulding.
- Use the technique you acquired in Install mouldings and Trims (Technique 8 Episode 1) to mount a framed picture on the wall.

Building a Flower Bed

Imagine that you have an area, roughly 30′ (w) × 8′ (d), in front of your house waiting for you to plant some trees, bushes, and flowers. You want to level the area with a retaining wall and turn this area into a flower bed. Use the tools and tool modes available in the VW program to create the most gorgeous flower bed in the world that your neighbors will be jealous of you.

Manipulate Texture Shaders

Create a new document. Go to Resource Manager – Create a new Renderworks Texture. In the Edit Texture window, create one of the following textures by manipulating four texture Shaders, (their options and perimeters). You may import an image or use an image existing in the VW program. You will experience trails-and-errors to get what you intended.

1. Sawdust Texture (Figure 8.26)
2. Wrinkly Foil Texture (Figure 8.27)
3. Frosted Plexiglass Texture (Figure 8.28)
4. Metallic Glitter Texture (Figure 8.29)
5. Pebble Stone Texture (Figure 8.30)

Figure 8.26 *Sawdust Texture*. Photo by Collab Media on Unsplash. *Unsplash*, 11 Jan. 2022, unsplash.com/photos/Qwem1LxlnBc.

Figure 8.27 *Wrinkly Foil Texture*

Figure 8.28 *Frosted Plexiglass Texture*

Figure 8.29 *Metallic Glitter Texture*

Figure 8.30 *Pebble Stone Texture*

Bibliography

Alan. *Creating a Swimming Pool in Vectorworks*. *YouTube*, YouTube, 12 June 2019,. Accessed 5 June 2022.

Allen, Kevin Lee. *Vectorworks for Entertainment Design: Using Vectorworks to Design and Document Scenery, Lighting, and Sound*. Routledge, 2021.

Appleton, Eric. *Drafting Fundamentals for the Entertainment Classroom: A Process-Based Introduction Integrating Hand Drafting, Vectorworks, and SketchUp*. Routledge/Taylor & Francis Group, 2022.

Baer, Tom. *Vectorworks 10 for Windows & Macintosh: Visual Quickstart Guide*. Peachpit Press, 2003.

Beautiful Life Studio. Fig. 1 and Fig. 12 *Wedding Photo*. Curtesy of Grace Lu and Bing Luo. 2022.

Callab Media. Fig. 8.26 *Sawdust Texture. Unsplash*, unsplash.com/photos/Qwem1LxlnBc. Accessed Jan.11 2022.

Jansenson, Daniel. *Remarkable Renderworks Ep. 13: Altering Textures with Displacement Mapping. YouTube*, Vectorworks, 20 Apr. 2017a, https://www.youtube.com/watch?v=J2h2bGDWzLg. Accessed 30 Dec. 2018.

Jansenson, Daniel. *Remarkable Renderworks Ep. 18: Applying Textures Pt. 2. YouTube*, Vectorworks, 20 Apr. 2017b, https://www.youtube.com/watch?v=F0EEkeBIgAQ. Accessed 2017.

Jansenson, Daniel. *Remarkable Renderworks Ep. 35: Grass. YouTube*, Vectorworks, 1 Aug. 2017c, https://www.youtube.com/watch?v=DUWaftzqhq8. Accessed 18 Jan. 2023.

Jansenson, Daniel. *Applying Textures Part 1. YouTube*, Vectorworks, 20 Apr. 2018, https://www.youtube.com/watch?v=GP33XXCkkCc. Accessed 8 Nov. 2017.

Jonathan Reeves, *Creating Complex Scenery, YouTube*, Vectorworks, 1 Aug. 2021, https://www.youtube.com/watch?v=kKMkh_a5Hfk. Accessed 19 May 2022.

Knu, Su. *7.2a Plant Tool - Vectorworks 2023. YouTube*, Vectorworks, 17 Feb. 2023, https://www.youtube.com/watch?v=Du9hRSF4_64. Accessed 1 July 2023.

Macluskie, Steve. *Vectorworks for Theatre*. Entertainment Technology Press, 2015.

McBeath, Geoff. *Vectorworks 2008 Fundamentals: Course Notes and Workbook*. Resolve Software Solutions, 2008.

Media, Collab. Fig. 8.23 *Sawdust Texture*. Photo by Collab Media on Unsplash." *Unsplash*, 11 Jan. 2022, unsplash.com/photos/Qwem1LxlnBc. Accessed 15 Apr. 2023.

Vectorworks. *Site Design - Creating Hardscape. YouTube*, YouTube, 12 Sept. 2017, https://www.youtube.com/watch?v=4zWmCimwH0g. Accessed 7 Jan. 2019.

Vectorworks. *Water Textures - Bump Shader. YouTube*, YouTube, 21 Aug. 2018, https://www.youtube.com/watch?v=v2x1qKftVQo. Accessed 25 Oct. 2021.

Vectorworks. *Water Textures - Colors. YouTube*, YouTube, 21 Aug. 2018, https://www.youtube.com/watch?v=IvLwEvxtAu0. Accessed 3 Apr. 2023.

Vectorworks. *Interiors – Designing a Home Office. YouTube*, Vectorworks, 10 May 2021, https://www.youtube.com/watch?v=D_RkNVZdPhI. Accessed 12 Mar. 2023.

Designers and Art Directors

DOI: 10.4324/9781003266242-9

evan alexander

van Alexander is a 3D concept artist and visualizer working across multiple industries, with a background n set and production design. His work has helped teams visualize project designs for five Super Bowl alftime shows, the 2016 Democratic National Convention, the 2019 MTV VMAs, Harry Potter and the Cursed hild, and concert tours for Imagine Dragons and the Spice Girls. He also works in architecture, product, nd automobile imagery helping companies like Apple and Peloton tell their story through visual imagery. former senior designer for MTV Networks, Evan also adjuncts at NYU's Tisch School of the Arts.

arisian Dining Room. Modeled in Vectorworks and rendered in Cinema4D.

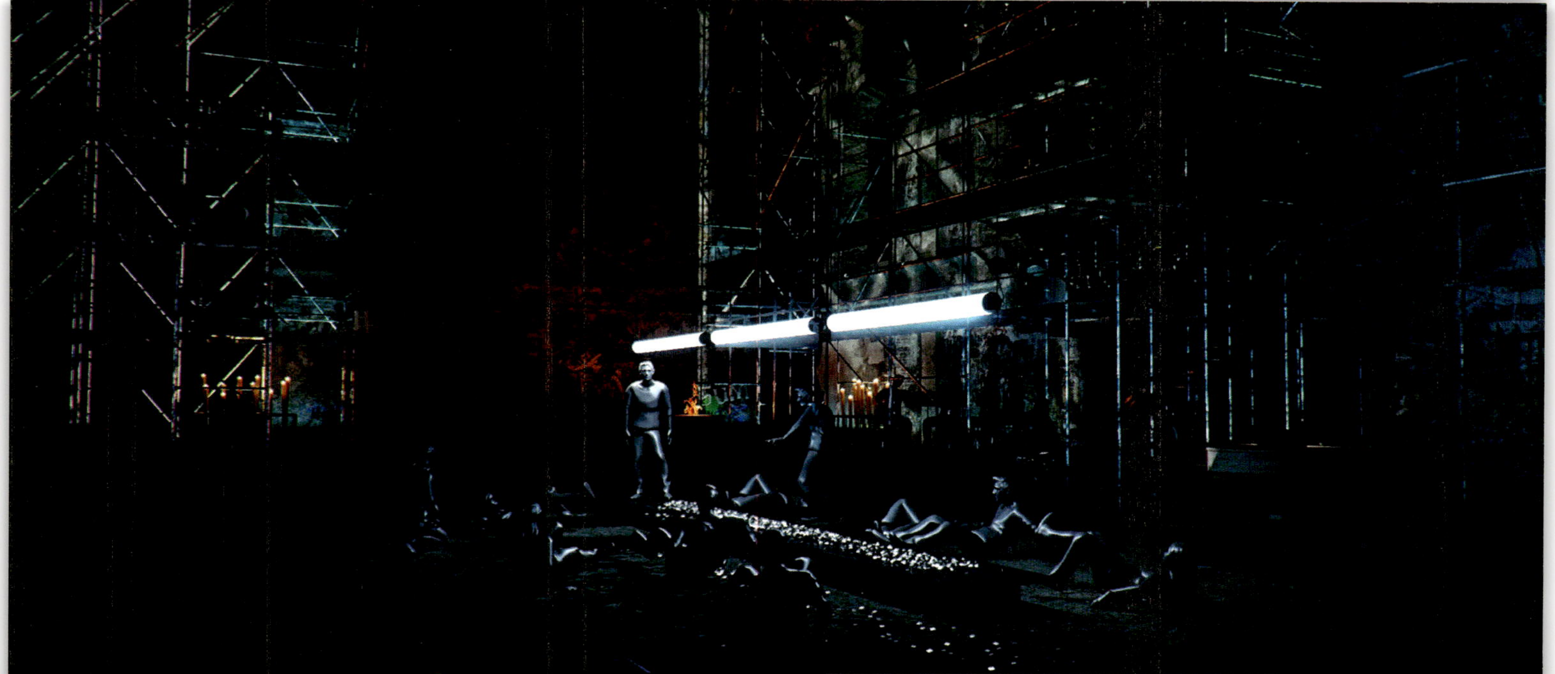

Jesus Christ Superstar: Live Production Design by Jason Ardizzone-West

Digital renderings modeled in Vectorworks and rendered in Cinema4D

La Vette Social Club Design by Evan Alexander & Christine Jones

Digital renderings modeled in Vectorworks and rendered in Cinema4D

Various Volumetric Lighting Studies

Light beams created using the Redshift Render Engine for Cinema4D.

Light beams are usually rendered separately and then laid into a rendering in Photoshop. This gives me the maximum amount control and lets us write cues and build layered looks in Photoshop faster then rendering each scene.

Interview with Evan Alexander

The following interview between Evan Alexander (Alexander), a veteran of and expert in the application of Vectorworks and Cinema4D, and Ming Chen (Chen), the author of this book, was conducted in the form of e-mail correspondences. The back-and-forth email messages took place between July 20 and August 18, 2023.

Chen: You received an MFA in Scene Design for theatre and opera, but ended up thriving in art direction, working on TV productions, and large events, such as Super Bowl Halftime shows, the 2016 DNC Convention, People's Choice Awards and, most recently, Summer for the City at Lincoln Center. What prompts you to make this switch?

Rachael Ray's 30 Minute Meals (TV Series). Digital Rendering. Set Design by Amy Gavin. Digital model and render by Evan Alexander. Converted Brooklyn loft space. 2019.

Alexander: I think it is more of an evolution than a distinct choice. I did work in theatre and opera for many years after grad school in New York, both as a designer and assistant. I worked with people like Christine Jones and Robin Wagner; drafting and model making as I tried to develop my own career as a designer. In Tom Lynch's studio, I taught myself Photoshop as we developed backdrops for Seattle Opera's Ring Cycle and eventually, I started doing more and more photoshop work as part of my overall design process. In 2001, my friend Andi Blady brought me into MTV Networks to help photoshop some sketches and a whole new world of event design was presented to me there. Here was a place where I could design really lavish environments with fewer restrictions, and much higher budgets, in shorter period of time than the theatre or opera world. I joined the staff there for many years and got an on-the-job education about event design. I liked that I could create spaces that people actually walked into instead of just being seen front on from the auditorium. From there, I worked at a firm that did museum and exhibit designs. Then, when I went back to freelancing, I started getting asked about helping with fashion shows, red carpets, and other design related environments that I had never dreamed of in school. So, it really happened by accident and organically over many years.

Study for DJ Set Up. An image modeled in Vectorworks and rendered in Cinema4D. Design and digital model and render by Evan Alexander. Study for creating digital audience members. 2017.

I was working on a corporate job where I first met Bruce Rodgers of Tribe Design. He introduced me to the world of concert design and that was finally the place where I felt all these different experiences and styles of work came together in a medium that I could really understand and do my best work. Through all of this, I developed more and more digital skills and am constantly trying to enhance and improve in those areas as I take on new and different projects. The story telling, concept development, and problem-solving skills I learned in school has always been the basis of each job, no matter what avenue it is being developed in, so I am grateful for my training and years in theatre to really round me out as a designer and illustrator.

Super Bowl Halftime Show: Bruno Mars. An image Modeled in Vectorworks and rendered in Cinema4D. Set Design by Bruce Rodgers, Tribe Design. Digital model and render by Evan Alexander. MetLife Stadium. 2014.

Super Bowl Halftime Show: Katy Perry. An image Modeled in Vectorworks and rendered in Cinema4D. Set Design by Bruce Rodgers, Tribe Design. Digital model and render by Evan Alexander. University of Phoenix Stadium. 2015.

Chen: You are teaching in the Design for Stage & Film department at NYU Tisch School of the Arts. Based on your professional experience, nowadays, what do you think are the essential skills an aspiring scenic designer, production designer, or art director needs to acquire while he/she is studying in school?

Alexander: I think a strong education in digital image creation, based on a traditional media foundation is the best. It's still important to learn how to draw and how to paint, even in the modern digital age we are in. Digital skillsets are based on the concepts and guidelines that traditional media teach us (color theory, composition, contrast, guiding the viewer's eye) so developing those skills are still incredibly important and valuable. Explore those ideas and concepts without complicated software on top of it first, then develop your digital skills. I still doodle my ideas out on paper before I ever pick up the mouse. Being able to draft a solid ground plan, section, and elevation of a design is key as well – these tools are critical to the design process. There are things we learn from doing these drawings that practicing on sketches can't really teach us. So, sketch and drafting go hand in hand. Drafting isn't just what you do at the end of the design process – it is a major part of development as you bring your larger conceptual ideas into the focus of reality.

People's Choice Awards 2018_1. An image modeled in Vectorworks and rendered in Cinema4D. Set Design by Jason Sherwood. Digital model and render by Evan Alexander. Barker Hangar.

I think all designers should learn these digital image making skills since it does force you, in a good way, to get the idea out of words and hand gestures and into a visual reality that can be shared with other people. You don't have to love it and maybe you will be a huge famous designer with a whole art department of people helping you develop your designs – but if you've done it yourself, your ability to work with that team, to move their work forward, to understand the technical process just enough and collaboratively develop a concept together will be much better and more efficient. Doing 3D renderings also makes set and production designers light their scenes and even make blocking and costume choices as well. Lighting your own set really makes you understand it in a way that physical models or hand sketches can't explore, and I think this makes for better scenery and certainly a better process with your collaborators. The same concept applies to cameras: once you have to frame a shot, pick the mm lens size for the camera, place actors and create a still, you see and understand the film in a whole different way. I think these skills are critical for all designers and they teach things about your ideas that you can't see or learn in any other ways.

Chen: When did you start using Vectorworks and why did you choose Vectorworks as your foundational tool for modeling and drafting over other available software, especially since many builders use AutoCAD for their construction drawings?

People's Choice Awards 2018_2. An image modeled in Vectorworks and rendered in Cinema4D. Set Design by Jason Sherwood. Digital model and render by Evan Alexander. Barker Hangar.

Alexander: When I started at MTV Networks in the early 2000s, I was first exposed to Vectorworks. I had been hand drafting all my projects up until that point and Vectorworks was the chosen software in that office. I love the simplicity of it and worked with it for many years only as a 2d tool before starting to develop my 3D skills with it. I tried to learn AutoCAD a few times, but Vectorworks always draws me back with its ease of use. Learning both is, of course, the best, as it makes you more employable and gives you the most options, but in entertainment, I've never run into problems with Vectorworks. I don't get religious about software, and I think people should use whatever works for them and their workflow. Both packages are fully capable, and I encourage people to try both with an open mind and see which they want to come back to.

Chen: You said that, in entertainment, you have never run into problems with Vectorworks. Is it because Vectorworks can easily be exported into different file formats that other programs, such as AutoCAD, can open the file, or is it because, from your experience, most of the collaborators, such as lighting designer and the people in the shop, also use Vectorworks?

Alexander: I have found most designers and firms I work with are Vectorworks based and most fabricators I work with are AutoCAD based. Certainly, Vectorwork's connection with Lightwrite makes it the standard in theatre, but most of the concert and event designers I work with are using it as well. There is very good file exchange though – I certainly receive most of my large venue files as DWG or if we are working with a large staging or tent company – those drawings are always DWG as well and Vectorworks imports them with ease. I export my drawings to DWG when asked and, so far, I've never had anyone come back to me with a problem. On *Jesus Christ Superstar: Live*, the Art Department was AutoCAD based and I and one other guy modeling for the design were using Vectorworks, but they took our models and converted them with no trouble for plating, so it doesn't seem to be much of an issue from my point of view. I'll say that I try to do as much Solid Modeling in Vectorworks as possible, and by this, I mean I model everything from scratch (with the exception of truss). I don't use the Wall, Roof, Slab tools or even any of the Stage Decking or Rigging tools which are all parametric. So, I don't know about the exchange with those kinds of Plug-in Objects – I tend to keep things as simple as possible. If I'm drawing a 40x60 stage deck – I will just draw a rectangle and extrude it. I know the fabricators are going to do their own drawings with steel deck, cross bracing, swivel feet, etc. and there is no need for me to draw that stuff unless it's a critical part of the designer's look in renderings.

Chen: Could you describe your standard Workflow?

Sam Smith – The Thrill of it All Tour_model. An image modeled in Vectorworks and rendered in Cinema4D. Set design by Jason Sherwood. Digital model by Evan Alexander. International Arena Tour. 2017.

Alexander: Usually, a designer will reach out to me about an upcoming project, and I ask for the venue drawings first so I can get started on building that while he or she meets with the client or director to get their initial ideas going. So, my first task is to build out the venue in 3D in Vectorworks and I use this time to set up the rest of the packet (title block, standard sheet size/scale, etc.). Once the designer downloads me with whatever information they are giving me (sketches, CADs, research) I build out a first pass of the design as much as I can within Vectorworks. This is all built out in 3D and I create the ground plan and section views from this model. I will usually screen grab various views of this in a shaded view and share these with the designer to make sure that proportions are correct, that they don't have questions, and that I understood their intentions correctly.

Sam Smith – The Thrill of it All Tour_Render. An image modeled in Vectorworks and rendered in Cinema4D. Set design by Jason Sherwood. Digital model by Evan Alexander. International Arena Tour. 2017.

The next step will be to move the model into Cinema4D where I can add in more finished details – things like furniture, figures, and foliage. I will put a simple lighting setup in, choose some preliminary camera placements, and share clay renders with the designer. From there, we go back and forth developing the design together. So, he or she will mark up preliminary renders and I will go back to the Vectorworks file, update or add more details and re-export to Cinema to update that model. While we are going back and forth, along the way, I start to add more detail to the Cinema4D model as things get more refined: I will start to apply textures and with each pass, lighting and cameras get more and more refined. This takes as many passes as needed but is influenced by calendar and budget realities as well. By the time we are ready to present first pass to the client or director, I will output an initial set of full color, lit renders to be shared. While those meetings are happening, I will break the 3D model down into plates of elevations and full-scale details. If the meeting goes really well, we are in a good place to share an initial packet of drafting with fabricators to start generating budget numbers. If the meeting does not go well, we at least have a good working template for the next round of drawings and we jump back into working it out. And we just continue this process of updating the Vectorworks plans and elevations and moving new geometry over to Cinema4D for new renders for as long as the project allows. Some projects happen rapidly over a few weeks and some projects take months or even years to develop. It's important to set up systems and templates that can easily be updated and revised as revisions is the name of the game. Every project will change and expand or shrink as it is developed, and my job is to make that as quick and painless for everyone as possible.

Ferrari Monza. Modeled by Saksham Kumar and rendered in Cinema4D. Digital render by Evan Alexander. 2022.

On a more technical note, with renderings: the base is always built out in Vectorworks, but I just build the geometry there and don't do any textures or lighting. All of that happens once it gets into Cinema4D. I budget a set amount for purchasing stock 3D models on each project, so if the designer wants a specific chair or table, we'll buy it online if possible. Renders are done in Cinema4D using the Corona render engine before finally landing in Photoshop. The post processing in Photoshop varies from sketch to sketch – sometimes it's just simple color balancing or adjustments, and other times we do a lot of heavy lifting in photoshop adding in special effects, adding talent, or changing screen content. The Photoshop files are built modular for revisions as well, so as design progresses, I can just slip a new render under all the other layers and with minimal work, update all the elements into a harmonious render.

Chen: Now that you are well versed in Vectorworks and Cinema4D, will you ever go back to make physical models and do renderings by hand, and why?

Alexander: I'm all-in on digital. I haven't made a physical model since 2001. There are plenty of shows I work on and do digital drafting and rendering for that a separate team of artists in the designer's studio still make physical models for. Some directors just need them and are totally in that mind set for understanding space, and I do understand that it can be easier to present a design to a large group of performers with a three-dimensional object in the room. Physical model making has advanced as well, so most of the studios I work with have 3D printers and laser cutters and can use my drawings to make the templates for cutting out parts and pieces for these physical builds. I still love sketching and do a lot of marker illustration work outside of entertainment, but my client work is all digitally based. Occasionally someone will ask for a hand drawn sketch, usually because they want the design to still present as rough and loose and not come at the director with a slick looking "finished" render that feels like it can't be changed. For these, however, I still build it all out in 3D so I can set my camera and play with placement and proportion first, then I will render it out and trace over it with pen and ink. I love those sketches and it's a nice change of pace from the day to day of endlessly staring at a screen.

Chen: Going over your portfolio posted online (http://www.evanalexander.com/), I was deeply impressed by the quality of your work, your versatility, and productivity. On the top of your work mentioned above, you also designed interiors, lighting, furniture items, theatre venues, and even cars. In addition, you created some artworks that are thought provoking. How did you find time to do all of them?

Wegner Elbow Chair. An image modeled and rendered in Cinema4D. Digital model and render by Evan Alexander. 2022.

Alexander: I am someone who must keep creating things and I can get bored easily. Some of these commercial projects can take years of development and it's hard for me to stay interested when I'm working on revisions number 237. I try to create a new personal piece every few days around my client work. Similar to Beeples' Everyday project: this is a playground for me to try new techniques and software. I can work without client or budget constraints and just have fun while I teach myself new things. I think of it as RnD work and all of these skills and techniques I learn and develop get folded back into the client work and makes me a better and always expanding artist. I think, the secret to life is to never stop learning. So, I try to create new things in different fields and areas to learn, to keep my sanity, and to stay fresh in my work. It also rounds out my portfolio and has help me overcome my fear of branching into newer, unknown fields when those clients approach me. There is no better way to learn a program than just hours spent in the software. You have to make a large body of work, and in that you will fail, or things won't go as expected, but this is really where the growth happens, and people shouldn't shy away from it.

Manta Mech. An image modeled and rendered in Cinema4D. Artist: Evan Alexander. 2019.

Chen: One can admire the simplicity of your art, while marvel at the sophistication of the digital modeling and rendering techniques that require you to produce these works. Did you ever get frustrated working with digital means? If so, how did you overcome the technical barriers?

Alexander: Absolutely! I get frustrated on something technical every day. Every project hits that point where I think – I don't know how to make that or how are we going to pull that off? But it always works out and there is always a solution. After doing this long enough, that fear really takes a back seat and I feel confident that I can deliver almost anything I might be asked to do, but it took a really long time to reach that point. Nothing is more frustrating than when you have an idea but are restricted because you don't know how to model the shape or get the lighting and reflections to bounce the way you want. It's all about trial and error on a day-to-day basis and you have to train yourself to get comfortable in that uncomfortable space. This, to me, is the very nature of design and everyone I have talked to, from students up to Oscar winning designers feel this on some level – it's totally normal. When I run into this, I've learned that walking away for a few moments is usually better than trying to force it. I'll take a walk or do some yoga and try to change my brain space. If I'm slammed, then I'll jump over to something more brainless for a while, but still needs to be done (updating title block, researching stock furniture to buy, etc.). When all else fails, go back to paper and pencil – those tools are so intuitive to your body, that you don't have to think about how to engage with them and you can focus on the idea. Also, never be afraid to ask for help. I call other designers and friends all the time to talk through a technique or approach. Most people are happy to share knowledge and experience if you are willing to do the same yourself.

Chen: You are operating a one-man shop; do you promote entrepreneurship to young designers?

Alexander: After years of working in firms, I found that, for me, working by myself was the best. But I used to employ a handful of people to work with me and while I could take on more projects, I found that I was spending my day doing admin and email, but really I just wanted to be making things. So, while I still have to run the business, being a one-man shop lets me be more hands on with the craft which is the part I am most interested in. This is a very personal thing for each person, and you really have to find this out for yourself. Some do better at a firm where someone else is finding clients and dealing with budgets and others need. Some find working with one or two people is ideal – there is no right or wrong. You have to find your place with this and the only way to do that is to try as many things as you can.

Chen: Since your wife is a lighting designer working on Broadway shows, could you elaborate on how lighting work hand in hand with solids, even vapor or fog, in your art and design?

Exploding Piano. An image modeled and rendered in Cinema4D. Artist: Evan Alexander. 2016.

Alexander: Jane has always said that lighting is everything and I am, finally, 100% onboard with this. The best sets, the best costumes, the best composition are meaningless with poor lighting, so I've really focused a lot of my energy on learning to be a better lighting designer in 3D spaces. It's the number one thing I see in renderings that could be improved and take the sketch to the next level. In concert design, lighting and volumetrics really are a part of the scenery, so I have also focused time in understanding how to control this and render it as realistic as possible to enhance the idea we are trying to get across.

Chen: Have you worked with your wife in a live show? If so, what kind of collaboration you two have in terms of workflow?

Alexander: We've never collaborated on a live show as we really work in different spaces, but we have done a lot of virtual lighting together and that is always fun and educational for us both. During COVID lockdown, I built a 3D lighting lab for her, and her Princeton students and we were able to have them write light cues in Cinema4D in real time together over Zoom, and while not the same as being in the room, it did really convey the ideas and foundational concepts they are learning about. There have been a few Broadway shows where I've built out the scenery for her and we can experiment with different lighting ideas together – one show she did was set inside a gold leaf room and we were able to really explore what the reflections and bounce light reactions would be for different positions and scenarios. I hope we get to do more work together – she is the best!

Chen: Indeed. Do you have anything else to say to our readers?

Alexander: It will sound cliché but find the work or industry that brings you joy. The rest will fall into place around that. I quit being a designer to focus purely on rendering and drafting for other creatives and everyone told me I was crazy, and it wouldn't work. But since it was the thing that I was most interested in, it drove me to really commit to it and dive deep and I think that shows in the work and is what draws people to want to work with me. It takes time, don't lose faith.

han lixun

Han Lixun is a visual artist who graduated from Shanghai Theatre Academy in 1985 with a degree in Stage Design. From 1991 to 1993, he studied in the master class of the National Academy of Fine Arts in Dusseldorf, Germany. He currently lives in Beijing. Han is the Chief Stage Designer for the Opening Ceremony of the 2008 Beijing Olympic Games, the celebrations of the return of Hong Kong and Macao and the 50th anniversary of the founding of the People's Republic of China. He has worked on hundreds of theatrical performances as a chief designer and artistic director. He has engaged in a wide variety of creative projects, including the event designs for the Opening Ceremonies of 95-United Nations World Conference on Women, 2000 World University Games, East Asian Games, and The Eleventh National Games, architectural-interior designs for Shanghai Tower and Free Trade Zone Complex, visual art in public spaces, installation art, multimedia art, and paintings. He is an Adjunct Professor at Shanghai Theatre Academy and has lectured at many universities in the U.S. He was the winner of the 2013 International Best Film Gold Award issued by the British International Visual Communication Association for his design of Bird's Nest – Attraction.

Producton photo of 2008 Beijing Olympics Opening Ceromeny, Beijing National Stadium, Beijing, China

Bird's Nest–Attractio
Chief Visual Designer:
Han Lixun
Medium: Digital mode
and render (top,
middle); Production
photo (bottom)
Performance Venue:
Beijing National
Stadium, Beijing, Chin
Opening Date: 2013

The Celestial Liquor-Making
Artistic Director / Chief Designer: Han Lixun
Mudium: Digital Render (top); Sketches (middle); Production Photo (bottom)
Performance Venue: Maotai Town, Guizhou Province, China
Opening Date: 2017

Architecture - A
/Business Compl
Chief Visual
Designer: Han
Lixun.
Medium: Digital
model (top),
Architecture pho
(middle), Interio
photo (bottom)
Location:
Shanghai Free
Trade Zone, Chin
Completion Date
2023

Interview with Han Lixun

It has been ten years since Han Lixun came to the United States for his lecture tour in 2013. After he designed for the opening ceremony of the 2008 Olympic Games, Han has continued to engage in large-scale design projects, including his stage designs for the performances of *Bird's Nest - Attraction* and *The Making of Celestial Liquor* as well as his visual designs for "Shanghai Tower" and the Art and Business Complex located in the Free Trade Zone in Pudong, Shanghai. The following is the transcription of the interview between Ming Chen (Chen), the author of this book, and Han Lixun (Han) conducted via WeChat video on July 23, 2023.

Chen: I am delighted to have this opportunity to learn about your behind-the-scenes work for some projects you have designed in recent years, especially the application of computer software in your design processes in hope to shade light on aspired designers. I know you have a studio in Beijing. When working on a large-scale project, you would use sketches or a physical model to express your design ideas, and then guide the team in your studio to translate your design in electronic formats for presentation and construction purposes. Am I correct?

Beijing Olympics – Production Photo. Chief Stage Designer: Han Lixun. Production photo. Beijing National Stadium (Bird's Nest), Beijing, China. 2008.

Han: You are right. In fact, we developed such a working method during the design process for the opening ceremony of the 2008 Olympic Games. At that time, the software products for designs were not user friendly and often incompatible to one another. I did not feel convenient to use for conception. However, my design intent must be understood by all those involved in the project, including people on the management and administrative teams, who did not have the knowledge in stage design. Because it was a gigantic team, any communication issues between me and the people on other teams will hinder the progress of my work. The impact of digital model and rendering on average layman prompted me to work with people who specialized in digital modeling, rendering, and drafting. After my design was translated into a digital form, it became more accessible to other teams. The various views of a digital model help the laymen to digest the 3D forms and space of the design. The digital renderings facilitate their understanding of how the 3D forms interact with lighting and with actor's performance. As a result, the digital means not only played an indispensable role in the communication between me and the relevant personnel of the project, but also built a substantive bridge between my artistic team and technical team, as both teams share the same digital language. Nowadays in China, this method of working became a norm for designing large-scale projects. In our country, to start a large-scale project, fundraising and passing screening process on various level conducted by non-professionals for a design are must. The digital models and renderings can play a crucial role in these processes because they not only produce realistic and immersive visual effects, but also supports physical production and performance.

Beijing Olympics – Digital Model. Chief Stage Designer: Han Lixun. Digital model. Beijing National Stadium (Bird's Nest), Beijing, China. 2008.

Chen: This kind of working method is also very common in the United States today.

Han: Actually, in my opinion, this working method has advantages and disadvantages. What I just talked about is its beneficial side. This also includes the fact that many people can involve in a creative process. As the old saying goes though, the strength of a thing is often its weakness. You know, visual creativity is a very personal thing. If there are too many people intervening, it might severely affect designer's authentic creative intention, because he/she is under the pressure of compromising and synthesizing other people's opinions. This might be okay for a short term. But in a long run, when this becomes a norm, it may inhibit the designer's enthusiasm and creativity.

Chen: Well, this scenario sounds problematic and is worthy of attention. Nevertheless, from my observation, the digital renderings and models of your designs are very close to your sketches. Even the images presented in the production photos often match your hand drawings quite well. *The Making of Celestial Liquor* and *Bird's Nest – Attraction* are such examples. The works are stunningly beautiful. Can I ask what software you use to make models, renderings, and produce designer's drafting?

Bird's Nest – Attraction – Sketch 1. Chief Visual Designer: Han Lixun. 2012.

Bird's Nest – Attraction – Digital Model. Chief Visual Designer: Han Lixun. 2012.

Han: We mainly used AutoCAD, 3ds Max, and Photoshop. AutoCad was used for modeling and drafting. After a model is complete, we would use 3ds Max and/or Photoshop to complete the renderings. In addition, for special effects, such as water and fire, we would write some small software programs to embody those ideas.

Chen: Likewise, AutoCAD is also a popular software in the United States, especially in the construction and engineering industries. The file conversion between Vectorworks and AutoCad is easy and seamless. I believe, AutoCAD is a more accurate software than is Vectorworks, but it is a heavier program to use and requires more rational brain work. In contrast, although Vectorworks is not as precise as AutoCAD, the operation of Vectorworks is more intuitive, and therefore it is a more suitable program for theatrical designers and artists alike.

Han: With today's technology, you can use the camera lens to display your digital model from various angles and directions. You can also make several renderings in a speedy manner for comparison. Directors like these computation functions because they help the communication between designers and directors and avoids many unnecessary misunderstandings. After all, digital models are virtually three-dimensional. It simulates physical entities. Moreover, one can generate countless models from one model instantaneously. The various schemes derived from these models are conducive to the selection of the best scheme.

Chen: What kind of performance is the *Bird's Nest - Attraction*? Does it involve acrobatics? Why, in your sketches, do people fly in the air? When you conceived your design, did you consider whether or not you can physically realize your conception?

Bird's Nest – Attraction – Sketch 2. Chief Visual Designer: Han Lixun. 2012.

Bird's Nest – Attraction – Sketch 3. Chief Visual Designer: Han Lixun. 2012.

Bird's Nest – Attraction – Digital Model and Render. Chief Visual Designer: Han Lixun. 2012.

Han: This show has its historical background. *Bird's Nest* is a stadium specially built for the 2008 Olympic Games. At that time, building huge stadiums specifically for the Olympics was controversial. Because, throughout the history, the stadiums built by other countries for the Olympic Games have not been used after the Games. They became ruins. It has caused extreme waste and environmental pollution. After the 2008 Olympic Games, we decided to create a large-scale performance for tourists coming from all over the world to Beijing. This is *Bird's Nest – Attraction*. This production has lived up to its name as a result. The original intention of this work is to experiment, in global arena, to find environmental and economical solution to the remaining stadium. In the process of creating this work, we tried not only to use the buildings, equipment, and materials left from the Olympic Games as much as possible, but also turn this theatrical production into a profitable tourism attraction in hope to enrich the lives of Beijing residents and attract people throughout the country and the world to travel to Beijing. The image with people flying in the air that you saw in my sketches reflect my intent to use the rigging system left from the opening ceremony of the Olympic Games, which is an example of environmental protection and cost saving. The technology used in this work covers anything ranging from sea, land, and sky. Acrobatics are of course part of it. But in the end, the use of technology still needs to serve the theme of the show. *The Nest - Attraction* tells a love story between a man and a fairy whose union is challenged by an evil force. The play reflects our understanding of nature and life. We want our audience to know our past as well as our present, including the thinking of our generation.

Chen: Your design for *Nadam Annual Convention* is visually arresting. You used scaffolding, like a skyscraper, and countless LED panels to capture the image of a galloping horse. What inspires you to create such an image?

Han: Actually, this project presented some challenges for us. Because we would be performing in an open-air grassland, a horse-racing venue to be more precise, the performance environment would change based on the changing weather. Strong wind, heavy rain, and sandstorms could all affect the performance. The wildness and uncouth feel of the grassland inspired my creation of a runaway wild horse. Yes, the main materials of this installation are scaffolding and LED panels. The choice of scaffolding and the free combination of the scaffolding units are in line with the visual expression of "wildness." They meet the blocking needs of large-scale performance and, at the same time, meet the needs of artistic presentation on LED display panels as well as the technical requirements for the installation of LED panels.

Chen: Do the LED panels display images during the show? If so, what role did computer software play in the creation and performance of this work?

Han: Yes, we used images on the LED panels. These images are naturally manipulated with the use of computer software. The standard LED panel is 40cm by 40cm. We utilized these panels to form screens of various sizes. Some of them were 1m x 1m, others were 2m x 3m and 3m x 4m, and so on. The result seen from the audience in distance is a galloping horse in mosaic style. The total area of the screen was about 3500 square meters (37.660 square feet), which turned out to be technically difficult to operate. I do not mean that the image was not bright enough due to insufficient electric current. Rather, it was the traffic/speed of image delivery that was giving us problems. For such a large-scale installation, it is rather challenging to display the images on every panel at the same time. Furthermore, the LED screen at that time had a low resolution; the images were not sharp. Fortunately, because the audience is watching the show from a great distance, they could still see the image shown on the screens despite its low resolution. In the early stage of creation, we built a 3D model of the LED panels with images on them. We set the camera angles to simulate the result of these images being viewed by audience from various perspectives. This helped us to judge the quality of the images in the real world and make choices on the size, angle, and brightness of the LED screens.

Nadam International Annual Convention – Digital Model and Render. Chief Stage Designer: Han Lixun. 2012.

Nadam International Annual Convention – Production Photo. Chief Stage Designer: Han Lixun. Ordos, Inner Mongolia, China. 2012.

Chen: What kind of work is *The Making of Celestial Liquor*?

Han: Through a first-generation master of liquor-making, Youyou (the narrator), *The Making of Celestial Liquor* tells an extraordinary story about the creation process of Moutai. This play embodies the Chinese people's spirit of excellence, perseverance, patience, and pursuit of perfection. Guided by the old man Youyou, the audience passes through five performance spaces one after another, symbolizing five layers of elevation in the ascending process of accomplishments. At the same time, they were fully immersed under the influence of Moutai culture formed through text, sound, light, and 3D moving images.

The Celestial Liquor-Making – Production Photo. Artistic Director/Chief Designer: Han Lixun. Maotai Town, Guizhou Province, China. 2017.

Chen: I heard that this performance used Volumatic Images (moving images floating in the air for the viewers to see at every angle). Volumatic Image is a relatively new technology. I am a layman in this technology. How did you do it seven years ago? Does this have anything to do with computer software development?

Han: Of course, the visual effect we had in our performance is inseparable from the software development for video production. Strictly speaking, what we used at that time cannot be called Volumatic Images. We employed fog as the projection screen. We used multiple 4K projectors to project video images onto the fog from different angles. Therefore, although the moving images were not holographic per say, if the audience views the performance from one side, this technique does have the visual effect of 3D dynamic images.

Chen: This is an interesting idea. In addition to designing for theatrical performances, your portfolio reveals your engagement in other kinds of design and art, even painting. Can you tell us about your visual design for the Art and Business Complex in Shanghai, including the project's purpose, scale, and application of digital technology.

Architecture – Art/Business Complex – Digital Model. Chief Visual Designer: Han Lixun. Digital model. Shanghai Free Trade Zone, Shanghai, China. 2023.

Han: The Complex is in the Free Trade Zone in Pudong, Shanghai. It was created against the background of the CIIE at that time. This is a multifunctional building covers an area of 250,000 square meters. The building includes showrooms for the cars, food shopping areas, catering areas, exhibition space, office space, experimental performance space, and press conference rooms. Because the building is situated in a place away from the city center, the transportation is not convenient. Therefore, as designers, we need to take into consideration of various needs by visitors and by people who work in the building. For this project, I oversaw the artistic side of the Complex. They also brought in an American architect, Reja Bakh, to collaborate with me on the project. In this building, a lot of digital technology, including AI technology, are used. For instance, in the Exhibit Hall, where the exhibition of vendors' products and the showcase performances occur. The interaction among images, between image and material, image and human being, and human being and material are all manipulated by machine pallets.

The project will be completed in September 2023. During the design process, we are already very mature in terms of software application. The workflow has been smooth, and the connection between the design team and the construction team can be described as seamless, especially when compared to the projects of this scale that I had engaged in previously.

Art/Business Complex – Interior Photo. Chief Visual Designer: Han Lixun. Digital model. Shanghai Free Trade Zone, Shanghai, China. 2023.

Chen: Knowing that you are still a visiting professor at the Shanghai Theatre Academy, do you have any suggestions for the readers of this book?

Painting No. 2. Artist: Han Lixun. 2022.

Han: My suggestion is that, while learning to use CAD to design, do not give up the training in hand-drawing skills. Of course, CAD software is much user friendly nowadays. It is a natural draw to the younger generation. However, I think that it is also a time to look back and contemplate. Not long ago, I visited a university in Italy. There is a department of stage design in their School of Journalism. To my surprise, hand drawing skills were still taught in traditional ways in their classrooms. Oh, my God! The technology is so advanced today. Who can still sit down and draw by hand? But they believed that being in an academy does not always mean one must look forward; it is also the responsibility of those who are in the academy to look backward. Only by understanding what happened in the past can we understand what is happening today and predict what will happen in the future. Personally, I believe that drawing by hand is different than drawing with computer. Drawing by hand is a perceptual act of the heart, while operating a computer to draw is a rational act of the brain. I think that there must be a reason for human beings to exist as independent individuals. The uncertainty in the world and the free souls has the right to be proud for their existence in the digital world.

matthew mccoy

Matthew McCoy has dedicated three decades to iconic, award-winning, and leading creative teams in the fields of architecture, attractions, and themed entertainment destinations. He has worked as a creative director/designer for large-scale international projects, such as Colorful Yunnan Paradise, Kunming Space City, and Robot Museum in China, Disney Paris in France, and Movie World Madrid (Warner Brother Park) in Spain. Characterized by their dynamic story-driven images and innovative design concepts, his work includes designs for National Museum of Patriotism, Mountasia, City Walk, Six Flag's theme parks and theatrical productions, Native American Heritage Center, Auto Heritage and Race Car Museum, Warner Brother Store, The Fun House Shop, Irish Pub, Coca Cola Store, Discovery Kingdomand a variety of Brand IP graphic designs.

Robot Museum – Render. Creative Direction/Design: Matthew L. McCoy. Digital Model and Render in Sketch Up. Shanghai, China. 2019.

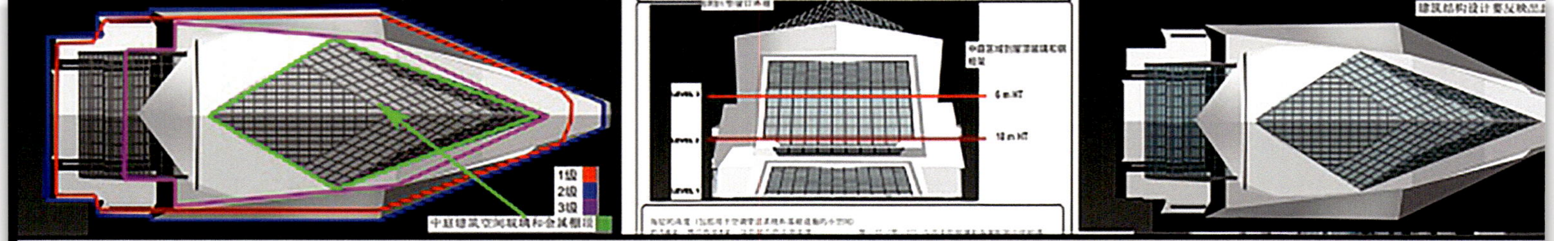

ROBOT MUSEUM

CREATIVE DESIGN DIRECTION

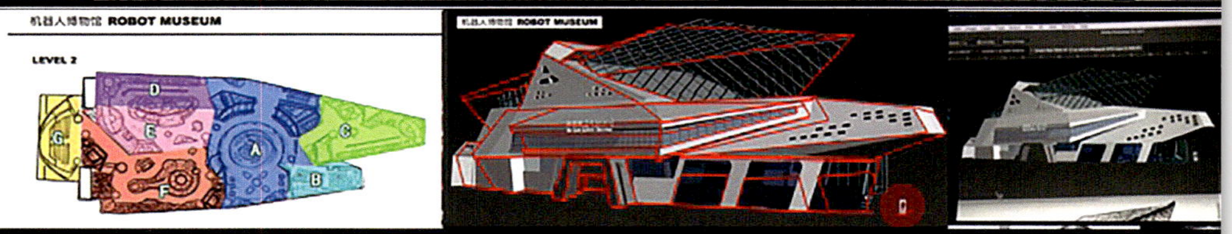

Robot Museum – Process. Creative Direction/Design by Matthew L. McCoy. Digital model (above) and render (below) in Sketch Up. Shanghai, China. 2019.

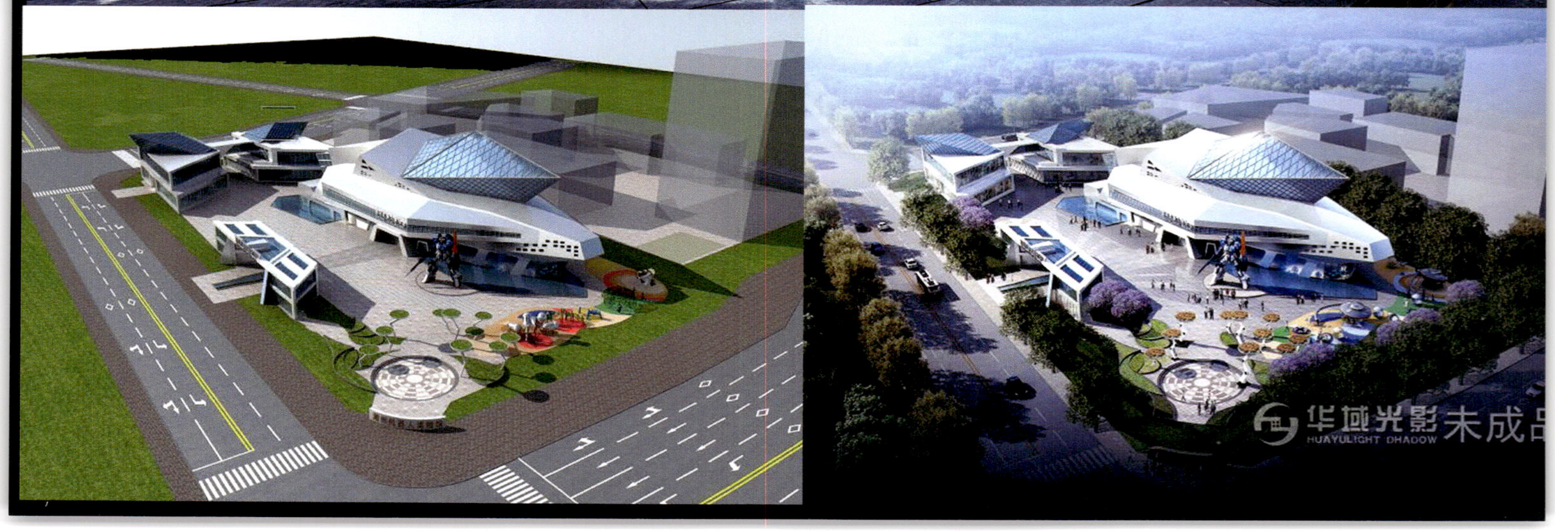

Irish Pub. Interior Design by Matthew L. McCoy. Product Photo. Georgia, USA. 2015.

OLDE BLIND DOG IRISH PUB
OLDE BLIND DOG®
INTERNATIONAL
IRISH PUB
OF THE YEAR
IRISH PUBS GLOBAL
2015
WINNER

Irish Pub of the Year

by Pubs Global Federation of Dublin, Ireland

We are very excited to share the news that Olde Blind Dog has been chosen "Irish Pub of the Year" by the Irish Pubs Global Federation of Dublin, Ireland! This is an international award, with over 6500 member pubs represented worldwide and sponsored by Guinness. The ceremony was held on Friday, Feb. 27, in Dublin, Ireland.

Olde Blind Dog is the first pub in the U.S. to win this coveted award. As you can see, it is a very significant award and accomplishment for our restaurants, our team and our patrons. We are thrilled and humbled by this honor. Click here to read the LA Times article.

Colorful Yunnan Paradise – Process. Creative Direction/ Design by Matthew L. McCoy. Digital master plan (above) and model (right) in Sketch Up and product photos (blow) Yunnan, China. 2015.

Interview with Matthew L. McCoy

The following conversations between Matthew L. McCoy (**McCoy**) and Ming Chen (**Chen**) were conducted in the form of e-mail correspondences dating from May 25 to September 10, 2023, as the artists were traveling intercontinentally among the United States, Asian countries, and Saudi Arabia.

Chen: With the vast experience you have in the design industries, do you see a trend nowadays in the use of Computer Aided Design/Drafting (CAD) programs during design and construction processes? Do you believe that digital drawing, modeling, rendering, and drafting skills are a must for aspired designers?

McCoy: As a Creative Design Director in themed and leisure-based industries, I see many in the teams that I worked with and many creatives in theme park facility design and Architects use Revit, SketchUp, 3D Studio Max, Navis-Works, Auto-CAD, etc. to create construction documents and/or early 3D concepts designs regularly. These include prop & signage designs for theme parks and resorts, theatrical settings for major dark-ride attractions, themed character shows, parades, and events, as well as master planning and iconic architecture.

Six Flags – Water Park Interior – Sanderson Group. Creative Direction/Design by Matthew L. McCoy. Digital Model and Render in SketchUp. Shanghai China. 2017.

Chen: Your portfolio (https://www.krop.com/mccoyexpdesign/) reveals that you are comfortable and eloquent in both traditional and digital means of artistic expression. What media and software do you normally employ to communicate your design concepts and ideas?

McCoy: I utilize many creative tools for ideations, planning, and design of themed leisure-based destinations and attractions. First, I use traditional hand-sketch to get the ideas out. This might be performed on yellow onion paper, drawing pads, or digitally, on a giant screen or small iPad. All digital drawings are created in layers on software programs, such as Photoshop, or Pro Create, Illustrator… The more detailed elements are then refined in SketchUp. The use of AI (Artificial Intelligence) enhanced "text to creative" tools are just breaking in and only used for ideation exploration.

Six Flags–DC Comics Superhero Brand Name Store. Creative Store Direction/Design by Matthew L. McCoy. Digital model and render in SketchUp. Six Flags Global Retail/USA. 2014.

As designers, we try to use the most advanced tools available to communicate design ideas to people in various disciplines and will be responsible for turning these design ideas into reality. However, in my opinion, both conceptual and architectural drawings are still best started through traditional hand-drawing methods. For 3D models and technical drawings, software such as Sketch-Up, RIVET, RHINO, 3ds Max, Sculpt-3D, and AutoCAD are used. In my field of themed leisure-based industries, including theme park architectures, themed restaurants, Casinos, and resort architecture, it is my observation that Sketch-Up is the "Go-To" software as it is versatile. The initial sketches can be easily transferred to AutoCAD and shown through VR (Virtual Reality) and fantasy realms in "Architecture in the Virtual World of Gaming."

However, most show-sets and show-props, parade floats, and dark-ride attraction props are designed either with traditional hand sketching or with SketchUp. Then these are transferred into AutoCAD for fabrication.

Rose Parade Float. Design by Matthew L. McCoy. Tempera on Bristol board. Pasadena, California, USA. 2023.

Chen: Have you ever used Vectorworks? If so, can you compare Sketch-Up to Vectorworks in terms of their versatility and compatibility with AutoCAD? I am asking this question because, in theatrical designs, Vectorworks is used by most of the lighting designers since the software company works with the lighting designers to develop the program. Therefore, it seems to me that Vectorworks should be a logical program for the set designers to use as well, because, as you know, seamless communication and teamwork is the core of the trade.

McCoy: Vectorworks is good for master-planning and layout of land and facilities, landscape planting plans and landscape visualization quickly. However, I do not use this software. I guide the teams that do.

Architecture designs are usually started with master planning. High-Poly 3D software, such as AutoCAD are difficult to navigate at that stage; ride construction vendors usually work with them. So, with this kind of software, find the angle of the scene you need and flatten the scene on a layer to be placed in a master plan. As a project moves into design development phases, high resolution models are a fantastic way to communicate designs to vendors and contractors.

Maya and Sculpt 3D are other software focused not on the direct creation of 3D characters but on world building and character design for theme parks. In addition, designers also utilize ZBrush, Blender, and Daz Studio, when they work in animations for further integration into major attraction set design and gamification.

Amusement Park Designs. Creative Direction/Design by Matthrew L. McCoy. Digital renders in SketchUp. Dragon Hill Park, Vietnam (top); Cool Town Shouxing, China (middle); Changsha Kids Park, China (bottom).

Chen: Could you elaborate on your standard working process?

McCoy: After a concept is put on the paper through hand-drawing, we take the idea into Sketch-Up with drawing of various viewing angles. Then, use layer functions in the program to recreate a 3D model of the design that is somewhat more accurate in dimension and scale. Based on this model we can then develop renderings. With that method, while the models and renderings still look conceptually driven with the artistic touches, they have a more accurate feel to them.

Chen: One of the photos you sent me shows that you were sketching on a large computer screen (Fig. 11.42). Is this sketch for a real project. If so, what is the software that you were using to produce the sketch and how easy it is for you or others to develop a 3D model from a rough sketch?

Singapore Pirate Show – Video Conference Presentation. Creative Direction/Design by Matthew L. McCoy. Photo of video conference – digital sketch on touch screen. Singapore. 2019.

McCoy: We mounted a large-scale monitor of digital touch screen in the board room wall that doubles for all other things as video conference calling and project viewing. I like designing this way for shows.

That particular sketch which you mentioned was part of the design for Worlds of Sonesta Singapore - Pirate Stunt Show, the sketch was later converted and integrated into 3D Modeling of the overall design.

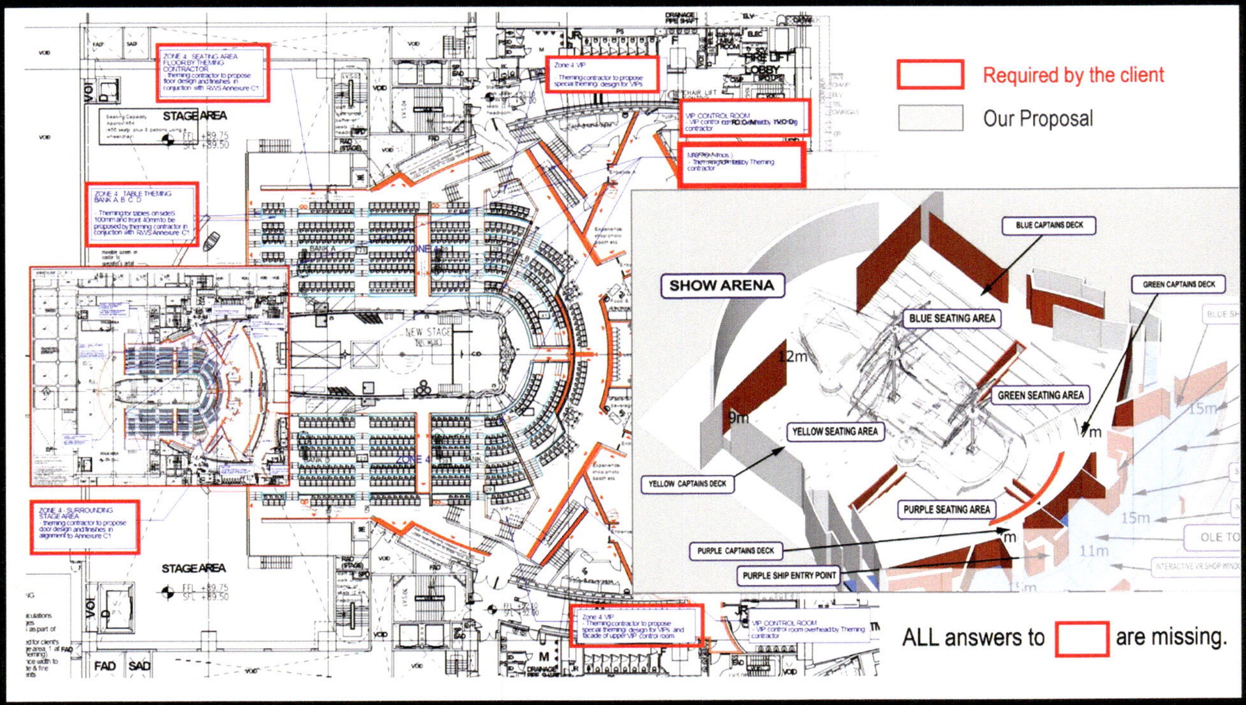

Singapore Pirate Show – Master Plan. Creative Direction/Design by Matthew L. McCoy. Digital sketch in SketchUp. Singapore. 2019.

Chen: I heard that, among 6500 member pubs represented worldwide, the restaurant that you worked on won Irish Pub of the year in 2015 for your interior design. This is an international award issued by Irish Pubs Global Federation of Dublin, Ireland. This design is unique, a bit weightier than the artistic style that you are accustomed to. What inspires you to create the interior. What tools and media do you use to communicate your design ideas to the construction team?

McCoy: The inspiration comes from history storytelling and the desire to design the BEST. Unlimited client funding helps this as well. They wanted the BEST. And to me, designing for themed interior restaurants and themed interior retail stores are very much like designing for the theatre. Yet, for an authentic storytelling of Pub restaurant as an "Old Blind Dog Irish Pub," we shopped for antiquities and high-end lighting fixture. In addition, we hired the best team of fabrication and faux finishing artisans.

When I was designing themed retails for Six Flags Parks in 1999, we won the first-place global award and used the same methodologies of themed details. The Promenade at Six Flags is the park's renovated main entrance, which included 7000 square feet of new retail space. The Looney Tunes™ Exposition capitalizes on Six Flags' cartoon properties. So, we utilize the same software tools as we used to design for theme park attractions, theatrical productions, etc. (See Fig. 11.41 for reference).

Chen: What kind of project is Colorful Yunnan Paradise in terms of its scale, purpose, and cultural relevance. Did you do research on the place (southwestern China) and their culture and architecture? If so, what did you find out through your research?

Colorful Yunnan Paradise Park by NorthStar Group. Creative Direction/Design by Matthew L. McCoy. Digital renders in SketchUp. China. 2015.

McCoy: We were contacted by the NorthStar Group in Yunnan, China about a theme park design with about 130 acres. They did not wish to partner with any global licensing, so we went and studied the cultural heritage of Yunnan, China, including the local stories, architecture, and landmarks of the region. We found the main park land characters and parkwide brand. We came up with compelling storylines based on the local stories and landmarks. We create zones and designate attraction shows, rides, and events based upon the adventure of those local stories. The Peacock, The Eagle, The White Elephant, and The Tiger (Tiger Leaping Gorge) in the park came from the main iconic characters of the southern region.

Chen: That is what I can see in your design for the park – The stories and myth of the southwest China.

McCoy: In addition to the project in Yunnan, I have also worked on the 90-million-dollar Monkey King – Dark Ride Attraction at SUNAC Theme Park in Guangzhou, China. The attraction is an immersive dark ride theme park inspired by Havoc in Heaven, a tale about the legendary Monkey King depicted in the 16th-century classic Chinese novel *Journey to the West*. The major conflict of the story is between the Jade Emperor and the Monkey King, which leads to the Monkey King's wrecking of the heavens, including a fight with Nezha, the Marshal of the Central Altar. In this Attraction, after making their way through the queue and pre-show's Heavenly depictions environment, the guests enter the Dark Ride and are engulfed by the world of the Monkey King. The design for this project incorporated the cutting-edge technology of robotic "Kuka" arm vehicles, synchronized SFX-effects, and media dome projection. Every attraction that I creative/art directed starts with a storyline. There are scenes very much like scenes in theatre. Some of these involve high-tech robotics and synced show controls.

Monkey King – Renders. Creative Direction/Design by Matthew L. McCoy. Digital Renders in Photoshop. A promo for the Attraction (top). A render of Scene 6 (bottom) during the cauldron part of the story where the Monkey King gets thrown in, gaining 30,000 years of wisdom and strength. Guang Zhou, China. 2021.

Monkey King – Process Photo. Creative Direction/Design by Matthew L. McCoy. A process photo taken on the technical set while syncing the robotic attraction-ride-vehicle to the 3D animation on the dome screen. Guang Zhou, China. 2021.

Chen: Of course, I know Monkey King Story by heart. I grew up with it. In fact, in 2006, I even brought a group of faculty and students from my university in the United States to perform *Monkey King*, a theatrical production, at Shanghai Theatre Festival.

Is "Robot Museum" and "Robot Show" the same project? There must be a lot of technology used in the project as well. Could you introduce a few of them?

Robot Museum. Creative Direction/Design: Matthew L. McCoy. Product Photo (top) Digital Renders (meddle and bottom). Shanghai, China. 2019.

McCoy: They are the same kind of projects. We partnered with other industry design groups on theme parks. Boston Dynamics Robotics and HRG Technology Group are involved in the Robot Museum. The Museum has a historical walk through of Pop-Culture Robots, Sci-Fi droids" and animatronics, as well as industry robotics in automotive manufacturing, farming robotics, robotics in medical fields, and more. Over the years, with high-cost theme park dark ride show attractions and high-tech museums, I have worked with motion-based platforms, and have co-created robotics as KUPA arms connected to tracks vehicles in roller coaster rides, character animatronics connected with show controls that synchronized with image mapping projection media, focal sounds, optical special effects, smell devices, and theatrical lighting. Everything was choreographed. Creative Direction involves going to the manufacturers as well as research and development.

Chen: Is the Robot Museum in Shanghai complete, or is it still under construction?

McCoy: Yes, the Robot Museum is currently still under construction.

Chen: Are the Images shown in *DC Comics Concept, Cool Town & Fantasy Anime World* real projects or are they just conceptual renderings came purely out of your imagination?

McCoy: These are real projects that either have happened or is currently taking place. As I was working on roller coaster designs for Six Flags and DC Comics, I developed ideas for DC comics superhero stunt shows, water park, retails stores, and attractions on the side.

Cool Town is a giant theme park connected to a huge Wave Hotel and Dumb Waterpark in Shaoxing, China. I worked on that with Sanderson Group as a Creative Design Director.

Anime World is a secret project name IUs, for a mega theme park in Riyadh, Saudi Arabia. I did the concept and core design for a 1,000,000 m^2 hub, involving Japanese brand characters. This includes developing concepts for a master plan of facilities, theme parks, and shows. This project is still under an NDA (non-disclosure agreement) and in continuation of construction. For this project I'm going through

Falcons Creative Group and Sanderson Group Global. You can see the Six Flags in Riyadh, which has already been developed as one of the other eight parks being built. There is also a giant water park being built in Riyadh. This is a giga-project.

Chen: Since you have worked in a variety of design fields, such as architecture, interior, themed attraction, and theatrical design, can you name one thing that is in common for all these design fields?

McCoy: We are place-makers, so we want to make sure our designs are made for human beings to inhabit and relate to. So how people fit in spaces and in the story-setting is very important. Everything we design needs to relates to the scale of a human.

Chen: Indeed, no matter which of these design areas you are working in, human is the reason and measure for our designs, even if we manipulate the scale of the setting in theatrical designs. The manipulation is for the comparison with a human and, ultimately, for human to see and to use. Is there anything else you would like to share with our readers?

McCoy: Designs for theme-based destination, theme restaurants, themed retail, and attractions are fundamentally theatrical designs. Experiential design, master planning, and layout can be performed with traditional drawings, yet digital software are contemporary tools of the trade.

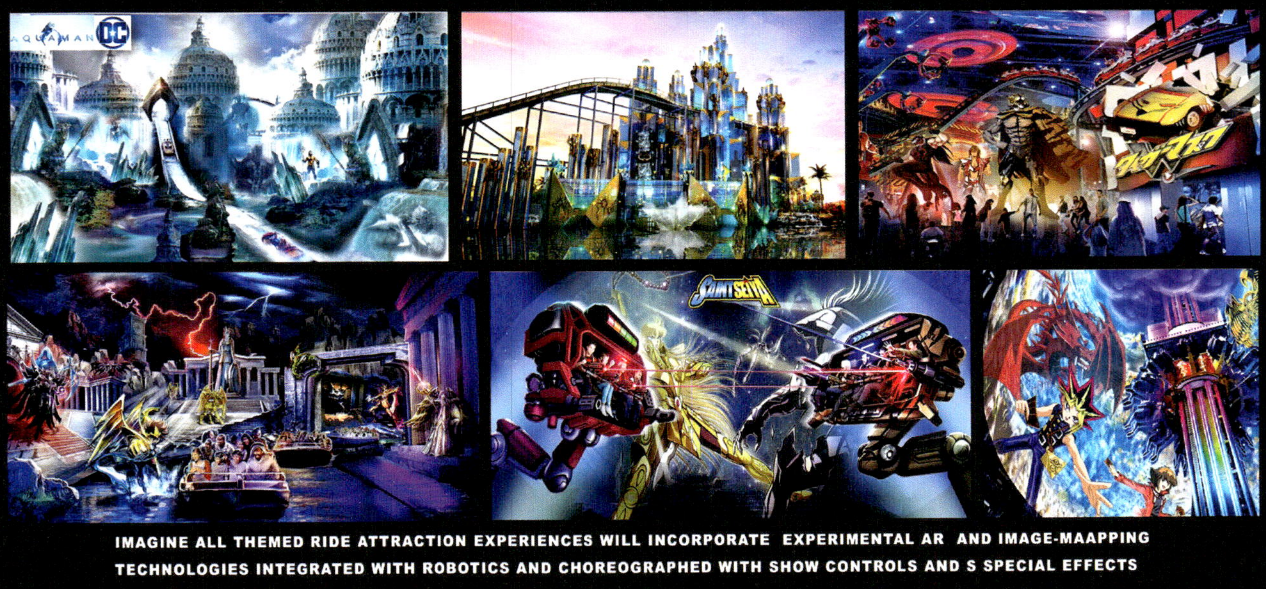

DC Comics Concept, Cool Town & Fantasy Anime World. Art by Matthew L. McCoy. Digital Renders in Photoshop. Six Flags Parks, USA, China, Saudi Arabia. 2021.

Bibliography

Alexander, Evan. Fig. 01 *Parisian Dining Room*. "Architecture." *EVAN ALEXANDER*, 2021. www.evanalexander.com/architecture. Accessed 29 Mar. 2024.

Alexander, Evan. Fig. 02 *Jesus Christ Superstar*. Live. "Performance." *EVAN ALEXANDER*, 2018, www.evanalexander.com/performance. Accessed 3 Apr. 2022.

Alexander, Evan. Fig. 03 *La Vette Social Club*. "La Vette Social Club." *EVAN ALEXANDER*, 2022, www.evanalexander.com/lavette. Accessed 15 Sep. 2021.

Alexander, Evan. Fig. 04 *Various Volumetric Lighting*. "Volumetrics." *EVAN ALEXANDER*, 2014-22, www.evanalexander.com/volumetrics. Accessed 9 Dec. 2020

Alexander, Evan. Fig. 05 *Rachael Ray's 30 Minutes Meals*. "Performance." *EVAN ALEXANDER*, 2019, www.evanalexander.com/performance. Accessed 3 Mar. 2020.

Alexander, Evan. Fig. 06 *Study for DJ Set Up*. "Performance." *EVAN ALEXANDER*, 2017, www.evanalexander.com/performance. Accessed 3 Mar. 2020.

Alexander, Evan. Fig. 07 *Super Bowl Halftime show Bruno Mars*. "Performance." *EVAN ALEXANDER*, 2014, www.evanalexander.com/performance. Accessed 3 Mar. 2020.

Alexander, Evan. Fig. 08 *Superbowl Halftime Show Katy Perry*. "Performance." *EVAN ALEXANDER*, 2015, www.evanalexander.com/performance. Accessed 9 Dec. 2020.

Alexander, Evan. Fig. 09 *People's Choice Awards 2018_1*. "Performance." *EVAN ALEXANDER*, 2018, www.evanalexander.com/performance. 9 Dec. 2020.

Alexander, Evan. Fig. 10 *People's Choice Awards 2018_2*. "Performance." *EVAN ALEXANDER*, 2018, www.evanalexander.com/performance. Accessed 9 Dec. 2020.

Alexander, Evan. Fig. 11 *Sam Smith – The Thrill of it All Tour*_model. "Performance." *EVAN ALEXANDER*, 2017, www.evanalexander.com/performance. Accessed 12 Sep. 2021.

Alexander, Evan. Fig. 12 *Sam Smith – The Trill of it All Tour*_render. "Performance." *EVAN ALEXANDER*, 2017, www.evanalexander.com/performance. Accessed 12 Sep. 2021.

Alexander, Evan. Fig. 13 *Ferrari Monza*. "Cars." *EVAN ALEXANDER*, 2022, www.evanalexander.com/cars-1. Accessed 15 Nov. 2023.

Alexander, Evan. Fig. 14 *Wegner Elbow Chair*. "Products & Furniture." *EVAN ALEXANDER*, 2022, www.evanalexander.com/products-furniture. Accessed 1 May, 2023.

Alexander, Evan. Fig. 15 *Manta Mech*. "Artwork." *EVAN ALEXANDER*, 2019, www.evanalexander.com/artwork. Accessed 5 Apr. 2023.

Alexander, Evan. Fig. 16 *Exploding Piano*. "Artwork." *EVAN ALEXANDER*, 2016, www.evanalexander.com/artwork. Accessed 5 Apr. 2023.

Han, Lixun. Fig. 17 *Beijing Olympics*. 2008. Photo courtesy of the artist.

Han, Lixun. Fig. 18 *Bird's Nest – Attraction*. 2012. Photo courtesy of the artist.

Han, Lixun. Fig. 19 *The Celestial Liquor-Making*. 2017. Photo courtesy of the artist.

Han, Lixun. Fig. 20 *Architecture – Art/Business Complex*. 2023. Photo courtesy of the artist.

Han, Lixun. Fig. 21 *Beijing Olympics Production Photo*. 2008. Photo courtesy of the artist.

Han, Lixun. Fig. 22 *Beijing Olympics Model*.2008. Photo courtesy of the artist.

Han, Lixun. Fig. 23 *Bird's Nest – Attraction – Sketch 1*. 2012. Photo courtesy of the artist.

Han, Lixun. Fig. 24 *Bird's Nest – Attraction – Digital Model*. 2012. Photo courtesy of the artist.

Han, Lixun. Fig. 25 *Bird's Nest – Attraction – Sketch 2*. 2012. Photo courtesy of the artist.

Han, Lixun. Fig. 26 *Bird's Nest – Attraction - Sketch 3*. 2012. Photo courtesy of the artist.

Han, Lixun. Fig. 27 *Bird's Nest – Attraction – Digital Model and Render*. 2012. Photo courtesy of the artist.

Han, Lixun. Fig. 28 *Nadam International Annual Convention – Model and Render*. 2012. Photo courtesy of the artist.

Han, Lixun. Fig. 29 *Nadam International Annual Convention – Production Photo*. 2012. Photo courtesy of the artist.

Han, Lixun. Fig. 30 *The Celestial Liquor-Making – Production Photo*. 2017. Photo courtesy of the artist.

Han, Lixun. Fig. 31 *Architecture - Art/Business Complex*. 2023. Photo courtesy of the artist.

Han, Lixun. Fig. 32 *Art/Business Complex – Interior Photo*. 2023. Photo courtesy of the artist.

Han, Lixun. Fig. 33 *Painting No. 2*. 2022. Photo courtesy of the artist.

McCoy, Matthew. Fig. 34 *Robot Museum – Render*. "M.L.McCoy Exp Design." *Exp Design*, 2019, www.krop.com/mccoyexpdesign/. Accessed 12 Mar. 2023.
McCoy, Matthew. Fig. 35 *Robot Museum – Process*. "M.L.McCoy Exp Design." *Exp Design*, 2019, www.krop.com/mccoyexpdesign/. Accessed 12 Mar. 2023.
McCoy, Matthew. Fig. 36 *Irish Pub*. "M.L.McCoy Exp Design." *Exp Design*, 2015, www.krop.com/mccoyexpdesign/. Accessed 12 Mar. 2023.
McCoy, Matthew. Fig. 37 *Colorful Yunnan Paradise – Process*. "M.L.McCoy Exp Design." *Exp Design*, 2015, www.krop.com/mccoyexpdesign/. Accessed 9 May. 2023.
McCoy, Matthew. Fig. 38 *Six Flags – Water Park Interior – Sanderson Group*. "M.L.McCoy Exp Design." *Exp Design*, 2017, www.krop.com/mccoyexpdesign/. Accessed 5 May. 2022.
McCoy, Matthew. Fig. 39 *Six Flags–DC Comics Superhero Brand Name Store*. "M.L.McCoy Exp Design." *Exp Design*, 2014, www.krop.com/mccoyexpdesign/. Accessed 15 May. 2023.
McCoy, Matthew. Fig. 40 *Rose Parade Float*. "M.L.McCoy Exp Design." *Exp Design*, 2023, www.krop.com/mccoyexpdesign/. Accessed 3 Dec. 2023.
McCoy, Matthew. Fig. 41 *Amusement Park Designs*. "M.L.McCoy Exp Design." *Exp Design*, 2015, 2018, and 2021, www.krop.com/mccoyexpdesign/. Accessed 12 May 2022.
McCoy, Matthew. Fig. 42 *Singapore Pirate Show – Video Conference Presentation*. "M.L.McCoy Exp Design." *Exp Design*, 2019, www.krop.com/mccoyexpdesign/. Accessed 12 May 2022.
McCoy, Matthew. Fig. 43 *Singapore Pirate Show – Master Plan*. "M.L.McCoy Exp Design." *Exp Design*, 2019, www.krop.com/mccoyexpdesign/. Accessed 1 May 2020.
McCoy, Matthew. Fig. 44 *Colorful Yunnan Paradise Park by NorthStar Group*. "M.L.McCoy Exp Design." *Exp Design*, 2015, www.krop.com/mccoyexpdesign/. Accessed 1 May 2020.
McCoy, Matthew. Fig. 45 *Monkey King – Renders*. "M.L.McCoy Exp Design." *Exp Design*, 2021, www.krop.com/mccoyexpdesign/. Accessed 3 Apr. 2022.
McCoy, Matthew. Fig. 46 *Monkey King – Process Photo*. "M.L.McCoy Exp Design." *Exp Design*, 2021, www.krop.com/mccoyexpdesign/. Accessed 3 Apr. 2022.
McCoy, Matthew. Fig. 47 *Robot Museum*. "M.L.McCoy Exp Design." *Exp Design*, 2019, www.krop.com/mccoyexpdesign/. Accessed 12 May 2022.
McCoy, Matthew. Fig. 48 *DC Comics Concept, Cool Town & Fantasy Anime World*. "M.L.McCoy Exp Design." *Exp Design*, 2021, www.krop.com/mccoyexpdesign/. Accessed 2 Mar. 2023..

CHAPTER 9

The Art and Logistics of Lighting

Vocabulary

Lighting Intensity
Dimmer
Lighting Direction
Lighting Angle
Footlight
Direct Light
Diffused Light
Diffusion Medium
Color Filter
Shutter
Iris
Gobo
Frequency
Follow Spot
Intelligent Light
Crossfading
Label Legend

Learning Objectives

- Describe and give examples of the important role light plays in various forms of visual art, including theatre.
- Memorize the controllable properties of stage lighting and explain ways of manipulating them on stage.
- Display capacity to use VW resources to set up lighting positions, place lighting instruments, and focus lights on a stage plan,
- Demonstrate the ability to create label legends.
- Practice the mechanics of producing a light plot and light schedules.

Light and Our Visual Experience

Volume–Light Interaction

The minute we are born, we learn to wake up in the morning and sleep at night. We are so used to taking advantage of natural light that we no longer pay attention to the important role light plays in our lives. Light brings visibility to our visual experience; without light, there would be no sensuality of lines and shapes, nor would there be excitement over color and visual texture. Light reveals lines, shapes, forms, spaces, textures, colors, objects, and even vapor around us and interacts with them. Look at Fig. 9.1 and imagine a world without light—how much we would have missed.

Light in Arts

Light in Paintings

To effectively organize our visual experience in two-dimensional art, master painters, such as Rembrandt Harmenszoon van Rijn, Jean Honore Fragonard, Pieter Claesz, and Claude Monet, made light a major subject of study in their works.

DOI: 10.4324/9781003266242-10

Figure 9.1 *Chapel of Notre-Dame-du-Haut, Ronchamp, France*. Architect: Le Corbusier. Building completed in 1954. Photo taken by Metaphox on June 13, 2010. CC BY 2.0 via Openverse.

In his oil painting, *Self-Portrait at the Easel* (Fig. 9.2), Rembrandt employs a single light source to bring a focus to the head.

While using exhaustive minute details to describe the facial features and headband that are well lit, he lets the shadowy part of the body fade into the dark void.

In his painting, *The Swing* (Fig. 9.3), Fragonard organizes the emphasized areas in a hierarchical order.

He skillfully picks the areas to be lit and arranges those areas in various lighting intensities to guide the viewers' eye movement in a circular fashion (Fig. 9.4).

Figure 9.2 *Self-Portrait at the Easel*. Artist: Rembrandt Harmenszoon van Rijn. Oil on canvas. The Musée du Louvre, Paris. 1660. PD via Wickmedia.

Figure 9.3 *The Swing*. Artist: Jean Honore Fragonard. Oil on canvas. 1766.

Figure 9.4 *The Swing – with Annotation*. Artist: Jean Honore Fragonard. Oil on canvas. 1766. The white lines in this diagram indicate the compositional structure of the painting.

In this way, he not only unifies a rather complex scene comprised of multiple figures in a landscape background but also retains the viewers' affixations on the painting for a longer period of time.

In exquisite details, Claesz vividly describes the way the various texture materials interact with light in his still-life painting shown in Fig. 9.5.

The glasses and silverware appear highly reflective and rigid with distinct highlights, while the textures of the bread, lemon skin, and tablecloth look duller and softer. The wine, beer, and lemon pieces are depicted with various degrees of transparency.

Unlike his processors, the impressionist painter, Claude Monet, examines how light interacts with ***Local Colors*** (the pigmentation inhabiting in the object) of objects in various contexts. He painted about twenty oils on the same subject of the Rouen Cathedral over a period of two years, each of which captures the atmosphere of the cathedral at a specific time of the day and under a particular weather condition. Fig. 9.6 presents a glimpse of Monet's Rouen Cathedral series, from which we discover how the quality of light can affect people's emotions.

The painting in Fig. 9.6a depicts the first ray of the sun that penetrates the early morning mist and awaits the world to wake up. The mysterious and dreamy quality of this painting forms a sharp contrast to the clear and crisp sunlight captured in Fig. 9.6b. Despite its vibrant color combination, the painting that portrays the sunset in Fig. 9.6c makes us feel exhilarated and yet sad at the same time, because we often associate aging with the fading brilliance of the sun at the end of the day.

Light in Sculpture and Architecture

Instead of describing light on a flat canvas as painters would do, sculptors and architects turn a physical light source to their advantages.

As early as human civilization was recorded, sculptors in ancient Greece already created beautiful statues with masses wedged and locked in positions of twists and turns. These sculptures receive light and cast shadow in arresting ways. The famous statue, *Venus de Milo*, by Greek sculptor Alexandros of Antioch is such an example (Fig. 9.7).

Figure 9.5 *Still Life*. Artist: Pieter Claesz. Oil on canvas. 1635.

(a) (b) (c)

Figure 9.6 *The Portal of Rouen Cathedral Series.* (a) *The Portal of Rouen Cathedral in Morning Light*. Artist: Claude Monet. Oil on canvas. Folkwang Museum. 1894. (b) *Rouen Cathedral: The Portal (Sunlight)*. Artist: Claude Monet. Oil on canvas. Metropolitan Museum of Art, New York. 1894. (c) *Rouen Cathedral, Sunset*. Artist: Claude Monet. Oil on canvas. The Musée Marmottan Monet. 1892. PD via Wikimedia Commons.

Figure 9.7 *Venus de Milo*. Sculptor: Alexandros. Photographer: Mattgirling. Marble statue. Antioch, Greece. C. 160 BC–c. 140 BC. CC BY-SA 3.0 via Wikimedia Commons.

By observing the buildings featured in Fig. 9.8, one would have no doubt that Frank Gehry was fully aware of the importance of light and the reflectivity of objects in the environment of his creation when he conceived the angles of the surfaces and the material used for the buildings.

The images featured in Fig. 9.8 demonstrate ways the light reveals the voluptuous forms and gives depth and shadow to the buildings. In addition, the colors in the surroundings, such as the grass and the sky, enrich viewer's experience of the architecture.

Light in Theatre

Completely opposite from the working methodology of a sculptor or an architect, a lighting designer, most of the time, works within an enclosed space that is devoid of any incidental light source coming from the outside of the theatre and takes full control of the lighting for theatrical productions.

Controllable Properties of Stage Lighting

In *The Lighting Art*, Richard Palmer identified controllable properties of stage lighting, which include intensity, direction, diffusion, color, form, frequency, motion, and luminousness. ***Luminousness*** refers to the glowing quality of light. Since the variations of this property are so subtle that the audience barely notices them, the following sections will investigate how a theatrical designer can manipulate properties other than luminousness to illuminate objects, sculpt actors, create a focus(es) on stage to guide audiences' affixation and eye movement, interact with other design elements, and convey moods and ideas on stage.

Intensity

Lighting Intensity refers to the density of light energy. In theatre, it is measured by the amount of light reflected from the stage floor. Lighting designers can control the intensity by several means, including the use of a ***Dimmer*** (a device designed to vary the brightness of light) and the choices on type, size, wattage, color, and the number of lighting instruments being used. Fig. 9.9 illustrates how a designer can bring focus to important characters on stage by means of lighting intensity.

In this image, the stage is barely lit with an ambient light of very low intensity (5%). A directional light of a higher intensity (70%) from SR picks up the character standing by the window, and a spotlight of even higher intensity (300%) from above picks up the character standing on SL, while leaving the character sitting in the middle in the shadow. She is hardly noticeable despite wearing clothes of lighter values.

Direction and Angle

Lighting direction **and** ***angle*** refer to the relative spatial relationships among the lighting instrument, the object being lit, and the audience. From an actor's standpoint, light can come from above (***downlight***), below (***footlight***), front (front light), back (backlight), and sides (side light) and from various angles.

The images shown in Fig. 9.10 inform us that lighting from different directions and/or angles can change the audience's perceptions of characters, sets, and the atmosphere of the scene.

(a)

(b)

Figure 9.8 *Architecture by Frank O. Gehry*. (a) *Neuer Zollhof*. Architect: Frank O. Gehry. Photographer: Fred Romero from Paris, France. The New Zollhof, located at Neuer Zollhof 2-6, Unterbilk, is a prominent landmark of Media Harbor, part of the redeveloped port of Düsseldorf, Germany. Building completion: 1998. CC BY 2.0 via Wikimedia Commons. (b) *Richard B. Fisher Center for the Performing Arts*. Architect: Frank Gehry. Photographer: Daderot. Bard College, Annandale-on-Hudson, New York, USA. Building completion: 2003. Photography: 2009. PD via Wikimedia Commons.

Figure 9.9 *Lighting – Intensity*. This scene was created in Vectorworks. An ambient light, a directional light, and a spotlight were used to illustrate how the light intensity can be varied to guide audiences' attention to certain part(s) of the stage.

Some general observations of Fig. 9.10 include:

- Front light(s) makes the character(s) and scenery look flat (middle-left). In contrast, sidelights from different angles (top-right, middle-right, bottom-left, and bottom-right) can sculpt the character(s) and the scenery and make them appear more three-dimensional.
- Front light(s) makes the stage look shallow (middle-left). Contrarily, both sidelight of steep angles and backlight can make the stage appear deeper (top-left, middle-right, and bottom left).
- Compared to the starkness that front-light(s) affords (middle-left), the atmosphere provided by downlight, backlight, or sidelight of steep angles is rather mysterious, romantic, or even horrifying (top-left, middle-right, and bottom-left).

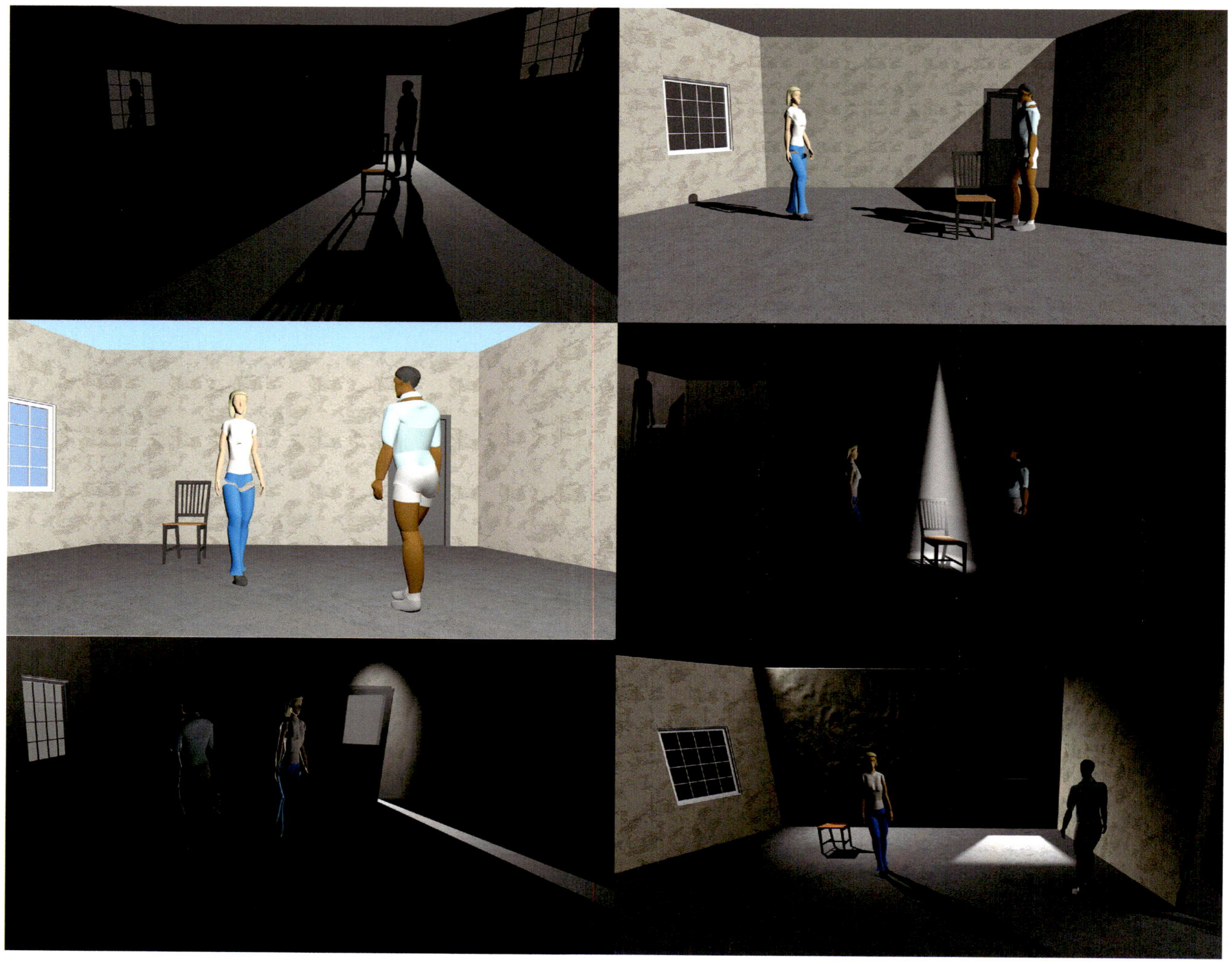

Figure 9.10 *Lighting Direction and Angle*. This series of images illustrates the manipulation of lighting direction and angle to create a variety of visual effects and moods.

- Lighting at steep angles can enhance the texture of the sets (bottom-right).
- Shadows can play an important part in the audience's visual experience of the scene (all the images in this series except for the one on the middle-left).

Diffusion

A light can be perceived as harsh or soft, or direct or diffused. In real life, sunlight can shine on an object with no obstruction or indirectly illuminate the object through its energy being bounced off from the surfaces surrounding the object. When a light illuminates an object without obstruction and with the intensity to cast harsh shadows, it is called ***Direct Light***; when a light illuminates an object indirectly or appears scattered and wraps around an object from all directions without casting distinctive shadows, it is called ***Diffused Light***. A direct light is relatively hash and intense, and, in theatre, it often comes with a small perceivable light beam or light source, whereas a diffused light is softer, often with a large scattering of light without a perceivable light source. That said, you do not need to see a light source to see direct light. By seeing distinct shadows of objects, you can tell where the direct light is coming from. A lighting designer can create artificial diffusion of light either by throwing instruments out of focus or by applying a ***Diffusion Medium*** at the gate of an instrument to soften the light beam and create an impression of scattered light.

In the digital rendering for *La Vette Social Club* (Fig. 9.11), the designers, Evan Alexander and Christine Jones, depict a room lit mostly by diffused light sources.

Although it appears to be a sunny day, which is observable by the warm light shone on the foliage outside of the window, the sunlight does not directly light the objects and cast shadows inside the room. The light coming from outside is rather environment lighting that bounces off the outdoor walls by the window and from the sky. Inside the room, the most obvious light source is the glowing tubes. You may argue that the objects in the room directly receive light from the tubes, but these glowing tubes send light in all directions and only cast a soft shadow when the illumination is intense. The room is well lit, maybe also by some scattered light sources hidden from the view, such as ambient light, so the objects in the room correspondingly receive the light bounces from other objects around.

Figure 9.11 *La Vette Social Club*. A digital rendering modeled in Vectorworks and rendered in Cinema 4D. Design, model, and render by Evan Alexander and Christine Jones. This rendering features a room lit by diffused light sources.

Color

Nowadays, in theatre, colored light can be created by a few means, including inserting a ***color filter*** (either gel or glass) into the gate of an instrument. Nonetheless, the hue, saturation, and value that we perceive in the audience are also influenced by other variables such as the local color of an object, the reflectivity of the object receiving the light, and the spectral profiles of different sources of illumination on stage. Colored light is best known for its ability to convey mood (atmosphere; emotional tone) on stage.

Compare images shown in Fig. 9.12a–c and ask yourself, "Does the change in color lights make you fell the scene differently?"

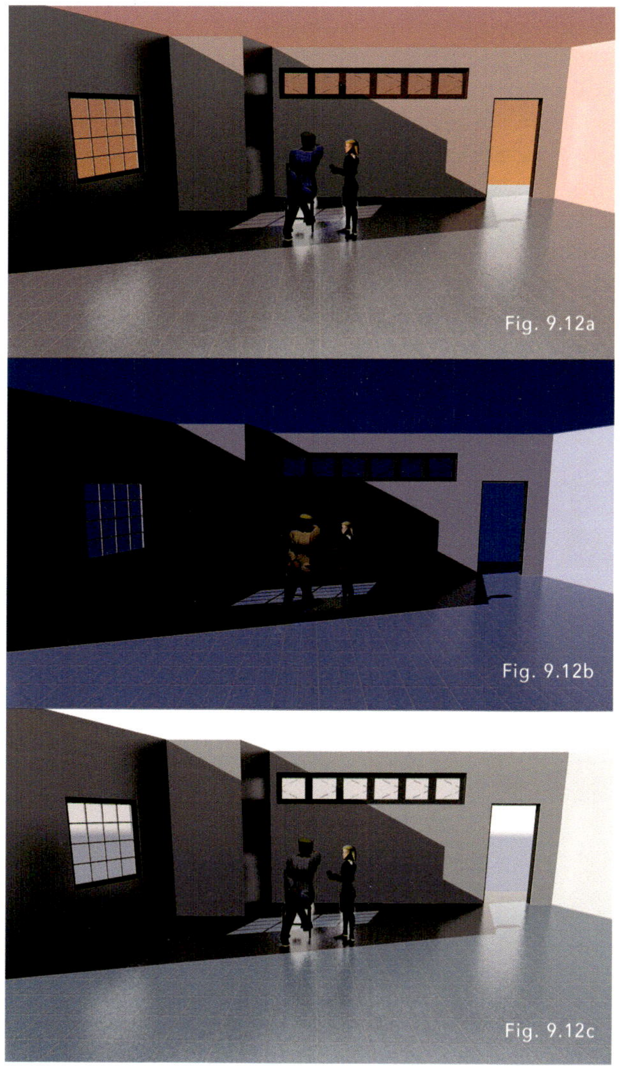

Figure 9.12 *Lighting – Color*. Color variations rendered in Vectorworks.

Instead of using color lights of various hues that will compete with the artists on stage, the renders of the design for the performance by Blue Man Group (see Fig. 9.13b and c) reveal the artist's strategy of varying intensity of light (value of different degrees) to bring focus to the signature color – blue – on the facial makeup of the artists.

Shape, Form, and Texture

With light, a designer can not only reveal and enhance the shape, form, and texture of objects placed on stage, but also create them through individual pools of light or through the use of a ***shutter*** (a metal device in the front of a profile spot that can change the shape of a light beam), an ***Iris*** (a device inside a lighting fixture that allows for the cylindrical narrowing of the beam to produce a smaller diameter of lighting on stage), a ***gobo*** (a metal or glass template inserted into the gate of an instrument and letting the light filter through to produce shape, pattern, and texture on stage), or a projector (a device that projects enlarged images onto a surface).

In his experiment (Fig. 9.14) titled *Motorcycle: Volumetric Study*, Evan Alexander demonstrates the way light reveals the texture and colors of the object and interacts with the water reflection on the ground and the droplets in the air.

Look at Fig. 9.15. In this image, (1) the form of a chair is featured by means of a spotlight; (2) this pool of downlight is cropped into the shape of a square by customizing the shutter in the lighting instrument; and (3) a gobo pattern is used to create texture, simulating a starry night sky, on the back wall of a room.

Frequency and Motion

Frequency is an aspect of motion in light and describes the number of times a light stops in each designated period. A strobe light, for instance, has a rhythmic short-frequency, while dimming for scenes has an irregular long-frequency.

Another way to achieve a sense of motion in light is to adopt a ***follow spot***, or an ***intelligent light***, that follows an actor by way of a controller or operator. In addition, the audience may also perceive the movement in lighting when the intensity, color, direction, or position of light is changed at a

(a)

(b)

(c)

Figure 9.13 *Blue Man Group: Speechless Tour*. Concept artist and draftsman: Evan Alexander. Design by: Jason Ardizzone-West. Modeled in Vectorworks. Rendered in Cinema 4D. North American Tour. 2019. (a) *Blue Man Group – Digital Model*. Modeled in Vectorworks. (b) *Blue Man Group – Digital Render 1*. Modeled in Vectorworks and rendered in Cinema 4D. (c) *Blue Man Group – Digital Render 2*. Modeled in Vectorworks and rendered in Cinema 4D.

Figure 9.14 *Motorcycle: Volumetric Study*. Illustrator: Evan Alexander. Learning how to render volumetric light. Volumetric light study in Cinema 4D with the Redshift render Engine.

noticeable pace; ***crossfading*** is one such example. This term describes a lighting technique that lowers the intensity of the preceding light on one area of the stage while raising the intensity of the following light on another area of the stage. Whether or not the audience can perceive the motion largely depends on the degree and speed of those changes.

Although this is not for a theatre project, Evan Alexander's digital lighting study in *Searching for Father* (Fig. 9.16a–c) experimented with the way lighting interacts with an interior room.

From morning, afternoon, to night, this series of images reflects the light change at different times of the day and informs us how the same room can be lit in a variety of ways to create moods and shape a story. With the knowledge you acquired in this chapter, can you describe the controllable properties used in this series and how the light changes from one scene to another as if these were scenes from a theatre or movie production?

Figure 9.15 *Lighting – Shape, Form, and Texture*. Model and render in Vectorworks. This image illustrates the way lighting reveals the form of a chair, casts the shape of a square on the floor, and creates starry texture on the wall of a room.

(a)

(b)

(c)

Figure 9.16 (a)–(c). *Searching for Father: Digital Lighting Study*. Based on Architecture by Buro511. Illustrator: Evan Alexander. Vectorworks Model: Rendered in Cinema 4D. 2020.

Lighting for Theatre Production

As mentioned previously, lighting for visual effects is different from lighting for a realized production. The following list describes the workflow of creating a light plot and generating color and instrument schedules in the VW program.

- **Set the Stage for Lighting**: Open the file with a set model created in an existing theatre space.
- **Create a Design Layer for Lighting**: Create a new Design Layer, name it "Lighting," and make it active.
- **Set Lighting Positions**: Install battens or trusses found in Resource Manager – VW Libraries and label them "electrics" using the Lighting Position Tool in Tool Sets.
- **Install a Lighting Instrument**: Import a lighting instrument found in VW Libraries and hook it on a batten.
- **Modify (customize) the Attributes for an Instrument**: Double-click on the instrument to set color, shutter, focus point, etc. for the instruments.
- **Create Label Legend for an Instrument**: Create a Label Legend in Top Menu – Spotlight – Label Legend – Label Legend Manager… to label position, color, and focus on the lighting instrument.
- **Duplicate and Distribute Instruments:** Use the Duplicate Tool in the Basic palette to duplicate the instrument; use the Align and Distribute Tool in Tool Sets – Lighting to distribute the instruments evenly on the battens; use the Move by Points Tool in the Basic palette to duplicate the 1st Electrics.
- **Number the Instruments**: Assign numbers to each instrument.
- **Bring Talents into the Space**: Insert human figures in the document. In VW, you can find human figures in Resource Manager – VW Libraries – Visualization – People. (Note: There are three types of People available in VW Libraries. One type is 2D symbols; the other two types are 3D symbols. However, within the 3D types, 3D Image Props are not made to interact with light. Only the People in Legacy Human Figures – Entourage Figures.vwx – 3D symbols can interact with light.)
- **Assign Focus Points**: Use the Focus Points Tool in Tool Sets – Lighting to place Focus Points on the stage.
- **Focus the lights**: Select an instrument and use the options and perimeters available in OIP to set the focus and customize the instrument.
- **Generate Paperwork**: Generate Paperwork such as Instruments and Color Schedules through Top Menu – Spotlight – Reports – Generate Paperwork…

Technique 9 – The Mechanics of Producing a Light Plot and Light Schedules

Technique 9 demonstrates how to create a symbolic Light Plot and generate paperwork for an Instrument Schedule and a Color Schedule from a Light Plot in Vectorworks.

Note: Technique 9 adopts and updates the process and technique explained in the instructional video published at https://www.youtube.com/watch?v=cah17sQ_o1A and applies them in the Stillwell Theatre context. This is to prepare for *Lighting a Scene for Stage* in Technique 10 – Episode One. It offers a shorter version and a longer version of this preparation. If you have taken Intro to Stage Lighting course and are interested in Lighting Design, the longer version will enhance your knowledge and digital skills in the area. For others, you may take the shortcut for this preparation. You will be reminded to stop when the time comes.

Prepare for a Light Plot

1. Open the file named "Mock Box Set," which you created previously.
2. Create a new Design Layer and name it "Light Plot."
3. In the Navigation palette, make the Light Plot layer active, the Set layer, Section layer, and Horizontal Masking layer invisible.
4. In the Layer Option dropdown menu, select Gray/Snap Others.
5. Save the document as "Mock Box Set_Light Plot" on your desktop for easy access.

Create Lighting Positions

To produce a Light Plot, you need to start with creating lighting positions. Lighting positions are the hanging points of the lighting instruments. They need to be established on a Light Plot Layer before the lighting instruments are placed. VW provides numerous lighting instruments. They are available in Resource Manager – VW Libraries.

Create a Horizontal Lighting Position

To create a horizontal lighting position, do the following:

1. Go to Top Menu – Tools – Workspace – Spotlight.
2. In Tool Sets – Rigging, click on the Lighting Pipe Tool.

3. On the Mode bar, select "Point Insertion Mode" and "Align Center Mode," and type 52′ in the Length slot.
4. Make a click on the point where the Centerline and 1st Electric position meet to set the 1st Electric hanging position.
5. Select the pipe, go to Top Menu – Spotlight – Object Conversion – Convert to Hanging Position. A dialog box opens.
6. Type "1st Electric" in the name slot to label the hanging position. When prompted, click on the "Create Symbol" button. The label of the hanging position appears on the pipe.
7. In OIP, set the "Z" height at 24′.
8. Switch to Front view to see the result of the pipe positioned high up in the air.

Create Vertical Lighting Positions

To create a vertical lighting position, take the following steps:

1. Switch back to Top/Plan view.
2. Go to Tool Sets – Rigging and click on the Lighting Pipe Tool.
3. Select the Point Insertion Mode and Align Left Mode and type 24′ in the Length slot.
4. In the house, use the click-drag method to draw a vertical line starting from the critical seat position on the left and going downward.
5. Select the pipe in house-left and go to Top Menu – Spotlight – Object Conversion – Convert to Hanging Position. A dialog box opens.
6. Type "FOH Vert 1" in the name slot to label the hanging position. When prompted, click on the "Create Symbol" button. The label of the hanging position appears on the pipe.
7. Go to OIP to set the Z height to 24′.
8. Switch to the Right Isometric view to see the result of the pipe positioned high up in the air.

Note: Beside pipes, VW also has trusses and other tools to create hanging positions.

Insert a Lighting Instrument and Assign It to a Hanging Position

To insert and hook up a lighting instrument on a batten, perform the following:

1. Switch back to the Top/Plan view.
2. Select the 1st Electric batten. Go to Resource Manager to search for a lighting instrument named "ETC Source 4 26deg" and double-click on it to select it.
3. To place the lighting instrument, click on the point where the Centerline and the 1st Electric pipe meet, and drag your cursor to rotate your instrument upward. Release your cursor to finish the insertion.
4. Check to make sure that the instrument is hooked up on the batten either by going to the Front view or by checking the Z height of the instrument in OIP.

Note: For those who decided to take the longer version of this process, skip this note section, and move on to the next section (*Modify an Instrument's Attributes*). For those who want to take a shortcut in this process, please do the following:

1. Use the same method that you used to create a hanging position on the 1st Electric to place two more hanging positions on the 2nd Electric and 3rd Electric and name the positions 2nd Electric and 3rd Electric.
2. Select the vertical hanging position in the house left, use the Mirror Tool to produce another vertical hanging position on the opposite side of the house, and go to OIP to rename this hanging position "FOH Vert 2".
3. Use the same method that you used to place the first lighting instrument on the 1st Electric to place more lighting instruments (ETC Source 4 26deg) in the following positions.
   a. Two instruments at the left side of the vertical position, which is located on the right side of the house.
   b. One instrument at the furthest left (SR) position on the 3rd Electric.
   c. One instrument at the furthest left (SR) position on the 2nd Electric.
   d. Save the document.

You are now prepared for the exercises in Technique 10 – Episode One: *Lighting a Scene for Stage* and can skip the rest of the process in Technique 9.

Modify an Instrument's Attributes

The attributes of an instrument can be modified either in OIP or by double-clicking on the instrument. In the pop-up window, the unit number, circuit number, channel, dimer, color, focus, wattage, beam/field angle, shutter, depth/angle, etc. can all be modified.

Set a Color

To set a color for the instrument, do the following:

1. Double-click on the instrument.
2. In the Lighting Device dialog box, click on the Light Information tab.
3. In "Color" slot, type R-302. If you do not know the code of a color, perform the following steps:
   a. Click on the "Color" dropdown menu and click on any of the "Pick a Color" icons located on the upper right corner.
   b. Select the color you want for your lighting instrument and click "OK."
   c. The color you picked appears in the Color slot.

Set a Shutter

To set a shutter for the instrument,

1. Click on the "Shutters" tab.
2. Adjust the Top Shutter – Shutter Depth to 25% and Shutter Angle to 0.
3. Click "OK" to save these adjustments and exit the Lighting Device window.

Set a Focus Point

A Focus Point sets the direction a light beam assembly will focus on. To focus a light beam assembly on an object or an area, a Focus Point needs to be assigned.

To assign a Focus Point, follow the steps below.

1. Create a new class and name it Focus Point Objects.
2. Go to Navigation palette to make the "Set" layer visible.
3. Go to Tool Sets – Lighting and click on "Focus Point."
4. In the drawing area, click on the center of the coffee table to place the Focus Point.
5. When a dialog box appears, name this Focus Point "A".
6. Type 2′ as the Focus Height and click "OK."
7. In the drawing area, click on the chair located downstage left to place a Focus Point.
8. When a dialog box appears, name this Focus Point "B."
9. Type 4′ as the Focus Height and click "OK."

To set a Focus Point for the instrument, you can double-click on the instrument. When the Light Device window opens, under the "Lighting Information" tab, select "A" in the Focus dropdown menu, and click "OK."

As an alternative, you can do the following:

1. Click on the lighting instrument.
2. Go to OIP and scroll down almost to the bottom of the list.
3. In the Focus slot, type "A".
4. Your instrument is now assigned to the Focus Point "A" position.

To see the result of setting this Focus Point, you can scroll back up to the middle of the list to check the "Draw Beam" box. If you move a Focus Point, the light beam assembly associated with this focus point will move with it. You can also uncheck the "Draw Beam" box to hide the beam.

Go to the Navigation palette to make the Set Layer invisible again.

Create a Label Legend

A ***Label Legend*** will display information about a specific lighting instrument in a design layer.

To create a label legend for the instrument, select the instrument.

1. Go to Top Menu – Spotlight – Label Legend – Label Legend Manager… When a dialog box appears, click "Add."
2. Name the label legend "LL-1".
3. On the first left column (Use in 2D), check the following items and deselect everything else:
   a. Position
   b. Color
   c. Focus

Note: You may check additional categories to label as needed.

4. Click on "Use Layout Symbol."
5. Click on the arrow to search for "ETC Source 4 26deg" (if it is different by default) and click "OK."
6. In the Label Legend Manager window, select LL-1, and click on "Edit 2D Layout."
7. In edit mode, drag "Position" below the instrument, "Color" above the instrument, and "Focus" in the middle of the instrument.
8. Exit Symbol Edit window.
9. Click on the lighting instrument.

10. Go to OIP, click on the "Shape" tab to make sure that the Position is on "1st Electric," the color is "R-302," the Focus is on "A," and select LL-1 in the Use Legend dropdown menu.
11. Now, the Label Legend for your first lighting instrument appears on and about the instrument.

Duplicate and Distribute Instruments

Horizontal Position

1. With the lighting instrument selected, go to Top Menu – Edit – Duplicate Array. A dialog window appears.
2. In "Shape" dropdown menu, select "Linear Array."
3. In "Number of Duplicates," type 8.
4. Check the "Cartesian Offset" box, X: 3′; Y: 1′.
5. Check "Retain" in the Original Object slot and click "OK." You now have 9 instruments in the Drawing Area.
6. Select all the instruments, go to Tool Sets – Lighting. Click on the "Align and Distribute Tool."
7. In the Align and Distribute mode bar, choose "Distribute Mode" and "Evenly Inside Points Mode."
8. In the drawing area, click on the left end of the lighting position, drag the mouse to the right end of the lighting position, and make the second click. The lighting instruments are now evenly distributed on the 1st Electric.
9. Next, we are going to use the 1st Electric position to create a few more positions.
    a. Select the 1st Electric and all the lighting instruments associated with it.
    b. Activate the "Move by Points" tool in the Basic palette.
    c. Select the Distribute Mode and Object Retention Mode on the Mode bar and set the Number of Duplicates to "2."
    d. Click once on the left end of the 1st Electric and move your cursor upward; press "tab" to get to the floating data bar; enter 5′ for the Length; and press "Enter" or "Return" twice. Now, you have three rows of instruments on your light plot.
10. Deselect everything by double-clicking on "x" key or clicking on the Drawing Area outside of objects.
11. Select 2nd Electric and all the lighting instruments associated with it. Drag and drop, while pressing the Shift key, to align them with the 2nd Electric batten position.
12. Select 3rd Electric and all the lighting instruments associated with it. Drag and drop, while pressing the Shift key, to align them with the 3rd Electric batten position.
13. In OIP, name the position "3rd Electric."
14. Select 2nd Electric in OIP, name the position "2nd Electric."
15. Next, let's switch some of the instruments to another type.
    a. Select all the instruments on the 3rd Electric.
    b. Go to Resource Manager to search for an instrument named ETC Source 4 PAR WFL, and double-click on the symbol to select it.
    c. Go to Top Menu – Spotlight – Replace Lighting Devise… A dialog window appears.
    d. Check "Replace Selected Instruments" and click on the arrows to select "ETC Source 4 PAR WFL." Click "OK" to exit the window. The new instruments appear on the 3rd Electric Batten.
    e. With the new instruments still selected, set the "Y Rotation" in the OIP to 180 (degrees).
16. Now, by double-clicking on any instrument, you can edit the focus, color, and brightness of the lighting beam in the Lighting Device window (under Light Information).

Vertical Position

The Vertical Position will have lights on both sides, representing lights that stack on top of each other. We will need two label legends for the vertical positions. To create two new Label legends:

1. Go to Spotlight – Label Legend – Label Legend Manager…
2. When the dialog box opens, click on "Add." Another dialog box appears.
3. Name the legend "LL-2," select the same attributes as "LL-1" (position, color, and focus), and click "OK."
4. In the Label Legend Manager dialog box, click on "Add" again. Another dialog box appears.
5. Name the legend "LL-3," select the same attributes as "LL-1" and "LL-2" (position, color, and focus).
6. Check Use Layout Symbol and click on the arrow to search for an instrument named "Light Instr ETC Source 4 26deg."
7. Double-click on the symbol to select it and click "OK" to exit the window.
8. In the Label Legend Manager dialog box, select "LL-2" and click on "Edit 2D layout." A dialog window pops up.
9. Select all the labels (position, color, and focus) and place them on the left side of the instrument.
10. Exit the Edit mode.
11. For "LL-3," go to Spotlight – Label Legend – Label Legend Manager.

12. In Label Legend Manager dialog box, select "LL-3" and click on "Edit 2D Layout." A dialog window pops up.
13. Select all the labels (position, color, and focus) and place them on the right side of the instrument.

Let's now place some instruments in the vertical lighting positions.

1. Go to Tool Sets – Lighting and click on Lighting Device Tool.
2. If the default lighting device symbol is not an "ETC Source 4 26deg" symbol, select it in Resource Manager by double-clicking on the instrument.
3. Place the instrument on the top left side of the FOH Vert 1.
4. Double-click on the instrument. Under the "Properties" tab, set the position to "FOH Vert 1."
5. Under the "Light Information" tab, set Focus to "A" and Color to "R-36" and click "OK.
6. In the Object Info palette, set the "Z" height to 24′.
7. Make 4 duplicates of this instrument using a duplicate array and align them on the left side of the position.
8. Distribute the instrument evenly, using the Align and Distribute tool in Tool Sets – Lighting.
9. Select all 5 instruments and use the mirror tool in the Basic palette to create 5 instruments on the opposite side of the lighting position.
10. Select all the instruments and the lighting position, and use the centerline to mirror them on the opposite side of the theatre.
11. Select the lighting position on the house right and name it "FOH Vert 2" in OIP.
12. Select all the instruments on FOH Vert 2 and click "Edit" on OIP.
13. Click on the "Light Information" tab and switch Focus to "B." Click "OK" to exit the window.
14. Assign LL-2 to the instruments on the left side of the lighting position by selecting the instruments, clicking on the "Edit" button in OIP, and clicking on the "Properties" tab to select "LL-2" in the "Use Legend" slot.
15. Assign LL-3 to the instruments on the right side of the lighting position by selecting the instruments, clicking on the Edit button in OIP, and clicking on the "Properties" tab to select "LL-3" in the "Use Legend" slot.
16. Repeat these assignments (LL-2 and LL-3) to instruments on the left and right sides of the position on the house left.

Number the Instruments

1. Select all the instruments in the horizontal positions.
2. Select "Spotlight – Spotlight Numbering…" A dialog box appears.
3. In the "Object" dropdown menu, select "Lighting Device."
4. In "Field List," place a check mark on the left side of "Unit Number." Set the Prefix to "S-" and the Start Number to "1." Click "OK" to close the dialog box.
5. From bottom right to top left, click on each instrument one by one. Then, double-click on the blank area to finish the numbering.
6. After the numbering process is finished, you should click on each instrument to check in OIP to make sure that they are all numbered correctly.
7. Repeat this process (Steps 1–6) for the Front-of-House Instruments (instruments in the vertical positions). In the Spotlight Numbering dialog box, you only need to change the Prefix from "S-" to "FOH-" to number the lighting instruments in the vertical positions.

Generate Paperwork

Vectorworks can generate Instrument Schedules, Hookups, and other paperwork. You can create Custom Reports as well.

To generate paperwork for this light plot, follow these steps.

1. Create a new Design Layer, name this layer "Paperwork," and click "OK."
2. In the new window, click on the "Scale" button to set the scale to 1:1 and click "OK" and "OK" again.
3. In the Navigation palette, make sure that the Paperwork layer is the active layer.
4. Go to Spotlight – Reports – Generate Paperwork…
5. In the Generate Paperwork dialog box, under Schedules, select Instrument Schedule and Color schedule, and click on the "Setup" button.
6. In the Schedule Formatting dialog box, select all the items under Column Order, and then click the "Move" button with the move-left arrow.
7. Then select and move "Position," "Unit Number," "Inst Type" and "Focus" in the Available Fields to the Column on the right using the "Move" button with the move-right arrow. Click "OK," "OK," and "OK" again. The schedules are now available in the Resource Manager, under your document file.

8. Go to Resource Manager and click on the home icon. Scroll down to see the Color Schedule and Instrument Schedule. Drag them to your Design Layer.
9. You may want to adjust the column width of the schedules. To do so, double-click on the schedule and make any modifications that are necessary.
10. Export your Paperwork to PDF file as "Mock Box Set_Light Schedules and save it on your computer.
11. Save your project (vwx file) on your computer desktop for easy access.

Project #5: Creating Light Plot and Light Schedules

Objectives

The goal of this project is as follows:

1. Develop a simple Light Plot in the VW environment that illustrates your ability to
   - adopt Legacy Human Figure(s) in the scene.
   - set lighting positions, choose lighting instruments, hook the instruments on the lighting positions, create a Label Legend for the lighting instruments, distribute the instruments, and number the instruments.
   - assign at least three lighting instruments to at least three Focus Points in the scene.
   - customize the instruments in terms of color and focus.
2. Generate the Instrument Schedule and Color Schedule from the light plot (on a Design Layer) to Sheet Layers using the resources and commands available in the VW program.

Tasks

To fulfill your goals for this project, you need to do the following:

1. Create a symbolic Light Plot for an imaginary scene played on the Box Set.
   - Set hanging positions for lighting instruments.
   - Hook the instruments to lighting positions.
   - Create a Label Legend for the instruments.
   - Number the instruments.
   - Place Legacy Human Figure(s) in the scene
   - Create at least three Focus Points, place them on the human figure/figures and/or scenery, and focus the lighting instruments on the focus points.
   - Modify the attributes of at least three instruments, including their intensity, colors, and focus points, etc.
2. Generate an instrument schedule and a color schedule from the light plot on Sheet Layers.
3. Save the Light Plot in a vwx.file format and save the light instrument and color schedules in a PDF file format.

Required Equipment and Materials

To complete this project, you will need a computer with internet access and Vectorworks Version 2023 installed.

Design Layer Scale

¼″ = 1′ – 0″

Procedure

1. Follow the steps suggested in Technique 9, "The Mechanics of Light Plot and Light Schedules.
2. Bring Legacy Human Figure(s) on the scene.
3. Customize the lighting instruments to light and focus the scene.
4. Save your plot in a vwx file format on your computer desktop. Name this plot "Box Set – Light."
5. Export your Instrument Schedule and Color Schedule to PDF files and save them on your computer desktop as "Box Set_Instrument Schedule" and "Box Set_Color Schedule.

Evaluation Criteria

Artistry

1. The Light Plot takes into consideration the visual presentation of the set model and the human figures.

Problem-Solving

1. The battens on stage are installed at the electric positions.
2. The lighting instruments are appropriately hooked on the batten, labeled, and numbered.
3. The required three lighting instruments have their own unique focus points (maybe also unique intensity and color choices).

Requirements and Presentation

1. The work is complete and meets the required components and formats.
2. The various components of the work are executed with accuracy and professionalism.

Student Work Samples

Figs. 9.17–9.19 showcase student work smples for Project #5 – Creating Light Plot and Light Schedules.

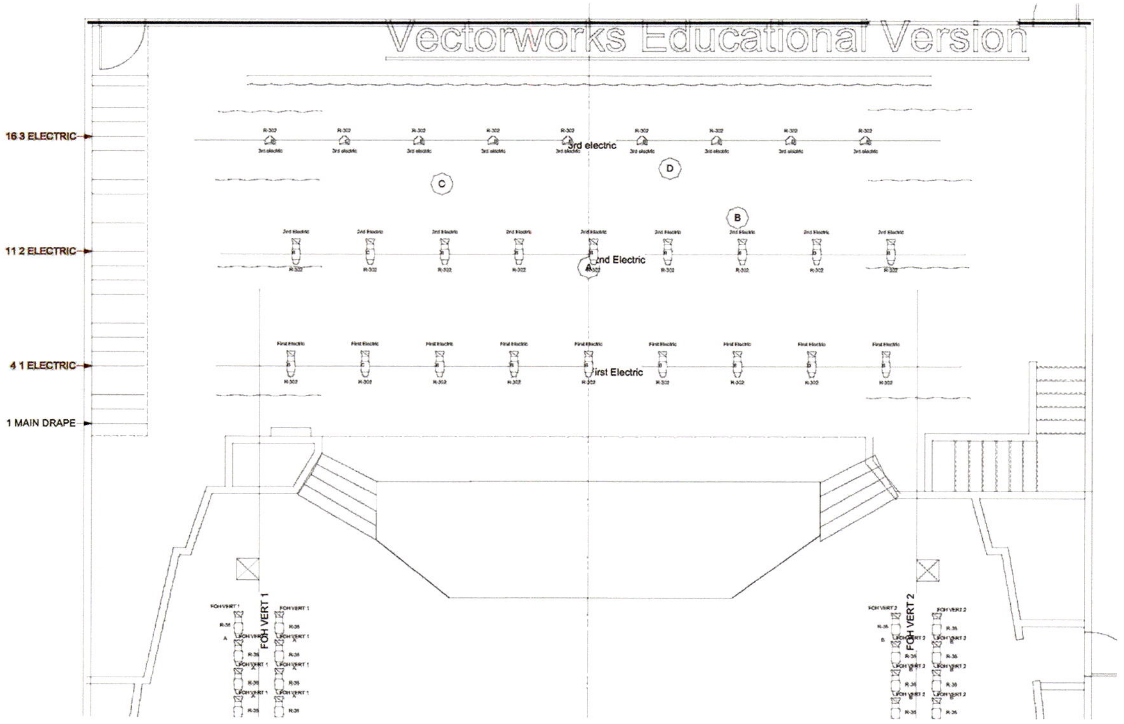

Color Schedule

Color	Position	Unit Number	Instrument Type	Frame Size
R-302	2nd Electric	S-16	ETC Source4 26deg	6.25"
	2nd Electric	S-15	ETC Source4 26deg	6.25"
	2nd Electric	S-18	ETC Source4 26deg	6.25"
	2nd Electric	S-17	ETC Source4 26deg	6.25"
	2nd Electric	S-14	ETC Source4 26deg	6.25"
	2nd Electric	S-11	ETC Source4 26deg	6.25"
	2nd Electric	S-10	ETC Source4 26deg	6.25"
	2nd Electric	S-13	ETC Source4 26deg	6.25"
	2nd Electric	S-12	ETC Source4 26deg	6.25"
	3rd electric	S-25	ETC CE Source4 PAR MCM (WFL)	7.5"
	3rd electric	S-24	ETC CE Source4 PAR MCM (WFL)	7.5"
	3rd electric	S-27	ETC CE Source4 PAR MCM (WFL)	7.5"
	3rd electric	S-26	ETC CE Source4 PAR MCM (WFL)	7.5"
	3rd electric	S-23	ETC CE Source4 PAR MCM (WFL)	7.5"
	3rd electric	S-20	ETC CE Source4 PAR MCM (WFL)	7.5"
	3rd electric	S-19	ETC CE Source4 PAR MCM (WFL)	7.5"
	3rd electric	S-22	ETC CE Source4 PAR MCM (WFL)	7.5"
	3rd electric	S-21	ETC CE Source4 PAR MCM (WFL)	7.5"
	First Electric	S-3	ETC Source4 26deg	6.25"
	First Electric	S-4	ETC Source4 26deg	6.25"
	First Electric	S-1	ETC Source4 26deg	6.25"
	First Electric	S-2	ETC Source4 26deg	6.25"
	First Electric	S-5	ETC Source4 26deg	6.25"
	First Electric	S-8	ETC Source4 26deg	6.25"
	First Electric	S-9	ETC Source4 26deg	6.25"
	First Electric	S-6	ETC Source4 26deg	6.25"
	First Electric	S-7	ETC Source4 26deg	6.25"
R-36	FOH VERT 1	FOH-41	ETC Source4 26deg	6.25"
	FOH VERT 1	FOH-42	ETC Source4 26deg	6.25"
	FOH VERT 1	FOH-40	ETC Source4 26deg	6.25"
	FOH VERT 1	FOH-38	ETC Source4 26deg	6.25"
	FOH VERT 1	FOH-39	ETC Source4 26deg	6.25"
	FOH VERT 1	FOH-46	ETC Source4 26deg	6.25"
	FOH VERT 1	FOH-47	ETC Source4 26deg	6.25"
	FOH VERT 1	FOH-45	ETC Source4 26deg	6.25"
	FOH VERT 1	FOH-43	ETC Source4 26deg	6.25"
	FOH VERT 1	FOH-45	ETC Source4 26deg	6.25"
	FOH VERT 2	FOH-36	ETC Source4 26deg	6.25"
	FOH VERT 2	FOH-37	ETC Source4 26deg	6.25"
	FOH VERT 2	FOH-35	ETC Source4 26deg	6.25"
	FOH VERT 2	FOH-33	ETC Source4 26deg	6.25"
	FOH VERT 2	FOH-34	ETC Source4 26deg	6.25"
	FOH VERT 2	FOH-31	ETC Source4 26deg	6.25"
	FOH VERT 2	FOH-32	ETC Source4 26deg	6.25"
	FOH VERT 2	FOH-30	ETC Source4 26deg	6.25"
	FOH VERT 2	FOH-28	ETC Source4 26deg	6.25"
	FOH VERT 2	FOH-29	ETC Source4 26deg	6.25"

Instrument Schedule

Position	Unit Number	Instrument Type	Focus
2nd Electric	S-10	ETC Source4 26deg	B
	S-11	ETC Source4 26deg	D
	S-12	ETC Source4 26deg	B
	S-13	ETC Source4 26deg	B
	S-14	ETC Source4 26deg	B
	S-15	ETC Source4 26deg	B
	S-16	ETC Source4 26deg	B
	S-17	ETC Source4 26deg	C
	S-18	ETC Source4 26deg	B
3rd electric	S-19	ETC CE Source4 PAR MCM (WFL)	B
	S-20	ETC CE Source4 PAR MCM (WFL)	D
	S-21	ETC CE Source4 PAR MCM (WFL)	B
	S-22	ETC CE Source4 PAR MCM (WFL)	B
	S-23	ETC CE Source4 PAR MCM (WFL)	B
	S-24	ETC CE Source4 PAR MCM (WFL)	B
	S-25	ETC CE Source4 PAR MCM (WFL)	B
	S-26	ETC CE Source4 PAR MCM (WFL)	C
	S-27	ETC CE Source4 PAR MCM (WFL)	B
FOH VERT 1	FOH-38	ETC Source4 26deg	A
	FOH-39	ETC Source4 26deg	A
	FOH-40	ETC Source4 26deg	A
	FOH-41	ETC Source4 26deg	A
	FOH-42	ETC Source4 26deg	A
	FOH-43	ETC Source4 26deg	A
	FOH-45	ETC Source4 26deg	A
	FOH-45	ETC Source4 26deg	A
	FOH-46	ETC Source4 26deg	A
	FOH-47	ETC Source4 26deg	A
FOH VERT 2	FOH-28	ETC Source4 26deg	B
	FOH-29	ETC Source4 26deg	B
	FOH-30	ETC Source4 26deg	B
	FOH-31	ETC Source4 26deg	B
	FOH-32	ETC Source4 26deg	B
	FOH-33	ETC Source4 26deg	B
	FOH-34	ETC Source4 26deg	B
	FOH-35	ETC Source4 26deg	B
	FOH-36	ETC Source4 26deg	B
	FOH-37	ETC Source4 26deg	B
First Electric	S-1	ETC Source4 26deg	B
	S-2	ETC Source4 26deg	D
	S-3	ETC Source4 26deg	B
	S-4	ETC Source4 26deg	B
	S-5	ETC Source4 26deg	B
	S-6	ETC Source4 26deg	B
	S-7	ETC Source4 26deg	B
	S-8	ETC Source4 26deg	C
	S-9	ETC Source4 26deg	B

Figure 9.17 *Light Plot and Light Schedule_1*. Created by Jessica Ford for the Light Plot, Light Schedule, and Walkthrough assignment.

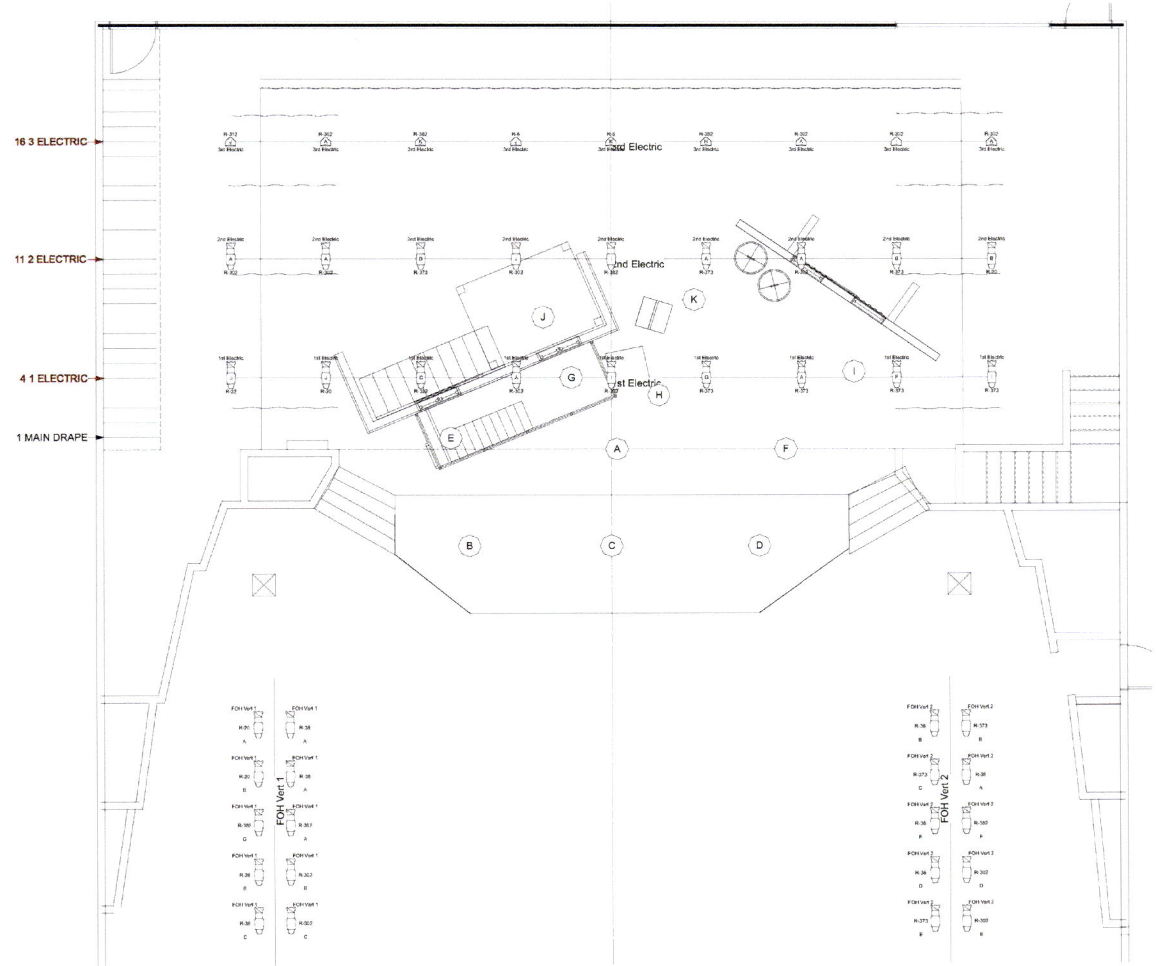

Instrument Schedule

Position	Unit Number	Instrument Type	Focus
1st Electric	S-1	ETC Source4 26deg	I
	S-2	ETC Source4 26deg	F
	S-3	ETC Source4 26deg	A
	S-4	ETC Source4 26deg	G
	S-5	ETC Source4 26deg	I
	S-6	ETC Source4 26deg	A
	S-7	ETC Source4 26deg	C
	S-8	ETC Source4 26deg	J
	S-9	ETC Source4 26deg	J
2nd Electric	S-10	ETC Source4 26deg	B
	S-11	ETC Source4 26deg	B
	S-12	ETC Source4 26deg	A
	S-13	ETC Source4 26deg	A
	S-14	ETC Source4 26deg	I
	S-15	ETC Source4 26deg	J
	S-16	ETC Source4 26deg	D
	S-17	ETC Source4 26deg	A
	S-18	ETC Source4 26deg	A
3rd Electric	S-19	ETC Source4 PAR WFL	A
	S-20	ETC Source4 PAR WFL	I
	S-21	ETC Source4 PAR WFL	A
	S-22	ETC Source4 PAR WFL	H
	S-23	ETC Source4 PAR WFL	K
	S-24	ETC Source4 PAR WFL	J
	S-25	ETC Source4 PAR WFL	K
	S-26	ETC Source4 PAR WFL	A
	S-27	ETC Source4 PAR WFL	J
FOH Vert 1	FOH-11	ETC Source4 26deg	C
	FOH-12	ETC Source4 26deg	C
	FOH-13	ETC Source4 26deg	B
	FOH-14	ETC Source4 26deg	B
	FOH-15	ETC Source4 26deg	A
	FOH-16	ETC Source4 26deg	G
	FOH-17	ETC Source4 26deg	A
	FOH-18	ETC Source4 26deg	B
	FOH-19	ETC Source4 26deg	A
	FOH-20	ETC Source4 26deg	A
FOH Vert 2	FOH-1	ETC Source4 26deg	E
	FOH-10	ETC Source4 26deg	B
	FOH-2	ETC Source4 26deg	E
	FOH-3	ETC Source4 26deg	D
	FOH-4	ETC Source4 26deg	D
	FOH-5	ETC Source4 26deg	F
	FOH-6	ETC Source4 26deg	F
	FOH-7	ETC Source4 26deg	A
	FOH-8	ETC Source4 26deg	C
	FOH-9	ETC Source4 26deg	B

Color Schedule

Color	Position	Unit Number	Instrument Type	Frame Size
R-20	1st Electric	S-8	ETC Source4 26deg	6.25"
	2nd Electric	S-10	ETC Source4 26deg	6.25"
	FOH Vert 1	FOH-18	ETC Source4 26deg	6.25"
	FOH Vert 1	FOH-20	ETC Source4 26deg	6.25"
R-22	1st Electric	S-9	ETC Source4 26deg	6.25"
R-302	1st Electric	S-5	ETC Source4 26deg	6.25"
	1st Electric	S-6	ETC Source4 26deg	6.25"
	2nd Electric	S-15	ETC Source4 26deg	6.25"
	2nd Electric	S-12	ETC Source4 26deg	6.25"
	2nd Electric	S-18	ETC Source4 26deg	6.25"
	2nd Electric	S-17	ETC Source4 26deg	6.25"
	3rd Electric	S-20	ETC Source4 PAR WFL	7.5"
	3rd Electric	S-19	ETC Source4 PAR WFL	7.5"
	3rd Electric	S-26	ETC Source4 PAR WFL	7.5"
	3rd Electric	S-21	ETC Source4 PAR WFL	7.5"
	FOH Vert 1	FOH-11	ETC Source4 26deg	6.25"
	FOH Vert 1	FOH-13	ETC Source4 26deg	6.25"
	FOH Vert 2	FOH-1	ETC Source4 26deg	6.25"
	FOH Vert 2	FOH-3	ETC Source4 26deg	6.25"
R-312	3rd Electric	S-27	ETC Source4 PAR WFL	7.5"
R-36	FOH Vert 1	FOH-19	ETC Source4 26deg	6.25"
	FOH Vert 1	FOH-17	ETC Source4 26deg	6.25"
	FOH Vert 1	FOH-14	ETC Source4 26deg	6.25"
	FOH Vert 1	FOH-12	ETC Source4 26deg	6.25"
	FOH Vert 2	FOH-6	ETC Source4 26deg	6.25"
	FOH Vert 2	FOH-4	ETC Source4 26deg	6.25"
	FOH Vert 2	FOH-7	ETC Source4 26deg	6.25"
	FOH Vert 2	FOH-10	ETC Source4 26deg	6.25"
R-373	1st Electric	S-2	ETC Source4 26deg	6.25"
	1st Electric	S-1	ETC Source4 26deg	6.25"
	1st Electric	S-4	ETC Source4 26deg	6.25"
	1st Electric	S-3	ETC Source4 26deg	6.25"
	2nd Electric	S-11	ETC Source4 26deg	6.25"
	2nd Electric	S-13	ETC Source4 26deg	6.25"
	2nd Electric	S-16	ETC Source4 26deg	6.25"
	FOH Vert 2	FOH-2	ETC Source4 26deg	6.25"
	FOH Vert 2	FOH-8	ETC Source4 26deg	6.25"
	FOH Vert 2	FOH-9	ETC Source4 26deg	6.25"
R-382	1st Electric	S-7	ETC Source4 26deg	6.25"
	2nd Electric	S-14	ETC Source4 26deg	6.25"
	3rd Electric	S-22	ETC Source4 PAR WFL	7.5"
	3rd Electric	S-25	ETC Source4 PAR WFL	7.5"
	FOH Vert 1	FOH-15	ETC Source4 26deg	6.25"
	FOH Vert 1	FOH-16	ETC Source4 26deg	6.25"
	FOH Vert 2	FOH-5	ETC Source4 26deg	6.25"
R-6	3rd Electric	S-23	ETC Source4 PAR WFL	7.5"
	3rd Electric	S-24	ETC Source4 PAR WFL	7.5"

Figure 9.18 *Light Plot and Light Schedule_2*. Created by Ameer Hashem for the Light Plot, Light Schedule, and Walkthrough assignment.

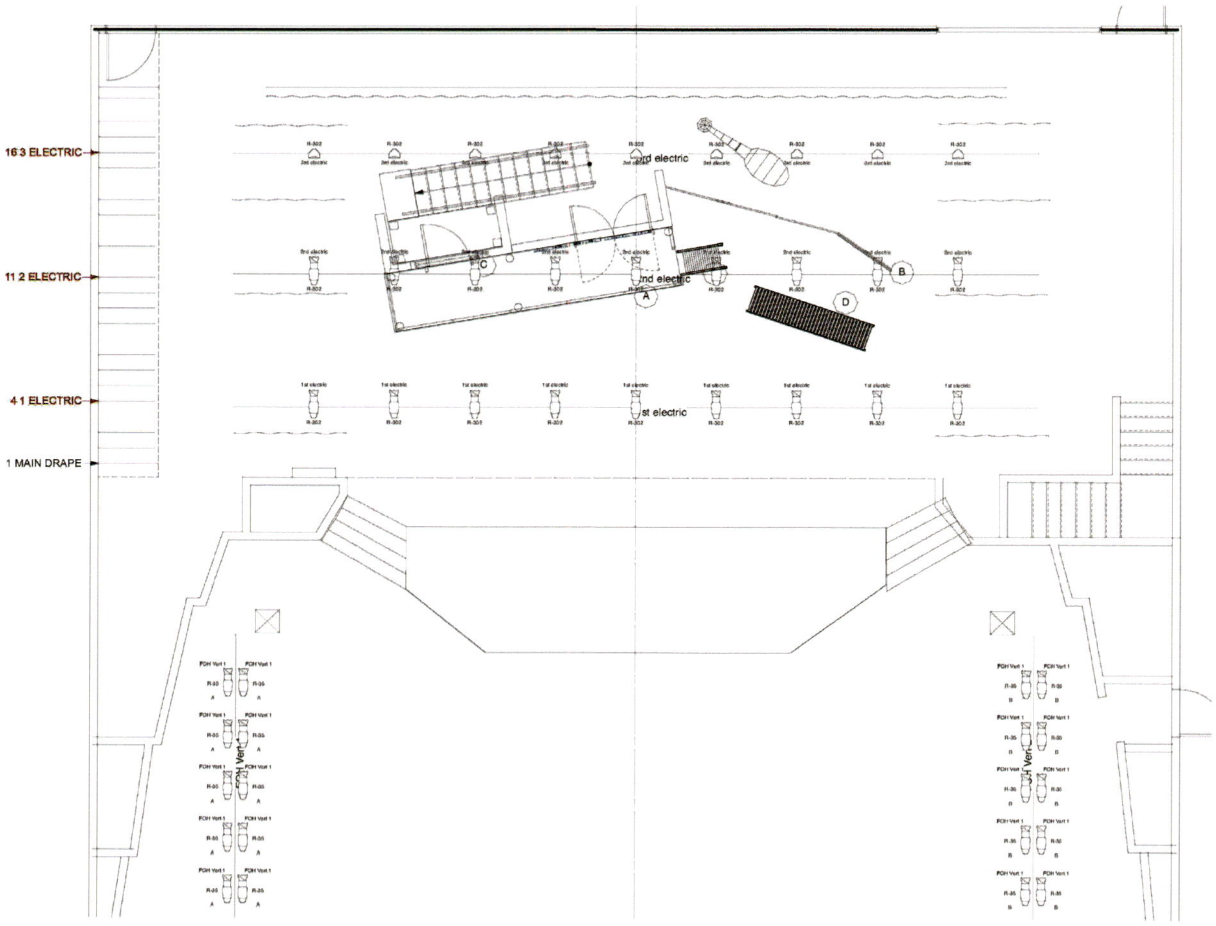

Color Schedule

Color	Position	Unit Number	Instrument Type	Frame Size
R-302	1st electric	S-3	ETC Source4 26deg	6.25"
	1st electric	S-4	ETC Source4 26deg	6.25"
	1st electric	S-1	ETC Source4 26deg	6.25"
	1st electric	S-2	ETC Source4 26deg	6.25"
	1st electric	S-5	ETC Source4 26deg	6.25"
	1st electric	S-8	ETC Source4 26deg	6.25"
	1st electric	S-9	ETC Source4 26deg	6.25"
	1st electric	S-6	ETC Source4 26deg	6.25"
	1st electric	S-7	ETC Source4 26deg	6.25"
	2nd electric	S-12	ETC Source4 26deg	6.25"
	2nd electric	S-13	ETC Source4 26deg	6.25"
	2nd electric	S-10	ETC Source4 26deg	6.25"
	2nd electric	S-11	ETC Source4 26deg	6.25"
	2nd electric	S-14	ETC Source4 26deg	6.25"
	2nd electric	S-17	ETC Source4 26deg	6.25"
	2nd electric	S-18	ETC Source4 26deg	6.25"
	2nd electric	S-15	ETC Source4 26deg	6.25"
	2nd electric	S-16	ETC Source4 26deg	6.25"
	3rd electric	S-21	ETC CE Source4 PAR MCM (WFL)	7.5"
	3rd electric	S-22	ETC CE Source4 PAR MCM (WFL)	7.5"
	3rd electric	S-19	ETC CE Source4 PAR MCM (WFL)	7.5"
	3rd electric	S-20	ETC CE Source4 PAR MCM (WFL)	7.5"
	3rd electric	S-23	ETC CE Source4 PAR MCM (WFL)	7.5"
	3rd electric	S-26	ETC CE Source4 PAR MCM (WFL)	7.5"
	3rd electric	S-27	ETC CE Source4 PAR MCM (WFL)	7.5"
	3rd electric	S-24	ETC CE Source4 PAR MCM (WFL)	7.5"
	3rd electric	S-25	ETC CE Source4 PAR MCM (WFL)	7.5"
R-36	FOH Vert 1	FOH-3	ETC Source4 26deg	6.25"
	FOH Vert 1	FOH-1	ETC Source4 26deg	6.25"
	FOH Vert 1	FOH-5	ETC Source4 26deg	6.25"
	FOH Vert 1	FOH-9	ETC Source4 26deg	6.25"
	FOH Vert 1	FOH-7	ETC Source4 26deg	6.25"
	FOH Vert 1	FOH-4	ETC Source4 26deg	6.25"
	FOH Vert 1	FOH-2	ETC Source4 26deg	6.25"
	FOH Vert 1	FOH-6	ETC Source4 26deg	6.25"
	FOH Vert 1	FOH-10	ETC Source4 26deg	6.25"
	FOH Vert 1	FOH-8	ETC Source4 26deg	6.25"
	FOH Vert 1	FOH-14	ETC Source4 26deg	6.25"
	FOH Vert 1	FOH-12	ETC Source4 26deg	6.25"
	FOH Vert 1	FOH-16	ETC Source4 26deg	6.25"
	FOH Vert 1	FOH-20	ETC Source4 26deg	6.25"
	FOH Vert 1	FOH-18	ETC Source4 26deg	6.25"
	FOH Vert 1	FOH-13	ETC Source4 26deg	6.25"
	FOH Vert 1	FOH-11	ETC Source4 26deg	6.25"
	FOH Vert 1	FOH-15	ETC Source4 26deg	6.25"
	FOH Vert 1	FOH-19	ETC Source4 26deg	6.25"
	FOH Vert 1	FOH-17	ETC Source4 26deg	6.25"

Instrument Schedule

Instrument Type	Unit Number	Position	Focus
ETC Source4 26deg	S-1	1st electric	
ETC Source4 26deg	S-2		
ETC Source4 26deg	S-3		
ETC Source4 26deg	S-4		
ETC Source4 26deg	S-5		
ETC Source4 26deg	S-6		
ETC Source4 26deg	S-7		
ETC Source4 26deg	S-8		
ETC Source4 26deg	S-9		
ETC Source4 26deg	S-10	2nd electric	
ETC Source4 26deg	S-11		
ETC Source4 26deg	S-12		
ETC Source4 26deg	S-13		
ETC Source4 26deg	S-14		
ETC Source4 26deg	S-15		
ETC Source4 26deg	S-16		
ETC Source4 26deg	S-17		
ETC Source4 26deg	S-18		
ETC CE Source4 PAR MCM (WFL)	S-19	3rd electric	
ETC CE Source4 PAR MCM (WFL)	S-20		
ETC CE Source4 PAR MCM (WFL)	S-21		
ETC CE Source4 PAR MCM (WFL)	S-22		
ETC CE Source4 PAR MCM (WFL)	S-23		
ETC CE Source4 PAR MCM (WFL)	S-24		
ETC CE Source4 PAR MCM (WFL)	S-25		
ETC CE Source4 PAR MCM (WFL)	S-26		
ETC CE Source4 PAR MCM (WFL)	S-27		
ETC Source4 26deg	FOH-1	FOH Vert 1	B
ETC Source4 26deg	FOH-10		B
ETC Source4 26deg	FOH-11		A
ETC Source4 26deg	FOH-12		A
ETC Source4 26deg	FOH-13		A
ETC Source4 26deg	FOH-14		A
ETC Source4 26deg	FOH-15		A
ETC Source4 26deg	FOH-16		A
ETC Source4 26deg	FOH-17		A
ETC Source4 26deg	FOH-18		A
ETC Source4 26deg	FOH-19		A
ETC Source4 26deg	FOH-2		B
ETC Source4 26deg	FOH-20		A
ETC Source4 26deg	FOH-3		B
ETC Source4 26deg	FOH-4		B
ETC Source4 26deg	FOH-5		B
ETC Source4 26deg	FOH-6		B
ETC Source4 26deg	FOH-7		B
ETC Source4 26deg	FOH-8		B
ETC Source4 26deg	FOH-9		B

Figure 9.19 *Light Plot and Light Schedule_3*. Created by Riley Tagliatela for the Light Plot, Light Schedule, and Walkthrough assignment.

Bibliography

Alexander, Evan (Concept artist and draftsman). Fig. 9.13a *Blue Man Group – Digital Model*. Design by: Jason Ardizzone-West. North American Tour. 2019.

Alexander, Evan (Concept artist and draftsman). Fig. 9.13b *Blue Man Group – Digital Render 1*. Design by: Jason Ardizzone-West. North American Tour. 2019.

Alexander, Evan (Concept artist and draftsman). Fig. 9.13c *Blue Man Group – Digital Render 2*. Design by: Jason Ardizzone-West. North American Tour. 2019.

Alexander, Evan (illustrator). Fig. 9.14 *Motorcycle: Volumetric Study*. Illustrator: Evan Alexander. Learning how to render volumetric light. Volumetric light study in Cinema 4D with the Redshift render Engine. 9 Mar. 2020.

Alexander, Evan (illustrator). Figs. 9.16a, 9.16b, and 9.16c. *Searching for Father: Digital lighting Study*. Based on Architecture by Buro511. Vectorworks Model: Rendered in Cinema 4D. 2020.

Alexander, Evan, and Christine Jones (designers and artists of digital model and rendering). Fig. 9.11 *La Vette Social Club*. Digital rendering modeled in Vectorworks and rendered in Cinema4D. 6 Dec. 2021.

Alexandros (sculptor) and Mattgirling (Photographer). Fig. 9.7 *Venus de Milo*. Marble statue. Antioch, Greece. C. 160 BC – c. 140 BC. (sculpture), 2011 (photography).

Anfam, David A., et al. *Techniques of the Great Masters of Art*. Chartwell Books Inc, 1993.

Bablet, Denis, et al. *Adolphe Appia, 1862–1928: Actor, Space, Light*. John Calder (Publishers), 1982.

Burian, Jarka. *The Scenography of Josef Svoboda*. Wesleyan University Press, 1971.

Chen, Ming. *Visual Literacy for Theatre*. Linus Publications, 2011.

Claesz, Pieter. Fig. 9.5 *Still Life*. Oil on canvas. 1635.

Corbusier, Le. Fig. 9.1 Chapel of Notre-Dame-du_ Haut, Ronchamp, France. Building completed in 1954. Photo taken by Metaphox on June 13, 2010.

Ford, Jessica. Fig. 9.17 *Light Plot and Light Schedules 1*. Design Skills class. 2021.

Fragonard, Jean Honore. Fig. 9.3 and Fig. 9.4 (with author's annotation) *The Swing*. Oil on canvas. 1766.

Gehry, Frank O (architect) and Fred Romero from Paris (Photographer). Fig. 9.8a *Neuer Zollhof*, Düsseldorf, Germany. Building completion: 1998.

Gehry, Frank O (architect) and Daderot (photographer). Fig. 9.8b *Richard B. Fisher Center for the Performing Arts*. Bard College, Annandale-on-Hudson, New York, USA. Building completion: 2003. Photography: 2009.

Harmenszoon, Rembrandt van Rijn. Fig. 9.2 *Self-Portrait at the Easel*. Oil on canvas. The Musée du Louvre, Paris. 1660.

Hashem, Ameer. Fig. 9.18 *Light Plot and Light Schedules 2*. Design Skills class. 2021.

Monet, Claude. Fig. 9.6a *The Portal of Rouen Cathedral in Morning Light*. Oil on canvas. Folkwang Museum. 1894.

Monet, Claude. Fig. 9.6b *Rouen Cathedral: The Portal (Sunlight)*. Oil on canvas. Metropolitan Museum of Art, New York. 1894.

Monet, Claude. Fig. 9.6c *Rouen Cathedral, Sunset*. Oil on canvas. The Musée Marmottan Monet. 1892.

Palmer, Richard H. *The Lighting Art: The Aesthetics of Stage Lighting Design*. Prentice-Hall, 1998.

Ragheb, J. Fiona, and Jean-Louis Cohen. *Frank Gehry, Architect*. Solomon R. Guggenheim Foundation, 2001.

Suler, John R., and Richard D. Zakia. *Perception and Imaging: Photography as a Way of Seeing*. Routledge, 2018.

Tagliatela, Riley. Fig. 9.19 *Light Plot and Light Schedules 3*. Design Skills class. 2021.

Vectorworks. "GSG - Vectorworks Spotlight 2015 - Drawing a Light Plot." *GSG*, YouTube, 6 Oct. 2014, www.youtube.com/watch?v=cah17sQ_o1A.

Vectorworks. "Vectorworks Lighting Rig Design Tutorial." *YouTube*, YouTube, 20 Dec. 2022, www.youtube.com/watch?v=ZTCEOgZUO-k.

CHAPTER 10

Presenting Scene Design with Light, Camera View, and Animation

Vocabulary

Ambient Light
Environment Lighting
Heliodon
Spot Light
Pan
Tilt
Lit Fog
Ambient Occlusion
Specials
Practical Light
Camera View
Walkthrough

Learning Objectives

1. Manipulate the properties of lights in the VW working environment to light a set model and human figures for a scene from a play.
2. Display capacity to capture a scene you created with Camera View for rendering and presentation.
3. Showcase ways to use resources available in the Sheet Layer working environment for design presentation.
4. Demonstrate the ability to utilize the Saved View function and the VW Walkthrough Tool to produce an animation for a model in video format.

Types of Luminaires in the VW Program

VW provides an abundance of luminaires. Heliodon and Light Tool in various modes are modular in nature. You can easily access them in Tool Sets and customize them in OIP to create lighting in your designs. There are also various readymade light symbols stored in Resource Manager – VW Libraries. These include lighting instruments and practical lighting fixtures, such as streetlamps and candelabras. In addition, light emitters may take forms other than light objects; they can come from your choices on texture shaders (a topic covered in Chapter 8), on ***Ambient Light*** (a form of diffused and indirect light), or on Renderworks Background.

The options on Ambient Light and Renderworks Background reside in Top Menu – View – Set Lighting Options (or Set Renderworks Background). These lighting options provide general lighting, as opposed to lighting that covers specific areas. Now, let us examine the functions of these luminaires.

Modular Light Tools

Heliodon (Tool Sets – Visualization)

A ***Heliodon*** provides you with a light source from one direction. It simulates the lighting from the sun. You can set the time frame and geographic location for the sun that you want to use for your model, and the Heliodon will give you the look of

DOI: 10.4324/9781003266242-11

that specific light. After a Heliodon is installed in your document, you can change its settings in OIP (under the Shape tab).

Light Tool (Tool Sets – Visualization)

Light Tool gives you more options and flexibilities in terms of controlling the properties of light. After a light is installed in a document, you can find these options, such as brightness, color, shadow, etc. in OIP (under Shape tab).

There are four tool modes available in Light Tool: Directional Light Mode, Point Light Mode, Spot Light Mode, and Custom Light Mode. Since the use of Custom Light Mode requires a distribution file, which is more complicated than the purpose of this book, the following discussion will only cover the functions of the other three modes.

- **Directional Light Mode**: As its name implies, a directional light, like Heliodon, lets you create a light source from one direction. The Light Object comes with two blue handles. The longer one lets you change the direction of the light source (azimuth). The shorter one allows you to change the angle of the light source (elevation). After a light is installed and selected, you can change its azimuth and elevation by using the sliders in OIP while observing the light change on the model instantaneously. In addition, other options, such as tool mode, brightness, color, shadow, and z height of the light, are all available for you to adjust.
- **Point Light Mode**: Unlike a directional light, a point light acts like a light bulb. It emits light from a point evenly in all directions. You can change the brightness, color, degree of realism, and Z height of the light source in OIP after the light is installed in your document.
- **Spot Light Mode**: A Spot Light in VW simulates the behavior of a spotlight as we know it in theatre. It casts a ray of light in one direction. Unlike a directional light, however, this light can have a defined and visible perimeter of illumination. After a spot light is installed in the document, you can fine-tune the light in OIP, including those in the settings. You can make the light cast a shadow, change its brightness, color, and degree of realism, and adjust its degree of spread and beam either by moving its spread and beam handles or by providing numeric degree angles in its Spread and Beam slots. You can provide a height to which the light is aimed at (in the Look to Height Slot). Just as in a camera, the term ***Pan*** in Spot Light refers to horizontal movement (swiveling side to side) from a central axis. The Term ***Tilt*** in Spot Light denotes vertical movement (pivoting up and down) from a central axis. In OIP, you may also adjust the Pan and Tilt of a Spot Light by either giving a degree angle in the Pan and Tilt slots or by using Pan and Tilt sliders while observing the lighting changes made to your model.

Light Symbols

Just as the way you adopt plants and furniture pieces from VW Libraries, you can adopt light objects in your designs. Professional lighting instruments and practical lighting fixtures, such as wall-mount lamps, chandeliers, etc. are available in VW Libraries. One thing to keep in mind though, as you search for light symbols in Resource Manager, is that some of the light symbols found in VW Libraries are actual light sources, which you can use to illuminate your model, while others do not have the capacity to emit light. The good news is that, when a lighting instrument or practical lighting fixture has the ability to emit light, it will be listed in the Visualization Palette (Top Menu – Window – Palette – Light).

Lighting Instruments (Resource Manager – VW Libraries – Entertainment – Lighting Instruments)

There is a difference between using a lighting instrument for rendering or presentation purposes and using it for a light plot, which will be executed in an actual production. If it is just for the visual effects to convey your lighting ideas, you do not need to worry about whether this lighting instrument is hooked up on a batten or truss position and wired for use. However, if you are plotting the lights for an actual production, a whole set of logistics, such as batten position, number and type of instruments, wiring, as well as labels and paperwork, all need to be taken into consideration. Due to the purpose of this book, our emphasis will be on lighting for presentation. That said, in Technique 9 of this chapter, we still touch on the mechanics of producing a simple light plot. This includes practice on how to place lighting positions, install instruments on these positions, focus and customize instruments, create label legends for the instruments, number the lighting instruments, and produce paperwork, such as instrument and color schedules.

If you want to test-use the lighting instruments available in VW Libraries, go to Resource Manager – Vectorworks Libraries – Entertainment – Lighting Instruments – ETC Source 4. Under ETC Source 4, you may pick any lighting instruments in the folders either named "Source 4," "Source 4 Par," or "Source 4 LED," as this will ensure that the symbols you selected for use do emit light. Double-clicking on a symbol allows you to activate the symbol. A symbol requires two mouse-clicks to install on your set. The first click determines the placement of the symbol. You can pivot the symbol before making the second click to decide the orientation of the symbol. Please note that the orientation of the symbol does not dictate the direction of the light that this symbol represents; the Focus Point of the lighting instrument does, instead. After the symbol is placed on the drawing, you can go to OIP to customize the light. Based on a particular instrument, most of the perimeters that you can change are listed on the OIP palette, but some may exist in OIP – Edit only. For example, as important as the lighting intensity is, you can only access the intensity perimeter of the Source 4 instruments by going to OIP and clicking on the "Edit" button.

Practical Lighting Fixture (Resource Manager – VW Libraries – Interior – Décor – Residential Lighting.vwx; Resource Manager – VW Libraries – Interior – Décor – Residential Lighting Floor Lamp.vwx; VW Libraries – Interior – Generics – Furniture – Scenic Elements-Lighting.vwx)

Like lighting instruments, some of the practical lighting fixtures do emit lights; others are decorative only. If a lamp from VW Libraries does not illuminate, but you like the style of the lamp and want it to light the room, you can install a modular light inside the lamp shade. No one can tell the difference.

Other Lighting Options

Indirect Lighting (Top Menu – View – Set Lighting Options...)

Indirect Lighting options include light bounces, ambient light, emitters, and environment lighting.

Light bounces emulate the way light behaves in real life, as objects receiving light absorb some light energy and bounce off others to objects nearby. Ambient light gives a general wash to your model. In VW, Ambient Light ON is the default setting. If you turn the Ambient Light off without using another type of luminaire, your model will appear completely black, because what you are dealing with is the absence of light. Aside from turning it "on" and "off," you can also set the brightness and color of the ambient light. Emitter options let you adjust the brightness and temperature of all light objects. You select "Use Emitter" and make changes. Environment lighting lets you select among the available environment lighting options to exert lighting influence on your model. Keep in mind that some of the available backgrounds do emit light, while others do not. Some of these background choices only work in Shaded rendering mode, while others only affect your model in Final Quality Renderworks.

Lighting from Renderworks Background (Top Menu – View – Set Renderworks Background...)

VW offers some background images for you to adopt in your design. These are images of the sky, clouds, a gradient of two colors, etc. By default, some of these backgrounds are luminaires and can provide environment lighting to your model, while others do not emit light. Some of the backgrounds are 2D images that you can apply in a Sheet Layer; but in the Design Layer, these 2D images will show their edges when viewing your model from different directions and angles. Some of the backgrounds are panoramic images that allow you to view your model from various angles and directions without perceiving the edges. That said, it is also possible to change the settings of existing images that do not emit light to make them luminaires. You can even create your own Renderworks background that is both panoramic and luminaires in the VW program.

To apply an existing Renderworks Background in the Design Layer, go to Top Menu – View – Set Renderworks Background. In the Renderworks Background dialog window, select a background. You may also access the Renderworks Background window by selecting the layer that you want to apply a background to in the Navigation palette, Right-Clicking (PC) or Ctrl±Clicking (Mac) your mouse and selecting "Edit" to make your choice of background

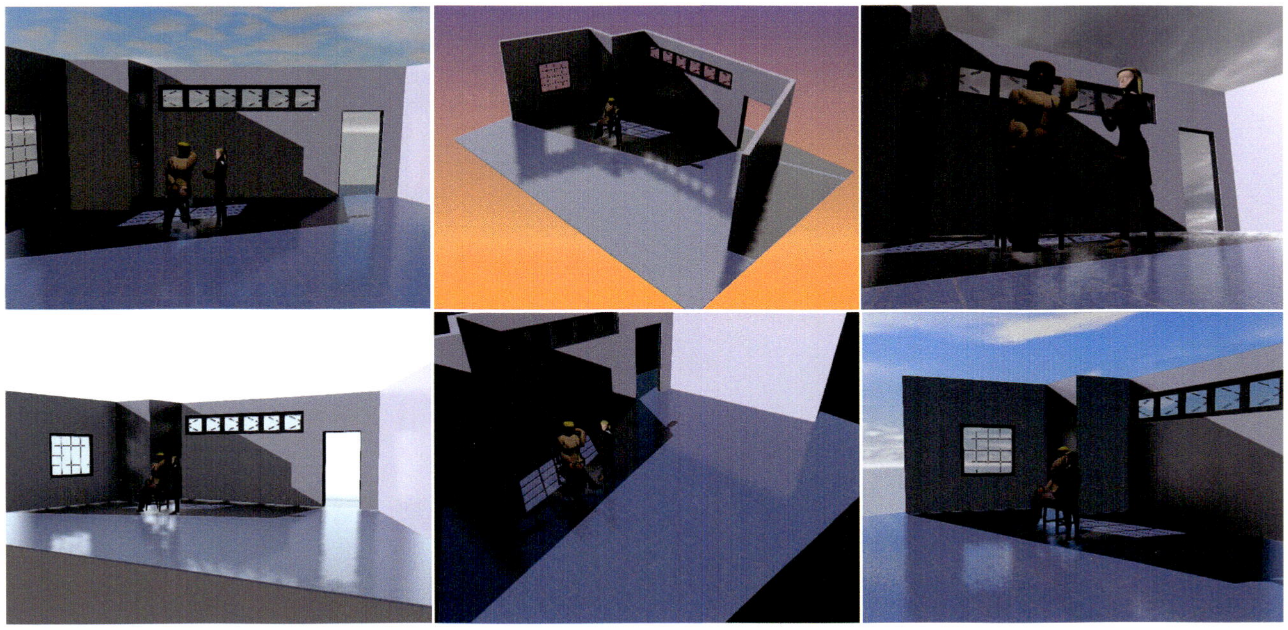

Figure 10.1 *Viewing Angles and Backgrounds*. An illustration of variations in viewing angle, direction, and background.

in the window. As a second alternative, you can go to Resource Manager – VW library – Visualization – Renderworks Background to drag-and-drop a background swatch to the drawing area. When prompted, choose to download the background image to your current document, as this will allow you to make some choices later in the process.

In a Sheet layer, Renderworks Background options are available in the RW Background dropdown menu. You can simply select a background in the dropdown menu. Setting a background in a Design Layer gives you a consistent background for your model, whereas setting a background in a Sheeting Layer allows you to set different backgrounds in different views of the model. This is especially helpful when you want to compare your model against different backgrounds or present a storyboard to the director or your clients. Fig. 10.1 is an example of such a practice.

To check whether the Renderworks Background you use can provide Environment Lighting, do the following:

- Go to Resource Manager and click on the "home" icon.
- Select the current document listed in the left column.
- Right-click (PC) or Ctrl+Click (Mac) on the Renderworks Background file that you are currently using.
- In the dropdown menu, select "Edit."
- In the Edit window, click on the "Option" button. A new window appears.
- In this window, if you see "Environmental Lighting Options" available to you, the Renderworks Background that you selected is a luminaire, and vice versa.

To adopt a Renderworks Background that emits light (see Fig. 10.2), you need to 1) select the right background (via one of the abovementioned methods) and 2) ensure that the "from current background" is checked in the Environment Lighting slot in the Lighting Options window (Top Menu – View – Set Lighting Options…).

Lit Fog (OIP, Directional Light – Spot Light Mode)

Like other options for a Spot Light object, the "Lit Fog" checkbox can be found in OIP. However, the "***Lit Fog***" option is worth mentioning here, not only because it creates special visual effects, such as beams and sheets of light and mist and fog in the air, all of which theatrical and production

Figure 10.2 *Background as Luminaire*. Set design for *East Texas Hot Links*. This image is modeled and rendered in Vectorworks with a background that emits light.

designers love, but also because it can interact with Renderworks Background in a disruptive way if you do not handle it properly.

For a light beam to be visible on stage, two components are crucial: light of high intensity and small particles of droplets in the hair. In the late 1960s, Josef Svoboda, a well-known stage and lighting designer from Czechoslovakia, experimented with this lighting technique that he coined "aerosol lighting" in the creation of light columns and light sheets while designing for *Tristan and Isolde* (Wiesbaden, Germany, 1967) and *Sicilian Vespers* (Hamburg, Germany, 1969). The result of these experiments was promising. In the digital world nowadays, "lit fog" is the command to create such a lighting effect. In VW, this command is available in OIP when you use a Light Tool of Point Light Mode or Spot Light Mode.

New users of the VW program may very well be surprised by a sudden change in the background of the model when they choose the "Lit Fog" option in OIP. This is because, by default, many Renderworks Background images are not set for the "Lit Fog" effect. You can fix this by going through the following steps:

- Go to Resource Manager and click on the "home" icon.
- Select the current document listed in the left column.
- Right-click (PC) or Ctrl+Click (Mac) on the icon of the Renderworks Background that you are currently using.
- In the dropdown menu, select "Edit."
- In the Edit window, check "Lit Fog" for the background and click "OK." Exit the window.
- Drag and drop the RB icon to your drawing area to restore the background and allow the "Lit Fog" effect to take place in your model.

Both Spot Light Mode and Point Light Mode have "Lit Fog" options. Spot Lights are rather flexible in creating a variety of foggy effects. Depending on your choices of lighting intensity, color (color temperature), beam, and spread in OIP, as well as fog density and consistency in the

(a)

(b)

Figure 10.3 *Lit Fog – Visual Effects*. An illustration of the different visual effects of Lit Fog. (a) *Lit Fog – Light Beam*. This image presents a clearly defined light beam by means of Lit Fog. (b) *Lit Fog – Mist*. This image features shapeless mist spread in the air by means of "Lit Fog."

Edit Renderworks Background window (Resource Manager), your fog can look thin or thick, well-defined or shapeless by varying settings for these properties. Fig. 10.3 illustrates two distinctive visual effects of Lit Fog.

Fig. 10.3a provides an example of using a spotlight (Spot Light Mode) of relatively higher intensity (150% brightness), narrower spread (14.20° for both spread and beam), higher fog density (100%), and smooth consistency to create a well-defined light beam against a dark background. With the same spotlight and dark background as used in Fig. 10.3a, b offers an example of choosing a relatively lower intensity (30% brightness), wider spread (150°), wider beam (58°), a much higher fog density (300%), and still smooth consistency to create the feel of mist in the air. To better reflect the environment lighting, a white color light is used for this image, as opposed to a warmer color light used in Fig. 10.3a.

Rendering and Presentation

Render with Light for Presentation

For a smooth lighting process, before installing lights in your document, you want to know how to setup light objects display mode, where to check lighting devices used in the current document, including their lighting status, and where to go to adjust the Ambient Light settings. You need to remember to create a separate Design Layer and name it "Lighting." You also want to open the frequently used palette, Visualization – Lights for easy access. In addition, if you are lighting for theatre productions, you might want to work in a Spotlight Workspace.

Setup Light Objects Display Mode

To set up a default Lighting Display mode, do the following:

1. Go to Top Menu – Tools – Options – Vectorworks Preferences…
2. When a dialog window appears, click "Display" listed on the left column.
3. In the right column, under the Display Light Objects dropdown menu, you can make a choice among "Always," "Only in Wireframe," and "Never."

To gain easy access to switching Light Objects Display Mode from one to another, do the following:

1. Click on the down-arrow located on the right end of the Mode bar. A list of choices appears in the dropdown menu.
2. Check Display Light Objects; a Display Light Object icon appears on the right side of the Mode bar. You can now easily switch from one mode to another during the lighting process.

If you choose "Always," you will see the light objects installed in the document all the time during the lighting process and in all rendering modes. If you choose "Never," you will not see the light objects installed in the document during your lighting process, no matter what rendering mode you select to render your model. If you choose "Only in Wireframe," the light objects installed in the document will be revealed only when you render your model in Wireframe rendering mode.

Check on Light Objects and Their Status

To easily check what light objects are currently installed in the document, learn their current lighting status, and select the light to edit, do the following. Go to Top Menu – Windows – Palettes – Visualization (or Lights). A Visualization – Lights palette appears. This is an expandable palette. It is best that you leave it there, as you will need it all the time during the lighting process. In this window, you can double-click on the name of a specific light to select it for edit in OIP; you can also access the lighting Edit window by right-clicking (PC) or Ctrl+Clicking (Mac) to select "Edit;" you can turn a light "on" and "off" by clicking the "On" column of the light; you can also make the light "cast shadow" or "not cast shadow" by clicking on the "Cast Shadow" column of the light.

Lighting for Visual Effects – Exterior and Interior

If you light for visual effects and realism is what you aim for, exterior lighting for a daytime scene is relatively less complex. You can install a Heliodon as the main source of lighting and set the time of day for the heliodon. A Renderworks Background can also be brought in to provide environment lighting for the scene. To fine-tune the lighting, a couple of light objects may be added. For example, to further soften the stark shadow of a Heliodon, you can install a directional light from the opposite direction of the Heliodon, but uncheck the cast shadow of that light because it will make the lighting appear unrealistic. Lighting for an interior scene is relatively more challenging in terms of controlling the brightness and color temperature of a light object because interior rooms are enclosed spaces and light bounces are sometimes harder to manage. This is where the Ambient Occlusion option comes in handy. ***Ambient Occlusion*** is a rendering option that darkens the corners where objects and planes meet or intersect. It helps viewers to see the walls and objects in the room more clearly and enhances the quality of the rendering. To select and adjust Ambient Occlusion, go to Top Menu – View – Set Lighting Options… When a dialog window opens, with the Ambient light turned on, check the "Ambient Occlusion" box and adjust the strength and size of the Ambient Occlusion.

Render with Camera View for Presentation

Set Cameras for Views

In VW, the Renderworks Camera Tool is available in Tool Set – Visualization. When you need to use a camera, in Top/Plan view, click on the tool and draw a line between the position of the camera and the center of the view you want the camera to capture, as this will set the camera's viewing direction. The first time you use a camera, the camera tool preference window will open. You can either set the default values for the camera and click "OK," or simply click "OK" to accept the program default." You can always go back to set the default values by clicking on the tool preference icon located on the Mode bar. After you set the camera's viewing direction, you can then click and drag its control points to change the position, look-to direction, and lens of the camera in an intuitive way. You can also change perimeters in many aspects of the camera in OIP. For instance, you can assign a height for the camera and a height for the main subject that your camera is viewing. You can set the projection and render modes for the camera, set the aspect ratio for the camera frame, name the camera, and assign the camera or cameras to a Class or a Design Layer. There are also several interesting camera effects that simulate the behavior of a real camera. The properties, such as "Exposure" and "Field of Depth" (the selection of a focal point in the scene)," etc. are all at your disposal. After you set the perimeters for the camera, you need to press the "Activate Camera View" button to see what your camera sees. You can also deactivate and reactivate the camera later as you wish. Especially convenient and user-friendly are the sliders available in the "Fine Tune Camera View" window. By clicking on the "Fine Tune Camera View" button, you can use the sliders in the window to adjust the camera while observing the result of the changes you are making instantaneously. In addition, you can use the Flyover Tool to set a view to your satisfaction, then click on the "March Current View" button and then the "Activate Camera View" button in OIP to capture your preferred view for rendering and presentation.

Present Views through Viewports on Sheet Layer

To present views of varying directions and angles of your model to the director or client, you can create Viewports for the views you captured with the camera in your design Layer and bring a camera with the view to the Sheet Layer. In this way, although the camera no longer exists in the Design Layer, you can make final changes to the view on the Sheet Layer. You can use multiple cameras for different views of the same model and send them to the same Sheet Layer for the presentation of your model, or you can duplicate an image on a Sheet Layer and set a different viewing angle for each if a camera is brought to the Sheet Layer.

Present Designs in Animation

VW Workthrough Tool (Tool Sets – Visualization) has four tool modes. The Walk Mode lets you use your mouse to walk in and around the model with ease. The Look Around Mode lets you use your mouse to change the viewing angle right, left, up, and down, as if you were standing still. The Elevator Mode lets you use your mouse to control your standing elevation while viewing, as if you are physically ascending and descending. The Gamer Mode allows you either use the arrow keys on your keyboard or use the mouse by clicking and draging to steel left and right and look up and down as you move in and around your model. In addition, you can customize the perimeters for the Gamer Mode in its Preferences window.

In the VW program, walking through your design via a path of Saved Views is a delightful experience. You just need to use the tool modes of the Walkthrough Tool to go through your preferred path in and around the model step by step while saving the views along the way using the Save Views command available on the View bar. Then, go to Model – Create Animation… – Create Walkthrough Path from Saved Views… to set the path in the popup window. You can preview the Workthrough by clicking on the Play button in OIP. If everything looks the way you intended, press the "Create Movie…" button. A movie of your design, if it is short, will be ready in a few minutes. Keep in mind that the longer the duration, the finer the rendering mode, and the bigger the frame size, the longer the output process of the movie will require. The method and procedure for creating a walkthrough of a model are available in the video format of Technique 9 – Episode Two.

In OIP, you can also find tools to edit the amination. If the preview of the animation reveals shortcomings, "animations can be edited from the Object Info palette and by manually manipulating the shape of the animation path, the number and location of keyframes, the camera's look-to point and viewing angle, and the camera's speed" (Vectorworks 2023 Help – Editing Animations).

Technique 10 – Episode One: Render with Light

Lighting Key Moments for a Scene Design Presentation

In this episode, we will practice the use of lighting resources available in VW to light key moments of the scenes to boost the visual effects of your model for a design presentation. Displayed here are two scenes happening on the same set for an imaginary play, one in the morning and the other at night. The lighting for these two scenes involves the use of various luminaires, including Ambient light, a Renderworks Background that emits light, theatrical lighting instruments, Glow texture, light tools of different modes, and practical lighting items of various kinds.

What you are seeing here is an updated render version of the model named "Box Set" (Figs. 10.4–10.7).

This series of images, along with captions and text boxes, detail the luminaires used to light the two scenes and the main settings for these luminaires.

Previously, after the model named "Mock Box Set" had been completed, you were asked to install moldings and trims on the walls, the furnishing items, such as a curtain and a framed picture, etc. In addition, you were asked to install hanging positions and lighting instruments. These images are taken from an updated version of the "Mock Box Set." As you might have noticed, some set props and set dressing details are added to the set. These include a metallic line sculpture on the SR wall, an area rug under the sofa, a floor lamp in the middle of the room, as well as the tiny items such as the books, the magazine, the cup, and the glasses. The model is also fully colored. That said, however, special attention should be given to the luminaires for the scene and the "characters" being brought in because our focus in this episode is lighting. Now let's get started.

Figure 10.4 *Morning Scene Lighting – Render*. This image displays a box set lit with a morning scene in mind. The photo of the park scene outside of the window is a Shutter Stock image by AlinaMD.

List of luminaires used to light the Morning Scene

- Ambient Lighting: Warm Gray (05%): Brightness (20%), with Ambient occlusion checked (50%).
- Renderworks Background (Environment Lighting): HDRI Morning.
- Renderworks Texture: Color Shader – Image; Reflectivity – Glow (Brightness: 100 with "Emit Light" checked.
- One Spot Light (Light Tool – Spot Light Mode): One Spot Light (brightness: 200%) is used to simulate the sunlight that casts long shadows on the floor as if the sun has just popped out from the horizon.
- One Point Light (Light Tool – Point Light Mode): One Point Light (brightness: 60%) is used in the middle of the stage to illuminate the line sculpture, cast shadows, and create texture on the SR wall.
- One practical light: A floor lamp used in the middle of the stage provides controlled illumination to the room.
- Two Candlelight Objects with Point Lights: Candlelight objects are used inside the fireplace to give a spark of glow to mimic the fire.

Preparation

1. Find a picture of a park under bright sunlight for the outdoor view seen through the window on SL and save it on your desktop.
2. Open the vwx file named "Mock Box Set – Light Plot" and save it on your desktop as "Mock Box Set – Lighting."
3. Go to Top Menu – Window – Palettes – Visualization. In Visualization, you can click on the Cameras icon or the Lights icon to toggle between the two modes.

   Note: This window shows you a list of lights used in your document. You can turn on and off a light by checking the "On" slot of the light.

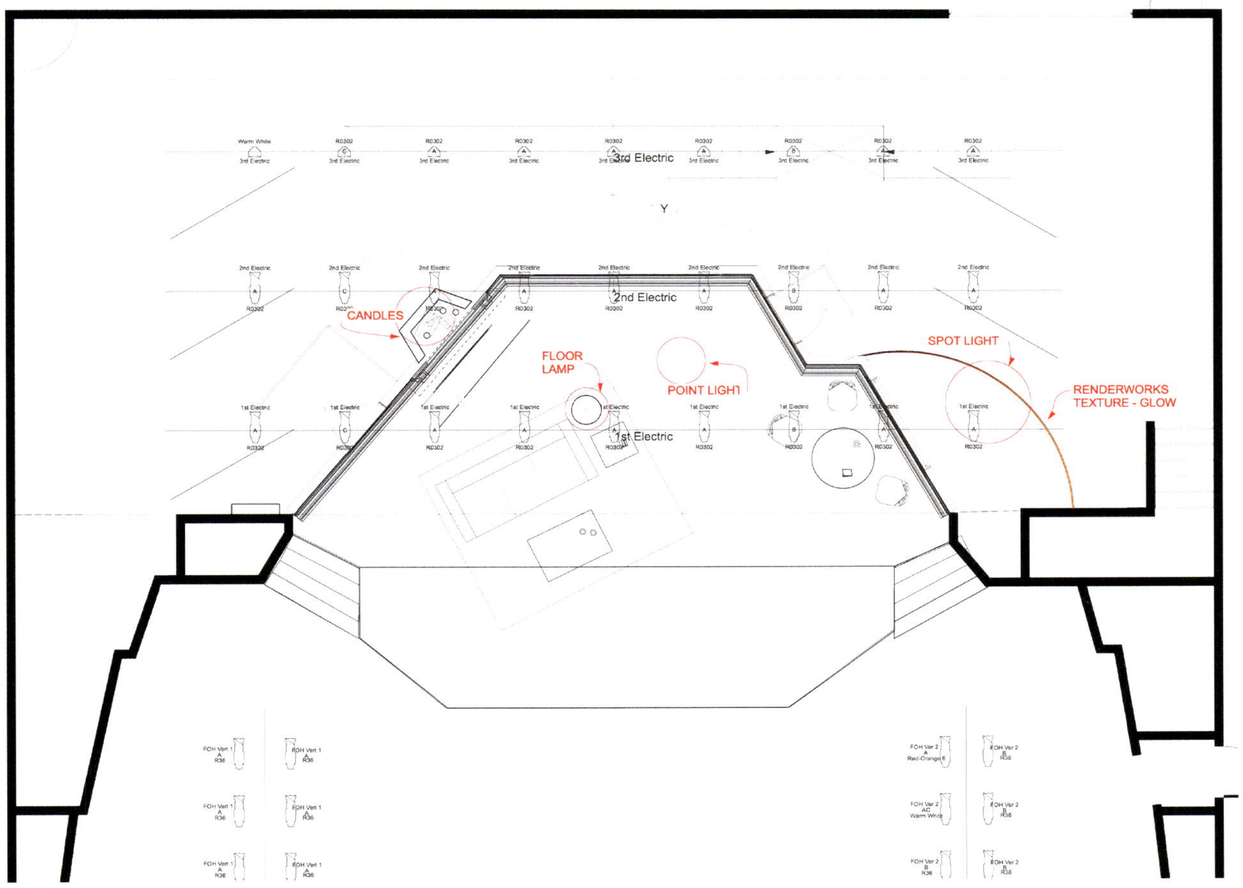

Figure 10.5 *Morning Scene Lighting – Luminaire Diagram*. This Top/Plan View reveals the Luminaires used in lighting the Morning Scene.

Figure 10.6 *Night Scene Lighting – Render*. This image displays a Box Set lit with a night scene in mind.

List of luminaires used to light the Night Scene

- Ambient Lighting: Warm Gray (05%); Brightness (20%), with Ambient occlusion checked (40%).
- Environment Lighting (Renderworks Background): HDRI Sky Night.
- One light blue Spot Light (brightness: 200%) from downstage left to simulate lighting from the street or from the moon.
- Two practical lights: 1) one is a gallery light used to illuminate the line sculpture to cast shadow and provide texture on the wall (brightness: 70%); 2) one is a floor lamp to provide controlled illumination to the room (brightness: 50).
- Two Candlelight Objects with Point Lights: Candlelight objects are used inside the fireplace to give a spark of glow to mimic the fire.
- Four lighting Instruments hooked on the battens: 1) one light from the right-hand side of the house to illuminate the characters sitting on the sofa and standing downstage; 2) one light from the right-hand side of the house to increase the intensity of the light on the character standing downstage; 3) one light from upstage-right behind the wall, using gobo to cast the shadow of a window on the upstage platform-floor; 4) one light from upstage-right aligned with the wall to illuminate the back wall and put the character standing in the upstage center in a silhouette.

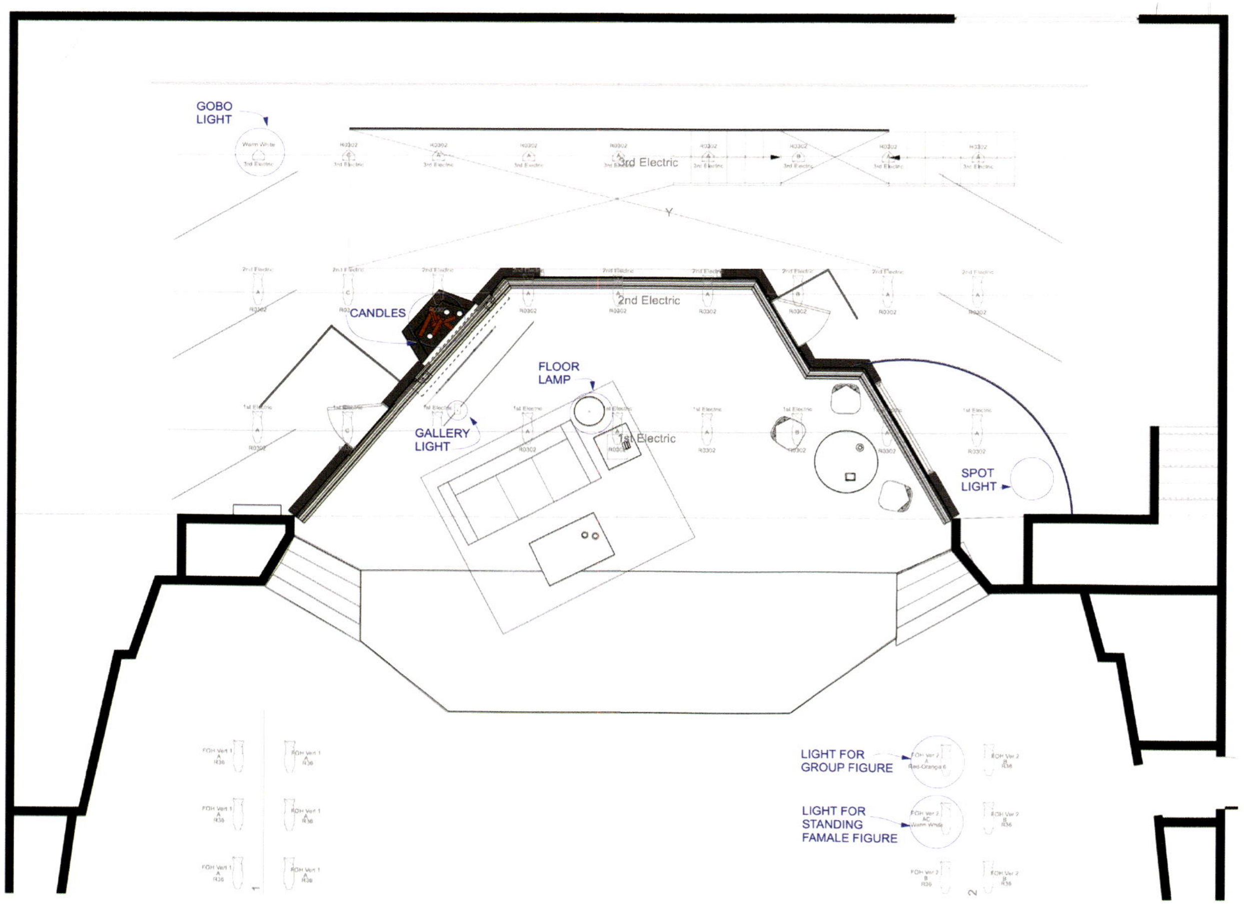

Figure 10.7 *Night Scene Lighting – Luminaire Diagram*. This Top/Plan View reveals the Luminaires used in lighting the Morning Scene.

Clicking on the "On" button will let you prioritize the list by the on/off state of the lights. If you click on the "Name" button, the lights will be listed based on the names of the instruments. This is the same as it is in the Camera window. In the following lighting process, we will sample a couple of luminaires for each type. If you are bothered by the existing Light Plot, you can make the Light Plot Layer invisible in the Navigation palette anytime during this process, as we would not use the lighting instruments on the light plot until the later part of this process. You will be reminded to switch it back to visible when the time comes.

4. Click on the down-arrow located at the end of the Mode bar and check "Display Light Objects" and "Default 3D Render Mode" to place the two icons on the Mode bar for easy access.
5. In "Display Light Object" dropdown menu, select "Display Light Object: Only in Wireframe." You can switch to another option whenever needed.
6. In "Default 3D Render Mode" dropdown menu, select "Shaded."
7. Click on the Teapot icon dropdown menu, select "Shaded," then "Shaded Options," and make the following choices. As an alternative, you can also select "Options for Other Render Modes" – "Shaded Options…" in the Teapot icon dropdown menu.
   a. Check "Textures," "Colors," Anti-aliasing," and "Shadows."
   b. Uncheck "On ground only" and "Draw edges."
   c. Check "Environment lighting," "Environment reflections," and "Object reflections."
   d. Select "High" in both "Details" and "Shadows" and click "OK."
8. Switch back to Top/Plan View. Use the Wall Tool – Curved Wall Mode to create a curved wall (Thickness: 1") to replace the additional masking flat behind the window for the Morning Scene.
   a. To draw a curved wall, deselect all snapping options on the Snapping palette.
   b. Go to Tool Sets – Building Shell – Wall Tool and select Arc Path Mode, Right Control Line Mode, and Three Points Mode.
   c. Click on the upstage corner of the window as a start point. Press and move the mouse slightly right, then release the mouse. Click on a point to end the wall.
9. Create a new Class and name it "Window Mask – Morning."
10. Click on the wall and assign it to the class named "Window Mask – Morning."
11. Select the curved wall and use the Off-Set Tool in the Basic Palette (off-set distance: 3") to produce another curved wall for the Night Scene.
12. While the new curved wall is still selected, go to the Attributes palette to select "Azure-Blue 10" for the color of this wall.
13. Create a new Class and name the blue wall "Window Mask – Night."
14. Click on the new wall and assign it to the class named "Window Mask – Night."
15. Create a 3D sculpture using the Line Tool and Extrude Along Path command (or a framed painting) above the fireplace.
16. Go to Front view, Perspective projection, and use the flyover tool to find a view that looks at the set from slightly above. Zoom in or out to include just everything on stage.
17. Go to View bar – Save View to save this view. You will need to come back to this view all the time during the lighting process.

Light the Morning Scene

For the Morning Scene, since there will be no theatrical lighting instruments involved, let's just practice turning on some ***Specials*** (lighting instruments, each used for a specific purpose other than as part of a system such as an area light or color wash) and adjust their perimeters.

Set the Ambient Lighting

1. In Spotlight Workspace, go to the Navigation palette to make the Light Plot Layer active.
2. Turn on "Show/Snap/Modify others."
3. To turn on and off the Ambient Light, go to Top Menu – View – Set Light Options… A dialog window opens.
4. Check "On" to turn on the ambient light if it is not already on.
5. In the Color dropdown menu, select "Warm Gray (05%)."

6. Set the Brightness to 20%.
7. Check "Ambient occlusion" box and set the strength to "50."
8. Under Environment Lighting, check "from current background," and click "OK" to exit the window.

Light the Environment with a Renderworks Background

1. Go to Top Menu – View – Set Renderworks Background…
2. In the dropdown menu, select HDRI Morning.

Light the Park with a Glow Texture

1. Go to the Navigation palette to ensure that the "Window Mask – Morning" Class is visible and the "Window Mask – Night" Class is invisible.
2. In Top/Plan view, select the white curved wall. Go to OIP and click on the "Render" tab.
3. Select "Texture" in the Texture dropdown menu.
4. Go to Resource Manager and click on the New Resources button. A dialog window appears.
5. Check Renderworks Texture and click the "Create" button. Another dialog box appears.
6. Name the Texture "Park" and select "Image" under the "Shaders – Color" dropdown menu.
7. When prompted, import the park picture you previously saved on your desktop.
8. When the image appears in the preview window, under the "Shaders – Reflectivity" dropdown menu, select Glow.
9. Click on the Edit button to make sure that the Brightness is set to 100% and the "Emit Light" box is checked.
10. Under both Size and Object Size, type in 12′ and click "OK" to create this luminaire.
11. View the scene in the saved view (Unified View-1).
12. If the Park picture does not show up on the curved wall, select the wall.
13. Go to OIP, under Render table – Texture, and click on the dropdown menu to select the texture named "Park."

    Note: In OIP, you may need to manually select the overall, left side, and right side of the wall one by one for the texture. You may also need to adjust the scale and position of the picture to make it fit the wall.

14. You should be able to see the result of this glowing piece in the saved view (Unified View-1).

Turn on a Spot Light for the Sunlight

1. In the Navigation palette, make the Light Plot Layer active.
2. In the Layer Option dropdown menu, select Gray/Snap Others.
3. In Top/Plan view, go to Tool Sets – Visualization – Light. Select the Spot Light Mode.
4. Drop a Spotlight in front of the curved wall, aiming directly at the window.
5. Go to OIP to make the following adjustments:
   a. Check both "Cast Shadows" and "Soft Shadows."
   b. Brightness: 300%.
   c. Color: White
   d. Spread: 85°
   e. Beam: 50°
   f. Z: 6′0″
   g. Look to Height: 1′4″
   h. Pan: 109°
   i. Tilt: 45°
6. See the Result in the saved view (Unified View-1). Go to OIP to fine-tune the light settings if needed.

Light the Room and the Art with a Point Light

1. Switch back to the Top/Plan view. Go to Tool Sets – Visualization – Light. Select the Point Light Mode.
2. Drop a Point Light in between the sofa and the SL door.
3. Go to OIP to make the following adjustments:
   a. Check "Cast Shadows" and "Soft Shadows."
   b. Set the brightness to 60%.
   c. Set the Z to 10′.
4. See the result in the saved view (Unified View-1).

Introduce a Floor Lamp

1. In Top/Plan view, go to Resource Manager, search in "All Resources" for a floor lamp, import the lamp named "Lighting Floor Contemporary," and place it behind the side table.
2. Go to OIP to set the brightness to 50%.

Note: If your room has a fireplace, you can put the firewood and drop candlelight objects with Point Lights inside to give it a spark of glow to mimic the burning firewood. Here is how you would do it:

1. Create a blank document.
2. Go to Resource Manager to search for "fireplace."
3. Double-click on the facade of a fireplace named "Fireplace Stone 03."

4. In your drawing area, click, drag, and rotate the fireplace to a counterclockwise 66° angle, then release the mouse to place the fireplace.
5. Go back to Resource Manager, scroll down to look for a fireplace interior named "Fireplace Majestic SHR36," and double-click to select it.
6. Place the interior on the back of the façade.
7. Go to the Attributes palette. In the Fill slot, select "Gray 70%" for the interior color.
8. Go back to Resource Manager to look for "fire wood" and double-click on the firewood named "Furn Outdoor Fire Wood 02" to select it.
9. Place the firewood in the interior of the fireplace and go to OIP to set the z to 9″.
10. Go back to Resource Manage to look for "tea light" and place a candlelight named "zNested Tea Light" in between the two parallel wood strips.
11. Go to OIP to set the z to 9″.
12. Go to Tool Sets – Visualization – Light and click on Point Light Mode.
13. Place a Point Light inside the tea light. If prompted, make the following choices. If not, go to OIP to make the following selections:
    a. Uncheck Cast Shadows.
    b. Brightness: 40%
    c. Color: Orange 1
    d. Z: 9″
14. Select both the Tea Light and the Point Light and copy and paste them to a hidden position among the wood strips.
15. Go to Tool Sets – Visualization – Light and click on Spot Light Mode.
16. Align a Spot Light with the top corner of the fireplace at a distance similar to the width of the fireplace façade, pointing the light beam towards the fireplace. If prompted, click "OK."
17. Go to OIP to make the following adjustments:
    a. Check "Cast Shadows."
    b. Brightness: 70%.
    c. Color: White
    d. Spread: 47°
    e. Beam: 20°
    f. Z: 12′
    g. Look to height: 5′
    h. Pan: 103°
    i. Tilt: 45°
18. Go to Top Menu – View – Set Light Options… to turn off the Ambient Light.
19. Go to Resource Manager. In VW Libraries, scroll down to the end to expand the Renderworks Backgrounds folder and click on the Renderworks Background.vwx icon.
20. In the display window, drag and drop the icon named "HDRI Spot Light Dome." When prompted, click "OK."
21. Click on the arrow located furthest right on the Mode bar to select "Display Light Objects" to place an icon on the Mode bar.
22. Click on the icon to select Display Light Objects Only in Wireframe.
23. View the result of the fireplace with a mimic of "glowing firewood" in Normal Perspective projection, Right isometric view, and Final Quality Renderworks rendering mode.

Capture a View

After you set the light for the Morning Scene, it is wise to export the render to a sheet layer so that you can keep a copy of the visual with lighting for that scene. In VW, you can save the settings for direction, angle, layer, class, render mode, etc. if you use the "Save View…" command, but you cannot save the lighting effect you created for that scene with the same command.

To keep a copy of the view with lighting effects, do the following:

1. In Top/Plan view, zoom out the Floor Plan to see the entire theatre.
2. Go to Tool Sets – Visualization – Renderworks Camera Tool and click on the tool to activate it.
3. Draw a straight line starting from the center of the house (camera's observation point) to the cyc by clicking–dragging–clicking.
4. Go to OIP and click on the "Activate Camera View" button. A view of the scene appears in your drawing area to show what the camera can see, including a suggested crop frame. After you send the view to Sheet Layer and select "Link to the Camera" when prompted, you can edit and fine-tune the camera on the Sheet Layer.
5. Go to Top Menu – View – Create Viewport. A dialog window opens.
6. Check "Linked to the Camera" and click "OK." Another dialog window opens.
7. In the "Create on Layer" dropdown menu, select "New Sheet Layer…," and follow the instructions to create the Sheet Layer. (Note: Leave the dpi at 72 to save the render time for this exercise.)
8. In the "Create Viewport" window, uncheck "Create drawing label" and click "OK" to exit the window. A copy of the render appears on a new Sheet Layer.

9. Go to OIP, and in the "Background Render" dropdown menu, select Shaded. You will come back to fine-tune the camera view later in the next section when we practice using Camera View on a Sheet Layer.

Light the Night Scene

For the Night Scene, we will bring characters to the scene. Since some of the light settings for the Night Scene share the light settings for the Morning scene, we just need to adjust the settings that do need a change for the Night Scene.

Preparation

1. In the Navigation palette, activate the Light Plot Layer.
2. In Top/Plan view, go to Resource Manager – VW Libraries – Visualization – People – Legacy Human Figures – Entourage Figures.vwx – 3D Symbols to look for a symbol named "Group 14."
3. Click on the symbol. Right-Click (PC) or Ctrl+Click (Mac) the symbol and select "Import" in the dropdown menu.
4. On your Drawing Area, click once to place the symbol on the sofa, rotate the figure to your desired angle, and make the second click to drop the symbol.
5. Repeat Step 1 and Step 2 for all the characters in the scene: Female 10 (downstage right), Female 22 (by the window), Male 07 (upstage center). You may need to adjust the characters' positions and rotations when seeing them from another viewing direction.
6. Go to the Navigation palette to make "Window Mask – Morning" invisible and "Window Mask – Night" visible.
7. Still in the Navigation palette, turn on any props needed for the scene.

Set the Ambient Lighting

1. Go to Top Menu – View – Set Light Options… A dialog window opens.
2. Change Ambient occlusion to 40% and click "OK" to exit the window.

Light the Environment with a Renderworks Background

1. Go to Top Menu – View – Set Renderworks Background…
2. In the dropdown menu, select HDRI Sky Night.

Use a Spot Light for the Moon

1. Go to Visualization – Light palette and turn off the ***Spot Light*** (spotlight) for the Morning Scene.
2. Go to Tool Sets – Visualization – Light. Select the Spot Light Mode.
3. Drop a Spotlight in front of the curved wall (on the downstage side of the other Spot Light), aiming at a steep angle at the short interior wall that is parallel with the front edge of the stage.
4. Go to OIP to make the following adjustments:
   a. Make sure that the light is on.
   b. Check both "Cast Shadow" and "Soft Shadow."
   c. Brightness: 200%.
   d. Color: Azure-Blue 5%.
   e. Spread: 50°
   f. Beam: 16°
   g. Z: 10′
   h. Look to Height: 3′
   i. Pan: 60°
   j. Tilt: 41°
5. Go to the Navigation palette to make the Window Mask – Morning invisible and Window Mask – Night visible.
6. See the Result in Front view and fine-tune the light settings if needed.
7. Save the view.

Light the Art with a Gallery Light

1. Go to Visualization – Light palette and turn off the Point Light for the Morning Scene.
2. In Top/Plan view, go to Resource Manager to search for a gallery light-track named "Light Fixt Lightolier Tangent Surf Track 8ft" and import the track.
3. Place the track about 1.5 feet away from the art but parallel with the wall.
4. Go to OIP to set the Z height of the track to 10′.
5. Go to the Attribute palette to select Black color for the track.
6. Go to Resource Manager to search for a gallery light named "Light Fixt Lightolier ProSpec Cylinder 3 3/4in."
7. Double-click on the symbol to import it.
8. In the Draw area, click once on the SR side of the pipe, rotate your cursor to find a suitable angle to light the art, and make the second click to drop the fixture.
9. Go to OIP, set the Z height of the fixture to 10′, and Brightness to 70%.

Note: For the Night Scene, the brightness of the floor lamp and the candles is the same as it is in the Morning Scene.

Light the Characters and Scenery with Stage Lighting Instruments

Set a Focus Point for an Instrument

1. Create a New Layer and Name it "Focus Point Objects."
2. In Top/Plan view, go to Tool Sets – Lighting – Focus Point Tool.
3. Place a Focus Point on the top of the Group Figure sitting on the Sofa. When prompted, name the Focus Point "AA," set the Focus Height to 3', and click "OK."
4. Use the tool to place another Focus Point on top of the female figure standing downstage left. When prompted, name the Focus Point "BB." Set the Focus Height to 5', and click "OK."
5. Use the tool again to place the third Focus Point near the middle of the upstage platform. When prompted, name the Focus Point "CC", set the Focus Height to 0, and click "OK."

Customize and Focus an Instrument on AA

1. Zoom out to see the entire theatre.
2. Go to the Navigation palette to activate the Light Plot Layer and make the Focus Point Layer invisible.
3. Go to FOH Vert 2 and select the instrument located on the first row of the left column.
4. Double-click on the lighting instrument, and a Lighting Device dialog window appears.
5. Under the "Light Information" tab, make the following selections for the instrument, then click "OK" to exit the window:
   a. Focus: AA
   b. Color: Red-Orange 6
   c. Check "On" to turn on the light.
   d. Check "Cast Shadows" and "Soft Shadows."
   e. Brightness: 150
6. Go to Front view to check if the light hits the characters sitting on the sofa.

   Note: If the beam does not hit the spot you intended, try some of the following troubleshooting tactics:

   a. You can set the focus at a different height off the ground.
   b. You can change the lighting instrument with a wider beam, for instance, Light Instr ETC Source 4 35deg. (The number of "deg" represents the beam spread of the instruments. The higher the number, the wider the spread is.)
   c. You can go to OIP, under "Mark," and check the "Draw Beam" box. Then, adjust the perimeters in the Pan and Tilt slots to see the changes.
   d. You can also go to various viewing angles and directions while fine-tuning the lighting focus in the Pan and Tilt slots.

Customize and Focus an Instrument on BB

1. Go to Top/Plan view and zoom out to see the entire theatre.
2. In the Navigation palette, make the Focus Point Objects Layer invisible.
3. Go to FOH Vert 2 and select the instrument located on the second row of the left column.
4. Double-click on the lighting instrument, and a Lighting Device dialog window appears.
5. Under the "Light Information" tab, make the following selections for the instrument, then click "OK" to exit the window.
   a. Focus: BB
   b. Color: Warm White
   c. Check "On" to turn on the light.
   d. Check "Cast Shadows" and "Soft Shadows."
   e. Brightness: 150
6. Go to Front view to see if the light hits the characters standing downstage. If not, refer to the note in the previous section (Step 6) for troubleshooting.

Customize and Focus an Instrument on CC

1. Go to Top/Plan view and double-click the furthest left instrument on 3rd Electric. A dialog window appears.
2. Click on the "Properties" tab and, under Instrument type, change the instrument to ETC Source 4 19deg.
3. Switch to the "Light Information" tab and make the following render choices.
   a. Color: Warm White
   b. Check "On" to turn on the light.
   c. Check "Cast shadows.
   d. Brightness: 80%

e. Check "Gobo 1" and click on the arrow key to get to the Resource Manager window.
f. Search for a gobo pattern named "617 Corporate Window 1" to select it. The gobo icon shows up in the Lighting Device window. Change the focus to CC and click "OK" to close the window.

Turn on an Additional Lighting Instrument

1. In Top/Plan view, click on the lighting instrument located furthest from Stage Right on the 2nd Electric.
2. Go to OIP and click on the "Edit" button. A Lighting Device dialog box opens.
3. Under the Lighting Information tab, change the focus to CC (if needed), turn the light "On," check "Cast shadows" and "Soft shadows," set the brightness to 100, and click "OK." This will light the hall behind the wall and will put the figure in the upstage center in silhouette.
4. See the Result in a Saved View.
5. Adjust the Pan and Tilt in OIP if needed.

Now, you have a Night Scene with some interesting lighting effects. To keep a copy of the view with this lighting effect, refer to the previous section on Capture a View.

Lit Fog

Lit Fog command can either cast a visible beam of light or create a foggy effect on stage, depending on the perimeter you set for the light. With a Light Tool, this option is only available in Spot Light Mode and Point Light Mode. That said, stage lighting instruments also have the "Lit Fog" option. If you double-click on an instrument, under the "Light Information" tab, you can check the "Lit Fog" option for the instrument. Please do remember that "Lit Fog" interacts with the Renderworks Background. Some of the RB choices allow "Lit Fog" effects; others do not by default. If you select the "Lit Fog" in OIP for a light and the background changes, you know you need to customize the background to make the "Lit Fog" command work for that background. To create the "Lit Fog" effect, do the following:

1. In Top/Plan view, go to Tool Set – Visualization – Light Tool, and click on Spot Light Mode.
2. Place a Spot Light on the top of the figure standing in upstage center.
3. Switch to Front view. In OIP, set the Z height to 24' and check "Lit Fog." You will immediately notice the light changes in the room. This is because the original RB does not allow "Lit Fog" by default. The background simply goes away.
4. To fix this, go to Resource Manager and click on the "home" icon to find the RB named "HDRI Sky Night."
5. Right Click (PC) or Ctrl+Click (Mac) to select "Edit…" When prompt, click "Yes" to get to the Edit RB window.
6. Check "Lit Fog" and click "OK."
7. Still in Resource manager, drag and drop the "HDRI Sky Night" RB to your Drawing Area to retrieve the original background for the Night Scene.
8. In the Visualization – Lights palette, find the Spot Light that you newly installed and turn it on if it is not already on.
9. Right-Click (PC) or Ctrl+Click (Mac) on the name of the instrument to open the Edit window and make the following changes. As you make the changes, the result immediately reflects in the drawing area.
   a. Brightness: 300%
   b. Spread: 8°
   c. Beam: 5°
   d. Use the Pan and Tilt sliders to adjust the direction and angle of the Spot Light and focus the light on the character.
   e. When you are satisfied with the result, click "OK" to exit the window.
10. Turn off the light instrument that casts the gobo pattern in the hallway and the one that lights the character downstage, both of which will help to give more focus to the character standing in the upstage center.
11. Select the Lamp and go to OIP to change the brightness to 10.
12. To keep a copy of the view with these lighting effects, refer to Capture a View (located in between "Light the Morning Scene" and "Light the Night Scene).

Technique 10 – Episode Two: Rendering and Presentation with Camera View and Animation

In this episode, we will explore some presentation techniques, using the Camera View and Animation functions available in Vectorworks.

Capturing Key Moments with Camera Views

Get Ready

1. Open the file named "Mock Box Set_Lighting."
2. Create a new Layer and name it "Lighting."
3. In Top/Plan view, select all the light objects and instruments you used to light the Morning Scene and Night Scene.
4. Go to OIP to assign them to a Layer named "Lighting."
5. Assign them to a class named "None."
6. Go to the Navigation palette to make the "None" class visible.
7. In the Navigation palette, make the "Lighting" Layer the active Layer and the "Light Plot" Layer invisible.
8. In the Layer Option Dropdown menu, select "Show/Snap/Modify Others."

Set, Adjust, and Fine-Tune the Camera View

1. In Top/Plan view, zoom out (if needed) to see the entire theatre.
2. Go to Tool Sets – Visualization to select the Renderworks Camera Tool.
3. Select Unconstrained Line Mode and draw a straight line from the position of the camera to the center of the camera view to set the viewing direction of the camera.
4. Now you can select the camera on your drawing area to adjust the camera's Position, Look To Point, and Field of View by dragging and dropping its handles.
5. You can go to OIP to change the other settings for the camera. These include Camera Height, Look to Height, Projection Mode, and Render Mode, among others. Camera Effects of different types, such as Depth of Field and Exposure, are also among the options.
6. Most importantly, you can render the model in Shaded render mode and click on the "Fine-Tune Camera View" button to use sliders in the Perspective View Controls window and see the changes made to your drawing area in real time as you slide the handles on the bars back and forth.
7. After you have made the adjustments and fine-tuned the camera, click "OK" to exit the window.
8. Click on the "Activate Camera View" button to see what the camera sees and where the frame of crop is going to land.
9. You can then change the aspect ratio of the camera frame if you like.

Match Camera View

As an alternative, while the camera is selected, you can use a combination of the standard view command (e.g., Front view or Right view) and the Pan Tool and Flyover Tool to set your favorite view and capture it with a Camera View.

1. Go to Right Isometric View.
2. Use the Pan Tool (Space bar or H key) and the Flyover tool (Shift C) to find a good view.
3. Go to OIP and click on the "Match Current View" button.
4. Click on the "Activate Camera View" button to view what the camera sees and where the frame of crop is going to land.

Set Up Multiple Camera Views

You can set up multiple cameras for the same scene. Since all the available Camera Views will be listed in Visualization – Cameras (palette), in that window, you can toggle among the views taken from various directions and angles to compare them.

1. In Top/Plan view, set up three cameras looking at different parts of the room.
2. Select Shaded Rendering Mode.
3. Go to the Visualization palette and click on the Cameras tab. All the cameras available show up on the list. You can now select among the cameras to see what each camera sees.
4. Select one of the views and adjust its aspect ratio.
5. When satisfied, go to Top Menu – View – Create Viewport… A dialog window appears.
6. Check "Linked to the camera" and click "OK." The Create Viewport dialog window opens.
7. Follow the instructions to create the camera view on a new Sheet Layer.

Organize a Design Presentation on a Sheet Layer

On a Sheet layer, you can make final adjustments to the images of your design and experiment with optimal ways to showcase your design. For instance, you can crop the image, switch on and off the lights available in the Visualization – Lights palette, you can make changes for the camera and fine-tune the camera views if you have chosen to link a camera to the Sheet Layer when creating a viewport from a camera view. You can also select viewing angles and directions, projection and render modes, as well as rendering styles and backgrounds on a Sheet Layer. Now, let's try some.

Crop, Scale, and Duplicate an Image

1. In the Sheet Layer, with an image taken from camera view, click on the "Update" button.
2. Right-Click (PC) or Ctrl+Click (Mac) on the image to open the Edit Viewport window.
3. Check "Crop" and click "OK." A Viewport Crop window appears.
4. Use the Rectangle Tool to define the area for cropping. The area that will be cropped will turn to GRAY in your Drawing Area.
5. If you are satisfied with the newly defined image, click on the "Exit Viewport Crop" button to execute the Crop command.
6. Go to OIP. In the Scale dropdown menu, select a scale that you think you can fit four images on the same sheet (e.g., 3/8 = 1′-0″). The image is now scaled to its size.
7. Make three copies of the new image and align them in a 2 x 2 image format.
8. Select all the images and update them by clicking on the "Update" button.

Render a Model with Different Lighting Effects

1. Leave the image at the top-left corner of the sheet intact, and select the image at the Top-right corner of the sheet.
2. Go to the Visualization – Light palette, turn on all the lights available in the palette and update the image.
3. Click on the image at the bottom-left corner of the sheet.
4. Switch off-and-on some lights to see the changes. If you like a lighting effect, update the image by clicking on the Update button in OIP.
5. Repeat Step 3 and Step 4 for the image at the bottom-right corner of the sheet.
6. When you are done with the four images, export the file and save it on your computer.

Fig. 10.8 provides an example of such a practice.

Render a Model with Camera Views Taken from Different Directions/Angles

1. Go back to the Design Layer and make the Lighting Layer active.
2. In Top/Plan view, find another camera and select it.
3. Activate that camera to fine-tune and adjust its aspect ratio.
4. When satisfied, go to Top Menu – Create Viewport… to create the new camera view on a new Sheet Layer.
5. Crop and scale the image, if needed, so that you can fit four images on the same sheet.
6. Make three copies of the new image and align them in a 2 x 2 image format.
7. Leave the image in the top-left corner of the sheet intact. Right Click (PC) or Ctrl+Click (Mac) on the image at the top-right corner of the Sheet to open the "Edit…" window.
8. When a dialog box opens, check the "Camera" box and click "OK."
9. In this window, you can use a combination of standard view and options available in OIP as well as in Fine-Tune Camera View window to capture an image viewing from a different direction/angle than that of the image on the top-left corner of the sheet.
10. After the new view is ready, click on the "Match Current View" button.
11. Click on the "Return to Viewport" button to execute the command.
12. Update the image by clicking on the "Update" button.
13. Repeat the process to create two views from different viewing directions/angles of the model at the bottom-left corner and bottom-right corner of the sheet (see Fig. 10.1 *Viewing Angles and Backgrounds* for a visual example).
14. When you are done with the four images, export the file and save it on your computer.

Render an Image with Different Render Modes, Styles, and Backgrounds

Since images with stage lighting will take forever to be converted to different modes, styles, and backgrounds, let us use a model without stage lighting to do this exercise.

Get Ready

1. Open your model named "Mock Box Set."
2. Make the Set Layer active, the CL Layer and Masking Layers visible, and the rest of the Layers invisible.
3. Use a Camera Tool to capture a front view of the model and activate the camera view.
4. Go to the Navigation palette to make all other layers but the Set layer invisible.
5. Adjust the view and its aspect ratio to your satisfaction.
6. Send the camera view to a new Sheet Layer.
7. In the Sheet Layer, crop, scale, and duplicate the view so that you will have four images on the same sheet.

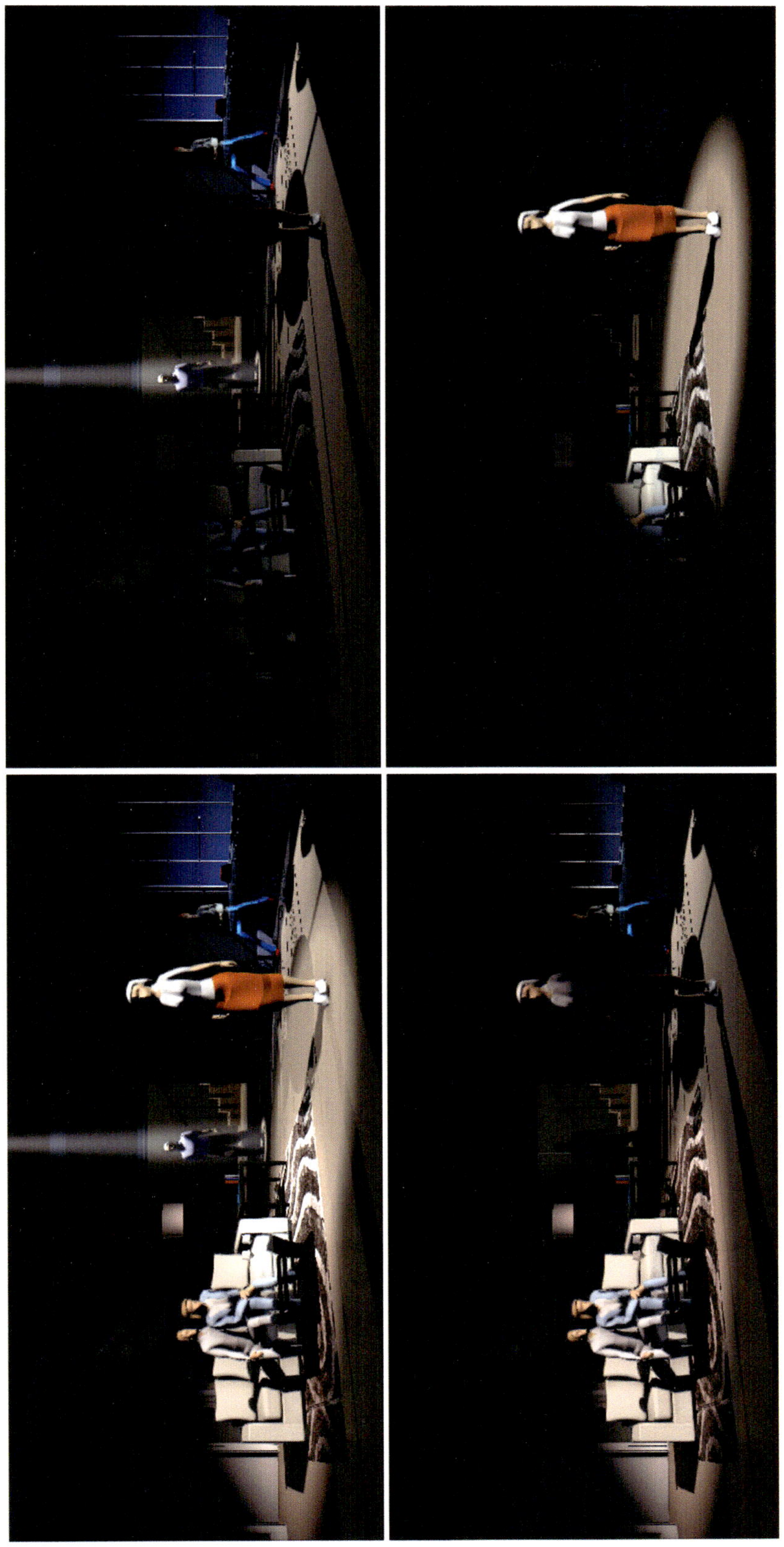

Figure 10.8 *Render Sample for Lighting Effects*. This image illustrates the use of resources in VW Sheet Layer to showcase a digital model through lighting effects.

Render the Model with Different Background Render Modes/Styles

1. Leave the image at the top-left corner of the sheet intact, and select the image at the bottom-left corner of the sheet.
2. Go to OIP, and in Background Render dropdown menu, select "Hidden Line."
3. In OIP, click on the "Update" button to update the render.
4. Select the image at the top-right corner of the sheet. Go to OIP, in the Background Render dropdown menu, select Renderworks Style – Artistic Pencil Thick Blue and update the render.
5. Select the image at the bottom-right corner of the sheet. Go to OIP, in the Background Render dropdown menu, select "Custom Renderworks" and update the render.

Select a RW Background for the Render

1. Select the image at the top-left corner of the sheet. Go to OIP, in the RW Background dropdown menu, select "HDRI Sky Day Mostly Sunny" and update the render.
2. Select the image at the bottom-left corner of the sheet. Use Rectangle Tool in Basic palette to draw a rectangle on the top of the image.
3. Go to the Attribute palette. In the "Fill" slot, select "Gradient."
4. On the right side of the gradient bar, click on the three dots to open the gradient option window.
5. Type 90 in the "Rotation" slot and update the render.
6. In the "Pen" slot, select "None."
7. Go to Top Menu – Modify – Send – Send to Back to send the gradient background to the back of the render.
8. Select the image at the top-right corner of the sheet. Use the Rectangle Tool in the Basic palette to draw a rectangle on top of the image.
9. Go to the Attributes palette. In the "Fill" dropdown menu, select "None" and update the render.
10. Select the image at the bottom-right corner of the sheet.
11. Go to OIP, in the RW Background dropdown menu, select "HDRI Sky Day High Cloud" and update the render.

Note: Rendering in Final Quality Renderworks will take a significant amount of time (possibly 40 min to 1 hr). The result will be a more refined and detailed image, but usually much brighter.

Fig. 10.9 provides an example of practices featured on this page.

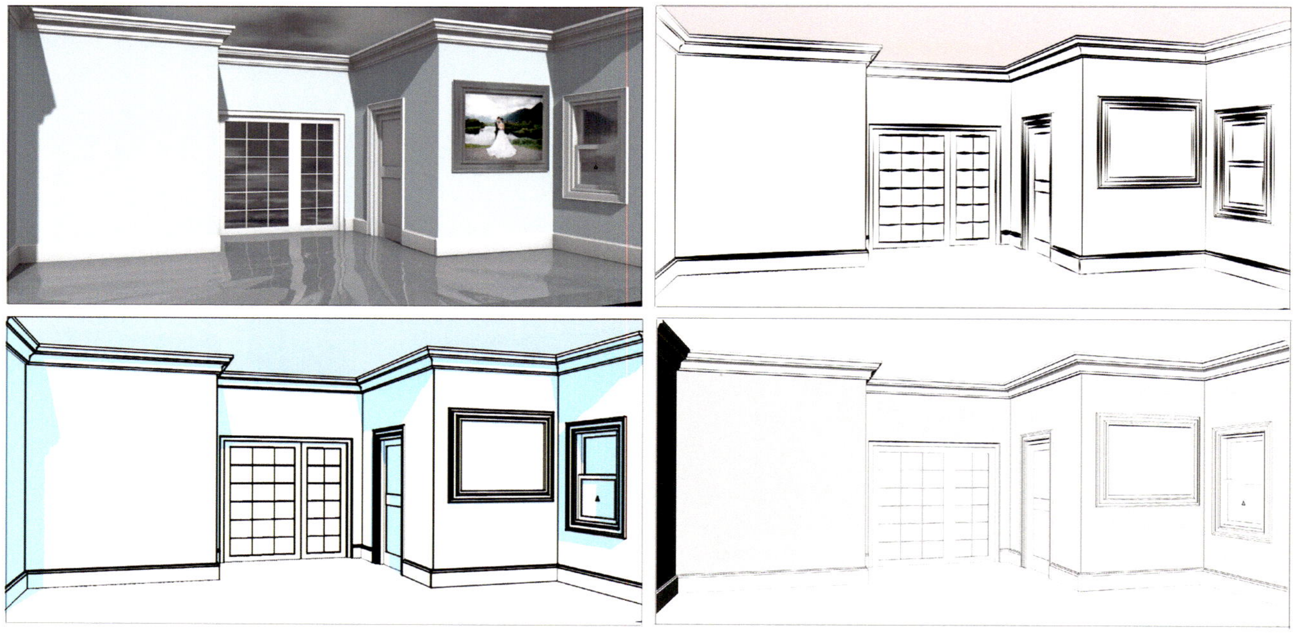

Figure 10.9 *Sample for Render Modes, Styles, and RW Backgrounds*. This image illustrates the use of the resources available in VW Sheet Layer for the exploration of Render Modes, Styles, and RW Backgrounds (Top-left: Final Quality Renderworks; Top-right: Renderworks Style – Artistic Tapper Thick Black; Bottom-left: Renderworks Style – Artistic Shadow Blue; Bottom-right: Final Shaded Polygon).

The value of organizing a design presentation on a Sheet Layer (as opposed to a Design Layer) is at least threefold. First, when making changes to a Sheet Layer, you will not mess up your original design in the Design Layers. Second, it allows you to compare different versions of the render in an immediate and efficient way. Third, rendering on a Sheet Layer allows you to present your design in a more fulsome manner.

Presenting a Design with a Motion Picture

Get Ready

To prepare for a walkthrough of your model, do the following:

1. Open your model and go to Tool – Workspace – Spotlight. Make sure that your set layer is the active layer and that your current projection is in Normal Perspective.
2. Go to Top Menu, in the "Current View" dropdown menu, select a view that looks at the set from the front.
3. Go to Tool Sets - Visualization and click on the Walkthrough Tool. The various walkthrough tool modes appear in the mode bar.
   a. The first mode (Walk) allows you to use the mouse to move the camera through the drawing.
   b. The second mode (Look Around) allows you to use the mouse to change the viewing angle up, down, right, and left while the camera remains stationary.
   c. The third mode (Elevator) allows you to use the mouse to raise and lower the camera's height.
   d. The fourth mode (Gamer) allows you to use the keyboard (to move) and the mouse (to steer left and right and look up and down) to move the camera through the drawing (a combination of the first two modes).
   e. The fifth mode (Preferences) lets you specify options for gamer mode.

Note: It may take you some practice to smoothly walk through your model along the path you prefer.

Save Views

The VW program lets you create a walkthrough path from saved views. A saved view is like a camera shot. A series of saved views playing in duration is the essence of animation.

Here is how you can save a series of views.

1. Select a desired view from the Top Menu – Current View dropdown menu (Front, Right Isometric, etc.) or use the Flyover Tool to customize a view. (Note: The drawing Projections must be set to a perspective view.)
2. Go to the View bar, click on the "Saved View" dropdown menu, and select "Save View." A "Save View" dialog box appears.
3. Give a name to the view and click "OK" to save this view as the opening view of the animation.
4. Switch to a front view, adjust the view to your satisfaction, and save this view again with a "Saved View" command.
5. Go to Tool Sets – Visualization and click on the Walkthrough icon.
6. Use the various Walkthrough modes to walk along your preferred path while saving a view for each stop along the path.

Note: For your first try, you might want to limit the number of views to 30 or less, as this will save time for video production.

Create a Walkthrough Path

1. After all the views are saved, go to the Top Menu bar – Model – Create Animation – Create Walkthrough Path from Saved Views… A Create Walkthrough Path dialog window appears.
2. Select all the saved views available (or select the views you like) in the left column.
3. Press the forward arrow in the middle to copy the saved views to the right column, and click "OK' to exit the window.
4. Now, a walkthrough path represented by a line and a camera represented by a triangular shape appear and are selected in the Drawing Area.

Preview and Save a Movie

1. In OIP, under the "Shape" tab, set the duration for the entire animation in the duration slot (e.g., 30 for 30 second)
2. Press the "Activate Camera View" button.
3. Under Preview, click "Play." You will see a preview of the walkthrough of your model in the Drawing Area.
4. After the completion of the preview, you can adjust the duration of the walkthrough and make other changes using the tools available in OIP. For details, please refer to Vectorworks Help: Edit Animations.

5. When everything looks good, scroll down to the end of the list in OIP and press the "Create Movie…" button. A Create Movie dialog box appears.
6. Check to confirm the info displayed in the window and click on the "Save Movie…" button. A window pops up to let you name the movie and select a location to save it.
7. Save the movie on your computer desktop for easy access.
8. Be patient and allow time for the process of the movie to complete.

Project #6: Presenting Scene Design with Light, Camera View, and Animation

Objectives

The goal of this project is as follows:

1. Create a Scene
   - Adopt an existing set model.
   - Introduce Legacy Human Figures
   - Apply at least three kinds of luminaires available in VW to light an imaginary scene with a distinctive time frame (morning, afternoon, or night).
   - Customize the instruments, aiming for interesting visual effects.
2. Set a Camera View(s) on the scene that you lit and customize the Camera(s) for a presentation of your set through Viewport on Sheet Layer, aiming for four distinctive looks of your model (various viewing angles and lighting effects are strongly encouraged).
3. Navigate inside and around a 3D model using the various modes of the Workthrough Tool and create a movie from the Saved View Path for your design.

Tasks and Procedures

To fulfill your goals for this project, you need do the following:

1. Create a scene.
   a. Open an existing set model.
   b. Introduce Legacy Human Figures.
   c. Light the scene with various luminaires, aiming for an interesting lighting effect (lighting from different directions/angles, intensity, color, etc.)
      i. Imagine the lighting effects that you want.
      ii. Set the focus points.
      iii. Create light objects (or designate existing lighting instruments), adjust their focus, and manipulate their attributes.
2. Bring the scene to a Sheet Layer.
   a. Capture the scene with a camera view.
   b. Fine-tune the view.
   c. Send the view to a Sheet Layer through Top Menu – View – Create Viewport… and choose "Linked to Camera" when prompted.
3. Create a design presentation board on a sheet layer.
   a. Crop, re-scale, and duplicate the view to result in four images on a sheet.
   b. Use resources available in the Sheet Layer working environment to make changes to the viewing direction/angle of the camera and/or lighting for duplicated views.
   c. Export and save the Sheet Layer in PDF format.
4. Create a rendered walkthrough movie of your set model.
   a. Use the Walkthrough Tool to walk inside and/or around the model while saving the views along the way.
   b. Select views for a movie.
   c. Preview, produce, and save the movie in MP4 format.
   d. Save your design in vwx file format.

Required Equipment and Materials

To complete this project, you will need a computer with internet access and Vectorworks Version 2023 installed.

Design Layer Scale

¼″ = 1′ – 0″

Evaluation Criteria

Artistry

1. The design demonstrates your ability to create a scene with human figures, meaningful and interesting lighting effects, and a distinctive time frame (morning, afternoon, or night).

Problem-Solving

1. The Presentation Board displays four different looks (variations in lighting effect, viewing direction/angle, rendering styles, and/or backgrounds) of the same model.
2. The work-through is well staged with varied viewing angles, directions, and elevations. It runs smoothly.

Requirements and Presentation

1. The work is complete and meets the required components and formats.
2. The various components of the work are executed with accuracy and professionalism.

Student Work Samples

Student work movie samples are available in the package for download.

Bibliography

AlinaMD. Photo of the park image in Fig. 10.4 *Morning Scene Lighting – Render.* Shutterstock. 25 Feb. 2018.

Gillette, J. Michael. *Theatrical Design and Production: An Introduction to Scene Design and Construction, Lighting, Sound, Costume, and Makeup*. McGraw Hill, 2012.

Gillette, J. Michael, and Michael McNamara. *Designing with Light: An Introduction to Stage Lighting*. Routledge, 2020.

Harvey, Michelle. "Vectorworks Rendering - Part 4 - Adding Lighting." *YouTube*, YouTube, 26 Apr. 2020, www.youtube.com/watch?v=9oLO1GoHEDA.

Jansenson, Daniel. "Remarkable Renderworks EP. 8: Overview Photo Realistic Renderworks." *Vectorworks*, YouTube, 2 Jan. 2017, www.youtube.com/watch?v=xEDyzFJ38Mg.

Jansenson, Daniel. "Remarkable Renderworks EP. 25: Lit Fog." *Vectorworks*, YouTube, 20 Apr. 2017, www.youtube.com/watch?v=guwrycromFY.

Jansenson, Daniel. "Remarkable Renderworks EP. 33: Ambient Occlusion." *Vectorworks*, YouTube, 1 Aug. 2017, www.youtube.com/watch?v=jZxNLLL7mA8.

Jansenson, Daniel. "Remarkable Renderworks EP. 26: Environment Lighting." *Vectorworks*, YouTube, 20 Apr. 2017, www.youtube.com/watch?v=sJrSWEaIF-E.

Jansenson, Daniel. "Remarkable Renderworks EP. 32: Ambient Light." *Vectorworks*, YouTube, 23 May 2017, www.youtube.com/watch?v=-wtEeSBeTS0.

Jansenson, Daniel. "Remarkable Renderworks EP. 36: Renderworks Camera Effects." *Vectorworks*, YouTube, 1 Aug. 2017, www.youtube.com/watch?v=-0JaB_Gd5jk.

Lévy, François. "Rendering and Lighting with Vectorworks." *Austin Vectorworks Community*, YouTube, 14 July 2022, www.youtube.com/watch?v=m-lJdu27HGQ.

Parker, W. Oren, and Harvey K. Smith. *Scene Design and Stage Lighting*. Harcourt Brace College Publishers, 1996.

Reeves, Jonathan. "Vectorworks 2023: Lighting & Rendering Tutorial (4K)." *Jonathan Reeves CAD*, YouTube, 26 Sept. 2022, www.youtube.com/watch?v=cYDSXGQZQR8.

Sean, O'Skea. "Fluorescent and Neon Lights in VW." *YouTube*, YouTube, 3 Mar. 2015, www.youtube.com/watch?v=ykz21dcKCns.

Unknown. The Forest image Fig. 10.2. *Background as Luminaire*. Shutter Stock. 19 Feb. 2018.

Vectorworks. "Backlighting/Halo Effect Light." *YouTube*, YouTube, 8 Jan. 2018, www.youtube.com/watch?v=LE4Lydlvk9w&t=186s.

Vectorworks. "Interiors – Designing a Home Office." *YouTube*, YouTube, 10 May 2021, www.youtube.com/watch?v=D_RkNVZdPhl&list=RDCMUCN7uzhu-ljLJOe6a0J-fBcQ.

Vectorworks. "Rendering in Vectorworks - Lights." *Vectorworks*, YouTube, 14 Sept. 2016, www.youtube.com/watch?v=3dmzNLd2KP4&t=12s.

Index

Note: Page references in *italics* denote figures.

For Product Safety Concerns and Information please contact our EU representative GPSR@taylorandfrancis.com Taylor & Francis Verlag GmbH, Kaufingerstraße 24, 80331 München, Germany

Batch number: 10722112

Printed by Printforce, the Netherlands